The BEST
USED BOAT
Notebook

The BEST USED BOAT Notebook

From the pages of SAILING Magazine,
a new collection of detailed reviews of 40 used boats

plus a look at 10 great new boats to sail around the world

JOHN KRETSCHMER

SHERIDAN HOUSE

First published 2007 by
Sheridan House Inc.
145 Palisade Street
Dobbs Ferry, NY 10522
www.sheridanhouse.com

The material is reprinted from articles published
under the title "Used Boat Notebook" and "Boat Test"
in SAILING Magazine

While all reasonable care has been taken in the publication
of this book, the publisher takes no responsibility for the
use of the methods or products described in the book.

Library of Congress Cataloging-in-Publication Data

The best used boat notebook : from the pages of Sailing magazine,
a new collection of detailed reviews of 40 used boats plus a look at
10 great new boats to sail around the world / John Kretschmer.
      p. cm.
   Includes bibliographical references and index.
   ISBN 978-1-57409-234-9 (pbk. : alk. paper)
  1. Used boats—Catalogs. 2. Sailboats—Catalogs.
3. Sailing ships—Catalogs. 4. Yachts—Catalogs.
I. Kretschmer, John. II. Sailing magazine.
   VM321.B434 2007
   623.822'3029—dc22   2007035785

ISBN 978-1-57409-234-9

Printed in the United States of America

CONTENTS

INTRODUCTION

Like most magazine columns "The Used Boat Notebook" sprang to life brimming with optimism and a bit of naiveté. Former *SAILING* Magazine Editor Micca Hutchins suggested I write a column about boats that would attempt to fill a void in the sailing press, and at the time, seemed anything but novel. What was different about her vision was the concept of writing about *used* boats. And it wasn't to be skimpy watered-down articles, but thoroughly researched, hard-hitting reviews of used boats.

"Let's present the good, the bad and the ugly, the information we all really crave," she said. "Kretschmer, you're ideal for this project. Who else has sailed as many different kinds of boats as you and has had as many problems along the way?"

I wasn't sure if that was a compliment or an insult, but the first column, a review of the Ted Brewer-designed Morgan 38, appeared in March 1996. It may seem odd to those outside the magazine publishing business, but the column was considered something of a risky venture. We were aware of the fact that many of our readers had purchased used boats, but we thought most were more interested in reading about the shiny new ones. After all, the sailing press is the major showplace for the latest in boats and equipment. To a lesser degree, we also worried about alienating *SAILING*'s new-boat advertisers. Our fears, as it turned out, were ungrounded. There was plenty of room between the magazine's oversized covers for new and used boat aficionados. In fact, boat-builders have been generous and helpful in supplying information about their old boats, some of which even compete with their new models in the marketplace.

It seems we had the right idea with "Used Boat Notebook," and many other publications have followed our lead. Only *Practical Sailor* was regularly offering used boat reviews when we began. Now most sailing periodicals offer some type of used boat news and evaluations. Today, over ten years and more than 100 reviews (and counting) later, the "Used Boat Notebook" has become one of *SAILING*'s most popular regular features.

The nuts and bolts of each review

The reviews are a combination of my sailing experience aboard a wide variety of boats, in-depth research and invaluable information provided by owners. I work closely with Greta Schanen, *SAILING*'s managing editor. An experienced sailor, having sailed a variety of boats the world over, she steers me in the right direction, especially when I'm tackling a performance boat. (She actually likes today's blunt-nosed, flat-bottomed rocket ships.) She is not only responsible for wrestling my words into shape every month but also suggests many of the boats profiled. Added into the mix is my experience conducting several boat buying workshops and working briefly as a yacht broker, which may not have been a noble calling, but it was a terrific way to learn about boats. As a yacht delivery skipper and a reviewer of new and used boats, I have sailed more than 100 different boats.

In general, the column targets affordable, good-quality, fiberglass production boats, steering clear of wood and metal boats. Most sell for less than $100,000 and some even sell for less than $10,000. Naturally, some of the boats larger than 40 feet and some of the higher quality boats sell for more. The bulk of the reviews, however, examine boats in the 30- to 40-foot range, with prices falling from $30,000 to $70,000. For the most part, the column covers boats that are popular and have had long production runs, making them widely available in the North American marketplace.

Each review follows the same basic format, while revealing the unique personality of the boat reviewed. A general overview of the boat, the designer and the builder opens the review, which is followed by **First Impressions**. This section is an initial glance as though I have just spotted an intriguing boat lying to a mooring or sitting on the hard in a boatyard and am struck by the profile.

I provide some design parameters and some statistics in this section, but the reviews are not all about numbers. I leave number crunching to yacht designers because practical experience has made me skeptical of the numbers listed on a spec sheet. Over the years I have found glaring inaccuracies between paper and fiberglass for statistics like displacement, draft and sail area. Accepting the design premise for what it is, be it a coastal cruiser, sport boat, casual daysailer or bluewater voyager, my objective is to analyze each boat for what it is meant to be and whether it hits the mark. This method is more valuable than simply putting a boat through a litmus test of what I consider to be desirable traits in a boat. We all have our own ideas of what we desire and need in a boat, I help by pointing out what works and what doesn't.

Under the heading **Construction**, the review answers such questions as, Is the hull solid glass or cored? Is the ballast internal or external? How is the hull and deck joined? Are molded liners used or are the bulkheads and furnishings fiberglassed to the hull? At the end of the day, the construction quality determines more about a boat's value than almost any other feature. Of course, boats can be overbuilt and as well as underbuilt, depending upon the design premise.

The next facet of the review, **What to look for**, may be the most important. What common problems have been documented by current or previous owners and how can they be avoided or repaired? I am always impressed by the candor of most owners. Although they invariably love their boats, they're not blind to their boats' faults and are willing to share them with other sailors. It is always enlightening to see what problems turn up in each review. Some problems are common to most boats, yet each has its own quirks. The aluminum fuel tanks can be a source of problems on the Pa-

cific Seacraft 37, according to some owners; water-logged rudders have plagued the CS 36 Traditional; and deck delamination may be an issue for the O'Day 37. The list goes on and on. Rarely do these problems eliminate a boat from consideration for used boat buyers, but they give you a heads up on what to look for when shopping. One of the Used Boat Notebook readers wrote that after reading a review he knew more about the boat he was looking at than the marine surveyor he had hired.

The reviews next take the reader **On deck**, examining the sail controls, spars and standing rigging, fittings and safety features. The layout of the cockpit receives scrutiny, both from a sailing and comfort point of view. Even a one-design rocket ship has to accommodate the crew with some measure of civility. Next we drop **Down below** and explore the interior. From layouts to storage, from joinerwork to engineering details, I point out various features of the cabin. Are the bunks actually long enough to sleep in? Will the sinks drain on both tacks? Are there fiddles, do the lockers latch securely, are the handholds accessible for short people?

Finally we move into propulsion and examine the **Engine**. I list the types of engines put into the boat during its production run and describe what kind of access there is for both routine maintenance and major repairs, including just how big a job it is to repower. **Under way** looks at a boat's sailing characteristics through a range of conditions. I have sailed many of the boats reviewed, but I also rely heavily on owner feedback. How high can the boat point? Does it make much leeway? At what wind range would you need to reef and shorten the headsail? How does the boat handle heavy weather and light air? These and more questions are answered.

After a brief **Conclusion**, which invariably includes a discussion about the boat's value on the market, I provide a unique quick reference **Value Guide**. This feature rates the boat in 10 categories, giving it from one to five sailboats in each category, with a five-boat rating being the best and extremely rare. The Value Guide also provides useful, updated resources for support and refits. The Value Guide lists the overall rating for the boat, with most of the boats reviewed falling between 2 and 3½ sailboats. The **Boats for Sale** guide is a list of current prices, both from the BUC Book (an industry standard guide to pricing used frequently by brokers) and from a analysis of boats listed on the open market

The "Used Boat Notebook" reviews are next best thing to actually sailing the boat and are designed to help readers zero in on a specific boat before committing funds to sea trials, haul outs and surveys.

The key to the **Used Boat Notebook** is that this book is about specific boats. You won't find a laundry list of what makes for a perfect boat and how to choose the one right for you. This book is for sailors farther along the learning curve. It is for those sailors who are ready to take the plunge and need information about specific boats. "The Used Boat Notebook" is a collection of honest and informed reviews covering a wide range of boats.

I have spent the past two decades sailing all over the world in an assortment of sailboats. Ironically, I haven't actually sailed around the world—there is a little chunk in the East Indian Ocean that I've missed. I have crossed the Atlantic 14 times, the Pacific three times and sailed most of the way across the Indian Ocean. I have sailed to near 60 degrees both north and south, from Stockholm to Cape Horn, and spent years plying the Mediterranean and Caribbean Seas. As a professional delivery captain I have logged 200,000 miles and spent more than 1,600 days and nights at sea. I recently compiled a list of the different boats I have sailed 1,000 miles or more in a single stretch. It's 35 and counting.

During all this sailing I have learned that boats come in all shapes and sizes, with individual personalities to match. Somewhere between these pages there is a boat that will not only fit your cruising budget, but more importantly, will fit your dreams.

PART I

Forty Great
Used Boats

West Wight Potter 19

Small but salty pocket cruiser that spawned large dreams

I collected sailboat brochures when was I a kid. I studied boat specs like other kids studied batting averages. I remember pouring over the brochure for the West Wight Potter 19. I know, I'm no spring chicken, but the Potter 19 has been in production in one form or another since 1971. I can still clearly picture the black-and-white single fold piece with a Potter 19 on the cover clipping along in a stiff breeze. There was something alluring about the boxy little trailersailer, it looked like a real cruiser but one that even a kid could handle.

There was also something exotic about the boat, it was named after the far away Isle of Wight. I had a notion to drop out of school and sail a Potter around the world and become famous, just like Robin Lee Graham did aboard DOVE. My mother, who took little pleasure in spoiling a kid's dream, did however remind me that although Potters were cheap, they were still a lot more than I had, which was nothing. She mentioned that I could quit the track team, get a job and save money to buy the boat, a thoroughly unromantic suggestion that made

the drudgery of school more tolerable. My sailing dreams would have to wait.

More than 1,600 West Wight Potter 19s have been launched during a 35-year production run. And while plenty of Potters have made impressive passages, most are sailed quietly on lakes, bays and coastline all over the country. Most importantly, they're almost universally admired by the folks who own them, and for good reason. The boat is stable in the water, it can stand up to a breeze, it's surprisingly commodious, it's easy to launch and can be trailed behind almost any vehicle. Mounted on its trailer the West Wight Potter 19 fits snugly in most garages, which eliminates the cost of dockage and winter storage.

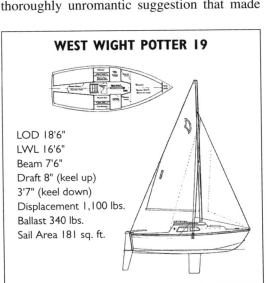

WEST WIGHT POTTER 19

LOD 18'6"
LWL 16'6"
Beam 7'6"
Draft 8" (keel up)
3'7" (keel down)
Displacement 1,100 lbs.
Ballast 340 lbs.
Sail Area 181 sq. ft.

First impressions

Designed by Herb Stewart, who originally bought the U.S. rights to the original Potter 14, the West Wight Potter 19 is a salty pocket cruiser. It was originally called the HMS 18. Stewart later sold the company to Joe Edwards. Edwards decided to include the outboard motor bracket in the measurement of LOA, and suddenly the boat grew a foot and became the West Wight Potter 19. From the springy sheerline to the forward chine, the boat has the look of other small English cruisers that were popular in the 1960s and 1970s.

There isn't much overhang—the LOA is 18 feet, 6 inches and the LWL is 16 feet, 6 inches resulting in a faster boat than many suspect, at least when the wind is blowing. The retractable keel lifts vertically into the hull. When fully raised the draft is just 8 inches. Together with the kick-up rudder the boat can be sailed right up on the beach. When the 300-pound keel is fully deployed the draft is 3 feet, 7 inches, although the keel can also be trimmed to various levels. The fractional rig supports a good size main and most boats on the used market have overlapping genoas in lieu of a working jib. Despite the small size, by all accounts the Potter 19 needs a bit of breeze to get up to speed.

Construction

One of the reasons the West Wight Potter 19 and her smaller sister, the 15, have endured while other small boats and small boat builders have come and gone is that the Potters are built solidly. International Marine, which has been building the boats since the early 1990s, upgraded the construction. While all the boats have solid fiberglass hulls, International Marine switched from plywood cored decks to balsa and refined the molding process. The centerboard is a simple, dependable design with no moving parts. Closed-cell foam enclosed fore and aft makes the 19 unsinkable, a design feature that all small boats should include.

What to look for

Some owners of older, mid-1980s boats have reported slight structural problems with the centerboard trunk. Early boats and later boats

WEST WIGHT POTTER 19 PRICE DATA			
		Low	High
BUC Retail Range	1985	$ 3,750	$ 4,350
	1995	$ 6,900	$ 9,980
		State	Asking
Boats For Sale	1986	MA	$ 3,500
	1998	MI	$ 7,700
	2004	GA	$12,900

had very sturdy trunks. Beefing it up with additional glass and epoxy is not an overwhelming project and to be fair, very few owners have noted this problem. There are many Potter sites online and one of the best is Judy B's West Wight Potter pages at **www.blumhorst. com/potterpages**. Owners discuss the good and the bad about the boats, but I must tell you there seem to be very few well-documented problems. Most Potter 19s are simply rigged and fitted out, items to watch for include all the normal age-related issues. International Marine has a good supply of applicable parts available, a big plus when buying an older used boat. Don't forget to carefully inspect the trailer too. The cost of a new trailer can spoil the savings made with a good boat buy.

On deck

The best design feature of the Potter 19 is the cockpit. Two adults have room to stretch their legs, the visibility is great and all the lines are typically led aft. The forward chine tends to deflect the water aside, keeping the cockpit relatively dry even in choppy conditions. Newer boats have a much improved nonskid pattern on deck and there are handrails on both the raised and lower sections of the cabin trunk. A husky bowsprit has always been part of the deck package and newer boats include a chain locker.

The mainsheet is a bit awkward. It angles down from the end of the boom, forcing the helmsman to keep clear. The jib sheets and the centerboard winch are well placed, making the 19 a perfect boat for sailing solo. The key

West Wight Potter 19

SAILING Magazine's Value Guide

 **PRICE:** You can find a Potter 19 that fits your budget, it's that simple. At any given time there are plenty of boats on the market and if you're really lucky, you might even find one at a garage sale and buy it for a ridiculous price.

 DESIGN QUALITY: The Potter 19 is a practical design. The boat can stand up to a blow and also be beached for swimming. It isn't fast or close winded, but it doesn't claim to be.

 CONSTRUCTION QUALITY: By trailersailer standards the Potter 19 is well built. The hulls are solid and heavily laid up. There is nothing sophisticated about the build but they hold up well.

 USER-FRIENDLINESS: The Potter 19 is an ideal boat for solo sailing. It is easy to handle. The interior is tight but all available space is well used. It is a good choice for camper sailing and can be towed by almost any vehicle.

 **SAFETY:** Safety is the Potter 19s strong suit. The boat can stand up to a breeze and is unsinkable.

 TYPICAL CONDITION: Condition depends on where the boat has been stored. If stranded on a trailer in the elements, it might be rough, if kept in the garage it might be pristine.

 **REFITTING:** The basic boat is very simple, and that's part of the allure. Typical projects include adding bimini tops, tiller pilots and additional battery storage.

 **SUPPORT:** Check out Judy B's West Wight Potter pages at www.blumhorst.com/potterpages and also the builder's site at www.westwightpotter.com.

 AVAILABILITY: More than 1,600 boats have been built. There are always Potter 19s on the market, all over the country.

 INVESTMENT AND RESALE: This rating is not a reflection of the Potter 19 as much as the reality of small sailboats. You don't buy a small boat to make money, you buy them for fun.

OVERALL 'SVG' RATING

to any trailerable boat is the degree of difficulty in raising the mast. The Potter 19 has an air draft of around 25 feet with a 22-foot, 6-inch mast section. Most owners report that they can be sailing in less than an hour from arriving at the launching ramp. A clever mast raising system lets one person hoist the stick. Many of the used 19s on the market include CDI flexible furling on the headstay.

Down below

Lets face it, there isn't much a designer or builder can do with a 19-foot boat's interior. Still, the Potter 19 will surprise you. The headroom is just five feet but that's better than most comparably sized trailersailers. The interior includes four berths, two forward and two quarterberths aft. A galley of sorts is sandwiched between the berths with a butane stove to starboard and sink to port. One of the impressive interior features is the amount of storage. There are lockers under the berths, under the sink and stove and seat back bins as well. There really is plenty of space for comfortable weekend sailing.

Think of the Potter 19 as a campersailer. There are many accounts of Potter 19s making long cruises. I encountered a 19 in the Abacos last summer, with a crew of three adults aboard and they were spending a month cheerfully cruising the Bahamas. If a previous owner has installed opening portlights be thankful and if not, consider adding them. Ditto for the forward hatch. Two items that I'd do away with include the indoor outdoor carpeting that decorates the sole of most used 19s and the porta potty located under the forward bunk. It is not only a waste of space, it stinks, and is a pain to deal with when it's full. Consider a bucket.

Engine

New West Wight Potters come standard with five-horsepower long-shaft Tohatsu outboards. Most used boats also have five- or six-horsepower outboards, although they might be a variety of makes. Nissan seems popular on several of the boats currently on the market. An adjustable motor bracket makes the outboard more efficient in the water and easier to lift completely out of the water when sailing. Also, an electric start engine allows the possibility of charging the batteries. Many Potters have had their electrical systems upgraded and include two batteries. Small solar panels are a logical addition to keep the batteries topped.

Underway

The West Wight Potter 19 is not going to win races but nobody buys it to win races. The boat needs a bit of breeze to get moving but that's not a bad thing in a trailerable boat and conversely the 19 can carry sail when other boats are fleeing back toward the launching ramp. The hull form limits heeling and is relatively dry— all 19-foot boats are wet when sailing upwind in any kind of seaway—but by way of comparison the 19 is downright comfortable. Owners report speeds of 5 knots in winds of 10-knots-plus when reaching. The boat is well balanced on a reach, and most owners suggest carrying as big a headsail as you can afford. New boats come standard with an overlapping headsail, which is 110 percent. Upwind sailing is the not the Potter 19's strong suit, it doesn't like to sail much closer than 50 degrees apparent.

Conclusion

The West Potter 19 is an enduring favorite among small boat sailors both in England and North America. It is well built and designed, simply rigged and safe to sail in blustery conditions. There are lively owner's associations and continued support from the factory. It can be towed and launched by a compact car from virtually any ramp. And it is affordable. Used prices range from less than $5,000 for the oldest models to around $12,000 for late models. What's not to like about this salty pocket cruiser?

Santana 22

This West Coast one-design, still actively raced, is a lot of boat for the buck

Here is a quick quiz question for connoisseurs of classic plastic boats. What was legendary naval architect Gary Mull's very first independent sailboat design? No, not the Ranger 26 or 22. Give up? It was the Santana 22, and it turned out to be one of his most enduring works. According to boatbuilder Tom Schock, Mull approached him in the men's room of the St. Francis Yacht Club during a break in the San Francisco Bay Big Boat Series nearly 40 years ago.

"I had no idea who Gary Mull was," Schock said with a laugh. "But he insisted that the drawings tucked under his arm would be a great boat for the bay. Mull explained that he was an apprentice with Sparkman & Stephens in New York, but he was really a California kid who grew up sailing on the bay. I took the drawings with me and after the series showed them to my father." The rest, as they say, is history. The Santana 22 went into production in 1966 and W.D. Schock Corp. built about 800 boats before it was finally taken off line in 1978.

In an unusual twist for an old boat, W.D. Schock Corp. took another look at the Santana 22 in 2001. "Retro is in," Schock said.

"Besides, people have been pestering us to build new 22s for years." The company gave the boat a complete makeover and put it back into production. The new boats have the same hull, keel shape and sailplan so they can compete in one-design racing against the first generation 22s, but they also feature updated hardware, materials and cosmetic changes. We'll review only the older boats, which are terrific values and can be purchased for about the same price as a decent life raft. However, it is nice to know that if you get hooked on the Santana 22 a new boat is a viable option. Ten new 22s have already been sold in less than a year.

First impressions

The Santana 22 is a handsome little boat with nicely proportioned lines. In some ways—and I know this will offend some—it is a better looking boat than the Cal 20, the Bill Lapworth classic that some say inspired Mull's design. Instead of a raised flush deck, it has a low-profile cabintrunk with two large portlights per side. Both boats feature long cockpits, but while the Cal 20 has an outboard rudder and transom tiller, the Santana 22 has a spade rudder and cockpit tiller.

Below the waterline, the Santana 22 has a sweptback fin keel that accounts for 1,230 pounds of ballast, creating a ballast-to-displacement ratio of almost 50 percent. Like the Cal 20, the Santana can stand up to a blow, and not surprisingly, there is an active fleet on blustery San Francisco Bay. Unlike the fractionally rigged Cal 20, the Santana 22 is a masthead sloop with a working sail area of 217 square feet. One of the best features of the boat is that it appeals to a wide range of sailors, from an inexperienced couple or family looking for a first boat to competitive

---

SANTANA 22

LOA 22'
LWL 18'8"
Beam 7'10"
Draft 3'6"
Displacement 2,600 lbs.
Ballast 1,230 lbs.
Sail Area 217 sq. ft.

sailors looking for an affordable and exciting one-design and PHRF racer.

Construction

Nothing defines original construction quality better than a careful look at how well a boat has held up after years of hard use. These small but tough boats have held up very well indeed.

"When we started the process to reintroduce the 22, we talked with the local fleets and looked at a lot of the old boats up and down the California coast," Schock said. "Many of the boats were more than 30 years old, and they are still sailing three nights a week. I guess it wasn't a bad idea to put so much glass into them."

The 22 hull is solid fiberglass and, like Schock says, heavily laid up. The deck is balsa cored. One of the improvements on the new 22 is a better hull-and-deck joint. On the old boats the joint was covered by a somewhat flimsy rubrail and vulnerable to impact.

The keel was cast iron, and the original keel bolts were galvanized iron. According to Schock these bolts had a life expectancy of about 30 years, and most boats have been retrofitted with stainless bolts. The mast is deck-stepped, and most boats have been fitted with a support post. That is another improvement on the new 22. Instead of a compression post, an athwartship fiberglass deck beam supports the mast and opens up the interior. The interior isn't fancy, but the two-compartment arrangement with four berths is all you need.

What to look for

Most Santana 22s have been raced hard for years, which is the perfect recipe for revealing a boat's flaws. Steve Seal, who was a consultant for the new 22 project and specializes in supplying parts and advice for old Cals and the Santana 22, (and who, incidentally, attended high school with Schock and Bill Lee) suggested carefully inspecting a used 22's spars and standing rigging. The original chainplates were aluminum and they tended to elongate and corrode over the years. A chainplate failure can lead to a dismasting. If the chainplates have not been changed to stainless steel, it should be

SANTANA 22 PRICE DATA			
		Low	High
BUC Retail Range	1970	$ 1,500	$ 2,200
	1980	$ 3,650	$ 4,400
		State	Asking
Boats For Sale	1967	CA	$ 1,200
	1973	CA	$ 3,500
	1978	MI	$ 4,100

the project on the top of your list. Seal also suggested upgrading the standing rigging, especially the lower stays that at times carry the most load. The original boom section was too light and occasionally failed under load. While it is likely that the section has either been replaced or upgraded, be sure to find out. The gooseneck fitting was also a bit undersized.

Other items to check include the previously mentioned keel bolts and rudder play, which seems to be a common problem. The stainless steel rudder post may need better bearing support in the fiberglass rudder tube, which is a hot topic of conversation on the Santana 22 owner's Web page.

On deck

The Santana 22 cockpit is ideal for racing but can get uncomfortable on longer sails. The coaming boards tend to hit you in the small of the back, and the shallow design of the well makes it hard to brace or stretch your legs. On the plus side, all major sail controls can be easily reached from the helm, and in fact, the boat is set up for easy singlehanding. The sheet winches are mounted on molded islands, and the mainsheet traveler is aft, allowing for efficient end-boom sheeting. Most boats are rigged with backstay adjusters within easy reach of the helmsman.

The side decks have a fair bit of camber, which seems awkward when the boat isn't heeled, but is really a practical feature while under sail and also creates more room below. There are usually two sets of headsail tracks,

Santana 22

 **PRICE:** A perfect five-boat rating doesn't appear often in the *Used Boat Notebook*, but the Santana 22 is really a steal. You can sometimes find a decent boat for less than $2,000!

 **DESIGN QUALITY:** Gary Mull's first independent design was a good one, and it has stood the test of time. The fact that W.D. Schock Corp. is bringing the boat back without altering the basic design is impressive.

 CONSTRUCTION QUALITY: The hull and deck were robustly built, although some of the hardware was questionable. The spars and rigging need to be upgraded, especially if you plan to race the boat.

 USER-FRIENDLINESS: The Santana is an easy, yet rewarding boat to sail. Controls are well placed. The cockpit and interior are not overly comfortable.

 SAFETY: Most 22s are set up for racing. Some don't have lifelines and the deck camber takes a bit of getting used to. Handrails are well placed.

 TYPICAL CONDITION: Most Santana 22s are at least 30 years old, and some are nearing 40. Naturally there will have been much wear and tear. Still, Santana owners are a devoted lot and many boats have been well cared for.

 REFITTING: Steve Seal of Seals Spars and Rigging, www.sealsspars.com, specializes in supplying parts and advice for old Santana 22s. This is a great service for Santana owners. Also, W.D. Schock Corp., www.wdschock.com, is supportive of its older boats.

 SUPPORT: Several Web sites are very useful for Santana owners and prospective buyers. The Class Web site is www.santana22.com.

 **AVAILABILITY:** With nearly 800 boats built, there are always 22s on the market. However, the vast majority of boats are in California. Other places to look for used Santanas are Oklahoma and Texas, where there are one-design fleets.

INVESTMENT AND RESALE: How wrong can you go financially when your initial investment is $3,000? The truth is you can have more fun in this boat than just about any other boat for the same money. And when you want to sell, there is a good market.

 **OVERALL 'SVG' RATING**

one on the coachroof for upwind work and another on the rail. There are teak grab rails on the coachroof and some owners have mounted another set on the foredeck, both for safety and for lashing sail bags.

Depending on how actively a boat has been raced, it may or may not be set up with lifelines. The nonskid on older boats is likely to be well worn. The stemhead fitting is rather small, and some owners have retrofitted a bow roller for cruising. Author John Vigor has a detailed description of this upgrade on the owner's Web page.

Down below

"We looked at several different interior options for the new 22 but finally decided that the original arrangement still worked the best," Schock said. Or as one owner put it, "Anyway you slice it, the interior is bare-bones." The interior consists of two full-length berths forward, two full-length settee berths in the saloon and a surprising amount of elbowroom. If you go back to the Cal 20 comparison, the Santana 22 seems downright spacious.

You will likely find a variety of owner modifications as some boats have been set up for cruising and may include an imaginative galley and even a fold-out table for navigation. There is good storage below each bunk and in lockers. Most boats are fitted with porta-potties, one of mankind's least noble inventions. The headroom is what manufacturers used to call with a straight face "full-sitting" headroom.

Engine

The Santana 22 is set up for an outboard engine. A clever cutout in the transom allows the motor to be efficiently mounted down low yet still easily lifted out of the water. Schock noted that the transom is strong enough to support the new four-stroke engines. Engines on most used boats will range from 4 to 10 horsepower.

Outboard engines are notoriously fickle, so if you have any doubts about the engine do yourself a favor, bite the bullet and purchase a new model. Performance under power is adequate, and the Santana 22 is so nimble under sail that powering is usually only required when maneuvering in close quarters or when trying to get home on a completely calm afternoon.

Underway

"There is no doubt in my mind that the reason the Santana 22 has remained so popular is that is a great performer," Schock said with more than a little pride. "The boat is well known for its ability to handle heavy weather, but it is not a slug in light air."

The San Francisco one-design association page on the Web is filled with advice for making the boat perform better throughout a range of conditions. John Skinner contributes an excellent piece on tuning the rig and making subtle adjustments while under way.

The Santana one-design association has two classes, one with spinnaker and one without. Both classes are popular, and races along the California coast will often see more than 20 boats turn up at the starting line. On the wind, the Santana 22 is fairly stiff, although it helps to be able to shift the crew to rail when working toward the windward mark. Off the wind, the boat has terrific steering control because the spade rudder is located well aft. The beam in the mid and aft hull sections also keeps the boat balanced and cuts down on rolling. The Santana 22 can carry sail in breezy conditions, and the masthead spinnaker really gives the boat punch while reaching.

Conclusion

The Santana 22 is what sailing should be all about. With new and used versions, it offers the proverbial best of both worlds. It is a well-built, spirited boat that can be purchased for less than $3,000 on the used boat market. It is a perfect first boat, and with active one-design associations, especially on the West Coast, you can develop and hone your sailing skills without breaking the bank. If you find that you love the boat but would like a new, less maintenance-intensive version, you can order a new one.

Com-Pac 23

A practical trailersailer in an affordable package
is perfect for coastal sailing adventures

"We just might be the longest running sailboat builder in the country under the original management," said Gerry Hutchins, who with his brother Richard, owns and operates Com-Pac Yachts in Clearwater, Florida. "I am not sure about that," he added with a laugh, "But we have been at this a long time."

Founded by their father Les, Com-Pac is a division of The Hutchins Co., which builds trailerable catboats, pocket cruisers and two larger models, the 27/2 and 35. The company's first boat, the salty Com-Pac 16, was launched in 1974. Designed by unheralded Clark Mills, whose other designs include the Windmill and the Optimist, it was fashioned after a lifeboat. With a springy sheer, jaunty bow and ample beam, the 16 was easy to trailer and stable in the water. It was an immediate success.

Five years later the company introduced a larger sistership, the Com-Pac 23. Also a Mills design, the 23 had an actual interior and was a bit livelier under sail. More than 600 boats have been built to date.

First impressions

Although the Com-Pac 23 is a very practical boat, its wide appeal comes from its traditional appearance. The sheerline sweeps aft from the short bowsprit before bending up again just before the transom-hung rudder.

The box cabintrunk, with round or oval bronze ports, flows naturally into the deck lines. From a distance the boat looks bigger than 23 feet. There is a shallow forefoot and a long, shoal keel with a draft of just 2 feet, 3 inches. Any more draft would make it difficult to launch on many ramps.

Although trailerability is a nice feature, most 23 owners keep the boat in the water all season. The aluminum rudder has a kick-up blade. Displacement is 3,000 pounds, of which 1,340 is ballast, accounting for the 23's stiffness. The mast stands 30 feet off the water.

Construction

Com-Pac farms out the molding of the 23's solid fiberglass hull and balsa-cored deck. The hull includes longitudinal stringers that encapsulate the bulkheads and stiffen the panels.

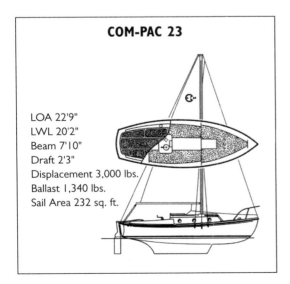

COM-PAC 23

LOA 22'9"
LWL 20'2"
Beam 7'10"
Draft 2'3"
Displacement 3,000 lbs.
Ballast 1,340 lbs.
Sail Area 232 sq. ft.

The crew at Com-Pac builds the interior and finishes the boat. Surprisingly, the interior components are handmade, including plywood bulkheads and surfaces with teak veneers.

The interior is not a symphony of stark molded components and the teak-and-holly sole is a very nice touch for a small boat. The workmanship is first rate, much better in fact than most small boat manufacturers. Com-Pac uses good quality materials throughout, and the company's construction philosophy has always been to build small boats like they were just short big boats.

COM-PAC 23 PRICE DATA				
			Low	High
BUC Retail Range	1985		$ 5,600	$ 6,400
	1990		$ 7,900	$10,500
			State	Asking
Boats For Sale	1980		VA	$ 9,400
	1989		FL	$ 8,900
	1994		ME	$19,500

What to look for

The condition of all used boats is directly related to the care they receive. However, this seems to be more relevant with trailerable boats. For some reason these boats can be forgotten and languish on their trailers for years. If they are well sealed, they may be moldy, but otherwise are lightly used gems that just require a good cleaning and represent a solid value.

On the other hand, if the boats have been leaking while shut up, you may push open the hatch to find rotting plywood and cabin soles among other problems. There are plenty of 23s on the market, and prospective owners can take the time to find a 23 that has been well cared for.

There were several changes with different models and you should be aware of the differences. The first changes occurred with the model 23/2, which took place in the mid-1980s. This is when the popular hide-away galley was added, the interior finishing was upgraded and the bowsprit was added for much needed additional sail area. In the early 1990s, the 23/3 was offered and this model change included mostly small tooling upgrades. Small round portlights were changed to larger, oval ones for example. One model to look for is the rare 23 D, which includes a 10-horsepower single cylinder Yanmar diesel. According to Gerry Hutchins, only about 35 of these boats were built and they are quite desirable on the used market.

On deck

The cockpit is the best design feature on the boat. It is long, more than seven feet, and surprisingly comfortable. Many pocket cruiser designs sacrifice cockpit space to increase the size of the cabin but unless you are sailing offshore, and few pocket cruisers are capable of that, it is a mistake. The cockpit is control central, this is where you spend your time in most small boats.

The 23's self-bailing cockpit includes two lockers and a bridgedeck. The original tiller was laminate mahogany and ash and there is good leg support when steering. Although the triangular mainsheet arrangement crowds the helmsman and isn't very efficient, a traveler would be more of an intrusion. The transom will likely have both an outboard motor bracket and swim ladder mounted, making it a bit crowded as well.

The stainless pulpits and stanchions are beefy by small boat standards. In contrast, the standing rigging seems a bit undersized, but remember, the mast was designed to be raised and lowered without gin pole.

Teak handrails on the cabintop and molded nonskid make getting around the boat safe and easy despite narrow side decks. Newer boats feature a chain pipe and divided chain locker. Most boats will include bronze cleats and small standard sheet winches.

Down below

While nobody buys a Com-Pac 23 based on the interior, most are surprised when they drop below. The cabin is spacious, this is where you appreciate the nearly eight-foot beam. The bulkheads have teak veneers and the cabin sides are covered with teak paneling. Two overhead hatches and six opening bronze portlights provide excellent ventilation.

Com-Pac 23

 **PRICE:** Compared with lower quality trailersailers the 23 may seem expensive, but when compared to any quality boat the value becomes obvious. Price is no excuse for not being able to sail, just find a nice used Com-Pac 23.

 DESIGN QUALITY: Clark Mills should be better known, how many people have learned to sail on Optis? The salty 23 sails adequately, is stable, has a roomy cockpit and utilitarian interior.

 **CONSTRUCTION QUALITY:** This small cruiser is well made. The hull is solid and the fit and finish are quite nice. Quality components complete the package. The 23 has aged well; a sign of good original construction.

 **USER-FRIENDLINESS:** The 23 is easy to handle and within its design limitations quite comfortable. The shallow draft contributes to its user-friendly nature.

 SAFETY: The Com-Pac was designed for coastal and shallow-water sailing. The large cockpit, which is one of the boat's best features, would make it vulnerable offshore. Handholds and well supported lifelines and stanchions make it safe on deck.

 TYPICAL CONDITION: Like any boat, condition depends on former ownership. Trailerable boats often suffer from neglect. However, most Com-Pac owners seem devoted to their boats.

 REFITTING: Smaller boats are harder to work on than bigger boats but much less costly to work on as well. Com-Pac is still doing well and although the 23 is still in production not many boats are built. Still, parts are available, a big plus.

 **SUPPORT:** There is an active owners' group at www.com-pacowners.com. There are several forums, including those set aside for the 23.

 **AVAILABILITY:** With more than 600 boats built there is always a good supply of 23s on the market. Although there seem to be more in Florida, they are well represented all around the country.

 INVESTMENT AND RESALE: No small, trailerable sailboat can ever be classified a good investment but 23s do seem to hold their value decently.

 OVERALL 'SVG' RATING

There is just one step down into the cabin and standing headroom is only under the companionway. The hide-away galley usually features a two-burner stovetop to port and a stainless sink to starboard. These cleverly fold and slide aft. A boat without these features is a pre-23/2 model. The interior really does sleep four with some comfort, including two settee berths and two berths forward. There is a storage compartment for a portable head between the forward berths. As undesirable as this arrangement is, sacrificing room for an enclosed head would waste far too much space. There are clever storage compartments throughout the boat. A portable table mounts on the bulkhead.

Engine

As noted earlier, the vast majority of boats came with outboard engines. A few, roughly 35, came with a 10-horsepower inboard diesel. While the inboard offers many obvious advantages, including the ability to efficiently charge batteries, don't set your hopes on finding one on the used market, and if you do, be prepared to pay for it. There is a bit of information on the Com-Pac owners Web site, **www.com-pacowners.com,** that discusses retrofitting a diesel. Unless you are committed to owning the boat a long time, it probably doesn't make sense.

Outboards offer a few advantages of their own, one being portability for repairs. If something goes wrong, just heft it into the trunk and take it to a mechanic. A very unscientific survey reveals that most 23s on the market have 8-horsepower outboards. All major manufacturers seem to be represented. Another advantage of an outboard is that you can actually afford to repower without breaking the bank.

A new four-stroke model would be a nice up-grade and a lot better for the water you sail in. A built-in locker is designed to house a six-gallon fuel tank.

Underway

The hull shape of the Com-Pac 23 is deceptive, the boat has a long 20-foot, 2-inch waterline. The theoretical hull speed is 6 knots and owners report hitting this fairly regularly on a reach. The hull shape is a bit prone to pitching but more importantly, it doesn't pound in a chop.

Although the 23 is nimble under sail it is not close winded. The sheeting angles are wide and it does develop a bit of weather helm when beating. So crack off a bit and enjoy the ride, the Com-Pac 23 is not a boat to race and it reaches beautifully. Besides, the 2-foot, 3-inch draft allows the 23 to skip across shallows that more weatherly deep-draft boats have to tack around.

Conclusion

The Com-Pac 23 blends quality construction, practical design features and a handsome appearance in an affordable package. Prices may range from $5,000 for an early boat to more than $20,000 for a recent model, however the bulk of the boats on the market are asking less than $10,000.

When you factor in the low cost of ownership, the 23 is genuinely affordable. If you live up north, you can trailer it south in the winter. It is an ideal boat for exploring the shimmering flats of the Florida Keys. It is also capable of crossing the Gulf Stream on a nice day, and is perfect for gunkholing the broad banks of the Bahamas.

Nimble Kodiak 26

Salty trailersailer for cold-water cruising

The Nimble Kodiak has always intrigued me. I confess, it's not the most beautiful boat to ever ply the high seas, or the highways for that matter. It is, however, one of the most unique. Designed by Ted Brewer and built by Nimble Boat Works, Inc. on the west coast of Florida, the company's motto aptly defines the quirky Kodiak, "a vote against boredom and mediocrity." The Kodiak, a versatile 26-foot pilothouse sloop or yawl that can be pulled behind most light trucks and launched with a minimum of fuss, opens up cruising grounds beyond the range of most boats.

The Kodiak is something of a cross between a sailboat, a small trawler and an RV. One thing is certain, those who have them love them.

"This is the best boat I have ever owned," writes Seattle-based Kodiak sailor Bill Varnson. The rugged double-ender was designed and built for sailing coasts and inland waters where the scenery is beautiful but the weather unpredictable. If you fancy the notion of sailing some of Canada's picturesque western lakes, gunkholing in Penobscot Bay, or exploring the boat's namesake region, the Pacific Northwest, but don't have the time or money to consider full-time cruising, the trailerable Kodiak is an alluring option.

Nimble Boat Works was founded by Jerry Koch in 1985. His first boat was the Nimble 20, a spry yawl that was a refreshing alternative to the small stamped-out trailersailers of the day. The next boat was a 30-footer that was raced successfully across the Atlantic. Innovative models like the Nomad, Arctic and Wanderer followed. The Kodiak, which is still available today, was introduced in 1993 and evolved directly from the Arctic. Koch, a former CNN photographer, was an innovator in trailerable sailboats. He and Brewer were a good team, creating rugged boats that blended purity of function with a dash of salty character. After Koch's untimely death in 2003, Ken McCleave, a former Nimble supplier, took over the company.

First impressions

The Nimble Kodiak commands your attention. The oversized pilothouse, dark green hull, sweeping sheer and canoe stern set the boat apart. The season-extending pilothouse is functional, and in its own boxy way, "cool." It's a feature that will either draw you to the boat or repulse you. You can't compare the Kodiak with boats that put performance first or even snappy little production boats. Naturally the numbers are not pretty: the sail area/displacement is 19.3; the displacement/length is 114; and ballast/displacement is 35 percent. However, the numbers don't tell the story. This is a boat meant for all matter of traveling, and the independent lifestyle that accompanies that ethos.

The stubby rig includes a mast on a tabernacle with an air draft of just less than 30 feet

NIMBLE KODIAK 26

LOA 26'6"
LOD 26'4½"
Beam 8'6"
Draft Shoal 34"
Draft Centerboard
  up 22" down 4'4"
Displacement
  4,100 lbs.
Ballast
  1,350 lbs.
Sail Area
  285 sq. ft.

on both the sloop and yawl models. The hull sections are flat, especially aft where the Kodiak is almost sharpielike, and there is a lot of flare forward. A couple of keel options are available—the more popular 22-inch shoal draft with a centerboard and the 34-inch fixed keel. The fixed keel is more of a challenge to launch from standard ramps.

Construction

Nimble does a fine job of laminating the Kodiak. The hull is foam cored, hand laid and vacuum bagged. The deck is also foam cored in most vertical surfaces and solid glass elsewhere—there's no core to rot. Top-quality materials are used, including vinylester resins in the outer skin layers to prevent blisters. Most boats are custom-built to some extent. The hull-and-deck joint is unique. The forward sections are joined on an outward flange while the aft sections employ the more common inward flange. The aluminum toerail, bolted on 6-inch centers, incorporates the joint. The fixed keel model has a 4-inch lead shoe that is bolted to a reinforced keel seat in the bottom of the stub. The outboard rudder is mounted with beefy pintles and gudgeons. The steering arrangement is interesting. The rudder is controlled either by a conventional tiller from the cockpit or by a hydraulic ram and a wheel in the pilothouse.

What to look for

No two Kodiaks are exactly the same. Also, remember that the Arctic, the model that preceded the Kodiak, is essentially the same hull. Further, there are only slight differences from the Nimble 24 and Wanderer models so if you can't find a Kodiak to suit your needs take a look at other Nimble options. The primary difference with the Kodiak is a larger pilothouse and more commodious interior. Be careful, some Kodiaks are sold as trawlers. Even if you don't ever raise a sail, at least with a mast you don't have to admit to being a member of the "dark side."

Most Kodiak sailors seem to prefer the yawl rig and shoal draft, so be sure just what model it is that you're considering. For the most part, there are few if any structural issues

NIMBLE KODIAK 26 PRICE DATA

BUC Retail Range		Low	High
	1995	$21,300	$23,600
	1997	$23,000	$25,600
Boats For Sale		State	Asking
	1993	AK	$39,500
	1994	AL	$24,500
	2002	FL	$55,800

with the Kodiak. The construction isn't fancy but it is muscular. One of the major differences between models is the engine arrangement. Most early boats have outboards, which fit neatly in dedicated wells astern, while later boats seem more likely to have inboard diesels, either Yanmars or Westerbekes. I prefer the diesel option because it allows for more efficient 12-volt charging, although it seems that owners are split on the subject.

On deck

The deep cockpit has a very secure feeling; almost too much so, and it takes some getting used to the lack of visibility. Eventually you realize that it's best not to try to look over or around the pilothouse but through it. Of course, this limitation is eliminated by steering from the inside station. The cockpit seats are long and angled for comfort. A wide coaming makes for a good perch when sailing. There are lockers to port and starboard. The mainsheet is usually led astern and the headsail sheet leads are within easy reach of the tiller.

Making your way forward is something of a challenge. It is a tight squeeze around the pilothouse and the side decks are narrow. It is almost easiest to skip below and pop up through the large forward hatch. Stout stainless steel handrails and a solid stainless rail in lieu of traditional lifelines lend security while moving about. This railing extends 17 inches. And once you're on the bow there is a terrific bulwark. A molded anchoring platform and large

Nimble Kodiak 26

 **PRICE:** The Nimble Kodiak is pricier than other comparable trailersailers, but this boat should not be compared with those. It's comparable to other quality 30-footers and represents a good value.

 DESIGN QUALITY: A unique Ted Brewer creation, the Kodiak is not meant to be all things to all sailors. As a genuine cruiser that can be towed behind a midsized SUV and double as an RV—it works.

 CONSTRUCTION QUALITY: Well built with quality components. One thing not often mentioned with trailerable boats, life on the road is hard; sometimes harder than life in the water.

 USER-FRIENDLINESS: While the cockpit is a bit awkward for boat handling, the pilothouse more than offsets this drawback.

 SAFETY: This rating reflects the design philosophy. The Kodiak is not a bluewater boat. Within the parameters of what it's meant for the boat is very safe indeed.

 TYPICAL CONDITION: Well built and relatively new translate into good quality used boats for sale. Also, owners are typically devoted to their Kodiaks.

 REFITTING: Not the easiest boat to work on simply because access is limited in places. However, good original quality makes adding components more rewarding.

 SUPPORT: Nimble Boat Works is still in business. Reach them at www.nimbleboat.net. There is plenty of information on the Web, be sure to google Kodiak and not Nimble 26.

 AVAILABILITY: The selection can be limited as these boats don't change hands often and production has always been limited. The Pacific Northwest seems to have the best selection.

 INVESTMENT AND RESALE: A unique boat is always something of a risk as a purchase, however the Nimble Kodiak has a solid reputation and a loyal following. Also, quality construction always minimizes risk and helps ensure resale value.

 OVERALL 'SVG' RATING

chain locker are well designed for a boat that has, as its mantra, thin-water exploration.

Down below

The clever interior arrangement includes several separate areas. The pilothouse has 6 feet, 7 inches of headroom, providing a sense of spaciousness that belies the Kodiak's 26-foot, 6-inch LOA. The inside helm station is to starboard and includes a comfy seat. The electrical panel and engine controls are easily accessed and the visibility is surprisingly good. Some boats have fold-up dinette arrangements behind the helm seat, while others have quarterberths to both port and starboard that make good sea berths. The finish is better than you might expect, with teak-and-holly cabin soles and nice teak trim work.

The stand up galley is to port, and usually includes a small sink, a hand pump for water and small stove. A chair behind the galley is the mate's perch. Just forward is a good-sized hanging locker that also houses the table, which can be set up aft of the helm. The V-berth is nearly 8 feet long and has terrific ventilation with an overhead hatch and several opening portlights.

Engine

As mentioned earlier, Kodiaks came with different engines. Of the six boats I was able to locate currently for sale, four had outboards, ranging from 8 horsepower to 15 horsepower, and two had diesels, including a two-cylinder 15-horsepower Yanmar and one with a 27-horsepower Westerbeke. Outboards are mounted in a fixed well aft of the tiller. While this is convenient, the lower unit must stay in the water all the time, and if the boat is left in the water it will lead to corrosion problems. Of course the key advantage of an outboard is that it can be easily removed and hauled into the shop for maintenance and repairs. The inboard is located under the companionway steps with average access. An 18-gallon fuel tank was standard issue, as was a water tank.

Underway

By all accounts, the Kodiak sails better than it looks like it will. That, of course, does not mean it's a good performer. Still, several owners report that they often top 6 knots on a reach and sail upwind in a decent wind at 5.5 knots or more. The nature of the hull shape and the pilothouse, which creates windage and precludes tight headsail sheeting angles, makes the Kodiak something of a slug to weather. But is that why you'd buy a Kodiak, for windward sailing? Of course not. This is a boat that craves a nice reach and a snug anchorage. The mizzen adds sail area but also weather helm. However, jogging along under jib and jigger is a nice way to keep a boat flat while riding out a strong breeze.

Conclusion

It doesn't take much imagination to see myself, white-haired and stooped, spending my last days cruising among the rocky islands of the Inside Passage or along the craggy coast of Nova Scotia. Don't be surprised to find your faithful correspondent, holed up in a shallow cove, reading a book and occasionally glancing out at the world from the pilothouse of a boat much like the Nimble Kodiak. Besides, with used prices ranging from about $25,000 to $50,000, including the trailer, I will be able to afford the gas required to drive from one great cruising ground to another.

Grampian 26

Not the prettiest girl at the dance,
but this inexpensive pocket-cruiser is just the ticket

What was the first Canadian production sailboat company? No, not C&C, not Hinterhoeller, not Whitby. Give up? Try Grampian Marine. That's right, Grampian, and they came of age at the right moment, during that brief but glorious epoch when styrene wafted from small factories across the land and sailboat production actually flourished in North America. Those golden years, which began in the mid-1960s and hung on into the early 1980s, produced some notable and a lot of forgettable boats. Despite the fact that it may not be the most handsome boat afloat, and that's putting it charitably, the Grampian 26 falls into the notable boat category. Why? For one thing, around 1,000 boats were launched during a 10-year production run making it Grampian's best seller, and for another, this roomy 26-footer was well-built, sailed better than it looked and has endured as something of a cult boat for those looking for a capable but inexpensive small cruiser.

The Grampian 26 was designed by Alex McGruer in 1967 and quickly went into pro-

duction. In fact, 200 boats were ordered the first year alone. McGruer's family had been building boats since 1911 on the Clyde Estuary in Scotland, and although Grampians were built in suburban Oakville, Ontario, McGruer longed for the Scottish countryside and named his designs after the Grampian Hills overlooking the weathered moors of his homeland.

McGruer's mandate was to design a boat big enough for a family of four, with six-foot headroom, and it had to be both seaworthy and trailerable—a tall order. While most 26s have fixed keels, a few centerboarders were built to meet this last requirement. And when it comes to seaworthy, at least one Grampian 26 has completed an Atlantic Circle and countless others have made the long trek from the Great Lakes to the Caribbean and back, and that qualifies as seaworthy.

First impressions

The Grampian 26 has a soft sheer and sweet hull shape with a spoon bow and counter stern. These features are often overlooked because of the high-sided, boxy cabintrunk and ample freeboard. However, the big cabin trunk was a major reason for the boat's popularity as it produced headroom, light and a sense of spaciousness below. By the numbers, a 21-foot LWL and 8-foot, 4-inch beam, the Grampian 26 is comparable to other small cruisers of its day. However, it seems bigger because of more volume belowdecks. The fixed-keel models featured an externally fastened cast iron section with a 4-foot, 3-inch draft. The centerboard models had a 3-foot fixed-keel and board down draft of 6 feet.

The displacement/length ratio of 242 and a sail area/displacement of 16.5 both describe a boat designed for coastal cruising, despite the manufacturer's heady comments about

GRAMPIAN 26

LOA 26'
LWL 21'9"
Beam 8'4"
Draft 4'3"-3'
Displacement
    5,600 lbs.
Ballast 2,600 lbs.
Sail Area
    325 sq. ft.

being a racing machine in the original brochure. The Grampian 26 is also a stiff boat, and the ballast/displacement ratio of 47 percent is no doubt partially responsible. The freestanding rudder is positioned well aft, especially for its day, and it offers good control off the wind. Almost all boats have tiller steering. The sloop rig supports a deck-stepped spar with an air draft of around 36 feet.

Construction

There was nothing fancy about the way the Grampian 26 was built, and that's not a complaint or a compliment. Like most boats of the day, the 26 was heavily laid up. Oil was cheap and there was no skimping on the fiberglass. A fiberglass molded pan was used to anchor the wooden facings for berths and cabinets. Joinerwork was workmanlike at best. Pans, especially in the early days, were not always well-secured to the hull. The keel was fastened with one-inch iron bolts. The centerboard and the rudder were both fiberglass. The rudder included a stainless post and rods forming a rib cage for the resin. Overall the fiberglass work typically featured thick gelcoat that was prone to cracking and crazing. The decks are cored and should be carefully checked for signs of delamination.

What to look for

Any boat that was built between 30 and 40 years ago is going to have some issues. There are several areas of concern with the Grampian 26. Be sure to check the condition of the keel bolts and backing plates, they may well be rusty and in need of love or replacement. Also, the keel may be loose or tweaked and the bolts may need to be taken up and the seal recaulked. If the boat is a centerboard model, the board may be stuck in the cavity and may need to be rebuilt. There is a good chance that there is deck compression around the base of the mast. Some owners have fitted their own mast support systems, some will be better than others. Also check for delamination in the deck and be wary of blisters when you haul. Many Grampians were sold and sailed in the Great Lakes and there are advantages to buying a freshwater boat over a saltwater boat.

GRAMPIAN 26 PRICE DATA

		Low	High
BUC Retail Range	1970	$ 4,900	$ 5,600
	1975	$ 5,350	$ 6,150
		State	Asking
Boats For Sale	1970	Canada	$ 5,400
	1975	NY	$ 9,953
	1980	WA	$10,165

This sounds like a terrible scenario but in truth it isn't. Remember, you can find a nice G26 for less than $10,000, in some cases much less, and if you are willing to invest a few bucks and some elbow grease you can come away with a nicely refurbished coastal cruiser for the price of a new 16-foot runabout sans engine. Other items to look for include changes during the production run. The biggest change came with the last boats built when the model was changed to the Discovery 7.9 that featured a raised deck to make it less boxy looking. The hull was unchanged, but few were launched. Other changes included swapping over to an aluminum toerail about halfway through the production, which allowed the stanchions to be bolted to the rail, freeing valuable side deck space. Most boats were outboard engine models. The inboards came with either a Palmer gasoline engine or an 8-horsepower Volvo diesel. Outboard models typically sell for less and are probably preferred as it makes repowering simply a matter of slashing the debit card, hefting the old one into the garage and the new one onto the boat.

On deck

The cockpit features long seats that are fairly comfortable. Tiller steering frees up space otherwise consumed by a wheel and pedestal. The outboard engine lies in a removable cutout on the transom, making the engine controls accessible. There are lockers to port and starboard, including a cockpit-accessible icebox. The original primary winches were under-

Grampian 26   SAILING Magazine's Value Guide

 PRICE: Most Grampian 26s on the market can be purchased for less than $10,000 and those priced higher have usually been upgraded. It's the proverbial a lot of boat for the buck.

 DESIGN QUALITY: McGruer's design works. It may not be beautiful but it provides plenty of interior space and performs pretty well.

 CONSTRUCTION QUALITY: Grampians were built like most boats of the period. The layup was heavy and finish was marginal. Still, the boats have held up well over the years, the sign of good initial construction.

 USER-FRIENDLINESS: The G26 is easy to handle in a variety of conditions and the interior is comfortable. It is, however, difficult to navigate the side decks and working on deck in general can be a bit awkward.

 SAFETY: The side deck issue and lack of a full bridgedeck are safety issues. However, the boat is solid and well proven on the ocean.

 TYPICAL CONDITION: This is as much an age issue as a maintenance issue. These boats are old, at least 30 years and often closer to 40.

 REFITTING: The G26 is well suited for retrofitting. One reason is that the interior finish was not great to begin with and also, there is elbowroom both above and below decks to renovate and update.

 SUPPORT: There is a lot of information available for Grampians. I am always impressed how some old boat companies are kept alive in spirit by their owners. The Grampian Owners Web site www.grampianowners.com is helpful.

 AVAILABILITY: There are always plenty of G26s on the market. The Great Lakes region, particularly Ontario, seems to have the best selection.

 INVESTMENT AND RESALE: The boats are cheap and may need some time and money invested to bring them up to speed. And while you may not get your money back out, you won't have much invested anyway.

 OVERALL 'SVG' RATING

---

sized, but they likely have been upgraded by now. Also, the original mainsheet was led aft, on a silly angle to a fixed point on the stern. If it hasn't been already, it should be led either to a traveler across the forward end of the cockpit or, and I can't believe I am suggesting this, to a traveler bridge over the companionway. Yes, I know, that's a midboom sheeting arrangement I am recommending, but the 26's loads are manageable.

The side decks are extremely narrow, that's one issue that can't be rectified, however the tradeoff is space below and it is something you get used to. There are teak handrails that line the cabin trunk making it a bit less daunting to go forward. As noted earlier, the single-spreader mast is deck stepped. Naturally, be sure to carefully inspect the standing rigging, chances are it is due for a replacement. The main boom was originally set up for roller reefing, one of the industry's worst ideas, and most owners will have converted over to slab reefing. This allows for the use of a solid vang, as well as being a much faster method of shortening sail.

Down below

To the younger crowd, the interior of the G26 will seem pre-historic. To me, it seems sensible. There was only so much space to work with and McGruer's plan was well received by the public. Indeed, the interior was considered downright luxurious when it was first introduced. When you drop below, the tiny galley with a single sink and single-burner stove is to starboard, just forward of a decent sized quarterberth. Opposite is a dinette arrangement that converts to a double berth, but is better suited as a single. There is a lot of storage under each bunk.

The head runs athwartship, a practical arrangement on a small boat. The V-berth is big enough for average-sized people to sleep comfortably and a full-length shelve is fitted above each side. There's an opening hatch above the bunk. The woodwork is nondescript. However, the key factor below is the 6 feet of headroom in the saloon. Affording most folks the ability to stand up, having a fully enclosed head and four legitimate berths made the Grampian 26 something special in 1967.

Engine

Most of the 1,000 boats launched came with an outboard engine. A robust 25-horsepower Chrysler outboard was standard issue for a while. Now boats on the used market will have smaller, more efficient outboards. A 9.9-horsepower four-stroke is an adequate outboard engine for the boat. Some 26s came standard with inboard engines. Early in the production run a Palmer gas engine was offered and later small one-cylinder diesels by Volvo and Yanmar.

Underway

Owner reports of the Grampian 26s performance vary, yet they all seem to agree that the boat is fairly well balanced, stiff and can carry sail in a blow. Like most spade rudder boats of the day, the tiller needs constant attention. The boat is not the "taut thoroughbred" the brochure claims it to be, and never really was, but it's not a cruising slouch either. Its PHRF rating is about the same as the Cal 25 and Pearson 26, two comparable boats of that time. It is possible to carry full sail to almost 20 knots, although it is more comfortable to reef sooner. Also, the 26 is not particularly close winded as the sheet leads are typically on the rail. Still, the boat is capable of ocean sailing. We saw a Grampian 26 in Lunenburg, Nova Scotia, this summer. It sailed over from Boston as part of the Marblehead to Halifax fleet and had apparently done well in the race.

Conclusion

The Grampian 26 is a roomy, well-built cruiser that can usually be purchased for less than $10,000. You may need to retrofit, or at least update the boat, but it's a boat worthy of a bit of TLC. This once popular pocket-cruiser represents a good buy on the used boat market.

Pearson 26

*This early fin keel and spade rudder
coastal cruiser makes a great first big boat*

The history of Pearson Yachts parallels the history of the American sailboat industry in many ways, at least until the 1990s when the once proud company gave up the ship in a sea of red ink. Cousins Everett and Clint Pearson launched their modest enterprise in 1956, first building dinghies and runabouts in an old textile plant in Bristol, Rhode Island. In 1959 the pair took a flyer and introduced the soon to be legendary 29-foot Triton. The boat was a huge success as the company took 17 orders at that year's New York boat show.

Other models followed and Pearson Yachts rode the wave of fiberglass boat construction to the very top, eventually becoming the largest sailboat builder in the country. Like so many other builders, however, Pearson was consumed by a conglomerate, in this case mammoth Grumman Allied Industries, which alienated its dealers and didn't adapt to the growing specialization that dominates today's sailboat market. As a result, the name Pearson, which once represented cutting-edge technology and quality construction, became staid and lost its appeal.

Pearson's legacy, however, does not lie with its muddled corporate history. No, the company will always be remembered for the many and varied boats it built. Early designs were by Alberg, Alden and Rhodes. In 1966 Bill Shaw took over as the general manager and chief designer. Shaw gradually changed the underwater profile of most of Pearson's lineup. The fin keel and spade rudders of the Pearson 26 and 30 replaced the cutaway full-keel shape, trademarks of the Vanguard, Invicta, Countess and others. Introduced in 1971, the 30 was an immediate success and more than 1,000 boats were built during a nine-year production run. The 26, which was first available in 1970, was another best seller. By the time Pearson took the boat off line in 1983, more than 1,700 had been launched, with another 400 or so built to a slightly modified deck design known first as the Weekender and later as the 26 One-Design.

First impressions

First impressions are long lasting, even if they do date their authors when revealed. There was a well-kept Pearson 26 moored just down the dock from my family's Sabre 28 on the Clinton River in Mount Clemens, Michigan. We're talking back in the early '70s. I remember clearly (despite my tender age) how it had a putrid green deck and cabintop. Seasick green we dubbed it. The Pearson 26 was one of the first boats available in different colors, and the shades offered were interesting to say the least. Still I liked the lines of the P26 then and continue to appreciate them today. The qualities that led to Pearson's popularity are evident in the 26. It is solidly constructed, handles well when

PEARSON 26

LOA 26'2"
LWL 21'8"
Beam 8'8"
Draft 4'
Displacement 5,400 lbs.
Ballast 2,200 lbs.
Sail Area 321 sq. ft.

the wind pipes up and is extremely user-friendly. It is also an excellent value.

The P26 has a modest sheer, typical of the times, and an unobtrusive stair step in the cabin-top that provides headroom and light below. The Weekender and the One-Design have a straight cabintop and consequently about 5 feet of headroom. The clean, gentle entry has a fair amount of overhang and leads to a rather flat forefoot. The fin keel is swept back as is the spade rudder. Displacement is 5,400 pounds, with 2,200 pounds of iron ballast providing a 40 percent ballast-to-displacement ratio, which partially accounts for the boat's stiffness. Sail area is 321 square feet, translating into an SA/D ratio of 16.6, a classic so-called coastal cruiser. Beam is a generous 8 feet, 8 inches and the draft is 4 feet. The sloop rig has an air draft of just over 35 feet. The boat motors smartly with a 9.9-horsepower outboard.

Construction

The Pearson 26 construction varies a bit from early boats like the Ariel, Wanderer and Pearson Alberg 35. Production techniques were becoming more efficient and Pearson didn't hesitate to employ them. The hull is solid fiberglass, and like almost all boats of that time, the deck is balsa cored. In fact, Everett Pearson was a pioneer in developing end-grain balsa as a coring material. The P26 makes use of molded liners, which are a blessing and a curse. While liners streamline production and offer a bit of hull rigidity and uniformity, they make accessing wiring and hull fittings very difficult and can also give the boat a sterile look.

The hull-and-deck joint is on an outward flange, sealed, through-bolted and covered with a vinyl rubrail. What is interesting about this joint is that it is fiberglassed from the inside. This makes it watertight, and few 26 owners complain about leaking hull-and-deck joints. However, the external joint is exposed to damage from smacking into docks and other things that boats occasionally smack into. If production efficiencies were responsible for this joint, then I would understand because it is easier to manufacture boats with external flanges. However, glassing over the joint from the inside is anything but efficient, and we all know what a bother vinyl rubrails can be. Still, it's important

PEARSON 26 PRICE DATA

		Low	High
BUC Retail Range	1975	$ 8,500	$ 9,750
	1980	$10,100	$11,500
		State	Asking
Boats For Sale	1972	OH	$ 4,000
	1975	VT	$ 6,900
	1980	GA	$ 7,500

to note that few 26 owners mention problems and replacement rails are available. The keel is cast iron, which is something of a maintenance headache, and externally fastened with eight hefty bolts.

What to look for

Let's first take a look at some changes made during 13 years of production. In 1975 the Weekender first went on the market. This model has the identical hull shape of the P26, but the cockpit is a couple of feet longer and the cabintop is a bit shorter, reducing interior volume. If you plan to strictly daysail the Weekender or the later One-Design, which had slightly tighter sheeting angles, might be the models to look for. Also in 1975, a separate shelf was added in the port locker for fuel tank storage. This was an important addition since it was otherwise possible for gas fumes to end up in the bilge. The Weekender was phased out in 1976 and the P26 One-Design was offered until the last year of production in 1983.

According to most P26 owners, the biggest maintenance issue on the boat is the rudder shaft and bearings. The rudder itself is a rather heavy blade made of solid fiberglass, and the stock is aluminum, a poor choice of material since it's soft and subject to wear. Fortunately, the problem has been around for a long time and many 26 owners have replaced the rudder and/or the bearings that slowly eat away at the stock, particularly on the bottom bearings. When evaluating a P26 be sure to carefully check the rudder stock when the boat is out of the water. New bearings can help solve the

Pearson 26

 PRICE: The P26 is inexpensive, not because it's a bad boat but simply because there are so many to choose from.

 **DESIGN QUALITY:** An early fin-and-spade-rudder boat, the P26 delivers good performance and will stand up to a stiff breeze.

 **CONSTRUCTION QUALITY:** The P26 employs molded linings and has an unusual hull-and-deck joint. Also the aluminum rudder stock was a cost-saving measure. Overall, however, the usual Pearson construction quality is evident, proven by how well most 26s have stood the test of time.

 **USER-FRIENDLINESS:** The P26 is forgiving and easy to handle under both sail and power. The interior isn't spacious, but it works. The boat is not system intensive, a good thing in an old boat.

 SAFETY: The rudder factor is worrisome and should be dealt with as soon as you purchase. The cockpit is vulnerable to a swamping. However, P26s are sailing all over the country, year after year.

 TYPICAL CONDITION: P26s seem to fall into two categories on the used boat market. Either they have been loved and upgraded or they have been forgotten and neglected. It is worth looking for a nice one, as prices don't vary much.

 REFITTING: The simplicity of the P26 makes most tasks on the boat a do-it-yourself project. However, the molded linings make access difficult and some projects, like changing the rudder bearings and repairing delamination, may require expert help.

 SUPPORT: Although Pearson is out of business, there is an active national owners association, the NPYOA (National Pearson Yacht Owner's Association). It publishes the Current, a newsletter packed with information. The best information on the P26 is definitely Dan Pfieffer's web site at www.en.com/users/danp/boat/boat.htm

 **AVAILABILITY:** The P26 is widely available all over the country.

 INVESTMENT AND RESALE: The P26 does not require much of an investment to begin with and returns a lot of fun for the dollar.

 OVERALL 'SVG' RATING

---

problem, and if necessary, a new rudder with a stainless stock can be purchased from Foss Foam Products, in Warwick, Rhode Island.

Other items to check for are a delaminated cockpit sole, keel bolt corrosion, keel corrosion and faulty wiring. There is also a plywood core under the maststep on deck that may be rotten. Of course, all age related items, from standing and running rigging to tired sails and outboard motors, should be inspected. Be wary of bargains, especially if you want to spend your time on the water, not in the yard bringing the boat up to speed.

On deck

The Pearson 26 has a roomy, relatively comfortable cockpit for three or four adults. As noted earlier, the Weekender and One-Design have slightly larger cockpits. All boats came with tiller steering, although I am sure somewhere in the world there is a 26 retrofitted with wheel steering. There are two sail lockers for storage, and the mainsheet traveler is aft, allowing for end-boom sheeting, which keeps the cockpit clear. There is not much of a bridgedeck—basically just a sill—but this is not a boat intended for offshore sailing. The cockpit seats are low and visibility from the helm over the deckhouse is not great, especially if you're short. The tradeoff is more room below and a drier boat.

There are teak handrails on the raised section of the deckhouse and double lifelines with well-supported stanchions. The boat feels bigger than 26 feet when you make your way forward. The nonskid may be quite worn and not particularly effective, although older Pearsons have aged well and you don't see the gelcoat crazing and cracking common on other boats. The mast is deck stepped, with a compression post below. Look carefully for a depression at the step; it may be sign of delamination. The genoa tracks allow for decent sheeting angles and many boats will be set up to fly spinnakers.

Down below

Few people buy the Pearson 26 for its spacious accommodations below. However, the interior plan is well-thought-out, and the boat has more room than you might think. Dropping below, the first thing you'll notice is the headroom, about 5 feet, 10 inches by my estimate. The galley is to port and the icebox faces forward, with the nav station opposite and the settee serving as the seat. Other details may vary as owners have made changes over the years. The boat I recently climbed through here in Fort Lauderdale had a two-burner stove and sink facing aft.

Most boats have a dinette arrangement to port in the saloon, which is a good use of space in a small boat. This can usually be converted into a double bunk. There is a straight settee to starboard with storage lockers behind. The head and hanging locker are private, with a large V-berth forward. Many boats have a 22-gallon water tank under the forward berth. Teak trim accents the molded white finish, and the overall effect is rather cozy. Two large ports light the saloon, while two smaller ports are in the head compartment. If you live where it's warm, converting these into opening portlights would be a good idea. There is a hatch over the forward cabin.

The boat was designed for an outboard motor, with a built-in motor well eliminating the need to mount a bracket astern and providing a solid, midtransom mounting platform. The fuel tank storage shelf accommodates a standard 6-gallon plastic tank rather nicely. The boat handles well under power, using the tiller for steering and the rudder can be completely turned around for control in reverse. Today's outboards,

especially four-strokes, are quiet, clean and reliable. They're also convenient. If you have a problem, you can toss the engine in the trunk and take it the mechanic. Although it is rare, I have heard of P26s fitted with inboards.

Underway

Owner comments reflect the forgiving nature of the P26. It's an ideal first "big" boat because it's easy to sail and will stand up in gusty conditions. The helmsperson can control the tiller and sheets, and with a bit of experience, it's ideal for singlehanding. Some owners refute the notion that the boat develops weather helm, arguing that if sailed on its lines and not wildly overcanvassed it is not an issue. The shape of the hull supports this claim as the P26 has a flat forefoot; the only effect of heeling will be to create leeway. The rudder is also large and located well aft, which serves to reduce helm. Several owners report that they race their boats locally under PHRF. By all accounts they perform best when the wind is more than 10 knots.

The P26 needs a headsail, since performance is marginal under main alone, and a large 130- to 150-percent genoa can be carried upwind with a full main in winds to about 15 knots. At that point shortening up the headsail flattens the boat and keeps the speed up. Most owners tie a reef in the main as the apparent wind inches toward 20 knots. The P26 handles well off the wind, and several owners describe surfing downwind at near double-digit speeds.

Conclusion

The Pearson 26 is an ideal boat to test the waters, so to speak, to see if sailing is indeed something you might enjoy. If you find you can't get enough time on the water, the P26 is not a boat you will quickly outgrow. It pleases on a variety of levels. With prices ranging from $6,000 to $11.500 it is hard to go wrong with this popular American-built favorite.

Bristol 27

This Alberg-designed sturdy cruiser
was the author's first love

My first boat was a Bristol 27. OK, I'll admit that was 28 short years ago. Yikes. It was a 1966 model with a dreadful name, Lobster Mobster. I spotted it lying on the hard in a small boatyard up the Clinton River in Mount Clemens, Michigan. I had dropped out of college again and my future was not looking all that bright. My mother offered me a deal. Instead of wasting money on another semester of school she would match what I raised that summer as long as I put it into buying a sailboat. She knew the only thing I wanted to do was sail. There was one condition however: Once I had the boat I had to take off and go cruising. Not surprisingly I took the deal. I sold my car, washed windows and worked in a muffler shop. It was late October by the time I raised $5,000. She chipped in $4,000 and there was just enough left over to ship the boat to Florida. I took the bus south, met the boat in Miami and I have been sailing ever since.

I remember my Bristol 27 fondly. Designed by Carl Alberg, she was robustly constructed and nice to look at. I kept the boat for two years, sailing all over the Keys and Bahamas, and I mean sailing. The outboard engine died soon after the boat arrived in Florida and I could never afford another. I remember tacking up the Miami River raising seven bridges along the way; yikes again. Although I was naive, luck was with me, I couldn't have a picked a better boat to cut my teeth on.

Clint Pearson, who along with his brother Everett had founded Pearson Yachts, created Bristol Yachts after selling Pearson in the mid-1960s. One of the company's first boats was the 27, which was shamelessly copied from the successful Pearson Triton, but was a good quality boat. The first 27 was launched in 1965 and was an immediate success. More than 170 were sold the first two years and although nobody is quite sure how many were finally built, most estimates put the number between 300 to 350 before production ceased in the mid-1970s. There is always a decent selection of Bristol 27s on the market and most are listed for under $12,000, making them darned good values.

First impressions

The Bristol 27 is a vintage Carl Alberg design. The hull shape has a short waterline with long overhangs, a sweet sheer, low freeboard and a stair step cabintrunk. It may not be a fast hull but it looks relaxed and quietly capable in the water. All of Alberg's designs have a DNA connection to the Scandinavian Folkboat, the small low-slung sea boat that emerged after the war and helped make sailing popular in Europe. Below the waterline the Bristol 27 features Alberg's classic cutaway full keel with an attached rudder that slopes aft. Draft is a moderate 4 feet. Inboard models house the prop in a completely protected aperture. The

BRISTOL 27

LOA 27'2"
LWL 19'9"
Beam 8'
Draft 4'
Displacement
  6,600 lbs.
Ballast 2,575 lbs.
Sail Area
  340 sq. ft.

low-aspect sloop rig includes a deck-stepped spar, a long boom and a whopping total sail area of 340 square feet.

Construction

Much has been written about the heavy construction of the first fiberglass boats. While that may not always be accurate, it was certainly true with early Bristols. In the two years I owned my 27 I never pumped the bilge—honest. Granted I had no engine and a porta potty for a head, (the only through-hull fitting was for the sink discharge) but it didn't leak a drop. And I gave it plenty of opportunities by going aground all over the Keys and Bahamas. The hull was Kretschmer-proof. The construction wasn't fancy but it was strong. The boat never flexed or groaned in a seaway. The 27 was built with a solid fiberglass hull and deck through-bolted on deck clamp. The deck and coachroof were an integral mold. A fiberglass liner was used overhead in the interior. Bulkheads were well tabbed to the hull. The lead ballast was encapsulated in the keel cavity.

What to look for

There were three different versions of the Bristol 27. The Weekender featured a long, 8-foot cockpit and was more of a daysailer with a very small interior. The standard model, sometimes called the cruising model, came with opposing settees and no table; that's the model I had. The dinette model included a table to starboard that eliminated the settee. The dinette model was the most popular. Early 27s also came standard with an outboard engine that was mounted in an enclosed well that was not the best idea. The lower unit remained in the water all the time and corroded quickly. Later boats offered inboards, usually an Atomic 4 or occasionally a one-cylinder, 10-horsepower Westerbeke diesel. Of the three, the diesel model is the most desirable. Look for a boat that has been recently repowered.

Other problems owners report include leaky hull-and-deck joints and gelcoat crazing. The hull-and-deck joint issue is not a surprise as most boats on the market are close to 40 years old. However, it is not an easy problem to solve short of pulling and rebedding each

BRISTOL 27 PRICE DATA

		Low	High
BUC Retail Range	1970	$10,200	$11,600
	1975	$13,800	$15,700
		State	Asking
Boats For Sale	1968	MI	$ 5,000
	1972	MA	$12,500
	1975	FL	$14,900

bolt, if you can get to them. Gelcoat cracks and crazes are not usually structural and can be filled and sanded when you repaint the deck. Surprisingly, many boats seem to be in near original condition, ranging from tiny sheet winches, to single lifelines, to plaid fabric on the seat cushions that belongs in a museum. Updating the boat can be costly.

On deck

The 27 has a 6-foot, 2-inch cockpit that seems more spacious because of tiller steering. I have a dear friend, he's in his 40s, and has been sailing 10 years, and he's never used a tiller. He's not unusual, just unfortunate. Steering with a tiller is an essential experience. From a practical standpoint, a pedestal and wheel takes up too much valuable space in a small, narrow boat like the Bristol 27. And besides, the wheel can't be large enough to offer much helming satisfaction. The cockpit includes lockers to port and starboard. The inboard models convert the large well aft into a welcome lazarette. Early models like mine had a stout bridgedeck. Later models reduced this to a small sill to make it easier to step over. I like the bridgedeck.

The side decks are narrow. Of course, the whole boat is narrow as the beam is only eight feet. Handholds are well placed on the cabin trunk but if it hasn't been done you should consider beefing up the stanchions and pulpits. The anodized spar, with an air draft of just over 36 feet is probably the original. It really is impressive how these aluminum sec-

Bristol 27

 PRICE: If you try, you can find a nice 27 for less than $10,000. If you are willing to tackle a fixer-upper project you may be able to find one for half that.

 DESIGN QUALITY: There is something timeless about older Alberg designs. They may heel a lot, they're not very fast, but they are seaworthy and handsome, and that counts.

CONSTRUCTION QUALITY:

 The Bristol 27 is a strong boat and was well constructed in its day. By today's standards it's overbuilt and unsophisticated. It does represent the enduring strength of old fiberglass boats.

 USER-FRIENDLINESS: The 27 is easy to sail and surprisingly nimble under sail. But it's small and cramped down below. A tradeoff.

SAFETY: Strong construction and seaworthy design make the 27 a safe boat, even offshore. The on-deck fittings should be beefed up.

TYPICAL CONDITION: These boats range from 30 to 40 years old. How much can you expect from a boat of that vintage? Even so, many have been well cared for and updated over the years. Sadly, many have not.

 REFITTING: Not an easy boat to work on, access is often poor and you must be creative when it comes to parts. Good original construction helps.

 SUPPORT: Bristol is kaput and even when they were in business they were more interested in selling new boats than helping their old customers. There is a good owners' association, www.bristolowners.org, with a lot of information.

 AVAILABILITY: There were a lot of boats built and that translates into boats for sale. The East Coast and Chesapeake seem like the best bets; Bristols were never big on the West Coast.

 INVESTMENT AND RESALE: You can't go too far wrong on an investment of $10,000—unless you go crazy and throw money at the boat that you won't get back out. But what the heck, it's a sailboat after all, they deserve some irrational love.

OVERALL 'SVG' RATING

tions on so many old boats have endured over the years. The boom featured roller reefing with a small worm gear at the gooseneck. If a slab reefing arrangement hasn't been added—do it immediately. Roller reefing never worked very well.

Down below

If you haven't been in a 1960s 27-foot boat in awhile, you are in for a surprise. There just isn't much room. A narrow beam, short waterline and relatively long cockpit all take space away from the interior. And to think I thought I was living in the lap of luxury; yikes again. The 27 does have decent headroom, at least in the saloon, which falls under the raised portion the coachroof, and the finish is workmanlike at best. While fairly large portlights help with

natural light, ventilation is sketchy. There is a hatch in the V-berth and that's it. Adding dorades, or better still, another hatch and a few opening portlights is a big improvement.

When you step below the tiny galley is under foot and to port. It includes a sink, stove, small counter and storage bin. The icebox/nav center is opposite. A clever feature that was not very practical was an access hatch to the icebox from the cockpit. Insulation was poor to begin with and this didn't help. My boat had two sea berths/settees in the saloon with shelves above. Continuing forward there was a small enclosed head, with a hanging locker opposite and a V-berth. The water tank was under the V-berth. The dinette model featured a swinging table to port that was removable to form another double berth, upping the berth total to an absurd five. Some boats included a quarterberth, just in case you needed to stuff one more person below. The weekender interior is not really worth mentioning, it is more of a cuddy cabin.

Engine

Most early boats were outboards. Mine originally had a 15-horsepower Chrysler and, when it ran, I lumbered along at 4 knots. I wasn't sad to see it die. The inboard models are preferred, not only for the obvious motoring advantages but also because they provided an alternator to power a real, if simple, electrical system. The Atomic 4, 30-horsepower gas engine was the most common and did a fine job of pushing the 27 through a chop. The Westerbeke 10-horsepower diesel, sometimes called the Pilot, was a bit on the small side. Although my boat was an outboard it did have a 22-gallon fuel tank mounted under the cockpit sole. Access to either inboard is from behind and below the companionway steps. It helps to be very small and agile when working on the engine.

Underway

Like most Alberg designs, the Bristol 27 heels easily, some say too easily. However, it does dig in at a point, usually somewhere between 15 and 20 degrees and then it becomes quite stiff indeed. That's just the nature of the design. You can ease the heeling by reefing the main but that does tend to de-power the boat. The 27 is faster than you might think, partially because when it does heel the 19-foot, 9-inch waterline suddenly becomes a lot longer. I remember crossing the Gulf Stream to Bimini in a snotty norther and clipping along at close to 6 knots for 10 hours. I also remember reaching out to the Dry Tortugas, 65 miles from Key West, and making landfall before darkness. The 27 does have a bit of weather helm and she rolls off wind. She can hobbyhorse in a chop too. However, her overall sea motion is soft and she rarely pounds.

Conclusion

The Bristol 27 eliminates a prime excuse for not buying a boat—that sailing is too expensive. You can find a nice Bristol 27, possibly with a newer diesel, for somewhere between $10,000 to $15,000. That's not much to spend for a handsome, capable, safe boat with a proud pedigree. The Bristol 27 is one of the better values in a good old used boat.

Catalina 27

*Good sailing, roomy interior and active owners
behind the popularity of this coastal cruiser*

The Catalina 27 is an American classic. First launched in 1971, more than 6,600 boats were built during a 20-year production run, making it possibly the best-selling 27-footer of all time. Frank Butler, the 27's co-designer, as well as the founder and driving force behind Catalina Yachts, has a uncanny knack for creating boats that people love and they show their love with their checkbooks. Catalina has built more than 60,000 boats, more than any other American sailboat company.

In many ways, the 27 was the model for a design and construction philosophy that continues to serve Catalina today. It is a simple but successful formula—build stylish but definitely affordable boats with semimodern hull shapes and high-volume interiors. Catalina builds its boats efficiently, which is often viewed as a sin by other builders that secretly envy the company's huge production runs. Catalina knows its customers and what they want. The company has an impressive ratio of repeat buyers, which is the ultimate compliment for any builder.

By the same token, used boat buyers also know what they're getting with the Catalina 27. It's a spacious, user-friendly family cruiser. A PHRF rating of around 210 means that it can be raced competitively on Wednesday nights or in active one-design fleets, although racing is not its forte. It is an ideal boat for the way most of us use our boats, that is daysailing and weekend outings. It isn't the best engineered boat in the marina, but it is, as one owner told me, a boat you can let your 16-year-old son take out with his friends and not worry about. And you can find a nice Catalina 27 with an outboard engine for well under $10,000.

First impressions

The Catalina 27 was a "big" boat when it was first introduced in 1971. In fact, at the time it was the queen of the Catalina fleet. The look is "California 1970s modern." This translates into an almost flat sheerline with a large but

CATALINA 27

LOA 26'10"
LWL 21'9"
Beam 8'10"
Draft 4';
  Wing Keel 3'5"
Ballast 2,700 lbs.
Displacement 6,850 lbs.
Sail Area 340 sq. ft.
  Tall Rig 364 sq. ft.

nicely blended cabintrunk and cockpit coamings. There is plenty of freeboard and nearly 9 feet of beam, which of course creates space below. Under the water, the high-aspect fin keel sweeps aft, as does the spade rudder. A wing keel shoal-draft model was offered in 1979, reducing the draft from 4 feet to 3 feet, 5 inches but requiring extra ballast. A tall rig option was available for light-air regions.

Construction

The Catalina 27 hull is solid fiberglass and the thickness tapers significantly from the waterline up. The deck is plywood cored, which is not the best material for the job, although deck delamination doesn't seem to be the common problem it is on many older boats. Catalina used molded hull and headliners, streamlining the manufacturing process.

I often lament the use of liners in my reviews because they make it difficult to access the hull and have structural limitations. However, for boats less than 30 feet, they make production sense provided that they are well bonded to the hull. The Catalina 27 was not designed or built to be a bluewater boat, and there is nothing wrong with that.

Some original construction details are more worrisome than the less than robust scantlings. Early boats were fitted with gate valves on below-the-waterline through-hull fittings and most deck hardware did not have backing plates. It is likely that these shortcomings have been addressed by owners along the way. The ballast is external and the iron keel bolts should be carefully examined. The ballast-to-displacement ratio is more than 40 percent.

What to look for

The first thing to look for is the right configuration that suits your needs from among the variables: standard or shoal draft, standard or tall rig, outboard or inboard engine, gas or diesel inboard. In addition to the wing keel offered in 1979, a 3-foot shoal draft was an option from the start. If you sail on Chesapeake Bay and plan to race the boat in the active one-design fleet in Annapolis, you might be best suited with a standard draft, tall rig, outboard engine, early model 27. These were the light-

CATALINA 27 PRICE DATA

		Low	High
BUC Retail Range	1975	$ 7,750	$ 8,900
	1985	$12,800	$14,600
		State	Asking
Boats For Sale	1973	WI	$ 7,900
	1980	AR	$14,000
	1987	NY	$16,700

est, fastest and cheapest boats. If you live in Florida and want to cross the Gulf Stream and cruise the Bahamas, the shoal draft, standard rig, inboard diesel model might be your best choice. There were many small changes made during the long production run, so the best acquisition strategy is to look at many different boats before making a choice.

In addition to finding the right configuration, there are several other problems to be wary of. Leaks are the bane of many 27s and water finds its way below through the hull-and-deck joint, the hatches, the chainplates and deck fittings. Chainplate leaks often result in bulkhead delamination.

Be sure to check the through-hull fittings and replace any gate valves with seacocks. Also, check for backing plates on deck fittings; occasionally owners have added these and sometimes by remounting the fittings they have inadvertently created leaks. The lack of backing plates allowed deck fittings to move, and the gelcoat around chocks, cleats, and other fittings is often crazed and cracked. Other items to inspect are the spreaders and particularly the cast aluminum spreader sockets as they're prone to failure. The result can be a mast toppling into the drink. Apparently Catalina is well aware of this problem and has a ready-made replacement kit available.

On deck

The Catalina 27 has a shallow but comfortable cockpit with a locker to port and aft lazarette. Tiller steering was standard, although I have seen some early boats retrofitted with a

Catalina 27

 PRICE: The Catalina is obviously a price-driven boat, but it delivers an awful lot of boat for the money. You can have your choice of 27s for less than $10,000.

 **DESIGN QUALITY:** Frank Butler and Robert Finch came up with an enduring favorite. The boat was intended to be a coastal cruiser and casual racer, and it pushes a lot of the right buttons.

 CONSTRUCTION QUALITY: The 27 is lightly built and corners were cut, yet most 27s are still sailing. Original fiberglass work was adequate. The problems are found in the details.

 USER-FRIENDLINESS: Easy to sail, comfortable on deck and below, the only real drawback is poor engine access on the inboard models, and the inefficiency of the outboard models.

SAFETY: The huge companionway is handy but dangerous in a blow. There is no bridgedeck, and stanchions were not well supported.

TYPICAL CONDITION: Of course with 6,600 27s built, the boats run the gamut in terms of condition. However, most owners seem to take care of their boats—Catalina owners are loyal to a fault.

 REFITTING: The use of hull and headliners makes refitting projects challenging. However, it is easy for many skilled owners to match or exceed original factory workmanship.

 **SUPPORT:** The International Catalina 27 Association provides much information on its Web site www.catalina27.org. Also, Catalina Direct, at www.catalinadirect.com, can supply parts and advice.

 AVAILABILITY: A quick look of boats for sale in the southeastern United States came up with 66 boats. If you want a Catalina 27 and are patient, you can find just the boat you want at just the price you want to pay.

 INVESTMENT AND RESALE: The 27 doesn't require much of an investment and is inexpensive to operate and maintain. The market is well defined, and if the boat is in good condition, you will be able to get most of your money back when you sell.

OVERALL 'SVG' RATING

pedestal and wheel. Late in the production run, wheel steering became an option and many boats after 1984 are equipped with wheels. The companionway is enormous and there is not a bridgedeck to speak of. Companionway leaks are common, especially on older models before a sea hood was added. The mainsheet arrangement shifted around over the years. Early boats lead the sheet aft, but the angle from the boom to the traveler is not very efficient and tends to interfere with the helmsman. Later boats mounted the traveler over the companionway; however this midboom sheeting really adds a lot of friction to the system and loads up a boom section that isn't very stout.

The headsail tracks are inboard, allowing close sheeting angles. The standard rigging requires a close inspection, and if it is older than 10 years consider updating it. Double lifelines became standard early, but the lifelines were

led to the base of the bow pulpit. This was fairly common in the 1960s and early 1970s, allowing the deck-sweeping genoas to roam freely. The forward hatch mounts flush, which is nice looking and saves a few toe bruises, but almost assures leaks when a wave sloshes aboard. A nice improvement was the molded external chain locker added on later models.

Down below

The interior is spacious and user-friendly. It doesn't feature elegant joinerwork, but so what, you don't buy a Catalina 27 for the craftsmanship, you buy it to have fun on the water. The huge companionway makes stepping below a breeze, which is not always the case in small boats. If you happen across an old boat that hasn't been updated, it is like stepping into a time capsule. Honest John, the 1974 model I examined in Fort Lauderdale, Florida, still had the original plaid cushion covers and weird orange brown shag carpeting. Still, the boat has more room below than my brother's Centurion 32 of the same vintage.

Catalina offered two basic interior plans. The standard layout includes a V-berth forward followed by an enclosed head. The saloon has two opposite settees and the galley is aft to port. The dinette interior layout places the galley alongside to port with a dinette to starboard and two quarterberths, which are the best sleeping berths on the boat. For cruising purposes the dinette arrangement is more convenient, although the standard plan is less cluttered. Both layouts include plenty of storage, although it is under the settees and something of a pain to access. Headroom is about 6 feet and ventilation is adequate. Most galleys will have small one- or two-burner alcohol stoves, and some may have 12-volt refrigeration, although this will likely have required a complete icebox rebuild as the original insulation was inadequate. The original icebox drain tends to back flow when heeled to port. The electrical panel is tucked away in the quarterberth.

Engine

When it comes to the engine, you'll find a great variety when you start looking at used Catalina 27s. Originally the boat was offered with either an outboard or an Atomic 4 gasoline engine. The outboard was designed to fit into the aft locker, or engine well, and while this kept the engine out of sight, it didn't make it easy to operate or maintain. Most owners fitted remote engine controls. The advantage of an outboard is that you can haul it off the boat, put it in the trunk and take it to a shop for repairs. And, when it's past its prime you simply buy a new one. The disadvantages include the lack of power (you need at least a 9.9-horsepower engine) difficulty in maneuvering in tight quarters and the inability to charge the batteries efficiently.

The inboard option is probably better, although the engine location under the cockpit is difficult to access, making even simple tasks like checking the oil a challenge. The Universal Atomic 4 at one time dominated the sail-

boat market and is plenty of engine for the Catalina 27. Although gasoline engines have gone out of fashion, Atomic 4 parts are readily available and cheap. You can actually buy a completely rebuilt Atomic 4 for less than a new 10-horsepower outboard. Diesels became an option in the late 1970s. Some boats were fitted with a 6-horsepower Petter, which is a cranky machine under the best of conditions and doesn't provide much oomph. Later boats had two-cylinder Universal diesels. If I could find a 27 with one of these, especially if it had low hours, I'd jump on it.

Under way

Naturally, the different hull and rig configurations influence the sailing characteristics. One of the most surprising features of the 27 is how nicely it sails. The boat is fairly well balanced, and according to several owner reports, thrives upwind in moderate conditions. In heavy air the 27 is a bit tender and one owner suggests putting the first reef in the main at 12 knots. Ironically, another says he sails his boat on breezy San Francisco Bay and is impressed with how stiff the boat is. Several owners who race the boat note that fairing the hull is critical, and another attributes his success to changing the wire rope halyards to Kevlar. My own experience is limited to a few sails on Michigan's Lake St. Clair long ago, but I clearly remember the boat being responsive, relatively fast and easy to sail.

The Catalina 27 fits the vague description of coastal cruiser and casual racer. With that said, several boats have made impressive passages. I remember talking with a young solo sailor in Bermuda who was heading toward the Caribbean in his 27, and I heard of another 27 that circumnavigated.

Conclusion

The Catalina 27 didn't become one of the most popular boats ever built without good reason. It offers good sailing, comfortable accommodations, one-design fleets and active owner's groups. With prices ranging from around $8,000 for old, tired 27s to less than $20,000 for late-model gems, the boat is also a terrific value.

Nor'Sea 27

A little cruising boat with big-boat
seaworthiness and a dedicated following

The Nor'Sea 27 was designed by Lyle Hess, and that fact alone makes the boat worthy of a close inspection. Hess, who died in 2002 at age 90, was a master of creating handsome, spirited, ocean-going small boats. When asked in an interview many years ago what the common quality in his designs was, he thoughtfully replied, "I feel that any boat that points her bow out to sea should be designed so that the crew need not worry about a safe return." That is a sound and timeless premise, one that should be tacked to the wall in every yacht designer's office and one that is certainly fulfilled by the capable Nor'Sea 27.

Hess cut his teeth designing and building wooden boats. The shrinking wooden boat market forced him out of the business in the 1950s, but the burgeoning fiberglass revolution opened the door to his return as a yacht designer in the 1960s. He is perhaps best known for his designs of Lynn and Larry Pardey's boats and the Bristol Channel Cutter, built by Sam L. Morse Company. In the mid-1970s, Dean Wixom approached Hess with a seemingly impossible set of design parameters; he wanted a small cruiser, capable of sailing any ocean but also capable of navigating the interstate on a trailer. As the story goes, Wixom wanted a boat for exploring the Sea of Cortez without the hassle of sailing all the way down the Mexican coast. According to Chuck Malseed in an article in *Cruising World* in 1977, Wixom told Hess that a boat with big-boat seaworthiness and small-boat trailerability would open many interesting cruising grounds to sailors with limited amounts of time. Hess was up to the challenge and the result was the Nor'Sea 27, a classic pocket cruiser with an extraordinary resume.

Although Wixom eventually sold his firm and went cruising in his own Nor'Sea 27, his concept struck a nerve with sailors across the country. The Nor'Sea 27 is still currently in production, available in either kit form or as a complete boat, and more than 450 are already sailing the oceans and inland seas. And when I say sailing I mean it—four of these small but robust cruisers have circumnavigated, one via Cape Horn, and hundreds of Atlantic and Pacific crossings have been logged.

First impressions

Most Nor'Sea 27s are, at least by definition, center cockpits. It might be more accurate to say that they have aft cabins. However you describe the boat, it is unique and appealing, especially to those who like the traditional, canoe stern look. Even a casual observer will quickly note the quality ethos that permeates every aspect of the boat. Although an aft cockpit model is also available, the salty little aft cabin sloop far outsells the aft cockpit model. Hess designed plenty of sheer into the hull line and one of the most distinguishing features of

NOR'SEA 27

LOA 27',
  31' with bowsprit
LWL 25'
Beam 8'
Draft 3'10"
Displacement
  8,100 lbs.
Ballast 3,100 lbs.
Sail Area
  394 sq. ft.

the Nor'Sea 27 is a molded lapstrake hull. In the water the boat seems larger than 27 feet and although the bowsprit extends the LOA to 31 feet, the boat still has a stately bearing and undeniably sweet lines.

Below the waterline, the Nor'Sea has a classic cutaway full keel hull shape and the large outboard rudder is attached to the trailing edge of the keel with an aperture for the prop. This shape allows for a relatively shallow draft of 3 feet, 10 inches and still provides ample stability and a nice motion in a seaway. It is also about the maximum draft that can still be launched from a trailer, although in reality the relatively few Nor'Seas that are trailered are usually towed to boatyards and popped in the water. It takes a truck with some oomph to haul the 8,000-pound Nor'Sea 27—the boat was not designed to be trailer-sailed frequently but instead to be "transportable" between cruising grounds. The 27 was offered with either a tall or short rig, depending upon your sailing agenda. The tall rig sail area is just under 400 square feet and, at least on early boats, carried a bit more ballast than the short rig.

Construction

The construction scantlings of the Nor'Sea 27 are most impressive. The one-piece, hand-laid, solid fiberglass hull includes up to 22 layers of mat and woven roving along the stem, keel and stern sections. Hull thickness tapers from $5/16$ inches at the turn of the deck to $3/4$ inches at the keel cavity. Molding a lapstrake hull is not something a typical production builder would tackle; it not only requires a more sophisticated and expensive plug, it also takes a lot more time to laminate. The lapstrake hull does more than just look salty, it adds considerable strength to hull form, a time-tested technique that is proven by many lapstrake wood folkboats still sailing all over the world. The deck is cored with plywood and through-bolted to the hull on 6-inch centers. For the most part, stainless steel backing plates are used to reinforce deck fittings.

The internal ballast is lead and, as noted above, the keel cavity is thick fiberglass for those inevitable groundings. The large rudder is fiberglass over a foam core. The pintles and gud-

NOR'SEA 27 PRICE DATA

		Low	High
BUC Retail Range	1980	$29,500	$32,000
	1986	$33,700	$37,400
		State	Asking
Boats For Sale	1983	IL	$52,000
	1984	AR	$38,500
	1987	FL	$74,900

geons are oversized and bolted through the thick transom. The bottom bearing is strapped to the trailing edge of the keel. The handsome tiller is made from ash and mahogany. A partial molded liner is used in the interior and all bulkheads are built from marine grade plywood.

What to look for

Although the early Nor'Sea 27s are approaching 30 years in age, in general the boat has held up extremely well. My friend Ed Hershman recently purchased a 1985 aft cockpit model in Marathon, Florida, and the surveyor was amazed at the condition of the boat, a tribute to first-rate original construction. Of course few Nor'Sea 27s are completely alike because many boats were sold in kit form. In fact, the boat is still available as a kit, and a nearly completed version that leaves the finishing trim to the owner is the company's most popular model. While the hull and deck are the same on all boats, the quality of finish can vary dramatically on kit boats. Not surprisingly, factory finished boats are the most desired. Another item to inspect is the diesel engine. Early boats were fitted with a nine-horsepower Farymann. Later the engine was changed to a two-cylinder Yanmar, a nice upgrade. Some owners have reported corrosion problems with the aluminum 30-gallon fuel tank.

As mentioned earlier, two rig plans were offered, however, the ballast was upped to 3,100 pounds for both plans in 1980 and has remained constant. The obvious factor to look for when considering a Nor'Sea 27 is the deck arrangement. Ed Hershman's boat is an aft

Nor'Sea 27

 PRICE: The high initial price is the biggest drawback to the Nor'Sea 27. But as the adage goes, "You get what you pay for." When compared to the cost of a comparable new boat the price becomes more palatable.

 **DESIGN QUALITY:** I'm partial to Lyle Hess pocket cruisers and the Nor'Sea maybe a bit quirky but it is still handsome, versatile and capable. The boat is just as intriguing today as it was 25 years ago.

 CONSTRUCTION QUALITY: This is one tough little boat, heavily built but also well engineered.

 **USER-FRIENDLINESS:** The boat is easy to handle, and while it is also easy to singlehand the clever interior arrangement makes it perfect for a couple.

 **SAFETY:** By almost all accounts this a safe little sea boat. The bulwarks, long handrails and well-supported stanchion secure the deck. The cockpit is small and a bridgedeck will keep water out of the cabin. A sweet motion is probably the most important safety feature on any cruising boat.

 TYPICAL CONDITION: There are a few too many 27s afloat to consider the boat a cult but owners are typically fanatical about taking care of their boats.

 REFITTING: Ironically, high quality boats are often more difficult to retrofit because a high skill level is required to maintain the original workmanship. Also, like most small cruisers that pack a lot of features into a small space, working on things after the fact is always challenging.

 SUPPORT: Support is available through the factory, which can be reached on the Web at www.norseayachts.com. The Northern California owners' association has good information online at www.vander-bend.com/norsea.

 **AVAILABILITY:** Although more than 400 boats have been built they are rare on the used boat market. The West Coast seems to have the best selection.

 **INVESTMENT AND RESALE:** The Nor'Sea 27 has held its value quite well, and with the escalating price of new boats and lack of small, top quality small cruisers being built, will continue to hold its value well into the future.

 **OVERALL 'SVG' RATING**

cockpit model, although the center cockpit model has been much more popular and outnumbers the aft cockpit model by nearly 7-to-1. A few pilothouse 27s were also produced. However, if you have your heart set on finding a used Nor'Sea 27 you might have to take what you can find, as these boats are highly sought after and rarely linger on the used boat market.

On deck

The cockpit of both models is surprisingly comfortable and very well designed. In the center cockpit the tiller stretches over the aft cabintrunk house and companionway but it's a workable arrangement after you get used to it.

Most boats include a husky teak and stainless or teak and bronze boom cradle that is also handy for supporting a cockpit sun cover. Not surprisingly the boat is well suited to single-handed sailing and most 27 owners have led the sail controls aft. The triangular mainsheet system may not be the most efficient arrangement but it does keep the small cockpit uncluttered. And although the cockpit is by necessity fairly compact, it can accommodate three or four people without feeling overloaded. There is a large bridgedeck and a substantial companionway hood. Author Wayne Carpenter sailed most of the way around the world in his Nor'Sea 27 and his crew consisted of his wife, two small children and mother-in-law!

A molded bulwark, terrific nonskid, long

teak handrails on the cabintrunk and well-supported stanchions with double lifelines lend a sense of security when moving about the narrow side decks. The bowsprit forward is not a structural part of the rig as the forestay is tied to the stemhead fitting, which makes engineering sense. The teak and stainless bowsprit, with two bronze anchor rollers, does, however, provide an ideal anchoring platform and the short stainless steel bobstay won't foul the rodes. Deck hardware is oversized, to say the least, and where necessary backed with stainless steel plates.

The single-spreader, deck-stepped spar carries a long boom, and although the boat is designed as a sloop, some cruisers have added an inner forestay for a staysail. The tall rig mast is just over 34 feet, while the short rig is 30 feet, 6 inches. The external chainplates are ¼-inch by 1½-inch stainless straps with five through-hull bolts. You would need dynamite to pull these out of the boat.

Down below

The center cockpit deck found on most 27s allows for a creative and functional interior plan. Let's look at this arrangement first. Forward is a small berth that can be used as a storage area or extended into a decent-sized berth by lowering it athwartship in the saloon. A centerline table with settees to port and starboard is next aft. The table on older boats could be raised and lowered on the mast compression post, while on more recent models it drops to form a large double berth. The enclosed head and stand up chart table are to port and the surprisingly large galley is opposite. The two single berths in the aft cabin are excellent sea berths. The aft cockpit model is similar except that two quarterberths take the place of the aft cabin.

The joinerwork on the fully finished factory boats is simply superb; Nor'Sea is proud of the fact that there is no visible fiberglass. The Nor'Sea 27 is reminiscent of the Bristol Channel Cutter down below with its blend of elegance and simplicity. One difference is that there is more elbow room in the Nor'Sea—the 6-foot headroom is surprising considering the overall low profile. The boat is loaded with storage compartments—more than 30 separate

lockers can easily stow a month's provisions. A clever pullout shelf just below the chart table offers additional counter and working space. There are handholds throughout and bronze opening portlights and aluminum hatches. The interior is really quite stunning—a couple, or even a small family can distance cruise a Nor'Sea 27 in comfort.

Underway

Just a couple of weeks ago, Ed Hershman sailed solo from Marathon to Ft. Myers, Florida, a 100-mile passage that served as his test sail. "Believe me," Ed said, "I learned a lot, but I will tell you, this is one sweet sailing boat."

Hershman is typical of many Nor'Sea owners; he is stepping down. His former boat was a Catalina 400. "I was looking for a true bluewater boat in a small package. I looked at the Pacific Seacraft Dana 25, the Cape Dory 25D and others, but nothing compared to the quality and charm of the Nor'Sea."

Hershman encountered 25-knot winds and lumpy following seas as he passed under the Seven Mile Bridge and shaped a course northwest. "The boat clipped along at 6 knots, with very little stress, and sometimes more as we rode the waves. The helm was light and pretty well balanced."

The wind continued to pipe up and the tiller pilot was misbehaving, but Hershman was delighted with the boat. "Even when the wind clocked and we had more of a beam sea I was impressed with the Nor'Seas' motion. The speed on a reach was surprising. My only complaint was that I couldn't leave the helm long enough to prepare a decent meal." Hershman noted that his GPS touched 7 knots as he came up on the wind, which is good going in any 27-footer. He negotiated the tricky Marco Island Pass in the dark and dropped the hook for the night. "I was thankful for the 3-foot, 10-inch draft, especially after years of sailing with almost 6 feet on my Catalina, there just isn't as much stress. And when a passing powerboater slowed down and shouted, 'Nice boat,' well, that was the perfect end to a great day of sailing."

Hershman's shakedown trip pales when compared to some of the notable passages recorded by other Nor'Sea 27s, but it paints a picture of why the boat is so appealing. It is easy to handle, capable in a blow and easy on the eyes.

Conclusion

The Nor'Sea 27 is an intriguing, high quality, small cruising boat. Sure it is expensive—you can expect to pay anywhere from $35,000 to $80,000 for a used one, depending on the year. Yet this boat can fulfill cruising dreams on many levels. One summer you might haul it north and sail on pristine waters of Great Slave Lake in Northern Canada before schlepping it south to the Sea of Cortez for the winter. Of course, if those road trips are getting old, you might just sell the truck, clear Cabo San Lucas and head for the South Pacific.

Newport 28

*Although inexpensively built, this weekend cruiser
has a spacious interior and nice sailing manners*

A casual glance at most sailing magazine brokerage or classified ad sections will invariably reveal a wide selection of Newport 28s on the used boat market. Built by Capital Yachts in Harbor City, California, nearly 1,000 Newport 28s were launched during a long production run that lasted from 1974 to 1987. Designed by C&C, back in the days when C&C was confident enough to farm out its design team to other builders, the Newport 28 was, and still is, a handsome boat.

Good looks, however, didn't necessarily translate into good quality, and nobody will ever accuse Capital Yachts of overbuilding the 28. In fact, many construction flaws and cost-cutting measures have been well documented over the years. At the same time, however, the boat was never intended to be an offshore cruiser or racer, being designed instead as an affordable family boat for club racing, daysailing and weekend cruising.

It is easy to pick on boats that were built with price in mind, but without the Newport 28s, Catalina 27s, Hunter 27s and others, there would be far fewer people on the water. Sailing desperately needs affordable, entry-level boats, and besides, the Newport 28 does have many attributes. The interior is spacious and well thought out. The boat performs admirably in light to moderate air and does well racing under PHRF. There are active one-design fleets, especially on the West Coast, and most boats have been consistently upgraded. In 1982, Capital Yachts introduced the modified 28 II, which included a deeper standard keel and a diesel engine among other changes.

First impressions

Not surprisingly, the Newport 28 has a profile similar to many C&Cs of the same period. The sheer has an attractive sweep, the freeboard is relatively low, with the concave cabintrunk and cockpit coamings blending naturally into the flow of the hull. The aluminum toerail and dark outlined ports also give it a C&C look. The underbody shows a rounded midships section, which accounts for the 28's initial tenderness despite a ballast-to-displacement ratio of more than 40 percent on both models. While the original 28 has a swept-back fin keel and spade rudder, the 28 II's keel has a high-aspect-ratio profile and is a more efficient section. Draft on the early boats was 4 feet, 6 inches. On the 28 II it was increased to 5 feet, 2 inches.

The single-spreader mast features a typical IOR rig with a relatively small mainsail and large foretriangle. The Newport 28, like most boats built in the 1970s, was designed to be sailed with an overlapping genoa. The air draft is less than 40 feet. The displacement is 7,000 pounds and working sail area is a shade less than 400 square feet, making the Newport 28 comparable in weight and sail area to other

NEWPORT 28

LOA 28'
LWL 23'
Beam 9'6"
Draft 4'6"
Displacement 7,000 lbs.
Ballast 3,000 lbs.
Sail Area 385 sq. ft.

boats of the period, such as the Irwin 28, Sabre 28, S2 8.5 and Hunter 28.5.

Construction

The Newport 28 was a production boat through and through, and although its scantlings were not dramatically lighter than other production boats of the time, Capital Yachts didn't waste any material. Most of the noted defects were in the details and fitting out, not the actual layups. It is interesting to note, however, that some 28s are over 30 years old and are still merrily sailing every season. There is an active fleet of Newport 28s in blustery San Francisco Bay where the boat has a loyal following. As legendary builder and designer Charley Morgan stated many years ago, "Fiberglass is truly a remarkable material for building boats: It's virtually indestructible." Countless fiberglass boats have stood up to 30 to 40 years of use and abuse and are still sailing with no end in sight. I suspect we'll be reviewing fiberglass boats when they're 50, 60, even 70 years old.

The Newport 28's hull is solid fiberglass while its deck is cored. The hull-to-deck joint is on a narrow flange and leaks are not uncommon. The ballast is external and the mast is stepped on deck. The bulkhead tabbing was a bit light and the interior moldings are often cracked from the lack of support as the hull twists. Hard spots in the hull are not uncommon and occasionally there is print-through, where the weave of underlying fabric is visible, especially if the hull is painted a dark color.

What to look for

The first item to consider in choosing a Newport 28 is whether you want an original model with the 4-foot, 6-inch draft and possibly an Atomic 4 gas engine, or the 28 II with a deeper, more efficient keel and a diesel. Naturally there is a price difference, but careful shopping will likely turn up a 28 II in your price range. There was also a shoal draft 28 II offered with a draft of 4 feet.

Some common problems to watch for as you inspect used boats include leaking hull-to-deck joints and delamination in the deck, especially around the chainplates. Also, if the

NEWPORT 28 PRICE DATA			
BUC Retail Range		Low	High
	1978	$11,500	$13,100
	1985	$16,000	$18,200
Boats For Sale		State	Asking
	1976	CA	$ 9,900
	1980	WA	$13,900
	1986	VA	$18,500

chainplates have been leaking, the bulkhead below may have some rot too.

Original fitting out in the factory included undersized plastic through-hull valves (gate valves at that), small cockpit drains and inadequate backing plates for most deck hardware. Many owners will have addressed these problems, and some repairs and refits will be better than others. Also, it seems that tiller to wheel conversions were a popular item, so be sure to check the installation. Finally, Newport 28 hulls seem to have had their share of blister problems, and it would be useful to know when and if a blister job was done.

On deck

The Newport 28 came standard with tiller steering, although as noted above, wheel steering was a popular option and refit item. Ironically, the tiller arrangement opens up the cockpit and makes sail handling more efficient. In addition to steering advantages, the tiller can either be lashed out of the way or even removed to free up space in the cockpit when not sailing. Overall the 28 cockpit is comfortable, especially for an older boat, and accommodates four adults with elbowroom to spare.

The mainsheet traveler is on a bridge above the companionway. The Newport 28 was one of the first boats to adopt midboom sheeting, and although I often gripe about the disadvantage of this arrangement, in a small boat where the loads are less and space is at a premium, it makes sense. Single lifelines leading to the aft base of the bow pulpit came standard. Double lifelines

Newport 28

PRICE: With prices ranging from $10,000 to $20,000 the Newport 28 is cheaper than a decent used car. It really does represent a lot of boat for the money.

DESIGN QUALITY: The C&C design is well conceived and has stood the test of time. The boat has a lovely sheer and the 28 II has a capable underwater profile.

CONSTRUCTION QUALITY: This is the major knock against this boat. Simply put, Capital Yachts could have done a much better job of putting the Newport 28 together.

USER-FRIENDLINESS: Easy to sail and quite spacious for its length and beam, the 28 remains popular as a result of these features.

SAFETY: This rating is connected to construction and some of the original details, including small cockpit drains and plastic gate valve fittings.

TYPICAL CONDITION: The Newport 28 has held up better than some might have predicted, although boats that have been raced hard will not show as well.

REFITTING: Some aspects of the design make working on the boat challenging, including repowering. However this complaint can be lodged against most small boats of this era.

SUPPORT: Although Capital Yachts is now out of business, there is an active owner's Web site hosted by Sailnet.com. Also, one-design fleets on the West Coast provide information and updates on the boat.

AVAILABILITY: With nearly 1,000 boats built there is always a good selection of boats for sale. The West Coast has the best selection.

INVESTMENT AND RESALE: The Newport 28 is a cheap boat, it doesn't represent a huge investment and there is a lively market for it on the used boat market.

OVERALL 'SVG' RATING

---

led to the pulpit rails are an excellent refit project. The full-length aluminum toerail serves as an outboard genoa track and spinnaker lead attachment point. An inboard track allows for tighter sheeting angles. There is an external anchor locker forward and fittings for a babystay. The original deck cleats were ridiculously small, and hopefully will have been upgraded on the boat you are considering.

Down below

Capital Yachts offered three different interior arrangements. The original 28 had the galley along the starboard side, while the 28 II model offered aft galleys to either port or starboard. All three versions include a large V-berth followed by an enclosed head, which was an unusual and attractive feature when the boat was first introduced. There's a good-sized hanging locker opposite. The original starboard side galley arrangement carried a settee opposite and a bulkhead-mounted, fold-down table. A fold-down table is a great idea on any boat under 30 feet. A decent-sized chart table to starboard, two quarterberths and a short settee seat aft of the galley completed this functional layout.

The aft galley arrangements eliminated one of the quarter berths, opting instead for opposing settees. The galley included a two-burner stove, a single sink and a large icebox compartment. All layouts are actually quite spacious for an older 28-footer. The terrific interior is no doubt a major reason for the 28's enduring popularity. The woodworking and finish detail was adequate, however, and the original checkered fabric on the cushions can really date the boat.

Engine

When the Newport 28 was first introduced a Universal Atomic 4 was the standard engine.

This workhorse gasoline engine has served many boats well over the years and is still viable as a power plant. Replacement parts are cheap and commonly available, and it provides plenty of oomph that pushes the 28 along at close to 6 knots. That being said, I would still look for a boat with a diesel. When the 28 II came along it was offered with either a Universal or Yanmar diesel, ranging from 11 to 18 horsepower. Again, if given the choice I'd lean toward the Yanmar. Engine access is adequate for a small boat, although servicing the stuffing box is especially challenging.

Underway

Although the Newport 28 has its faults, it is by most accounts a very nice sailing boat, which makes up for a lot of warts. It is initially tender and heels early before stiffening up. Owners report that with a single reef in the main, the boat can carry a 100-percent headsail to weather in a stiff breeze and still track effi-ciently. Several owners report that the boat can point high, although claims of being able to sail cleanly at 30 degrees apparent seem a bit exaggerated. The boat is well balanced, adapting easily to a small autopilot. If not overloaded with gear, the easily driven Newport 28 sails very well in light air. This is an underrated attribute. The truth is, light days outnumber heavy-air days and nothing is more frustrating than trying to coax a clumsy boat along in what should be a decent sailing breeze. Many 28s on the used boat market are equipped with roller-furling headsail systems and jiffy reefing on the main.

Conclusion

The Newport 28 is a good sailing boat with a spacious, well-thought-out interior. Best of all it's affordable. Sure, it's a production boat and the construction detailing is not the best. But for those looking for an entry-level boat in this size range, the Newport 28 represents a fine value.

Catalina 28

Popular coastal cruiser with a big interior
makes a great first 'big' boat

The Catalina 28 underscores why Catalina has built more sailboats than any other American builder—more than 60,000 and counting. This versatile sloop is easy to handle and sails surprisingly well. There is nothing extreme about the design and it's relatively simple to maintain. The high-volume interior has more room than many 32-foot boats. There is excellent factory support, an active owner's group and parts and services are readily available. The 28 is affordable to buy and to operate. Furthermore, when you want to move up or down there is a well defined market for selling the boat. This adds up to a formula for success in an industry where failure can be the norm.

Catalina, based in Southern California, is famous for long production runs. Introduced in 1991 the 28 (and with the 270 that was launched a year later) replaced the legendary Catalina 27 as the all-time best selling keel boat. An updated version in 1995, the 28 MK II is still in production. If you're

looking for a first "big" boat to introduce your family to sailing, or simply looking for one of the best values in the 28- to 30-foot range, you owe it to yourself to look closely at a used Catalina 28. With prices ranging from less than $30,000 for an older model to just under $60,000 for an almost new boat, the 28 is a lot of boat for the buck.

First impressions

Designed by Gerry Douglas and his in-house design team, the 28 sports the distinct Catalina profile. The sheerline is flat, the bow overhang is moderate, the broad transom is reversed and there is ample freeboard. The sloping cabin-trunk extends well into the foredeck and the dark portlights are vintage Catalina. This is a big 28-foot boat, and not just because the LOA is actually 28 feet, 6 inches. The beam is a healthy 10 feet, 2 inches and it's carried well aft, especially in the MK II, and the bilges are full, creating a voluminous hull.

Below the waterline, the forefoot is relatively shallow, the fin keel angles aft and the rudder is balanced, another example of Catalina's well-honed hull shape that provides decent performance through a range of conditions. The standard draft is 5 feet, 3 inches; however, the 3-foot, 8-inch shoal-draft wing

CATALINA 28

LOA 28'6"
LWL 23'10"
Beam 10'2"
Draft 5'3"
Displacement
  8,300 lbs.
Ballast
  3,200 lbs.
Sail Area
  396 sq. ft.

keel was a popular option and seems to be widely available on the used boat market. The iron ballast weighs in at 3,200 pounds for the standard fin keel model, the wing keel is slightly heavier. The fin keel model displaces 8,300 pounds. A double-spreader sloop, the 28 was offered with either a standard or a tall rig. By most accounts the boat is stiff in a blow, and unless you sail on San Francisco Bay, the tall rig, which has an air draft of 44 feet, 4 inches, is the preferred option. The fin-keel standard-rig 28 has a sail area-to-displacement ratio of 14.21, while the tall rig bumps it up to 15.46. Either way, the 28 will not be a demon in light air.

Construction

Catalina uses its production scale to build boats efficiently. For example, they use the same hatches and deck fittings on several different models, streamlining production costs and for the most part, passing savings on to consumers. That does not mean the company's boats are not well built. On the contrary, while smaller Catalinas less than 40 feet are not specifically built for crossing oceans, they hold up very well under most cruising conditions. And of course, plenty of Catalinas have completed impressive bluewater voyages, including circumnavigations. Catalina owners are loyal. It is safe to say that more owners stay with Catalinas when they move up to a larger model than with any other manufacturer. This simply would not be the case if its boats were poorly built.

The 28's construction is fairly typical of the entire Catalina line. The hull is solid fiberglass, hand layed and the deck is balsa cored. The hull and deck are joined with an overlapping, shoe box joint that also incorporates the aluminum toerail. This is a good technique for limiting leaks but it does expose this critical joint to side impacts. The bulkheads are marine plywood with hardwood veneers. The bulkheads are slotted into the deck liner as molded liners are used throughout the boat. Over the years I have observed that some of the secondary bonding is not as robust as it might be. The iron keel is externally fastened. Fiberglass stringers stiffen the hull and provide athwartship support.

CATALINA 28 PRICE DATA

		Low	High
BUC Retail Range	1992	$ 25,400	$ 28,200
	1998	$ 32,300	$ 37,100
		State	Asking
Boats For Sale	1992	MI	$ 39,000
	1997	MA	$ 49,000
	2000	NY	$ 54,000

What to look for

The first item to consider is whether or not the MK II is worth the extra money, typically you will pay 25 to 35 percent more than an original 28. Several changes were introduced with the updated model in late 1995. The aft hull section was widened slightly, making the aft cabin more commodious. The galley was redesigned and sail controls were fine tuned. John Cairns, who sails TALISMAN, a 1992 Catalina 28, on Lake Erie, says with a laugh, "They addressed all my petty concerns with the MK II." Some of those issues include an inaccessible refrigeration compartment, inadequate locker latches, the location of the batteries in the stern and poor ventilation in the aft cabin. Cairns is right, these are slight problems and easily corrected. "Overall," he told me, "I am impressed with the boat, it has held up very well." Other owners have reported gelcoat cracking and crazing and annoying leaks, including around the base of the pedestal.

On deck

The Catalina 28 has a terrific T-shaped cockpit with wheel steering, and there is room for four adults to sit comfortably while under way. The 32-inch destroyer wheel is by Edson and the primary winches are Lewmar 30s. The walk-through transom allows easy access to the water and the dinghy via a narrow stern platform and the ladder cleverly folds up to form the stern rail. The mainsheet traveler is forward, over the companionway, and although this creates a lot of load on the boom,

Catalina 28

 **PRICE:** There is no denying that Catalinas are price boats, and the 28 is affordable. Hey, it's a virtue not a vice.

 **DESIGN QUALITY:** You have to appreciate the 28 for what it is intended to be, a roomy, comfortable daysailer and summer cruiser, and it's well designed for those intentions.

CONSTRUCTION QUALITY: Judging by the Catalina 28s on the used market, the boat is holding up well although Catalina can't be accused of overbuilding its boats.

USER-FRIENDLINESS: The 28 is easy and rewarding to sail and comfortable on deck and below. That's a good definition of user-friendliness.

SAFETY: Features that make the 28 appealing also can be construed as safety concerns, i.e., a large open cockpit, wide companionway and beamy, flat-bottomed hull.

 TYPICAL CONDITION: The Catalina 28 has only been in production a dozen years, which isn't long by Catalina standards. Most boats are still in decent condition.

 **REFITTING:** The 28 was designed with refitting in mind, and considering the use of molded liners, access is generally very good. Parts and services are widely available.

 **SUPPORT:** Catalina's support network is a good reason for buying a 28. There is an active owners group and a list-serve group. Helpful Web sites include www.catalinayachts.com and www.sailnet.com.

 AVAILABILITY: Catalina builds in vast numbers, a search on the site www.yachtworld.com showed 34 boats for sale.

INVESTMENT AND RESALE: For a production-built boat, Catalinas hold their values surprisingly well. One reason is that the company keeps its boats in production a long time and doesn't make changes just for the sake of changing.

 **OVERALL 'SVG' RATING**

---

it really opens up the cockpit and allows easy companionway access. Most 28s will have all sail controls led aft, including a single-line reefing system. I have used this system on several different Catalina models over the years and am not a big fan of it because a single-line system has to overcome too much friction. I think it's faster and ultimately safer to reef the main from the base of the mast where the leverage is best. Because the aft cabin is tucked beneath the cockpit there isn't a cockpit locker. New models however have wonderful seats mounted on the stern rail, a great perch when under sail.

The 28 has fairly wide side decks and the chainplates are mounted inboard for easy maneuvering and tight sheeting angles. The original 28s have teak handrails on the coachroof, while the newer boats have stainless steel. In fact, the elimination of all exterior brightwork was one of the successes of

the MK II design. The deck-stepped mast is well supported with fore and aft lower shrouds, a rare sight these days. Check around the mast base for deck depression, a factor if the rig has been over tightened. Catalina was one of the first builders to make double lifelines standard and the stanchions and pulpits are well supported on the 28, although they could be a bit taller.

Down below

The interior layout offers two genuine sleeping cabins, a spacious saloon, a full galley and head and a nav station, all in a 28-foot boat. "Two couples can comfortably cruise the boat, at least for awhile," Cairn said. The forward V-berth is good sized and an overhead hatch provides ventilation. This hatch is located on the sloping section of the trunkhouse, which makes it good for catching air and water. It needs to be dogged while under way. The saloon has facing settees and a centerline table that drapes the mast compression post. With the table open four people can eat in style.

The galley is immediately to starboard and includes a large sink, plenty of counter space, and in most cases, a two-burner stove. Be wary of pressurized alcohol stoves on the older models. Also, the icebox, which is under the nav desk, is deep and difficult to access. The head is opposite the galley and includes a shower. Most boats will have hot and cold pressure water. The aft cabin is entered from behind the galley and offers an athwartship double bunk. The only ventilation on the original 28 was through a small port opening into the cockpit. A couple of 12-volt cabin fans will help with this problem. Elegant yet functional, the interior workmanship is surprisingly nice.

Engine

The first 28s were fitted with Universal M3-20 diesels, while the later models have been upgraded to 3-cylinder, 26-horsepower Universal model 25XS. Access to the engine is excellent although the sound insulation needs to be improved on older models. Access to the stuffing box is through the aft cabin and requires tearing the berth apart to reach. Cairns said that his Universal 20 pushes the boat along at 5 knots at 2,000 rpm. And it's economical. "I haven't used a tankful of fuel yet in a season, and I use the boat a lot. Of course I sail whenever I can," he said. Fuel capacity is 19 gallons.

Underway

"What I like best about my boat is the way she sails," said Cairns, an experienced sailor who recently sailed around Cape Horn. "But not in my 28," he hastened to add. In a 10-knot beam reach the boat balances very well. "That's why I haven't purchased an autopilot, I can leave the wheel and she'll steer herself for extended periods." Cairns said that the helm is light in most conditions, even hard on the wind. The boat is relatively close winded and has a nice turn of speed off the wind. Cairns says he thinks about shortening sail when the wind hits 17 to 18 knots but that things don't get to be a handful until the wind is steady at more than 20 knots. Several owners note that the 28 is stiff in a blow, making it an ideal boat for a family or new sailor as it does not require micromanagement.

Conclusion

The Catalina 28 is a perfect example of why sailing should be more popular, there isn't much not to like about this boat. It isn't an offshore cruiser and it isn't going to win races. It is, however, an affordable cruiser that's easy to sail and comfortable on deck and below. The Catalina 28 should be high on your list if you're looking for a used boat in the $30,000 to $50,000 range.

J / 29

One-design that's as good as new with an active racing fleet and Johnstone-designed style and speed

The J/29 is an enduring favorite in the usually fickle world of one-design racing. Boat speed has always been the mantra for one-design sailors, and today's boats have pushed this concept to another level. A friend who campaigns a Melges 24 recently told me that his crew clocked 18 knots surfing down modest waves. And they weren't even pushing the boat. Speed usually means employing the very latest go-fast technology, something that rarely ages gracefully. Nothing seems older than outdated performance boats. Just picture the many IOR boats from the early 70s lying forlornly in marinas all over the country. Old boats are slow, or so the thinking goes, so what good are they? Unfortunately for the new-is-better crowd, the J/29, although "old," is anything but slow, especially if upwind sailing is thrown into the mix.

Introduced in 1982, the Rod Johnstone-designed J/29 was considered the logical step up for sailors who cut their teeth blasting around the buoys in J/24s. Although the J/30 was already in production, J/24 sailors were looking for a larger version of what they already loved, basically a bigger, faster J/24. They didn't need a boat with accommodations, and they didn't want to pay for it either.

The J/29, which sold for around $30,000 when new, offered affordable, high-level, one-design competition with enough of an interior to make an overnight or even a weekend ocean race doable. Built by Tillotson-Pearson in Fall River, Massachusetts, about 300 boats were launched during a five-year production run. Today there is still an active class association, and one-design fleets are thriving. The J/29 is also a terrific boat to consider for spirited daysailing, if racing is not your cup of tea.

First impressions

Johnstone has always had an uncanny ability to design incredibly fast boats that manage to sail well across the spectrum and also maintain a handsome bearing on the water. Many of today's fast boats are almost garish in appearance with their plumb bows and abrupt hull shapes designed for downwind flying. It's as if they are craving attention, like a teenager's tattoos, declaring, "Look at me, I'm fast." I suspect in 10 or 15 years, these boats will look completely outdated, replaced by the latest and greatest ideas for generating boat speed.

Johnstone's boats on the other hand look like boats, not platforms designed to skid across the water faster than the next platform. And as we all know, most sailing is upwind, an area in which his boats often excel. The J/29 is able to carry a full main in 15-plus knots, making 6.5 knots of boat speed.

The 29 began life as a modified J/30 and the rakish lines are quite similar. On the 29, however, Johnstone lowered the freeboard, re-

J/29

LOA 29'6"
LWL 25'
Beam 11'
Draft 5'6"
Ballast 2,100 lbs.
Displacement
   6,000 lbs.
Sail Area
   Fractional 453 sq. ft.
   Masthead 450 sq. ft.

designed the keel and trimmed the weight. Although it has 4 inches less LOA and the same 11-foot beam, the 29 weighs 1,000 pounds less and has almost as much sail area. Naturally, the 29's vertical center of gravity is lower than the 30's. And although most 29s were built with fractional rigs, a masthead rig was an option. Simplicity was hard-wired into the boat: From an outboard motor for auxiliary power, to the outboard rudder, to a lack of runners on the fractional rig, the J/29 has always been a boat that you can jump aboard and sail because not a lot of set-up is required. The boat sails well under main alone, and even with a moderately size genoa, the loads are rarely excessive. It is an easy boat to sail well.

Construction

The J/29 was never intended to be a ULDB, at least in comparison to West Coast boats, and the construction reflects this philosophy. The similarly sized Olson 30, for example, displaces just 4,000 pounds, while the J/29 tips the scales at 6,000 pounds. Within the framework of being a performance boat, the build is actually rather robust. The hull and deck are balsa cored and joined on a typical inner flange, incorporating the teak toerail where applicable. Tillotson-Pearson, which has since pioneered the SCRIMP manufacturing process, has always done good glass work, and the 29 has some interesting beefed-up specifications. The main bulkhead, a well documented problem in the J/24, and the keel floors are actually culled from the same scantlings as the J/36.

A large fiberglass molding is used as a floor and furniture pan, which helps stiffen the hull and originally streamlined the manufacturing process. The high-aspect outboard rudder is attached to the transom with stainless steel pintles and gudgeons. Most of the deck hardware is through-bolted and accessible, an important feature on a boat where the fittings may need to be replaced and updated due to regular racing wear and tear.

What to look for

The J/29 has held up extremely well over the years, considering that most of the boats have

J/29 PRICE DATA

BUC Retail Range		Low	High
	1983	$21,900	$24,400
	1986	$25,100	$27,900

Boats For Sale		State	Asking
	1982	ME	$12,500
	1984	TX	$18,750
	1987	NY	$29,000

been sailed hard and often put away wet. Of course, since many 29s are 20 years old and over, all age-related problems should be thoroughly inspected before making a decision to buy. Don't overpay for an impressive but old sail wardrobe. In fact, you should consider new sails a given when buying a J/29 because nothing breathes life into this racer like new sails. This is where the boat's simplicity makes it appealing.

The rudder pintles and gudgeons are a bit on the light side, and should be replaced if they look at all suspicious, although on the 1983 model I climbed through in Fort Lauderdale, Florida, they were clearly original and in good condition. If the gudgeons have been leaking, be sure to check the transom for delamination since some water may have penetrated the core. Several of the deck fittings on the boat I looked at were cracked, including the aluminum cleats. The hatch cover was also cracked, apparently from being stood on, and the teak handrails were loose. These are all areas that should be carefully examined since deck fitting problems often metamorphose into deck delamination problems. A bit of stomping around revealed some degree of delamination around the sheet winches and in the cockpit.

Inside the boat, the molded liner was cracked in several places, obviously from the hull being tweaked now and then. The tabbing on the other hand, at least where I could see, was in good shape. The chainplates also leaked and had soiled the main bulkhead. J Boats had its share of blisters, and some have suggested that the constant fairing of its hulls by owners contributed to the problem by skimming away at the gelcoat. This seems rather

J/29

 **PRICE:** With prices hovering on either side of $20,000, the J/29 is an excellent value. Aside from the interior, the 29 is every boat the 30 is in size yet performs better. It is also less expensive.

 **DESIGN QUALITY:** Rod Johnstone's design has an enduring quality, proven by the 29's continuing popularity. The boat is a brilliant example of a very fast hull that is easily controlled and can actually sail upwind.

 **CONSTRUCTION QUALITY:** Tillotson-Pearson builds fine boats and the J/29 is no exception. However, beware of problems with the coring.

 **USER-FRIENDLINESS:** This rating is based on the fact that the J/29 was conceived as a one-design racer without any pretenses of being a cruiser. Yet the boat is easy to handle, simply rigged and well-set-up.

 SAFETY: The J/29 has a better motion in a seaway than many modern sport boats. However, the nature of the design is not as safe as a more traditional boat.

TYPICAL CONDITION: J/29s seem to have held up well despite being raced hard. Owners have often upgraded to stay competitive, so there is good chance you will have to spend some money if you want to race and win.

 REFITTING: The overall simplicity of the boat makes refitting less of a challenge. Some problems are serious, including delamination in the hull and deck.

SUPPORT: J Boats Inc. is one of the few new boatbuilders that still actively and openly supports its used boats. The J/29 Web page is actually found through the J Boats page, at www.Jboats.com/j29. The class association is also helpful.

AVAILABILITY: With about 300 boats built, there is usually a good selection on the used boat market. Long Island Sound, the Chesapeake Bay, the Great Lakes and San Francisco Bay are good places to look for boats.

 INVESTMENT AND RESALE: J Boats continues to thrive as a company, and this always helps the company's used boats. As long as the class association stays viable, the J/29 will likely not depreciate much further and should be considered a good value.

 OVERALL 'SVG' RATING

---

unlikely since blisters begin in the laminate. But even so, it is a good idea to find out if and when an epoxy bottom repair job was done.

On deck

Because of the J/29's racing pedigree, the deck is well-designed for ease of handling, but the cockpit is not especially comfortable since you actually sit on the aft deck more than in the cockpit, which can be wet to say the least. The mainsheet traveler spans the cockpit and is easily controlled from the tiller. The sheet winches are forward of the traveler, making it a bit awkward for a singlehander, but the boat is ideal for a couple when not racing. The tiller

head is stainless steel and the tiller itself is oak and robust. Dual compasses are often set into the coachroof bulkhead, and there is room for instrument displays as well.

Double lifelines were standard. The stanchions bases are backed and well-supported, but are often the source of leaks. The pulpits are a bit undersized, and the original nonskid is likely to be worn nearly smooth. Naturally, the headsail tracks are close inboard, and all boats will be set up with spinnaker gear since the 29 predates J Boat's introduction of the retractable sprit. The mast and boom were built by Sparcraft in 4060 aluminum sections. The fractional rig has an air draft of 47 feet, 6 inches while the masthead rig is 4 feet shorter.

Down below

The interior of the J/29 is spartan but functional. Low freeboard and a sleek, low-slung coachroof results in a distinct lack of headroom—about 5 feet, 4 inches. The layout includes two quarter berths aft and two settees in the main cabin, perfect for a racing crew. The forward locker may be a sail locker, or it may have been converted into a double berth. Some boats were fitted with manual heads, although most will have porta potties. At least the boat complies with EPA regulations. The galley originally consisted of an Igloo cooler and a sink. There is actually a fair bit of teak below, including veneers on the main bulkhead, a teak-and-holly sole and teak companionway steps. I imagine that when refinished the boat can look rather smart.

Engine

Although an inboard diesel was an option, J Boats emphasized outboard motors when marketing the boat, again stressing the simplicity theme. As a result most boats have outboards, which are really very practical. Mounted on a transom bracket, a relatively small and light engine pushes the boat at 6 knots. It is also easily removed or stored below for racing. Another advantage of an outboard is that when it is broken you can pop it into the trunk and take it home or drop it off at the shop.

Underway

This is what it's all about with a J/29. The boat is fast on all points of sail and truly excels upwind. By all accounts, with the rig tuned the boat can carry a full main and No. 1 genoa in 15 knots true while making 6.5 knots and staying on her feet. The J/29 sails better under mainsail alone than other comparably sized cruiser/racers do with a main and headsail. Trimming up the main generally requires keeping the top battens parallel to the boom, unless it is extremely light, and then the leach must be opened to prevent stalling. In heavy going, the sail needs to be flattened with the backstay and the mainsheet eased to reduce weather helm and excessive heel.

Typically headsails are changed before the main is reefed, and the boat is quite stiff in 25 knots with a No. 3 and full main. Reefing the main is reserved for gales. According to the J/29 class association, it is common to fly a No. 1 genoa in up to 20 knots apparent before dropping to the No. 2. The boat handles beautifully under spinnaker, sustaining surfing runs in double digits without undue stress. This point can't be overemphasized; the J/29 is a very controllable, well-built boat that can sail at exhilarating speeds without the accompanying heart palpitations.

Conclusion

The J/29 represents an excellent value if you're looking for solid performance but can't bear the thought of new boat prices. With a proud pedigree, good company support, an active one-design class, and prices ranging generally from $20,000 to 30,000, the J/29 is hard to beat.

Alberg 30

*Forgiving yet capable of crossing oceans,
this traditional cruiser has built an avid following*

When Canadian builder Kurt Hansen commissioned Carl Alberg to design a 30-foot sloop for his Whitby Boat Works back in 1962 few would have predicted that the boat would stay in production for more than 20 years. By the time Whitby finally closed its doors in 1988, more than 700 Alberg 30s had been built. The Alberg 30 was inspired by a handful of Folkboat sailors from Toronto. They approached Hansen to build a suitable boat for one-design racing but also capable of extended cruising. In essence they wanted a larger Folkboat. When word of the new Alberg 30 reached the Chesapeake Bay area sailing clubs, two different groups of sailors turned up on Hansen's doorstep. They placed more than two dozen orders before retreating back across the border. Thus the Alberg 30 sprang to life in a flourish. By the end of the first year, a completed boat was rolling off the production line every three days.

While many older boats have a quiet following, nurtured by a few dedicated owners, Alberg 30 owners can be defined as a full-blown cult. They love their boats and maintain several active class associations. The Chesapeake Bay Alberg 30 Association boasts 250 boats on its registry and publishes an informative monthly newsletter, a maintenance manual and hosts well-attended seminars every February. There are other active classes, including a Great Lakes fleet based in Toronto. Every year, the Chesapeake and Great Lakes groups race, alternating host countries in this international competition. Very few significant changes were made during the long production run, and an early 1960s boat can sail boat-for-boat with an early 1980s boat, making the Alberg 30 one of the largest keelboat one-design fleets anywhere.

First impressions

The Alberg 30 bears the unmistakable signature of Carl Alberg, a look evident in so many boats from this period, including the Pearson Triton, Bristol 27 and Alberg 37. The look, which was modern in its day, is now considered traditional, at least when defined in terms of fiberglass boats. The long overhangs, springy sheer, low freeboard, cutaway full keel with an attached rudder, narrow beam, stair-stepped cabintrunk and moderate sailplan are trademark Alberg.

It is safe to say that the Alberg 30 traces its roots to the Scandinavian Folkboat, as most of Alberg's designs do, and the hull shape represents the transition that was taking place as builders switched from wood to fiberglass construction. The Alberg 30 may not be the quickest boat afloat, especially in light air, but don't be misled by the specs. With slack bilges and just 8 feet, 9 inches of beam, the boat is initially tender. The short waterline increases as the boat heels and the Alberg 30 finds its stride when other boats are being overpowered. The boat has

ALBERG 30

LOA 30'3"
LWL 21'8"
Beam 8'9"
Draft 4'3"
Displacement 9,000 lbs.
Ballast 3,300 lbs.
Sail Area 410 sq. ft.

a seakindly motion, although it can hobbyhorse in a seaway. The Alberg 30 is a proven blue water cruiser; indeed, Yves Gelinas circumnavigated in one by way of Cape Horn in his Alberg 30 JEAN DU SUD.

Construction

Most Alberg 30s have held up very well over the years, a tribute to Whitby's solid construction. There was nothing fancy about the building process, but like other early fiberglass boats, there was no shortage of material used in the 30's hull and deck. The hull is hand-laid, solid fiberglass bonded with polyester resin. Early decks and cabintrunks were partially cored with Masonite, while those built after 1970 used more common balsa coring.

Early boats used a laminated wood beam to support the mast, while later boats were fitted with an aluminum beam encased in a fiberglass liner. Later boats also incorporated a fiberglass pan for the cabin sole and as a base for the furniture. Whitby made similar changes in its other successful Alberg design, the 37. The ballast is iron, encapsulated in the keel cavity. According to some reports, Alberg specified lead ballast and a few of the earliest boats were quite tender until extra ballast was added.

What to look for

Like any boat, there are a few items to watch for when inspecting used Alberg 30s. Unlike other boats, however, the Alberg 30's flaws have not only been well documented by respective class associations over the years, but solutions to the problems are just as well documented. If you are looking at a pre-1970 boat, for example, be sure to check the wooden mast support beam. The beam may well be cracked after years of flexing under load, and it is not unusual to find a retrofitted aluminum plate to beef up the support. Be sure to probe around on deck to see if depressions are evident around the maststep.

Deck delamination is another problem to watch for, so carefully sound the decks, listening for the telltale creaking sounds that reveal rot in the core. Again, this seems more common in older boats, and don't overreact to a bit

ALBERG 30 PRICE DATA			
BUC Retail Range		Low	High
	1970	$17,200	$19,500
	1975	$19,500	$23,700
Boats For Sale		State	Asking
	1967	MD	$18,000
	1973	NC	$18,800
	1979	CA	$18,500

of deck delamination as almost every old boat has it to some degree.

Another common problem is the attachment of the forward lower chainplates, which are not well supported belowdecks. In fact, JEAN DU SUD lost her mast in the Pacific when a chainplate pulled out. Naturally, be sure to inspect all the components of the standing rigging, including the chainplates themselves, which can be bent and fatigued after years of hard use.

The type of engine may influence your buying decision since the need to repower the boat will certainly skew your budget. In fact, adding a new diesel can cost almost as much as the boat itself when you include the cost of installation. The earliest boats were fitted with 22-horsepower Gray Marine gas engines. Most Alberg 30s, however, came standard with a 30-horsepower Universal Atomic 4 gas engine, the workhorse of the industry for many years. Some of the later boats came with diesels, either a single cylinder Bukh or a two-cylinder Volvo.

On deck

The Alberg 30's cockpit is fairly large and the seats are long enough to stretch out on. There is good leg support on either tack, but the mahogany coaming board does get you in the small of the back after a while. Tiller steering was standard, and while there must be some wheel-steered 30s, I haven't seen one. There is a stout bridgedeck, typical of all Alberg designs. Circumnavigator Gelinas notes that he

Alberg 30

 **PRICE:** It is possible to find an Alberg 30 in good shape for little over $15,000—what else needs to be said?

 DESIGN QUALITY: This design cannot be compared to modern boats. It is traditional, capable and handsome.

 CONSTRUCTION QUALITY: Most 30s have been sailed hard and put away wet and yet they hold up very well. The original construction was simple and stout, although some better materials might have been used.

USER-FRIENDLINESS: The 30 is easy to sail, and once the main is reefed, forgiving and seakindly. The interior isn't overly comfortable, but that isn't why you buy an Alberg 30 in the first place.

SAFETY: The tough construction and well-designed cockpit make the boat safe. However the deck can be tricky to navigate, especially because the boat is often sailed well heeled.

TYPICAL CONDITION: The Alberg 30 has aged well, owing to solid construction, a good design, and for the most part a group of dedicated owners.

 **REFITTING:** Like many old boats, the 30 isn't easy to work on and Whitby is out of business, which makes finding parts more challenging.

 SUPPORT: The Alberg 30 Owners Association at www.Alberg30.org and various owner's groups offer terrific support and information.

 **AVAILABILITY:** With more than 700 boats built there are always many used 30s on the market. The biggest concentration of boats is definitely on the Chesapeake Bay followed by the Great Lakes.

 INVESTMENT AND RESALE: The Alberg 30 doesn't require much of an investment and you will likely be able to sell the boat for what you paid. This boat delivers a huge dividend in fun.

OVERALL 'SVG' RATING

can fit two folding bikes in the cockpit lockers. There is also a lazarette astern. The boat can be wet when sailing upwind and a spray dodger is a useful addition.

Like many CCA-influenced designs, the Alberg 30 has a long boom and the mainsheet features end-boom sheeting, usually led to a traveler aft of the cockpit. It's likely the sheet winches have been upgraded, although it isn't necessary as the headsail loads are not overly heavy. The 30 is not a close-winded boat and the headsail tracks are on the rail to clear the shrouds. The single-spreader sloop rig carries 410 square feet of sail, with more than half of that area in the mainsail. The lifelines and low stanchions are not designed to keep an adult from going overboard, but there are teak handrails on the raised portion of the cabin-trunk. The nonskid may be worn, and if the decks have been painted they may be slick when wet. The mooring hardware is more than adequate.

Down below

The Alberg 30's interior seems incredibly small by modern standards—it isn't much of a stretch to say that there is more room in a new Hunter 260, heck maybe even the 240. But then of course, the comparison is absurd, since the Alberg 30 is a completely different animal. The interior arrangement is straightforward, and nobody will ever accuse Alberg of resorting to gimmicks. There is a V-berth forward with an enclosed head aft to port with a hanging locker opposite. The saloon has settees port and starboard and a clever portable dining table mounted on an aluminum Z-shaped leg.

When not in use, the table stows over the V-berth. A small galley is to starboard, usually with a single sink facing aft and a two-burner stove next to it. A good-sized icebox is located to port and early boats had an access hatch from the cockpit.

The interior may be small, but the workmanship is good, and it has a snug feeling to it. The large saloon ports keep it well lit although the ventilation usually consists of only the forward-opening deck hatch, which of course is usually secured when underway. There is a lot of storage, with drawers and lockers throughout.

Engine

As mentioned earlier, the first boats were equipped with a 22-horsepower Gray Marine gas engines (the infamous Sea Scout). Early on, however, the standard engine became the Universal Atomic 4, which can still be found in many boats. Bukh and Volvo diesels were used late in the production run. Efficient motoring and engine access were not priorities in most Alberg designs, and the 30 is no exception. The engine is accessible from behind the companionway, although not particularly friendly to work on. The stuffing box, on the other hand, takes a contortionist and a special set of wrenches to change the packing, making the 30 a prime candidate for a dripless stuffing box. I would push a boat with a newer, refit diesel to the top of my list when searching for a used Alberg 30.

Underway

Older boats that maintain loyal and active followings invariably share one key trait—they sail well. The Alberg 30 is easy to handle, will stand up to a blow and has a nice motion. The boat balances well with the main and working jib, although weather helm can be an issue when flying a genoa. All owners agree that the 30 sails best when the main is reefed early because of the initial tenderness. A rule of thumb is change or furl the headsail to keep the decks clear of water and then hold on for the ride. The Alberg 30 is designed to sail on its ear, yet the boat feels incredibly solid in the water. The old line about sailing on rails is most apropos.

Gelinas, who by the way is the manufacturer of the well-respected Cape Horn self-steering vane, has owned JEAN DU SUD for over 30 years and has logged some 50,000 miles. He notes that the boat's hull shape has a great motion at sea, although he too suggests that you reef the main early. Gelinas dispensed with his Atomic 4 engine to free up storage space, and even today only uses an outboard perched on the stern for the rare times he finds powering necessary.

Conclusion

With prices ranging from the high $10,000 to around $25,000, it's easy to see why the Alberg 30 is an enduring favorite. It's an ideal boat for families wanting to test the waters of sailing, or for singlehanders and couples looking for an inexpensive but capable boat for cruising. Another alluring feature of the Alberg 30 is that with the right trailer and SUV it can be hauled by road to out-of-the-way cruising grounds. "To me the Alberg 30 is very close to the ideal boat: solid enough to sail around Cape Horn but small enough to carried on the road to the cruising ground of my choice," Gelinas said.

Dufour Arpege 30

*A good-quality French-built bluewater cruiser
that is at its best in heavy weather*

It is easy to forget, now that the combined might of Beneteau and Jeanneau dominate sailboat imports, that 30 years ago another French builder was the leading European exporter into the U.S. market. Michel Dufour, an innovative designer and builder produced several models and all were widely distributed in North America. These boats preceded those offered by Dufour and its Gib'Sea line today, which after a long hiatus, is back in the sailboat business. In the 1970s the Dufour Safari 27 and Dufour 35 were popular boats on this side of the Atlantic as was, to a lesser extent, the Dufour 41, which at the time was one of the largest production boats available anywhere. The most successful Dufour import, however, was the Arpege 30.

I confess that the Arpege 30, which was introduced in 1966 and had a fairly long production run of approximately 1,500 boats, had fallen off my personal radar screen of sailboats until two recent and far-flung trips. Last April I was in Oakland, California, attending the Pacific Sail Expo when, weary of

the hype and hoopla of the show, I was out wandering, and I came across an Arpege 30 at a nearby dock, where it had been temporarily displaced from her usual berth by the show's shiny new models.

"I wouldn't trade this boat for any one of those over there," said a bearded man in the cockpit, sipping coffee and gesturing toward the flapping banners. "I've been out to Hawaii and down to Mexico more times than I can count. This boat never lets me down." I pride myself on my knowledge of sailboats, and while I recognized the boat as an old Dufour, I couldn't quite place the model. "It's an Arpege 30," the man said helpfully, "built in '68, and still going strong."

A couple of months later I was in Brittany on the northwest corner of France, which is wonderfully indented with seaports, large and small. My writing assignment was complete, yet I still had a couple of days and a few hundred kilometers to use up on my rental car. I made my way northeast from the shipbuilding center of St. Nazaire to Vannes, meandering along the coast. In the holiday city of Pornichet, which drapes around a narrow, congested harbor, I stumbled upon a fleet of Dufour Arpeges. Unfortunately, my spoken French is limited to about 15 words, significantly reducing my usually adept conversational skills. Still, the language of sailors is universal, I was quickly invited aboard one of the boats and soon raising a glass of wine and proclaiming everything to be *"bon."*

First impressions

The Arpege 30 looks more like an American boat from the IOR era than the Euro-style boats that began flooding the market in the 1980s. Although the bow entry is quite sharp, there is also a sizable overhang. The sheerline

DUFOUR ARPEGE 30

LOA 30'4"
LWL 22'
Beam 9'11"
Draft Standard 4'5"
Draft Deep 5'4"
Displacement
   8,000 lbs.
Ballast 3,050 lbs.
Sail Area
   516 sq. ft.

is subtle and the counter stern is raised and pinched. The hull has a bit of tumblehome and looks well proportioned in the water. The coachroof has a step with a single dark Plexiglas portlight on each side. The single spreader sloop rig has a working sail area of 516 square feet, comparable to the C&C 30, a boat designed around the same time.

Below the water, the Arpege has a fairly shallow forefoot and fin keel with an exaggerated bulb that trails aft, almost as though the designer was adding a signature to the keel. Two keels were offered: a 4-foot, 5-inch standard version and a 5-foot, 4-inch deep version. Most boats in the United States seem to have the standard keel. The rudder is hung on an incredibly narrow but full-length skeg. It seems Dufour was not quite ready to commit to even a partial skeg in the mid-1960s when the boat was designed. The ballast-to-displacement ratio of just under 40 percent helps account for the Arpege's stiffness and seakindliness. Although the boat was moderately successful as a half-tonner, it came to be known as a small but capable bluewater cruiser. Several Arpeges have crossed the Atlantic, and at least one has circumnavigated.

Construction

The Arpege has held up very well through the years. In fact, Dufour recently purchased hull No. 1 and is in the process of restoring it for a company display. The Arpege hull is solid fiberglass and the deck may or may not have been cored. Michel Dufour was a pioneer in using molded liners to greatly streamline production. Liners are a mixed blessing, but in small boats, at least those less than 35 feet and under 10,000 pounds, they make a lot of sense, even if they do limit hull access. If the liner is well bonded to the hull, the pan, as it is sometimes called, can be a very sound way of supporting the hull and prefabricating furniture.

African mahogany was used for bulkheads that were well tabbed to the hull. The mast was stepped on the keel. The externally fastened keel is cast iron and fitted into a small recessed mold on a stub. The Arpege was really one of the first production boats to be sold in large numbers worldwide, and the overall construction was stout and efficient.

DUFOUR ARPEGE 30 PRICE DATA

BUC Retail Range		Low	High
	1970	$11,800	$13,400
	1973	$15,300	$17,400

Boats For Sale		State	Asking
	1970	MI	$19,500
	1971	Canada	$25,800
	1973	Canada	$23,800

What to look for

While an owner in Maine reports that his boat has never had osmotic blisters in its 30-plus year life span, another in Florida warns to expect to do an epoxy blister repair job if it hasn't been done already. Older Dufours have had their share of blisters. One thing is certain, grinding or sandblasting the iron keel and treating it with epoxy is a good idea. Naturally any boat of this vintage (the youngest Arpege is at least 30 years old) will need to have all age-related items carefully checked. From standing and running rigging, to deck leaks and electrical wiring, updates may well be in order. Even if a boat was rerigged once, it may be ready again. Interestingly, my brother recently purchased a 1973 Wauquiez Centurion for a very good price and has spent the past year refitting her for ocean sailing. Like the Arpege, the Centurion was built in France and the original construction is impressive. I understand this may be an apples-to-oranges comparison, but an older, good-quality French-built boat may be well worth the cost of a retrofit, especially if the initial purchase price is low.

Be aware that the deck nonskid will likely be well worn, and the quality of painted nonskid repairs will vary. Some owners have applied synthetic nonskid like Treadmaster. The boat originally came with gate valves on through-hull fittings, although it is unlikely any of those original valves are still operational.

On deck

A rather short but stout tiller was standard, and I have not heard of any boat that has been

Dufour Arpege 30

PRICE: BUC prices range from less than $12,000 to around $18,000 for a 1973 model. Any way you look at it, the Arpege 30 is a lot of boat for that kind of money.

DESIGN QUALITY: Michel Dufour's design, which was intended as a fast half-tonner has morphed into a fine bluewater cruising boat that is still fun to race PHRF.

CONSTRUCTION QUALITY: Typically I would moan and groan about an old boat built with fiberglass liners, but the Arpege has aged well and that is the best expression of construction quality.

USER-FRIENDLINESS: The Arpege is an easy boat to sail and fairly forgiving and stiff in a blow. The interior is innovative, and while it doesn't compare to a more modern boat with its space usage, it was well thought out for its day.

SAFETY: By all accounts the Arpege is a good boat in heavy weather with a seakindly motion. The stanchions and lifelines could be better supported.

TYPICAL CONDITION: Considering that most Arpeges on the market are around 30 years old, the boats have really held up well. But some may need some serious upgrades.

REFITTING: The age of the boat and foreign construction complicates the refit process. However, the basic systems are quite simple.

SUPPORT: Although Dufour is back in business, it is not the same company that built these wonderful old boats. There are owner groups all over the world, with the group in England being the most helpful. The group's Web page is www.dufour.org.uk/html/arpege.html

AVAILABILITY: The Arpege had a huge production run, and many boats were imported to the United States and Canada, but it is still a bit hard to find a large supply on the used boat market.

INVESTMENT AND RESALE: If you buy an older Arpege and upgrade the boat, there is a good likelihood you will get most of your money back when you sell.

OVERALL 'SVG' RATING

---

converted to wheel steering, although surely some must have been. Doing so really doesn't make any sense, because the small cockpit is ideal for a tiller. Quarterberths to port and starboard below mean there are no cockpit lockers, but there is a good-size lazarette astern. The boat I was aboard in France had converted this to a propane locker, with the bottles squeezed in amidst dock lines and fenders. The mainsheet traveler runs across the bridgedeck, restricting access to the companionway when underway but making the main convenient for efficient trimming.

The Arpege was considered beamy for its day, and the result is that the side decks are fairly wide, considering this is just a 30-foot boat. Originally the single lifelines tapered to the deck forward instead of connecting to the pulpit. Chances are good that double lifelines running to the pulpit have been retrofitted along the way. Most deck hardware was orig-

inally by Goiot and it has likely held up very well. There are opening hatches above the saloon and the head. Chances are the original mast and boom are still standing; it really is impressive how well anodized-aluminum sections have stood up in the harsh marine environment.

Down below

Michel Dufour was quite innovative when it came to interior layouts, and the Arpege was no exception. Instead of squeezing in a double berth forward, the small forepeak was dedicated to sail and other storage. A private athwartships head is aft of the forepeak. The saloon features opposite facing settees with pilot berths above. I like this arrangement. When coupled with a lee cloth, pilot berths are excellent sea berths located out of the traffic flow. I always commandeer a pilot berth if it's available.

The Arpege has an impressive galley for a 1960s-era 30-footer. Opposite the galley is the nav station, again an unusual feature in an older small boat, and the nav desk is large enough to work comfortably. The galley and the nav station can be closed off from the saloon for added privacy. There are quarterberths port and starboard, and if you can resist filling them up with gear, they make great sea berths. There is adequate storage below the settees and, of course, excellent storage in the forepeak. The table is designed to be stowed away and can also be used as a cockpit table. The finish work is really quite nice, trimmed in mahogany. There's even a built-in wine rack.

Engine

Most original Arpeges came with a Volvo diesel, which was very common for many smaller European boats, since Volvo owned the auxiliary market for years. The most common power plant was a two-cylinder 25-horsepower model that if well maintained should still run fine. It may be loud and a bit smoky, but if it's running, I wouldn't hasten to replace it. Repowering, however, seems to have been rather common and of the five boats I located on the secondhand market on the East Coast all had 2GM 20-horsepower Yanmars. Be sure to check this installation carefully. Either engine gives the Arpege adequate performance. The hull is easily driven and you should be able to motor along at more than 5 knots.

Access to the engine is decent from behind the companionway steps and through the quarter berths. Reaching the stuffing box is more challenging. The original plastic fuel tank held 11 gallons, although this has likely been replaced.

Underway

Two of the owners that I managed to communicate with in France explained that they sailed all over the Bay of Biscay every year and that the Arpege is really at its best in heavy weather. The chap I spoke with in Oakland, who has sailed his Arpege extensively offshore, confirmed this notion.

Mike Addelman owns a 1973 model that he sails on Biscayne Bay in Miami. When asked about the boat's performance parameters, Addelman told me via e-mail that he is surprised how well the Arpege points and not surprised that it tracks well too. While it doesn't accelerate like a modern boat, it doesn't slow down easily either. He noted that several years ago, he finished third in class in the Columbus Day Regatta despite a weekend of very light wind. Although he has not sailed his boat beyond the Bahamas, he has experienced some stiff breezes in the Gulf Stream. His only complaint is that the boat tends to develop weather helm. He flies an asymmetrical chute and claims that the boat steers very well off the wind, with 7 knots being his top speed on a reach.

Conclusion

The Dufour Arpege 30 is one of those old fiberglass boats that seems to have fallen through the cracks on the used boat market. It is a good quality, offshore capable boat that can usually be purchased for less than $20,000. It is an interesting alternative to more familiar American-built boats.

Contessa 32

*This oceangoing dynamo has a special place
in the author's history and heart*

Indulge me and try to understand—for me, the Contessa 32 is not just another fiberglass production boat. I cut my teeth on a Contessa 32, and the boat occupies a coveted spot in my brain's hard drive. The Contessa 32 tolerated my youthful mistakes, fueled my burgeoning dreams and always returned me safely to port after many long passages. There isn't much more you can ask of a boat. Like all fine boats, the Contessa 32 is forgiving and surprisingly rewarding to sail. Winsome and just 24 feet on the waterline, the 32 is easy to underestimate if you are not aware of its formidable reputation for seaworthiness.

Few boats can post more impressive curricula vitae. The Contessa 32 ASSENT was the quiet hero of the infamous storm-ravaged 1979 Fastnet race. It was a Contessa 32 that escorted 15-year-old solo sailor Seb Clover across the Atlantic just a few years ago. At the other end of the spectrum, IMAGINE, a 1980 model, was sailed by 65-year-old singlehander Bill Williamson across the Atlantic and back. Contessa 32s have been everywhere from the Arctic to Zanzibar. And it was a Contessa 32 named GIGI, which was one of the last English-built boats, that carried me around Cape Horn, east to west against the wind 20 years ago.

However, the Contessa 32 is not just a bluewater passagemaker. Most 32 owners sail their boats locally, race in one-design or PHRF classes and simply enjoy its soft motion in a seaway and ability to carry canvas when other boats are reefed to the nines. There is no denying that the tiller-steered 32s can produce biceps-building weather helm and ship plenty of water on deck when sailing upwind under full canvas.

Contessa 32 owners, who are not blind to their boat's quirks, are unusually devoted. When you buy a used Contessa you are not just buying a boat, you're buying a classic. You're also joining a cult. I recently attended a meeting of the Contessa 32 Owner's Association, which included a regatta on the south coast of England, and I was reminded what a unique breed Contessa 32 sailors are.

The first two Contessa 32 hulls were molded in builder Jeremy Rogers' small shop on the southern coast of England in late 1970 and launched in 1971. CONTESSA CATHERINE, owned by designer David Sadler, is still racing competitively today, in fact she competed in the recent regatta and did very well. The other boat, RED HERRING, was owned by Jeremy Rogers and went on to win her class in that year's Cowes week. The rest, as they say, is history.

The Contessa 32 was the London Boat Show boat of the year in 1972 and more than 700 boats were built before production stopped when Rogers went out of business in 1983. Also, like the famed Contessa 26, the 32 was built on license in Canada. J.J. Taylor and Sons of Ontario produced 90 or so Contessa

CONTESSA 32

LOA 32'
LWL 24'
Beam 9'6"
Draft 5'6"
Displacement 9,600 lbs.
Ballast 4,600 lbs.
Sail Area 417 sq. ft.

32s before closing its doors in 1990. Although plenty of English Contessas have sailed to our side of the Atlantic, many of the 32s for sale in the North American market are Canadian-built boats. Don't be put off by this fact for there is very little if any quality difference. In fact, the Canadian boats have a slightly modified interior along with other features that U.S. sailors tend to prefer.

First impressions

The Contessa 32 is a very handsome boat. It has been described with the best of adjectives over the years. The sheerline is deceptive—it almost looks to be reverse until you train your eye on the sweet lines. The bow is fine with a knifelike overhang. The stern is pinched in the style of the IOR boats of the early 1970s, but still attractive. The hull has pronounced tumblehome and the cabin profile and overall freeboard are low. Low as in 28 inches of freeboard, and as I remember, doing the dishes offshore was a matter of simply reaching over the side. Sadler mixed these ingredients just right and came up with a boat that is universally admired. I can't ever recall sailing into a harbor without receiving compliments about the boat.

Below the water the 32 has a powerful fin keel, a skeg-hung rudder and a deep forefoot. I have logged more than 30,000 miles aboard Contessa 32s, most of them upwind, and I have never felt the boat pound in a seaway. It does ship water over the deck and is affectionately known as a "submarine with sails." The ballast of 4,500 pounds is nearly 50 percent of the overall displacement, and although the boat does heel a bit, it is incredibly stable. The IMS stability curve puts the Contessa 32's limit of positive stability near 130 degrees.

Construction

The Contessa 32 is not overbuilt. Although, it is solidly constructed and well-engineered, it doesn't sport the massive fixtures of a Westsail or Valiant. Rogers was, and still is, extremely talented when it comes to molding fiberglass. I remember when we wanted to upgrade the size of the standing rigging before our Cape

CONTESSA 32 PRICE DATA

		Low	High
BUC Retail Range	1975	$42,300	$47,000
	1981	$34,500	$43,000

		State	Asking
Boats For Sale	1972	VA	$52,000
	1976	Canada	$56,000
	1981	Canada	$34,500

Horn adventure. He tried to point out that the fiberglass deck had only so much tensile strength and that beefing up the rigging was a waste of money.

The hull is solid fiberglass and on the English boats so is the deck. Americans are accustomed to cored decks and it is bit unnerving to feel the deck flex, especially on a legendary oceangoing boat. There is, however, no core to delaminate and flexibility is one of the great advantages of fiberglass. Canadian boats, at least later in the production run, went to balsa-cored decks. We had GIGI's deck cored with Airex, another waste of money according to Rogers.

Roger's layup was very well done, and although the hulls are thick by today's standards, every effort was made to keep the weight under control when they were built. These boats were designed for racing success as well as ocean cruising. The overall weight of 9,600 pounds made the Contessa a moderate displacement boat in its day. The Canadian boats were also built to Lloyds' specs and, if anything, are slightly heavier than their English cousins. The ballast is internal lead, and the rudder is solid fiberglass. The stock is stainless steel.

What to look for

Despite its legendary status, the Contessa 32 has a few items to carefully inspect. The Contessa 32 owners' association Web site is a valuable tool for probing into the inner workings of the 32. Also, Rogers, who has been for

Contessa 32

 **PRICE:** This rating would be higher but the dollar has plunged recently against the English pound making English boats 20 percent higher than just last year. Still, 32s on this side of the Atlantic can usually be had for less than $40,000, which is a good deal.

 DESIGN QUALITY: The only thing keeping this from being a rare five-sailboat rating is the lack of comfort below. Few if any boats of this size handle a variety conditions as well as the Contessa 32.

 **CONSTRUCTION QUALITY:** Contessa is a well-engineered boat, which is always better than simply being heavily constructed. The 32 has stood the test of time and has proven itself on every ocean.

 **USER-FRIENDLINESS:** The 32 is easy to sail, even for novices, as I proved with my early voyages. The rig is simple, the loads are not extreme and it is very forgiving. It is also rewarding for experienced sailors, a rare combination. Again, only the interior limits this rating.

 SAFETY: The 32 is extremely seaworthy, capable of standing up to severe conditions. That is the final measure of safety.

 TYPICAL CONDITION: 32s typically have been sailed hard. This is not a boat to baby, so many used boats have tired sails and gear.

 **REFITTING:** Not the easiest boat to work on because access is tight, however, parts are still widely available and there is a lot of documentation and information available.

 SUPPORT: The Contessa owners' association is an excellent resource, contact them at www.co32.org. Also, contact Jeremy Rogers at www.jeremyrogers.co.uk.

 AVAILABILITY: There is always a good selection of boats for sail in Europe but less so in North America. An Internet search turned up five boats for sale, all in Canada or on the U.S. East Coast. 32s are rare on the West Coast.

 **INVESTMENT AND RESALE:** Although the 32 holds its value fairly well, it is not an easy boat to sell in the U.S. where the small interior really hurts.

OVERALL 'SVG' RATING

---

years refurbishing old 32s (and has recently started building new 32s on a limited basis), is a font of knowledge. He is a wonderful man, modest, very gentlemanly and very accessible.

The first thing to look for is a boat that has been repowered. Although the Contessa 32 has never been a great boat under power, some engines are definitely better than others. A variety of diesels were used including Petter, Farymann, Bukh, Volvo and Yanmar. A 32 with a fairly recent three-cylinder Yanmar is worth paying a premium for.

Another item to look at is the water tank in the bilge. The large inspection plate usually leaks, letting bilge water into the tank. Some owners have done away with the inspection plates, or just given up on this as a fresh water tank. Also, check the hatches for signs of silicone and other sealants, the boat ships a lot of

green water and the hatches tend to leak. The electrical system, especially on the older English boats, will need upgrading to accommodate today's digital gizmos. One final note, many 32s had factory colored hulls that will need to be painted, possibly for the second or third time.

On deck

The 32 has a deceptively large and fairly comfortable cockpit. I spent many hours tucked up behind the dodger, which was at times the only dry spot on deck, and many others sprawled against the deep coamings reading while the windvane steered.

Tiller steering is de rigueur, at least on English boats. Canadian boats were occasionally fitted with wheels. There are small coamings and a good-sized locker to port for stowing gear. The mainsheet traveler is mounted on the bridgedeck just aft of the companionway. The helmsman can reach all sail controls without stretching. Two scuppers adequately drain the cockpit when water slops aboard.

There are low teak grabrails on the coachroof and double lifelines and well-supported stanchions are standard. The molded nonskid surface is not aggressive and may be well worn on older boats. A small bulwark that rises forward is an excellent safety feature and looks nice too. The chain locker is external and can house decent-sized ground tackle, although few boats have a good set-up for anchoring.

The mast on the new boats is from Selden. Older boats will likely have Sparcraft or Kemp spars. The chainplates are U-bolts, secured through the deck and by the hull. While they seem undersized, few if any 32s have lost their rigs due to turnbuckle failure. Winches will likely be Lewmar and most boats will have upgraded to self-tailers along the way. Most of the hardware on GIGI was also Lewmar, although we did have one of the early Harken headsail furling systems. A feature I liked was the two-way bulkhead mounted compasses that could also be viewed from down below.

Down below

The Contessa 32 interior is the reason the boat was never more popular in North America. It is small. Really small. It is easy to think you've stumbled onto a 27-foot boat when you drop below. Although Contessa brochures claimed there was 6 feet of headroom it was only the spot just below the companionway. As you stepped forward it was time to duck. British boats were finished nicely with teak interiors, while the Canadians opted for molded liners and components—practical but not as attractive. The Canadian boats do have a slightly wider cabin sole that helps make up for the narrow beam.

These boats were designed for northern sailing and ventilation is an issue. The overhead hatches in the saloon and forepeak are only adequate, and while opening portlights would help, the freeboard is so low that they would be impossible to open underway except in light conditions.

The interior plan is predictable. A double that is best suited for very good friends is forward, followed by the head to port and a locker opposite. The head is compact to say the least. Most older Contessa 32s have excellent Lavac pressure heads. The saloon features a wraparound settee and table to port and settee/sea berth to starboard. There is decent storage beneath the settees. The small galley is to port and usually includes two sinks, a two-burner gas stove and a small icebox. The best aspect of the interior is the nav station located opposite the galley. There is plenty of room for instrument repeaters and the electrical panel is also mounted here. Overall the interior works well for passage-making and has enough space for a couple to cruise with some degree of comfort.

Engine

As noted earlier, 32s came with a variety of engines. GIGI was fitted with a two-cylinder 15-horsepower Yanmar that performed brilliantly for more than 30,000 miles. We rarely motored at more than 5 knots but the engine was stingy with fuel, and we typically stretched our modest 12 gallons into 30 or 40 hours of motoring. Access is from behind the companionway and through a panel in the quarter cabin. GIGI, like most 32s, was fitted with a conventional stuffing box, including a grease gland, and a fixed two-bladed prop.

Underway

Contessa 32 voyages have been well documented but voyaging accounts don't dwell on handling characteristics. Simply put, the reason to buy a Contessa 32 is because it sails beautifully. The boat is close-winded, does not make leeway, never pounds in a chop, is fast with respect to a 24-foot waterline and handles extreme sea conditions. The boat is easy to daysail, exciting to race and cruises with a confidence few other boats can match.

Typically, most racers carry full sail until the wind tops 25 knots and deal with puffs by feathering the main. When cruising, shortening up sail results in a very well behaved boat in most conditions. Downwind sailing under spinnaker can be exciting. Most passagemakers report flying either a single or double poled out headsails in trades. Sailing from the Canary Islands to Antigua we poled out our 150 percent genoa and eased along at 6 knots day after day with little stress.

The 32 really shines in heavy going. Read Adlard Coles' classic book, *Heavy Weather Sailing,* for an account of how ASSENT handled the wild conditions that ultimately claimed 15 lives during the 1979 Fastnet Race disaster. We used similar tactics several times during our windward rounding of Cape Horn.

Conclusion

Prices for used Contessa 32s range from around $30,000 to $50,000. This is a small price to pay for a boat you can sail to the ends of the earth and back. However, like all boats, the 32 is a compromise. Its legendary seakeeping traits are offset by a lack of creature comforts. At the end of the day, the Contessa 32 is about sailing and nothing else and that's why it is a classic.

Freedom 32

*This well-built and spacious bluewater cruiser
pegs the user-friendly meter*

The Freedom 32 was something of a transition boat for Gary Hoyt and Freedom Yachts. Introduced in 1983, the 32 married Hoyt's devotion to the free-standing catboat rig with the benefits of a self-tending headsail. Hoyt conceded that there were advantages to the slot created by a jib, especially sailing upwind, and when the 32 proved successful at sea and in the marketplace, "cat sloops" became the future of Freedom Yachts. Some boats, like some people, find an identity later in life. The Freedom 32 has not only aged well but it has also completed many ocean crossings and has evolved into something of a cult boat among open-minded bluewater sailors. With its easy handling rig, roomy interior and low maintenance, it is an ideal boat to consider for a sailing sabbatical.

Hoyt was a breath of fresh air for the sailing industry when he launched Freedom Yachts in 1976. Hoyt wanted to make sailing simple and more accessible to those who had not been born to boats. Combining an unstayed cat rig

with modern fiberglass materials and construction technology, his first boat was the quirky but popular Freedom 40, a cat ketch. Although the 40 was designed for easy handling, its lively performance was a bonus and the prototype won the cruising class in the 1977 Rolex Cup in the Virgin Islands and others performed very well in various Bermuda races.

The Freedom 40 was followed by a 44 designed for short-handed offshore racing and several smaller cat ketches, including a Ron Holland-designed 39. The Freedom 21 and 25 were Hoyt's first single mast boats and the 32 followed shortly after. In addition to the clever vestigial jib, the 32 also included a carbon fiber spar and the innovative gun mount, which allows the spinnaker to be raised and dropped from the cockpit. The 32 remained in production for four years and more than 90 boats were launched, making it one of the company's best-selling models.

First impressions

The Freedom 32 is deceptive; at first glance it doesn't look like a boat to buy for sailing across the Atlantic. It isn't heavy on teak and doesn't have a heavy-duty sheen caused by oversized bronze hardware. It's also not a boat that is usually lavished with adjectives like

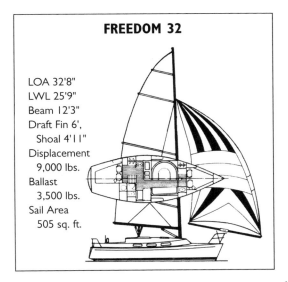

FREEDOM 32

LOA 32'8"
LWL 25'9"
Beam 12'3"
Draft Fin 6',
  Shoal 4'11"
Displacement
  9,000 lbs.
Ballast
  3,500 lbs.
Sail Area
  505 sq. ft.

beautiful and handsome, although it certainly has a unique bearing in the water. Aside from the rig, the most striking features are the wrap-around cabintrunk and long coamings, both of which are often painted a solid, contrasting color that gives the boat a distinctive profile.

Like any good catboat, the hull shape is beamy although the hull narrows at the waterline and the canoe shaped underbody has low wetted surface area. What you don't notice until you probe around is the very solid construction by Tillotson-Pearson. Two keels were available with drafts of either 4 feet, 11 inches or 6 feet. The lead ballast of 3,500 pounds translates into a ballast-to-displacement ratio near 40 percent. When you crunch the displacement of 9,000 pounds with the moderate waterline of 25 feet, 9 inches you come up with a displacement-to-length ratio of 258, which is a very good number for a cruising boat. Theoretically at least, it is light enough to be easily driven and yet heavy enough to stand up to a blow and also able to carry a reasonable amount of stores. Most of the 505 square feet of sail area is carried in the roachy, full-batten mainsail.

Construction

The Freedom 32 was built by TPI in Warren, Rhode Island. However, it predates the development of the company's patented Scrimp method of construction. The hull is balsa cored, which, as regular readers of *Used Boat Notebook* know only too well, is a construction technique I am not wild about. However, when balsa coring is done well it creates a very strong and light hull. TPI's original construction was excellent and there have been few reported problems. However, delamination issues can arise when new through-hull fittings are added or changed. It is important to make every effort to keep the core material dry. The deck is also balsa-cored. On the positive side, TPI was one of the first builders to use vinylester resins in the outer laminate to limit blisters and the builder's attention to detail is superb.

The ballast is lead and the tapered carbon fiber spar is stepped on the keel. The mast was guaranteed for life for the original owner, which of course doesn't do used boat

FREEDOM 32 PRICE DATA

		Low	High
BUC Retail Range	1985	$35,800	$39,700
	1990	$41,800	$46,500
		State	Asking
Boats For Sale	1984	CT	$40,000
	1986	RI	$45,000
	1990	MI	$57,000

buyers much good. The balanced fiberglass rudder has a stainless post. The bulkheads are stout plywood with teak veneers and securely bonded to the hull. The interior workmanship is solid if not overly showy, just the way I like it.

What to look for

The Freedom 32 has aged very well and the boat doesn't have a litany of items to be wary of. Naturally, be sure to have the hull and deck carefully inspected by a surveyor to make sure that the coring is in good shape. Also, a knowledgeable rigger should check the carbon fiber spar. Freedom developed its own spars and there were a few problems with early boats. Most masts are now 20 years old. One age related issue that is not a problem for the Freedom 32 is the standing rigging. However, the running rigging, lifelines terminals and keel bolts should be checked. Also, any evidence of deck leaks should be attended to without delay.

On deck

The cockpit is control central for the 32 and all sail controls, including the spinnaker, are led aft. There are clutches to port and starboard on the aft end of the trunkhouse and usually No. 23 Barient self-tailing winches. A molding is provided for a spray dodger. The cockpit is large and comfortable with nicely shaped seats and seatbacks. Freedom was one of the first builders to incorporate proper ergonomics in

Freedom 32

SAILING Magazine's Value Guide

PRICE: With prices ranging from $40,000 to $55,000 there is no denying that the Freedom 32 is expensive when compared to other 20-year-old, 32-foot boats. However, the boat is big for its length and well built.

DESIGN QUALITY: Some sailors just can't accept the free-standing rig, so they don't like the design. If you accept Hoyt's premises, than you must admit that the 32's design is brilliant.

CONSTRUCTION QUALITY: The 32 is well built by TPI. The balsa-cored hull is viewed as a positive by some and a negative by others. Good quality materials and fittings are used throughout.

USER-FRIENDLINESS: Yes, this is one of the rare 5s ever issued in the Used Boat Notebook but when it comes to user-friendliness the 32 is at the top of the charts. From a simple-to-handle sailplan, including the gun mount, to a very comfortable interior and cockpit, the 32 is all about being user-friendly.

SAFETY: Not having to leave the cockpit translates into safety. However the hull shape stability numbers don't necessarily meet offshore standards and the rig makes it impossible to heave to.

TYPICAL CONDITION: Most 32s have been well cared for and the nature of the boat doesn't really allow for it to be driven hard. The boat has aged well.

REFITTING: With a spacious interior and reasonable access, the 32 is not a difficult boat to work on. Freedom Yachts is still very much in business, so there is factory support.

SUPPORT: As noted above the company is still building boats and offers good factory support. There is also a helpful owners group at the Web site www.freedomyachts.com.

AVAILABILITY: Only 90 boats were built so availability will always be somewhat limited. However, there are currently at least 10 boats on the market today, including four in Rhode Island.

INVESTMENT AND RESALE: The 32 has held its value well over the years. Resale is governed to a degree by the fact that many sailors don't want to consider free-standing rigs.

 OVERALL 'SVG' RATING

---

its designs. There is a serious bridgedeck and the mainsheet traveler is forward of the companionway, freeing up cockpit space. The Edson wheel and pedestal is located well aft with a raised and curved helmsman seat. There are small cubbies to port and starboard and a decent-size locker to starboard. The aft cabin has a portlight that opens into the cockpit.

If you are not used to a free-standing rig you'll notice the absence of stays and shrouds the first time you make your way forward—there is nothing to hold on to. You will get used to it and the 32 does have long grab rails along the trunkhouse and well supported stanchions and lifelines. The nonskid may be worn and the boat I looked at in Fort Lauderdale had added treadmaster in select places. Freedom didn't cut corners and used good quality deck hardware. The bow pulpit, which houses the

gun-mount spinnaker pole, is especially robust, although the tube itself is a large contraption on deck.

Down below

Next to easy sail handling, the spacious interior is the feature owners like best about the 32. The plan includes two private double cabins, 6-foot, 2-inch headroom, a comfortable saloon and a functional, seagoing galley. Add excellent ventilation and quality joinerwork and you end up with a terrific interior, especially for a 32-foot boat.

The 32 was one of the first boats to sneak a full double cabin aft, tucked under the cockpit, a design concept that would eventually sweep the industry. The aft cabin is to port and is entered from the galley. Hoyt was able to expand the aft cabin by locating the engine amidships, under the aft dinette settee, which also helps center weight. The aft cabin includes a hanging locker and adequate storage under the bunk. The L-shaped galley features a two-burner stove and oven outboard, a large fridge/icebox and two good-sized sinks. Pressure hot and cold water was standard. Counter space is at a premium although the boat I inspected had a removable panel that fit over the stovetop. Storage is limited to small lockers behind the stove. In fact, that's one issue owners note consistently: it is challenging finding enough room to stow provisions for long passages.

Opposite the galley is a head with shower and just forward of that is a stand-up nav station, which allows for storage underneath. My current boat has a stand-up nav station and I confess, I prefer a more traditional sit-down arrangement. The saloon includes either a folding or half-moon-shaped table with a wraparound settee to port. The starboard settee makes the best sea berth and should be fitted with a lee cloth. An additional head and basin were options in the V-berth cabin; however that option does not seem popular, at least not with the 10 boats currently for sale on **www.yachtworld.com**.

Engine

The standard engine was the 22-horsepower, 3-cylinder Yanmar 3GMF diesel. This is a sweet little engine, reliable and fuel efficient, although it is on the small size for the 32. Although most boats on the market still have their original engines the two that have repowered have opted for the 27-horsepower Yanmar. Access is excellent, the engine is tucked under the port side dinette settee. The 32-gallon fuel tank is located under the forward dinette settee.

Underway

Although Hoyt was always interested in speed (as a champion one-design sailor he had racing in his blood) the Freedom 32 was really a cruising boat from the get-go. Easy sail handling is the essence of the boat. With the self-tending

jib and main, tacking is simply a matter of turning the wheel, come through the wind, fill the sails and straighten things out. No sheets to release and trim, no winches to grind. The 105-square-foot jib includes a flexible batten that maintains shape on any heading, Hoyt called this arrangement a Camberspar jib. The lack of a backstay means that the mainsail can have an extra large roach and it's the workhorse sail. The main is set up with single line slab reefing and the small headsail makes a natural storm jib. Heaving-to is not a viable option for a cat-sloop, although heaving-to is not a viable option for most modern fin keel sloops anyway.

Several 32s have crossed the Atlantic and one owner reported averaging better than 135 miles a day on an Atlantic Circle. That's great going for a boat with a LWL of less than 26 feet. Owners note that like all catboats, the 32 develops weather helm upwind, although a bit of helm usually allows for better self-steering. The 12-foot, 3-inch beam creates plenty of initial stability and limits heeling to a degree. The 32 is at its best reaching and watching the knotmeter arc past 7 knots is not uncommon. The 32 is nimble, and it's able to sail in and out of the dock. One of the more interesting features is the gun mount, which allows short-handed crews and singlehanders to raise and drop the chute from the cockpit. This system, which has been copied and tweaked by other builders, employs a short yard that extends from a tube mounted on the pulpit. The spinnaker clews are attached to each end of the yard, and the halyard is led aft. Yank up the halyard and trim the sheets. A chute scooper cleans up when it's time to drop the sail and finally the yard is retracted—a brilliant idea.

Conclusion

The Freedom 32 is an intriguing option as a small but capable bluewater cruiser. Prices hover around $45,000, which may seem a bit expensive for a 20-year-old, 32-foot boat. However, the boat is deceptively big, well built and cleverly designed. It is an easy boat to handle and well proven at sea. A couple planning to take a year off should take a good hard look at the Freedom 32.

Jeanneau Attalia 32

This lightweight sloop was one of the first to blend spaciousness with performance

Jeanneau, a division of Groupe Beneteau, is a key part of the largest sailboat manufacturing company in the world. Today Jeanneau builds a range of quality cruising and performance boats from 20 to 54 feet and aggressively markets its line in North America. Jeanneau, however, had a long history before consolidating with Beneteau in 1995. The French builder was one of the first European companies to gain a toehold in the U.S. market more than 20 years ago when European boats, especially the modern French variety, were still something of a novelty.

Founded by M. Henri Jeanneau in 1956, the company originally built wooden motorboats before switching to fiberglass a few years later. In 1970 Jeanneau began production of its first successful sailboat design the Sangria, a 25-foot sloop that sold nearly 3,000 boats during a long production run. Later that year Jeanneau sold out to Bangor Punta, an American Conglomerate that also owned O'Day, Ranger and Cal. That connec-

tion opened the door for exports into the United States.

In the early and mid-1980s Jeanneau offered several models on this side of the Atlantic, all with somewhat unusual names that didn't sound quite right to American sailors accustomed to identifying boats simply by the manufacturer and length overall. The Jeanneau Aquila, Arcadia, Melody, Symphonie and Gin Fizz sold in modest numbers. A lightweight sloop available with either a fixed keel or centerboard, the Attalia 32 was probably the most popular of the lot. Several hundred Attalias were built from 1982 through 1987 and there is usually a decent selection of boats available on the North American used boat market.

First impressions

The prolific team of Michel Joubert and Bernard Nivelt, who in those days specialized in boats less than 35 feet long, designed the Attalia 32 and patterned it closely after their 1981 half-ton world champion, AIR BIGOUDEN. The Attalia, which has an LOD of 30 feet, 2 inches and an LOA of 31 feet, 10 inches, blends a performance hull shape with a surprisingly comfortable interior, a concept that French builders would essentially patent over the next 20 years.

There isn't much sheer, but there is plenty of freeboard, and at first glance, the Attalia seems to bob on the water. The trunkhouse is fairly low and features dark Plexiglas portlights. Under the water, the forefoot is quite narrow, the iron fin keel has a relatively short cord and the rudder is mounted on a partial skeg. Although the majority of boats had fixed keels, Attalia's centerboard option with a board-up draft of just 3 feet, 8 inches accounted for its popularity in the United States. The standard draft is 5 feet, 9 inches. The design displacement is 7,500 pounds. By way of comparison, the Hunter 30 of

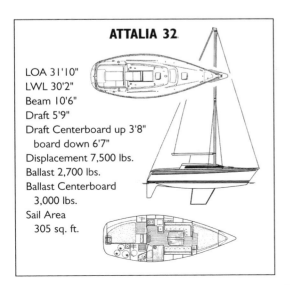

ATTALIA 32

LOA 31'10"
LWL 30'2"
Beam 10'6"
Draft 5'9"
Draft Centerboard up 3'8"
  board down 6'7"
Displacement 7,500 lbs.
Ballast 2,700 lbs.
Ballast Centerboard
  3,000 lbs.
Sail Area
  305 sq. ft.

the same period displaces 9,700 pounds and the Catalina 30 weighs 10,200 pounds. Of course, the Attalia seems downright heavy compared to a ULDB like the Olson 30, which displaces only 3,600 pounds.

Construction

Although the Attalia was a thoroughly modern design in 1981, the boat was built conservatively. The hand-laid hull is solid fiberglass, and the deck is balsa cored. The hull and deck are joined on a flange and bonded both chemically and mechanically. The joint is also sealed with a layer of fiberglass making it strong and essentially watertight. The iron keel is epoxy-coated and bolted to the hull. The keel bolts are then fiberglassed-over, a good technique for keeping the bolts dry but not for replacing them or dropping the keel. The rudder is glassed-over wood with stainless steel drift pins. The rudder stock is stainless steel as well.

Jeanneau has always done excellent fiberglass work, and one of its trademarks is to bond all the interior components to each other. The bulkheads are securely tabbed to the hull, and the settees and lockers are tabbed to the bulkheads. The result is that the interior furnishings act as structural members.

I have had plenty of personal experience sailing Jeanneaus of this era. My mother sailed her 1978 Gin Fizz sloop most of the way around the world in the early 1980s, and I later sailed it across the Atlantic twice. It was a standard production boat that held up incredibly well. Neither of us had encountered structural problems. In fact, another owner sailed the same boat around the world again in the early 1990s. The Attalia is not considered a bluewater cruiser, but it was built to similar scantlings. Bernard Belisle sailed his Attalia from Mexico to Quebec City and had nothing but praise for the boat.

What to look for

Owner comments tend to compliment the Attalia's construction, and by almost all accounts, the boat has aged well. There are, of course, a few common problems to look for. I was amazed that the Plexiglas ports on the Gin Fizz didn't leak, but several Attalia owners re-

JEANNEAU ATTALIA 32 PRICE DATA

BUC Retail Range		Low	High
	1984	$22,300	$24,800
	1987	$29,500	$33,200

Boats For Sale		State	Asking
	1984	Canada	$38,900
	1985	OR	$34,000
	1987	RI	$37,000

ported leaks, cracks, crazing and the need to replace the ports on the Attalia. The nature of the hull shape results in a shallow bilge that is difficult to drain, especially because the limber holes clog easily. Also, any water in the bilge tends to slosh onto the sole when heeled, and although the sole is glassed-over on the bottom, this water will eventually cause some delamination. Jeanneau also used fabric and vinyl for liners and locker covers that become droopy when the adhesive gives out, making repair difficult. One owner also noted that the icebox needed better insulation when he installed 12-volt refrigeration. Another owner complained about the difficulty in finding metric replacement parts. Probably the most common complaint about the Attalia is that it is underpowered. The standard engines were either a two-cylinder Yanmar or a Volvo, both around 13-horsepower. Naturally some Attalias have been repowered, and if you find one with a larger engine, consider it a bonus.

On deck

Most European Attalias came from the factory with tiller steering, which is my preference for two reasons. First, the boat is light and responsive and you can feel the rudder in your hands with a tiller. Second, the tiller is mounted well aft and can be pivoted to open up the cockpit when at anchor. Speaking of the cockpit, it isn't huge, but then again it is easy to forget that this is just a 30-foot boat. The seat backs are a bit abrupt, but the fairly deep well and bridgedeck make the cockpit secure in a blow. There is a large locker and a clever life raft

Jeanneau Attalia 32   SAILING Magazine's Value Guide

 **PRICE:** Attalia asking prices range from just over $20,000 to around $35,000 for a newer model in top condition.

 DESIGN QUALITY: Joubert/Nivelt combined to create a lively performer with a very roomy interior. The high freeboard is a bit unsightly, and you either like or don't like the flat-lined French look. The centerboard model offers the option of shoal draft.

 CONSTRUCTION QUALITY: For a production builder Jeanneau builds strong boats. Although the Attalia's design was modern in its day, the construction techniques were tried and tested.

 USER-FRIENDLINESS: The Attalia is easy to sail with all lines led aft. The interior is well thought out and comfortable. The shallow bilge means that even a little bit of water will slosh onto the sole when heeled.

 SAFETY: Although the boat is a bit tender by design, it is well constructed. The deck is easy to navigate, although the nonskid is likely well worn. There is a bridgedeck and a special life raft locker for offshore sailing.

 TYPICAL CONDITION: By most accounts Attalias age well, but they vary widely. Most boats were imported while others were sailed across the Atlantic on their own bottoms.

 REFITTING: The Attalia is not the easiest boat to work on and finding parts, especially special metric parts, takes a bit of patience and persistence. The Attalias were not built with refitting in mind.

 SUPPORT: Like most production builders, Jeanneau focuses on new models, although the company Web site provides good information about old boats. A useful Jeanneau owner's page can be found at http://jeanneau.tripod.com/owners/id217.htm on the Web.

 AVAILABILITY: Although hundreds were built, Attalias were exported in limited quantities. Fortunately, for buyers anyway, the boat is not well known so they tend to linger on the market. Be sure to include Canada in your search.

 INVESTMENT AND RESALE: Attalias have held their value adequately over the years and most of the depreciation has been absorbed. This is a good time to buy an Attalia.

OVERALL 'SVG' RATING

locker under the helmsman's seat. Two scuppers are located in the transom.

The mainsheet traveler runs across the bridgedeck, like most boats of this vintage. If you simply can't live with this arrangement, it's possible to convert to midboom sheeting with a traveler over the companionway. There is a good possibility the original two-speed sheet winches have been upgraded. The Attalia was one of the first production boats to lead all sail controls, including halyards, aft to the cockpit.

Spinnaker gear was standard. The genoa tracks are inboard, as are the chainplates, allowing for tight sheeting angles. The single-spreader, deck-stepped anodized aluminum mast and boom are likely by Isomat and feature internal halyards and slab reefing. Most deck hardware is by Goiot and above average

in quality. The nonskid is likely a little worn, but the side decks are fairly wide. Full-length teak grab rails are mounted on the cabintrunk and double lifelines were standard. The Attalia also came from the factory with a stout stemhead fitting that included double bow rollers, a chain stop and a large external chain locker.

Down below

The Attalia interior plan is deceiving. It would be easy to think the boat was designed in 1991 or even 2001, not 1981. The overall spaciousness is a result of high freeboard, a beamy hull shape that is carried aft and clever design work. The cabin is trimmed in teak and workmanship is good for a production boat. A light headliner with teak battens and forward-facing portlights really help brighten things up below.

The forward cabin has a large double berth with storage below and narrow shelves alongside. There is a hanging locker to starboard and an overhead hatch for ventilation. A sliding door offers privacy and takes up less space than a hinged door. The saloon includes a centerline table with leaves that fold up to accommodate six. In the centerboard version, the housing is located in the table. The port side settee is L-shaped with a wine cabinet above and a bladder water tank underneath. The back rests lift up and there is storage behind. The French have always offered distinguishing touches like blinds on the hatches and ports and panoramic roof screens. The headroom is just a pinch less than 6 feet.

The L-shaped galley is to port and includes a single stainless sink. Pressure water was standard, which wasn't always the case 20 years ago. A seawater foot pump was also standard on most old Jeanneaus but never worked well. There is a two-burner stove and oven, usually by Plastimo, and the icebox is decent sized but poorly insulated. The nav station is opposite the galley and the chart table is quite large for a boat this size. The fuel tank is located beneath the nav station. The head is aft to starboard and includes a wet locker. This is the best place to squeeze in the head on a small boat. The aft cabin is tucked under the cockpit to port and is surprisingly commodious. There is a full-sized double berth, a hanging locker and shelves for storage.

Engine

As stated earlier, the engine is a bit undersized, although it was designed for docking and close quarter maneuvers only, not for long motoring trips as evidenced by the 12-gallon fuel capacity. Owners report motoring at around 5 knots, and both engines are extremely stingy on fuel. The engine box is well insulated with foam soundproofing and access is excellent from behind the companionway steps and through a panel in the aft cabin. The stuffing box and batteries are easy to service from under the aft cabin mattress. Unfortunately, the Jeanneau engine control panel uses idiot lights instead of gauges.

Underway

The Attalia is a bit tender and sails best on her lines, avoiding excessive heeling. The boat is close-winded and easily driven. Although the centerboard model has slightly more ballast, the keel model is stiffer. Approximately 70 percent of the boats were built with keels. Two owners reported that they were surprised at the lack of pounding, although I suspect that beating into a choppy seaway you'd feel the shallow forefoot. Another owner who sails in Alaska notes that the helm is well balanced and is easily steered with a Tillermate autopilot even when reaching in 20-plus knots of wind. On the wind, he strongly recommends reefing early to keep the boat flat. Weather helm does not appear to be a common problem.

Bernard Belisle, who completed a 5,000-mile passage, agrees that the Attalia lacks punch under power, but that it doesn't affect passagemaking much. "I don't worry about the power situation because I prefer to sail the boat and don't motor unless I have to. It sails well in light air," Belisle said. Although most Attalias are used for cruising and casual PHRF racing these days, several boats were actively campaigned in Europe when the boat was first introduced. The Attalia will respond to aggressive sailing and that can be very rewarding.

Conclusion

The Jeanneau Attalia is surprising boat. Because it hovers just off the radar screen for most U.S. sailors, it is an excellent value. The Attalia delivers comfort, performance and quality construction at a most affordable price.

Islander 32 MK II

A good-sailing, good-looking family cruiser and a sound value

Searching for reliable material about Islanders is something of a challenge. The company, which began life as McGlasson Boat Company, was one of the early production sailboat builders. Later known as Wayfarer Marine, the company was firmly established as Islander Yachts by the time the Bob Perry-designed 32 MK II was introduced in 1976. Around 200 Islander 32 MK IIs were built during a four-year production run. Unfortunately, after Islander Yachts went out of business in 1986 most of the Costa Mesa, California, builder's records were lost or destroyed.

Although there is not much of a written record to draw on, the floating record is impressive, you'll find old Islanders at marinas all over the country. Like other West Coast builders Columbia, Cal and Ericson, Islander was a major player in the United States sailboat business for two decades. It produced many handsome designs, including Perry's popular 28, Alan Gurney's classic 36 and Ted Brewer's handsome 48-foot cruiser.

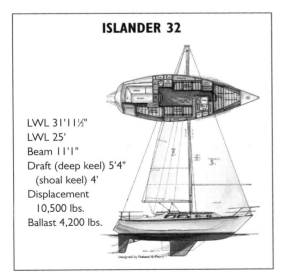

ISLANDER 32

LWL 31'11½"
LWL 25'
Beam 11'1"
Draft (deep keel) 5'4"
   (shoal keel) 4'
Displacement
   10,500 lbs.
Ballast 4,200 lbs.

Designed by Robert H. Perry

Perry told me recently that the 32 MK II was inspired by his earlier design, the Islander 28. "The team at Islander thought that the 28 was too tender so we went after a stiffer hull form with a harder turn to the bilge," Perry said. "Hank McCormick (Islander's marketing man) thought we should add 2 inches to my original drawings for more room below, so I did. The day the boat was launched we stood on the dock and watched the boat power around. As it took a run straight at us Hank said, 'It's good but it would have been better with 2 inches less freeboard.' "

First impressions

The Islander 32 MK II is a good-looking boat, and although the design is 27 years old, it could almost pass as a contemporary production boat. The bow is always the giveaway, most of today's new boats have snub bows that extend the waterline and flatten the forefoot for a pinch of extra speed. The tradeoff is that modern boats often pound the fillings right out of your teeth when sailing upwind. The Islander 32's bow is nicely raked without looking overly traditional and there is a subtle sheer that softens the otherwise modern profile. The reverse transom flows naturally in the hull line and the moderate beam is extended well aft, at least by mid 1970s standards. The cabintrunk includes two long ports aft and two smaller ones forward. When first observed, it is easy to mistake the MK II for a larger boat. Of course, there is about 2 inches too much freeboard.

There are no steep buttock lines below the waterline and the leading edge of the relatively deep fin keel is raked aft. Supposedly, East Coast sailors thought the draft of 5 feet, 4 inches was a bit excessive for a 32-foot boat, prompting the development of the 4-foot shoal-draft model. The large semibalanced rudder is positioned well aft for excellent steering control. The Islander 32 MK II is a fairly stiff boat with a ballast to displacement ratio of 40 percent. A masthead sloop rig, the 32 has a keel-stepped spar, with an air draft of 47 feet on the tall rig.

What to look for

Don't confuse the Islander 32 MK II, which as mentioned earlier was introduced in 1977, with the 1960's narrow-beam long-keel Islander 32. If you spot a used 32 with a great asking price it's probably the older 32. MK II prices typically range from the low 20s to the mid-30s. Another version of the 32 built by Iona is also confused with the MK II. Several different engines were used during the production run including the popular 30-horsepower Universal Atomic 4 gas engine, a single cylinder 7-horsepower Volvo, a more common two-cylinder 13-horsepower Volvo and the preferred 25-horsepower Westerbeke L 25.

Islander was hard hit by the dreaded pox, and many 32 MK IIs have had blister problems at one time. Try to find out if, when and to what extent a bottom job was completed and what barrier coat system was applied. Also, check the main bulkhead below, some 32 MK II owners have reported problems. The decks were cored with plywood and should be carefully sounded for signs of delamination. Leaks in the hull-to-deck joint were not uncommon and sloppy bedding compound along the toe-rail is an indicator of this problem. Finally, check the age-related issues, particularly the standing rigging and steering cables.

Construction

The true measure of a boat's construction is how well it holds up over time. For the most part the Islander 32 MK is going strong—it was a well-built boat. Several MK II's have completed impressive offshore passages, including one documented circumnavigation, and others sail regularly on windy San Francisco Bay. The hull is solid fiberglass and as mentioned earlier the deck is plywood cored. The construction is typical of the period with hand-laid hull and polyester resin. The hull-to-deck joint includes the aluminum toerail that runs nearly the entire length of the deck, an Is-

ISLANDER MK II PRICE DATA

BUC Retail Range		Low	High
	1976	$24,500	$27,200
	1980	$27,400	$30,500

Boats For Sale		State	Asking
	1976	ME	$28,000
	1977	FL	$26,700
	1978	CA	$25,500

lander trademark. The ballast is lead. Bulkheads are tabbed to the hull, the floors are stout and use of liners is limited.

On deck

The MK II has a spacious, comfortable cockpit that was a major improvement over the earlier 32s. The pedestal is placed well aft, which opens up the rest of the cockpit, yet the primaries remain within easy reach of the helm. The MK II was one of the first boats to offer optional midboom sheeting with the traveler over the companionway, although many boats still have the mainsheet led aft of the helm. There isn't much of a bridgedeck, and in heavy weather, prudence dictates leaving the bottom washboard in place. There are lockers aft, to port and starboard. The engine control panel on the boat I inspected was inconveniently located underneath the helmsman's seat.

The shrouds are mounted inboard, making it easy to navigate the side decks and also improving the sheeting angles. It seems that some boats came from the factory with full double backstays. The single-spreader spar is keel stepped. The nonskid may well be worn smooth. Deck hardware tends to be a bit undersized. Most boats are setup with a single anchor roller forward and an external anchor locker. The securing latch for the anchor locker is inadequate as are the small deck-mounted forward running lights.

Down below

Like its big sister, the Islander 36, the interior was a major reason for the 32 MK II's popu-

Islander 32 MK II

SAILING Magazine's Value Guide

 **PRICE:** Prices range from the low 20s for early boats with gas engines to mid 30s for late model 32 MK IIs with 25-horsepower diesels. Either way, it is a good quality boat for the price of a midsized new car.

 DESIGN QUALITY: Perry's design not only continues to look good but the 32 MK II performs well and has proven itself to be seaworthy.

 **CONSTRUCTION QUALITY:** Overall the MK II has held up well, which is the sign of good initial construction. Blisters were common and some deck fittings were undersized.

 USER-FRIENDLINESS: Relatively easy to handle under power and sail, the cockpit and interior are comfortable and spacious.

SAFETY: There is not much of a bridgedeck, which can allow green water below. Also, the interior could use a few more handholds. Its easy motion in a seaway is an important and often overlooked safety feature.

 TYPICAL CONDITION: Most 32 MK IIs have been used for family sailing and coastal cruising, which is easier on a boat than racing.

 REFITTING: Not a particularly difficult boat to work on although original parts are hard if not impossible to locate.

 SUPPORT: Unlike other Islander models, the 32 does not have an active owners group. There is a 32 MK II Web site, which can be found at www.geocities.com/nbh4nh/islanderhome.html although there isn't much information available as company records were lost.

 AVAILABILITY: Although around 200 32 MKs were built, used boat availability is average at best. The selection of boats is best on the West Coast.

 INVESTMENT AND RESALE: With a solid pedigree the MK II is a sound used boat value, and likely will remain so well into the future.

OVERALL 'SVG' RATING

---

larity. Almost every owner comments on the spaciousness, comfort and ample storage down below. The finish is classic late 1970's dark teak but the workmanship is first rate and large portlights help brighten things up. The interior arrangement is conventional but half bulkheads aft and a fold-away table in the saloon create a feeling of roominess—the 32 MK II seems like a bigger boat than it really is.

The forward V-berth is a good-sized double with storage below. Next aft is a hanging locker to port with the head opposite. The saloon features offset settees, both capable sea berths, and the table folds onto the main bulkhead. Cane faced lockers above the settees are deceptively large, attractive and practical as they allow the lockers to breath. An L-shaped galley is to port and includes a two- or three-burner stove outboard, a single sink and decent sized icebox/refrigerator. Drawers and lockers

swallow up provisions and there is enough counter space for most seagoing cooks.

The electrical panel is tucked away on the aft bulkhead just to port of the companionway and a quarterberth is to starboard. The only thing missing from the interior is a chart table.

Engine

The engine is tucked away under the companionway and access is adequate. Ironically, the boats with small Volvo diesels are a little easier to work on, although they're less desirable on the used market. If you find a 32 MK II with an Atomic 4 don't automatically scratch it off your list. Parts are still widely available and cheap, the engines are fairly reliable and the asking price might be a lot less than a comparable boat with a diesel. As noted earlier, the Westerbeke L 25 is the preferred model as most owners with the smaller diesels say the boat is under powered. Fuel capacity is approximately 30 gallons.

Underway

Like many older boats selected for the Used Boat Notebook, the most enduring feature of the Islander 32 MK II is its sailing ability. By almost all accounts the 32 MK is nimble, well balanced, fairly fast and able to stand up to a blow—what more can you want from a boat. Most owners note that the boat is quite seaworthy and typically doesn't require a reef until the wind pipes up over 20 knots. Consequently it can be a bit sluggish in light air. One owner notes that there is just enough weather helm so that it adapts well to his Monitor self-steering windvane. Owners who have cruised long-distance on the boats complain of a shallow bilge that easily soaks the cabin sole and praise its stout construction and ability to sail well upwind. Although primarily used as a coastal cruiser a generous PHRF rating of around 180 makes the boat competitive around the buoys.

Conclusion

The Islander 32 MK has much to commend it. It is a solid, good sailing boat with a comfortable interior. It can fill many needs, from a family weekender to inexpensive cruiser. And with asking prices usually in the mid- to high-20s, it is also a sound used boat value.

Caliber 33

*A used boat sleeper, this little big boat
elicits strong owner loyalty*

The Caliber 33 is a big boat tucked into a small package. Designed by company co-founder, Michael McCreary, the 33 is a solidly built cruiser of moderate to slightly heavy proportions and well respected by sailors around the country. First launched in 1985, approximately 70 boats were completed in Caliber's small but efficient plant in Clearwater, Florida.

The boat evolved into the Caliber 35 in 1990 when a reverse transom stretched the LOA. That's an intriguing feature about the 33, it is in many ways the same boat as the 35. Although Caliber has upgraded and refined the 35, and today's model, the 35LRC is a world-class yacht, the original 33 continues to represent an excellent value on the used boat market. Combined production of the 33 and 35 is more than 100 boats.

Fresh out of college, Michael McCreary and his brother George founded Caliber Yachts on a shoestring in 1980. Michael was a naval architect and engineering type while George majored in business and had a knack for marketing,

an ideal but rare combination in the boat business. Their first boat was a well-received 28-foot coastal cruiser that was loaded with the features that would ultimately come to define Caliber. It was solidly built and spacious without compromising sailing qualities or aesthetics. Their next project was the 33, which they launched during the recession of 1985. Quality always wins out, or so they say, and despite the hard times the 33 was a success.

First impressions

The Caliber 33 looks better in the water than it does on paper. Although I like the hull shape design—heck, it's the kind of shape I've been scribbling on cocktail napkins for years—most lines appear razor straight in the drawings. The sheerline looks like it was drawn with a ruler, as does the run of the coachroof and cockpit coamings. In the water, the softer side of the

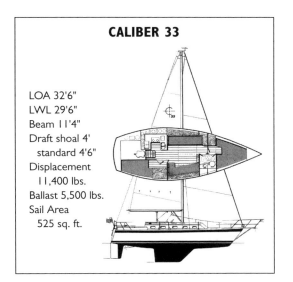

CALIBER 33

LOA 32'6"
LWL 29'6"
Beam 11'4"
Draft shoal 4'
   standard 4'6"
Displacement
   11,400 lbs.
Ballast 5,500 lbs.
Sail Area
   525 sq. ft.

33 becomes apparent. The slope of the forward end of the coachroof flows naturally out of the deck, the radius of the coamings becomes obvious, and the straight rake of the stem is muted a bit by the bowsprit. It's been noted that the appearance of the 33 is a curious blend between traditional and modern and I concur but it's a look I like.

Below the waterline the 33 has fairly flat forefoot that abruptly turns south at the leading edge of the large fin keel section. The standard draft is 4 feet, 6 inches and a 4-foot shoal-draft keel was also offered. The west coast of Florida pretty well demands a draft of less than 5 feet and many builders in the area have been influenced by local conditions. The rudder is supported by a full skeg and mounted well aft. Although various sources list slightly different figures, by any terms the 33 is a stiff, stable hull.

As a delivery skipper I have long been skeptical of published specifications for secondhand boats that invariably tip the scales well above their designed fighting weights. Immersion factors and different sail configurations further skew the numbers so I generally don't put much stock in ratios. Still, one figure that jumps off the 33's spec sheet is an impressive ballast/displacement ratio of 47 percent. A masthead sloop rig, the 33 carries 525 square feet of working sail. One of the best features added to later 35 models was the addition of an easily removed cutter stay.

Construction

Caliber builds its boats the old fashioned way and that's a compliment. Although they are not quite a custom builder, they're anything but a mass production builder. Caliber eschews molded liners and pans, instead it painstakingly laminates specific components into its hand-laid solid fiberglass hulls. The 33 has beefy, closely spaced floors glassed directly to the hull, providing support and rigidity. The teak-and-plywood furniture fittings and bulkheads are also glassed in place with structural bulkheads receiving added attention. The 33's hull-and-deck joint is one of the best I've seen. Set on an inward flange, the joint is made with 3M 5200 and through bolted on six-inch centers. A gasket is then formed around the in-

CALIBER 33 PRICE DATA

BUC Retail Range		Low	High
	1987	$47,000	$51,800
	1990	$51,800	$57,300

Boats For Sale		State	Asking
	1986	RI	$55,000
	1987	SC	$57,900
	1987	FL	$60,000

board edge of the joint where any leaks might occur. The toerail and stainless steel rubrail are also incorporated into the joint. Square headed carriage bolts, instead of pan head bolts, fit securely into the rail and won't easily loosen or twist when being tightened.

The deck is cored with small plywood sections that are extremely strong but heavy and can delaminate when wet. However, deck problems don't seem to be an issue, probably because Caliber goes to great lengths to keep its boats dry. Still, it is a good idea to carefully inspect and occasionally re-bed deck hardware. The lead ballast is encapsulated in the keel cavity. Quality material and hardware are used throughout the boat, a key reason why older 33s have aged very well.

What to look for

Documented problems with Caliber 33s are actually few and far between. The original bowsprit, which is actually just an anchoring platform, was not husky enough and in some cases came apart. Caliber recognized the problem and beefed up the platform and switched to heavier tubing as well. One of the owners I corresponded with mentioned that the standard prop is too small and another noted the shaft had come loose from the coupler. Still, it's fairly impressive how few common complaints I heard.

Like all boats, be on the lookout for age-related issues. All 33s are at least 15 years old, and some are over 20 years old. Check the standing rigging, especially the original swage

Caliber 33   SAILING Magazine's Value Guide

PRICE: The Caliber 33 is a bit pricey when you compare it against like-sized production boats. However, when you compare it against some top-quality boats it's a pretty good value.

DESIGN QUALITY: McCreary's design combines a seakindly hull shape with comfortable accommodations. There are some compromises, of course, but overall the design achieves its objective.

CONSTRUCTION QUALITY: The Caliber 33 is a very well-built boat. It's not sophistically constructed but it is a small boat built like a large one, everything is put in to stay in.

USER-FRIENDLINESS: The cockpit isn't all that comfortable, but otherwise this boat is very easy to handle. The interior plan is innovative and ideal for couple cruising with private accommodations for occasional guests.

SAFETY: Safety and construction are closely linked, throw in a seaworthy design and you have the makings of a safe boat. I'd like to see a better bridgedeck. Handrails are well placed above and below decks.

TYPICAL CONDITION: Many 33s seem to be one owner boats, and one owner boats are usually well taken care off. Also, good initial quality has helped the 33s age gracefully.

REFITTING: The fact that the Caliber 35 is still very much in production means that in some cases parts and particulars are still available from the factory. Boats without pans and liners are easier to access and consequently easier to work on.

SUPPORT: Although there isn't an active owners' association, the factory consults with used boat owners all the time. Contact Caliber Yachts, at (727) 573 0627, or www.caliberyacht.com.

AVAILABILITY: With just 70 boats built, there are never more than a few 33s on the market at any one time. If you include 35s in your search more boats will be available. Florida and the Chesapeake are well represented with used 33s.

INVESTMENT AND RESALE: The 33 has held its value quite well over the last 10 years. Like many quality boats, once the initial depreciation is over—usually in the first couple of years—the boats maintain their value. The fact that Calibers are still in production helps.

OVERALL 'SVG' RATING

---

fittings. Many Calibers appear to be one-owner boats, which is a nice testament but longtime owners are often blind to problems. Also, Calibers were not spared during the blister woes of the early to mid-1980s—try to find out when and if an epoxy bottom job was last done.

On deck

The cockpit of the 33 is a little bit cramped; this is where you remember this is just a 33-foot boat, after all. There also isn't much of a bridgedeck but I confess this worried me more 20 years ago than it does today. The cockpit seats are narrow, although they're also nicely scooped to allow access to the helm seat.

Wheel steering was standard and most pedestals are equipped with a teak table. All sail controls are led aft, usually to control stations on the coachroof that are complete with stoppers and a winch. The primary sheet winches can be easily reached from the helm. The traveler is out of the way, mounted forward of the companionway with midboom sheeting arrangement. I recognize this is a compromise that loads up the boom, yet in a boat of this size it makes sense from a space perspective. There is good storage in the port lazarette and under the helm seat.

The sturdy aluminum mast is deck stepped, another indication of the big boat mentality of the Caliber 33, and the standing rigging is oversized. Chainplates are set inboard enough for good sheeting angles. Caliber specs called for quality deck gear, from winches to hatches. The nonskid is fairly aggressive and teak handrails on the coachroof are well placed. A large chain locker can hold a couple of anchors and rodes, and the boat I inspected in Miami had rigged a nice wash-down system. I am not usually a fan of bowsprits but I'm okay with the arrangement on the 33. Although the updated version is well supported, it's primarily an anchoring platform and the rig is structurally supported at stem, not via the sprit and bobstay. And, it is nice to stow and deploy the anchors from the platform.

Down below

The interior of the Caliber 33 is very nicely finished in teak and innovatively laid out. The companionway steps are wide and there is good headroom throughout, an advantage of a less than sleek coachroof. The white headliner brightens the cabin and nicely offsets the otherwise all-teak interior. The galley is immediately to port as you drop below. Unlike a lot of boats under 35 feet, Caliber built in drawers and lockers instead of resorting to bins. Double stainless sinks with both pressure water and a backup foot pump were standard. The stove and oven are outboard and the icebox is aft. Counter space is more than adequate.

The aft quarter cabin arrangement is quite clever. A bi-fold door allows the cabin to be closed for privacy without the encumbrance of a full door. The nav station is tucked away in this cabin, an arrangement that I have on my 47-foot cutter, and it works well, although the chart desk is a bit small. The bunk is a bit snug for two, but it does make an ideal sea berth. The saloon is spacious. A fold-up, bulkhead mounted table is a great idea on any boat under 40 feet. The port settee is straight while the starboard is L-shaped. There's storage behind and under the seat backs and there are full-length shelves above. The teak-and-holly sole adds a bit of elegance.

The head, which is to starboard, is quite large for a 33-footer and includes an integral shower. It can be entered from both the saloon and the forward cabin. The V-berth is long, more than 7 feet and has nicely fitted drawers below. There is a decent-sized hanging locker to port. Ventilation throughout the boat is terrific with stainless steel opening ports. Tropical sailors know that portlights are more useful for airflow than overhead hatches. The Caliber 33 interior is certainly large and comfortable enough for a couple to contemplate long-term cruising.

Engine

The standard original power plant in the 33 was the reliable Yanmar 3GM30F, a three-cylinder 27-horsepower diesel. As noted earlier, the original prop was a bit undersized and some owners have switched to feathering models, an expensive but worthwhile upgrade. The horsepower is only just adequate for the 33, which is no lightweight, but what you lose in speed you make up for in fuel economy. The 26-gallon fuel tank will likely translate into nearly 50 hours of motoring. One of the key upgrades in the new LRC Calibers is increased tank size. Access to the engine is good from behind the companionway, although reaching the stuffing box still requires a bit of flexibility through the cockpit sail locker.

Underway

Several years ago I delivered a 1992 Caliber 35 from Key West to Fort Lauderdale, Florida, and later that same year I took a Caliber 38 from Punta Gorda, Florida, up to Charleston, South Carolina. Although I haven't specifically sailed the 33, I have a good feeling about how Calibers handle. Also, I corresponded with several owners, who incidentally were almost universally pleased with their boats. On my deliveries, we had a range of conditions, from flat calms to a nasty Gulf Stream squall, and the boats coped with the conditions without missing a beat. In fact, we reeled off a 200-mile day on the way to Charleston with an assist from the current. Sailing the 35 we had fresh winds the entire way and completed the 170-mile passage in 30 hours.

Owners report that although the 33 is stiff, it develops a fair bit of weather helm when winds approach 20 knots. That's fair enough, and a single reef in the main solves the problem. The boat is not overly close winded and the shoal draft model in particular makes a bit of leeway when sailing hard on the wind. I don't dispute the merits of shoal draft but I still don't like it. The flat forefoot can occasionally pound in a chop but overall the boat has soft motion, which is among the most important features for any cruising boat. The 33 is, however, a bit sluggish in light air.

Conclusion

The Caliber 33 is something of a sleeper on the used boat market. It's a high-quality boat, quite comfortable, and when given a bit of wind, it's a decent performer. It will also stand up to a blow and hold up to the rigors of the cruising life. It's an ideal small boat for a Caribbean sabbatical; it was made for the trade winds. With prices ranging from $45,000 to $70,000 it is also a good value.

Pacific Seacraft 34

*Handsome high-quality cruiser
made for crossing oceans in style*

The Pacific Seacraft 34 forces you to confront your cruising dreams head on, and that may or may not be a good thing. This capable canoe-stern cutter can carry you as far as your imagination can go. This is a genuine oceangoing sailboat wrapped up in a small package. It is expensive, too—a 15-year-old model can sell for close to or more than $100,000. However, the advantage of a quality small cruiser is the price can be managed, especially for a short-term cruising sabbatical. Do the math. The payments for a year or two at 6 percent are doable.

The PS 34 is ideal for a cruising couple or a good choice for the singlehander. The boat will stand up to the moods of Neptune and is easy to handle. A 34-foot boat is also relatively inexpensive to operate. The PS 34 holds its value well, and when the dream changes, or is completed or aborted, sail back to the harbor, spread some elbow grease and sell the boat for about what you paid for it. The Pacific Seacraft 34 eliminates excuses. Do you really want to go cruising, or do you just want to keep talking about it?

Bill Crealock designed the PS 34 and it is in many ways a scaled down version of his popular PS 37 according to his design comments. Hull No. 1 hit the water in 1978 and today, nearly 400 hulls later, the 34 is still in production. Pacific Seacraft Corporation of Fullerton, California, is a refreshing, enduring and unfortunately rare success story in the capricious sailboat industry. Cited by *Fortune Magazine* for building one of America's best product lines, the company has maintained a commitment to quality construction for 25 years. As a used boat buyer it is nice to know that the factory is still operating and even better that the model you're considering is still in production.

First impressions

The PS 34 has a traditional profile and deck layout that's blended with a fin and skeg underbody mixing old and new design traits. The concept, inspired to a large degree by Bob Perry's Valiant 40, caught on with many West Coast and Taiwan builders in the 1970s and 1980s and offers an insight into the mixed-up mindset of many sailors. There is something irresistible about a traditional sailboat with a sweeping sheerline and a canoe stern—it just seems right for bluewater sailing. There is also something appealing about better performance and the ease of handling offered by a more modern underbody. The marriage of these unlikely design parameters has produced some of America's best-loved boats, including the Pacific Seacraft 34 and its sisterships.

The PS 34 has a proud sheerline and a raked bow, with an overhang ratio of 23 percent. Yet the optional cutter rig, with a gener-

---

PACIFIC SEACRAFT 34

LOA 34' 1"
LWL 26' 3"
Beam 10'
Draft standard 4' 11"
Draft shoal 4' 1"
Sail Area 534 sq. ft.

ous 649-square-foot sail area, and the 13,200-pound displacement, makes for a moderate offshore cruiser. The external lead ballast of 4,800 pounds translates into a ballast-to-displacement ratio of 36 percent. The PS 34 sails surprisingly well and owners report that that hull is more easily driven than one might suspect. The single spreader aluminum spar has an air draft of 44 feet, 3 inches and an optional shoal-draft Scheel keel reduces the standard draft from reasonable 4 feet, 11 inches to gunkholer's fantasy at 4 feet, 1 inch.

Construction

The PS 34 has a solid fiberglass hull. The hull is stiffened with a full-length molded liner. Unlike other builders, Pacific Seacraft does an excellent job of providing openings in the liner for hull access and securely bonding the liner to the hull, creating almost a hull within a hull. The liner allows form fitting for components like tanks, furniture facings, structural floors and the engine beds. The deck is balsa cored except in areas of high load where plywood is used. The hull and deck are through bolted on a double flange that allows for the 5-inch deck bulwark and is covered by a beefy teak caprail. It is a muscular and almost always watertight union. And, just in case you ding up the caprail, it is installed in short 5-foot sections, secured with a "butterfly joint," allowing for easy and affordable sectional replacement.

Bulkheads are well tabbed in place and also through-bolted from the deck via a teak beam, making them extremely rigid. The rudder is robustly constructed with a steel backbone (or web) that is welded to the stainless steel shaft. A hefty bronze gudgeon is through-bolted to the steel reinforced skeg and offers lower bearing support for the rudder.

The keel is a molded stubby with external lead ballast through-bolted, arguably the best solution to the question of which is better: internal or external ballast. Pacific Seacraft pays attention to details. Small items like molded angled platforms ease the load on cockpit locker hinges and aligned screw and bolt heads are a nice touch and typical of the original factory workmanship still evident on older boats.

PACIFIC SEACRAFT 34 PRICE DATA

		Low	High
BUC Retail Range	1990	$ 89,600	$ 98,500
	1995	$119,000	$131,000
		State	Asking
Boats For Sale	1989	CA	$119,000
	1994	CT	$ 99,000
	2000	MD	$179,000

What to look for

The quality of the PS 34 jumps out at you the first time you amble alongside, from the chromed bronze ports to the stout bronze and stainless deck hardware. However, like every used boat there are certain items to check for. The most common problem, according to Tor Pinney, a longtime Pacific Seacraft dealer who has also logged thousands of miles aboard the 34, is the aluminum fuel tank. Located under the saloon bilge, the tank bottom sags after time and is exposed to both seawater and the stainless steel keel bolts, a sure recipe for electrolysis.

"If you smell diesel when you step below, the tank may well be leaking," Pinney said. Typical of Pacific Seacraft, the tank is easily removed through cockpit sole hatches without major surgery. The same fiberglass tank that is standard on new boats can be retrofitted in a couple of hours. The 1990 model that Pinney and I crawled though in Fort Lauderdale had the original tank and there was no sign of electrolysis or leaks.

If you are looking at a boat older than 15 years, be alert for signs of hull blistering. Pacific Seacraft, like virtually every manufacturer, had its share of blister boats in the early and mid-1980s, and some bottom treatments were better than others.

Also, one more item to be aware of is that some 34s came from the factory with tiller steering, not many, but you can usually spot them in the sale listings because they invariably have lower asking prices. If you prefer or can

Pacific Seacraft 34

 PRICE: The PS 34 is pricey, there is no denying it. However, that old adage, "you get what you pay for" applies; you pay for its quality.

 **DESIGN QUALITY:** Crealock's handsome design is well proven at sea. Performance is better than a heavy, long-keeled cruiser. The narrow beam limits interior volume.

 **CONSTRUCTION QUALITY:** Pacific Seacraft does an outstanding job of building boats and the quality really becomes apparent when you look at used boats; they hold up very well.

 **USER-FRIENDLINESS:** It's a very easy boat to handle, especially for one so capable. The interior is small but well thought out and comfortable for a couple.

 **SAFETY:** It is apparent that Pacific Seacraft goes to great lengths to make its boats safe. From oversized deck fittings, to 30-inch lifelines, to the molded bulwark, to well-placed handholds above and below, this is one safe boat.

 **TYPICAL CONDITION:** These boats are usually well maintained by their owners. The only reason this isn't a higher rating is simply because many boats have actually taken their owners cruising and show signs of wear.

 **REFITTING:** Pacific Seacraft does a good job of providing access to items that will typically need to be refit.

 **SUPPORT:** The national PS owner's e-mail list can be found at www.sailnet.com and the factory, www.pacificseacraft.com, is supportive both with advice and parts.

 **AVAILABILITY:** The problem with many quality cruisers is that they're hard to find on the used boat market. This is not the case with the PS 34. Currently there are about 20 for sale on www.yachtworld.com alone.

 **INVESTMENT AND RESALE:** The PS 34 is expensive but it holds its value as well as any production boat. Also, because the initial quality is high, it is usually not an expensive boat to operate.

 **OVERALL 'SVG' RATING**

---

live with a tiller, you can save a few shekels on a used 34.

On deck

The PS 34 cockpit is fairly deep and roomy, especially considering the space lost as the canoe stern curves inward. The seats are 6 feet, 5 inches long and are good for sleeping although the backs are a bit abrupt. The bridgedeck is well designed as it will keep water out of the cabin and is wide enough not to limit foot room in the cockpit well.

The primary sheet winches are just forward of the helm. Most 34s lead the sail controls aft, which is part of the popular but optional Singlehander's or Voyager's package.

Most 34s on the used market will have self-tailing Lewmar primaries, but new boats now come standard with Harken winches.

The PS 34 sports deck hardware usually found on larger boats. The stern cleats are 10 inches long and the bronze stern chocks are equally robust. The bow and stern pulpits are beefy and the stanchions are mounted both vertically and horizontally for strength. Double lifelines are 30 inches high. The 5-inch bulwark, aggressive molded nonskid and teak grab rails on the cabintrunk make navigating the side decks a safe and secure operation. The chain locker is internal and can only be accessed from the forepeak. The forward hawsepipes run through the bulkhead, a feature that would please the pilots in the Panama Canal Zone.

The mainsheet traveler is located just forward of the hatch, and is a midboom sheeting arrangement that keeps the cockpit uncluttered. It also allows for mounting a spray dodger that can stretch well back into the cockpit, two good reasons for putting up with the inefficiency and extra loads created by midboom sheeting. The spar is deck-stepped and the massive chainplates are mounted outboard. Some boats will have a fixed staysail headstay and others will opt for a mobile arrangement, which is preferred as it allows the option of sailing as a sloop with an overlapping genoa in light air.

Down below

The layout belowdecks is conventional and it works very well. The forward V-berth is of good size, the berths are 6 feet, 6 inches long and 5 feet, 11 inches across at the widest spot. Bookshelves line both sides. The bunk is a molded section with storage below. The head is next aft to port with a large hanging locker opposite. The saloon includes straight settees that make good sea berths and the port settee converts into a double. Most boats will have a fixed centerline table but some will have a foldaway bulkhead table that can really open up the boat.

Although the beam is only 10 feet the interior feels spacious due to 6-feet, 3-inch headroom and numerous opening portlights and overhead hatches. The headliner is a soft, foam-backed vinyl that can be unzipped to access deck fittings. The joinerwork is clean and functional and the generous use of hand-rubbed teak offsets the production boat look that liners create.

The shallow U-shaped galley is aft to port and usually includes a Force 10 two-burner stove outboard, double stainless sinks forward, and a well-insulated six-cubic-foot icebox aft. This boat was conceived as a cruiser and there is clever storage everywhere, including a hinged dish locker above the icebox, although there isn't room for much counter space. A large forward-facing nav station is opposite with the electrical panel outboard. Behind is a good-sized quarterberth, which often ends up as another storage area.

Engine

Most 34s on the used market are fitted with a three-cylinder 34 to 37-horsepower Yanmar diesel. The horsepower rating depends on the year of the engine. This model, the 3JH2E is a terrific machine and is very efficient. The standard fuel tank holds just 37 gallons, which will likely translate into 60-plus hours of motoring.

One of the best features of the PS 34 is engine access, which is about as good as it gets for a small cruising boat. While the front of the engine is reached by removing the companionway steps, a cockpit access hatch allows access to the back of the engine and the stuffing box. It also floods the compartment with light. Pacific Seacraft did not shoehorn the engine in place, there is plenty of room to work, and if re-powering is necessary, the engine can be easily removed through the cockpit hatch.

Underway

Comfort is defined different ways, and to Crealock, comfort is directly related to motion under sail, or lack thereof. The hull shape of the PS 34 will treat you kindly, even in choppy, lumpy conditions, and that makes the boat comfortable in the most important environment of all, at sea.

"The 34 will surprise you with its speed," Pinney said, "It has logged impressive runs crossing the Pacific." The cutter rig adds more than 100 square feet of working sail, although that balances out on the sloop rig if a genoa is used. If you do set up the boat as a cutter you will need to rig running backstays, which are part of the package.

Michael Rowen sails his PS 34 in breezy San Francisco Bay. Surprisingly he has elected to forego furling headsails and is content with the options that his hanked-on 130-percent genoa, high-cut working jib and staysail offer.

"I never feel like I can't quickly set up the right combination and I don't mind going forward to change headsails, it keeps me young."

He usually shortens down to the yankee when the winds near 20 knots. He ties in the first reef in the main when wind pipes up to 22 knots apparent.

Crealock notes that the canoe stern enables the boat to maintain surfing speeds when running before large ocean rollers while maintaining control and easy steering. My experience has shown that canoe sterns are not as fast off the wind but they do in fact keep the stern from wandering. On the wind, the 34 is not particularly close-winded but tracks well and weather helm does not seem to be a common complaint.

Pinney noted that the 34 has an impressive bluewater track record, including more than one circumnavigation.

Conclusion

The PS 34 is an excellent example of a quality, small cruising boat, designed and built to sail anywhere. Its best feature just may be that it eliminates any excuses to delay that much talked about cruising sabbatical.

Sabre 34

*Good looking and well-built family cruiser
that 'sails like a dream'*

Sabre Yachts is one of the survivors in the mercurial sailboat business. The company, founded by Roger Hewson in 1969, launched the first of nearly 600 Sabre 28s in 1970 and it continued production of the boat for 16 years. The Sabre 28 is still the company's best-known boat and it was recently inducted into the American Sailboat Hall of Fame. Although Hewson, like most of his peers, eventually went bankrupt, a team of investors rescued the company in the early 1990s. Today, the Maine-based company builds four models, ranging from 36 feet to 45 feet.

During the 1970s and 1980s Sabre carved a niche in the market by consistently producing handsome, high-quality boats that were nicely finished below and sailed well in a variety of conditions. This was the heyday of dual-purpose boats and Sabre competed with Tartan, C&C and other quality production builders. In 1976, Sabre expanded its line with the introduction of the 34. More than 200 boats were built before a significantly modified edition (called the Sabre 34 MK II and

later the 34 Targa) was launched in 1986. This article will examine the original 34, the MK I, which in terms of numbers is one of Sabre's most successful models. The boat originally appealed to those who admired the 28 but wanted more elbowroom. Today, with prices ranging from less than $30,000 to around $60,000, it appeals to those looking for a sound value in the used boat marketplace.

First impressions

It is hard to imagine that a 34-foot boat with a 10-foot, 6-inch beam was considered spacious in 1976, but such was the case when the Sabre 34 was launched. Spacious, however, is a relative term, and Sabres have never been considered roomy cruisers. The 34 evolved from the design parameters Hewson developed for the 28, although the added waterline translates into better overall lines. There is nothing showy about the profile, the sheer is slight, the amidships sections are rounded and the cabin-trunk is a bit boxy. The entry has a moderate rake and the stern is slightly reversed. Blended together, the overall look is classy. That's the mystery of yacht design—mix the ingredients and see what happens.

The Sabre 34 carries 507 square feet of sail area, just a shade less than the Tartan 33, a boat with the same LOA introduced a couple years later and about the same as the Cal 34, a model introduced a few years earlier. The air draft is 51 feet.

Below the water, the Sabre 34 features the predictable sweptback fin keel, a moderate forefoot and a partially balanced rudder. The underwater design is pure 1970s and there is nothing wrong with that. A displacement of 11,400 pounds made the 34 a bit heavier than some of its competitors, however 4,600 pounds of lead ballast helped the boat stand up

SABRE 34

LOA 33'8"
LWL 26'3"
Beam 10'6"
Draft Shoal
   Centerboard 3'11" to 7'9"
   Deep Keel 5'6"
Displacement
   Centerboard 11,700 lbs.
   Deep Keel 11,400 lbs.
Ballast
   Shoal 4,900 lbs.
   Deep Keel
     4,600 lbs.
Sail Area 507 sq. ft.

in a blow. How many times have you heard that old saw that every boat is a compromise?

Construction

The early Sabre 34s were built with solid fiberglass hulls with balsa-cored decks. In 1978 the 34 was modified and produced with a balsa-cored hull as well. Sabres have held their values well, one of the surest signs of good original construction. The hulls were hand laid, using mat and roving with polyester resin—the typical materials of the day—but the workmanship was excellent. The decks are generally cored with ⅜-inch and half-inch end grained balsa, although plywood is used in high-load areas. The hull-and-deck joint is an inward flange and through-bolted. Floors, knees, bulkheads and most structural members are well supported. The external lead ballast is fastened with stainless keel bolts, which in turn are supported by a reinforced fiberglass fillet. The nuts are visible in the bilge and should be examined. The 34 was also offered as a center-boarder and a careful inspection of the center-board apparatus should be a vital aspect of the marine survey.

What to look for

The first thing to look for is either the standard, 5-foot, 6-inch keel or the centerboard model that offers a board-up draft of just 3 feet, 11 inches. Dick Coerse, who sails EARLY LIGHT, hull No. 160, advises prospective buyers to look for the deep-draft model if windward performance is high on their priority list. Shoal draft, especially in the fast evaporating Great Lakes, offers its own advantages and centerboard problems don't seem to be an issue. The production run seems to be well divided, so finding either keel version is possible.

Delamination, especially around leaky handrails lining the cabintop, has been reported as problem, although none of the owners I corresponded with mentioned it. Hull blistering, the plague of many production boats built during this era, is a more likely problem. Blisters, however, just don't cause the stir they once did and in most cases, rightly so. Chances are that former owners have con-

SABRE 34 PRICE DATA

BUC Retail Range		Low	High
	1980	$35,700	$39,700
	1985	$48,300	$53,100

Boats For Sale		State	Asking
	1980	OH	$44,000
	1982	NH	$56,900
	1987	NY	$67,600

fronted this issue and if the boat you are looking at has blisters it usually is the responsibility of the seller to correct the problem. Blisters almost never cause structural problems.

Nearly all the Sabre MK I 34s you inspect will be at least 20 years old. The standing rigging should probably be replaced and be sure to carefully check hoses, pumps and wiring. Changing the wire-and-rope halyards to all line is a nice upgrade. Several owners noted that the original 12-volt electrical system was undersized and prone to overloading as new instruments were added. Swapping out the fuse panel for one with circuit breakers is a big job, best left to electricians.

Also be sure to check the engine carefully. The early boats may have the ubiquitous Universal Atomic 4 gasoline engine, which is much less desirable than the diesels that came later. Most boats will have either a 27-horse-power Westerbeke or a 23-horsepower Volvo. Interestingly, several owners note that the Westerbeke is greedy at consuming zincs. A boat that has been repowered should receive an asterisk or maybe two, on the listing sheet.

On deck

The cockpit is comfortable, especially for 1976. This was the era when designers and builders conspired to throw out as many backs as possible. The seats are slightly scooped to allow access around the 28-inch standard wheel. The boat is well suited for a spray dodger, although this limits visibility, naturally. Most boats came standard with

Sabre 34   SAILING Magazine's Value Guide

 PRICE: You can buy cheaper 34-foot used boats, but it is hard to buy a better quality boat for less than $50,000. Also, asking prices are once again becoming negotiable; it is a good time to be in the used boat market.

 DESIGN QUALITY: Hewson and the Sabre team did a nice job blending performance and comfort while maintaining a handsome look. The boat has aged gracefully.

 CONSTRUCTION QUALITY: The original construction was excellent and the boats have held up well. This is what you are paying for with a used Sabre.

 USER-FRIENDLINESS: A good all-around performer usually translates into a user-friendly boat. The motion is relatively soft. The cockpit is comfortable and most sail control lines are led aft. Interior uses available space well.

 SAFETY: There are well-placed handholds above and below, although the narrow side decks need to be navigated with care. The bridgedeck is adequate. Quality construction is a prime safety feature.

 TYPICAL CONDITION: Sabre owners tend to keep their boats a long time and lavish them with care. Also, the boats have aged well and the middle-of-the-road design does not seem out of date.

 REFITTING: Sabre's fine finish is a mixed blessing when it comes to refits—access is not terrific. Rewiring is a common project and something of a challenge.

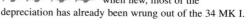 **SUPPORT:** While the 34 does not have a hyperactive owner's group like some other boats, there is plenty of information available in print and online. Also, Sabre Yachts does a good job of offering support and advice for used boat owners. Contact them at www.sabreyachts.com. Also, check out the Sabre list at sailnet.com.

 AVAILABILITY: There are usually a good selection of 34 MK Is on the market. A quick glance at Yachtworld.com turned up 10 boats. The best selection is on the East Coast and Great Lakes.

INVESTMENT AND RESALE: Sabres hold their value well. Expensive when new, most of the depreciation has already been wrung out of the 34 MK I.

OVERALL 'SVG' RATING

Lewmar primary winches. Consider it fortuitous if they have been upgraded in size and to self-tailing models. The mainsheet is usually led to a traveler over the companionway, which helps keep the cockpit uncluttered. A small but adequate bridgedeck lends security when sailing offshore and there is good storage in a couple of lockers.

Teak handrails line the cabintrunk. These should be carefully inspected, especially on boats that have spent considerable time in Florida or the tropics as they may be rotten. Double lifelines with well-supported stanchions were standard. The nonskid may be worn or ineffective, especially if the deck has been painted. There is a small anchor locker forward. However, if serious cruising is in your plans, the stemhead fitting will need to be modified to carry beefier ground tackle. The

mast and boom are anodized aluminum, although one owner notes that he painted his spar and it has held up well. As noted earlier, be sure to carefully inspect the standing rigging, especially the original swage fittings.

Down below

Much of Sabre's original success was due to the fine joinerwork in the cabin. Although the layout of the 34 is anything but innovative, it is nicely executed. Bulkheads, panels and trim are Burmese teak for the most part, which can make the boat seem dark. The countertops in the galley and head are often lighter Formica. The cabin sole is teak and holly. The headroom in the saloon is more than 6 feet. There are full-length overhead handrails in the saloon. Ventilation is adequate in the standard arrangement with a couple of decent-sized opening hatches. If opening portlights have been added, and the job was well done, consider it a plus.

The interior plan includes a V-berth double cabin forward. Once the filler cushion is fitted this a good-sized bunk. A door closing off the saloon provides privacy both for the cabin and the head, which is to starboard and a bit cramped. A large hanging locker and drawers are opposite the head. The saloon has port and starboard settees with storage behind and water tanks below, totaling 40 gallons. The best feature of the interior design is the bulkhead-mounted table that folds out of the way creating open space. The double leaf table sits four comfortably when in use and usually hinges from a handsome teak cabinet.

The galley is to starboard and unfortunately, like on many older boats, part of the counter space doubles as part of the companionway. Still, the shallow C-shaped galley cleverly uses available space with a sliding counter section over the stove and a built-in wastebasket. Most 34s have a single sink that faces forward with the large icebox behind. The stove on early boats used pressured alcohol for fuel; hopefully it has been converted or replaced. There is storage behind the stove and below the sink. The nav station is opposite the galley and the head of the quarterberth serves as the seat. The chart desk is good sized with chart storage underneath and small drawers on the side. The single quarterberth is an excellent sea berth, that is if you resist turning this space into the garage.

Engine

The earliest Sabre 34 MK Is came standard with Universal Atomic 4 gasoline engines. Early in the production run diesels became standard, and most boats either have a 27-horsepower Westerbeke or a 23-horsepower Volvo. The two-cylinder Volvo is a bit loud but both engines provide plenty of punch to keep

the boat moving at 5 or 6 knots. Access is decent, at least by 1976 standards, from behind the companionway, although reaching the stuffing box requires acrobatics. One aluminum fuel tank holds just 20 gallons, and several owners note that they would like to retrofit a larger tank.

Underway

"The Sabre 34 MK I sails like a dream," says Dick Coerse who sails EARLY LIGHT on the East Coast. "It has no quirky qualities." Coerse notes that the boat is initially a bit tender but once heeled to about 12 degrees stiffens up dramatically. He has sailed the boat through a range of conditions including steady 35 knots with gusts to 40, and has nothing but praise for the way the boat handles. Coerse likes his standard keel, especially when sailing upwind. However, several owners also noted that the centerboard model also tracks well. Weather helm is not much of an issue and owners report that the helm is balanced and responds well to autopilots.

The 34 MK I is a bit sluggish in light air, finds its stride in 8 to 10 knots apparent, and usually needs a reef just before 20 knots. The displacement-to-length ratio is 278 and the sail area displacement ratio is 16, numbers that make the boat cruising more today, but that were fairly typical of most dual-purpose racer-cruiser boats in the 1970s. Still, the 34 MK I is a good candidate to retrofit for a cruising sabbatical and several boats have completed bluewater voyages.

Conclusion

The Sabre 34 MK I is a handsome, high-quality boat that has maintained its value. Prices range from the mid $30,000 to the $60,000, with most of the used boats falling the mid $40,000 range. The boat is well suited for family sailing, casual racing and can also be retrofitted for cruising. It is nice to have options.

Hallberg-Rassy 34

*Simple design and finish belie the
bluewater quality of this versatile cruiser*

When most North Americans think of Hallberg-Rassy yachts they conjure up visions of husky, 40-foot and up center-cockpit world cruisers. Yet one of the company's most successful models, the HR 34, features an aft cockpit, a nimble fin-keel hull shape and a fractional rig. Don't get the wrong idea, the 34 does have a lot in common with its robust sisterships, including intelligent construction techniques, excellent engineering and a German Frers design pedigree. Introduced in 1990, the 34 remained in production until 2005 with more than 500 boats launched, making it one of the company's best sellers.

Hallberg-Rassy has been building boats on the west coast of Sweden for 50 years, just not always as one company. Cristoph Rassy and Harold Hallberg were never partners. In fact, they were competitors until Rassy purchased retiring Hallberg's yard in 1972. Since then, the firm of Hallberg-Rassy has carved a coveted niche in the sailboat industry. There is no disputing that it's in the top tier of sailboat manufacturers. Hallberg-Rassys, with their trademark windscreens and hard tops are fixtures at cruising crossroads the world over. The company builds about 170 yachts a year and the wait time for a new model can be up to a year. That's why, if you're in the market for a mid-30s Hallberg-Rassy, it pays to look at used boats. And pay is the right word because Hallberg-Rassys don't come cheap. You will likely need to spend more than $150,000 to purchase a used HR 34. But then again, you get what you pay for.

First impressions

The HR 34 is refreshingly versatile. It is certainly a capable bluewater boat with many documented ocean crossings to its credit but it is also right at home as an occasional PHRF competitor and a family cruiser. A 1995 model was recently hauled out at the boatyard just across the street from my house. It has an attractive profile. The sheerline is subtle, accentuated by a wide covestripe and a healthy amount of freeboard. The bow entry is raked but the overhang is still moderate. The reverse transom helps extend the LWL to 28 feet, 6 inches. The overhang ratio, or the LWL as a percentage of the LOA is around 16.5 percent, typical of many of Frers' best designs. The fin keel has a shorter cord than you might guess for a bluewater boat and the rudder is, more or less, freestanding, although the top bearing edge is nicely flared into the rocker section. The displacement of 11,684 pounds leans toward the heavy side of moderate and the lead ballast of 4,630 translates into a 35-percent ballast-to-displacement ratio. Sloop rigged, the working sail area is 592 square feet, although a more accurate number is with the common 125-percent furling genoa, or 667 square feet.

HALLBERG-RASSY 34

LOA 33'9"
LWL 28'6"
Beam 11'3"
Draft 6'1"
Displacement 11,684 lbs.
Sail Area 592 sq. ft.

Construction

I must confess, I am partial to Scandinavian-built boats. For the most part these boats are highly capable, well thought out and finished in a simple yet elegant if understated way. Nothing screams at you when you examine the HR 34, there's just a quiet sense of well-executed quality as you make your way around on deck and below. The hull is solid fiberglass although the sections above the waterline are foam insulated, so in this way the hull is cored. The hull is well supported by a grid system of fiberglass floors and stringers. There is a deep bilge sump, a good feature on any boat but especially an offshore cruising boat.

The lead keel is attached on a diagonal to a short stub with 10 stainless steel bolts. The battle about whether internal or external ballast is better continues to rage. I like internal ballast. However, more and more boats are fitted with external ballast and it certainly is well proven. It also streamlines the manufacturing process and allows for more flexibility in keel shapes. The large fiberglass rudder is wrapped around a beefy stainless steel stock with heavy-duty roller bearings.

The hull-and-deck joint is mechanical and chemical and fiberglassed over to prevent leaks. In fact, Hallberg-Rassys are well known for their lack of leaking. The hull and coachroof sections are composite, cored with either balsa or foam. The mast is deck-stepped, which makes perfect sense on a 34-foot boat. This eliminates a leak source and allows for easier stepping.

What to look for

Hallberg-Rassy continually upgraded the 34 during its long production run and several important changes were made along the way. The first boats did not have the fixed windscreen. Also, in 1994 the transom was opened to allow for a molded swim platform. Boats without this feature are less desirable on the used market. The cockpit was shortened in the mid-1990s, which of course means that the interior was extended. The cockpit is still good sized, with seats longer than six feet for stretching out on.

The interiors of early boats features a long, straight galley opposite the settee, which cre-

HALLBERG-RASSY 34 PRICE DATA				
BUC Retail Range			Low	High
	1985		$120,900	$142,000
	1990		$145,600	$151,000
Boats For Sale		State		Asking
	1982	MD		$133,000
	1989	NY		$173,000
	1994	Mediterranean		$179,000

ated more room for the aft cabin but was not practical for cooking while underway. Later boats featured an L-shaped galley aft to port. Other small changes were made and these are noted on the Web site, www.hallberg-rassy.se. Many of these upgrades were to comply with new European Union rules to qualify as a Category A boat, implying that it is capable of unlimited voyages.

If the HR 34 you are inspecting has wheel steering, check the installation carefully. Most 34s came with tiller steering and the pedestal and wheel were typically a retrofit. Incidentally, the standard tiller boats have a lot more cockpit space. Also, be sure to check the seal around the lower unit of the saildrive transmission. The standard engine was the Volvo MD 2030, and included a saildrive transmission. These lower units often corrode. Also, HRs were not immune to hull blisters, especially when first exposed to tropical waters, but it is not a widespread problem.

On deck

The HR 34 cockpit is fairly spacious and surprisingly comfortable. During the production run changes were made to make the cockpit more comfortable, including softening the angle of the seat backs. Visibility from the helm is adequate, but if the windshield is old and clouded, it can be hard to see when sitting. Lewmar deck hardware and hatches were often used and the quality was excellent. The mainsheet traveler spans the cockpit bridgedeck, which is nice for controlling the

Hallberg-Rassy 34

 **PRICE:** This is an expensive boat. But like a Volvo or a Saab, you pay for quality. I suspect that even if you buy a 15-year-old 34, you will be able to keep it for a lifetime.

 **DESIGN QUALITY:** This Frers design is all about versatility. Some may consider that too much of a compromise, I consider it a virtue and the hallmark of a good design.

 **CONSTRUCTION QUALITY:** This is one of the best-constructed boats we've featured in the Used Boat Notebook, with solid and intelligent engineering.

 USER-FRIENDLINESS: A well-protected cockpit with all sail controls led aft and a safe, friendly deck make handling the boat a pleasure. The interior is well done given the available space.

 **SAFETY:** Good construction and safety are always linked. The 34 includes plenty of handrails, built-in harness attachment points and other features that need to be added to most other used boats.

 TYPICAL CONDITION: Most used HR 34s are in good to excellent condition. This is mostly due to the original quality that was put into them but also because typical owners have the resources to keep them up.

 REFITTING: Not always an easy boat to work on. Although liners are kept to a minimum the ample use of wood makes accessing some areas challenging. Also, if you do decide to launch into a project you better do a good job or it will be obvious it's a DIY job.

 SUPPORT: The HR Web site, www.hallberg-rassy.se, is good, and the owner network is also well organized. However, the fact that the factory is in Sweden, and most boats are in Europe, doesn't lend itself to easy support.

 **AVAILABILITY:** Although there were plenty of 34s built, most are in Europe. There are always some 34s for sale in North America, although it's more likely to find them on the East Coast or Pacific Northwest.

 INVESTMENT AND RESALE: Hallberg-Rassys hold their value better than most boats, but the initial investment required is steep.

 OVERALL 'SVG' RATING

main but inconvenient for dropping below. Some boats have retrofitted midboom sheeting arrangements; be sure to carefully inspect how this was done.

Double-spreader Seldon spars were standard and these invariably hold up well. The 34 is fractionally rigged, but only just. It's seven-eighths rigged, which has always made me wonder, why bother? At least you don't need running backstays. A sleek spinnaker arrangement, with the pole stored on the mast, was standard. Most boats came standard with all sail controls led aft through jammers and a single-line mainsail reefing system. The stainless steel stemhead fitting is more than adequate with a single roller. The anchor locker is external and quite large. A small molded bulwark and an intricate molded nonskid make it safe to navigate the deck even when it's blowing.

Down below

Anyone familiar with Hallberg-Rassy will associate its interiors with a matte-finished, red-brown mahogany. The workmanship is excellent as every joint is made to last, but the overall atmosphere is spare. There's nothing ornate about the HR 34's interior, and that's fine with me. I really like the way these boats are finished. There isn't any visible fiberglass but at the same time the extensive use of wood doesn't feel oppressive. It's like a Swedish cottage, and of course that conjures up all sorts of images better left unsaid.

The interior plan also changed along the

way. When the cockpit was shortened, the interior became user-friendly. Although the aft bulkhead was extended just 10 inches, that translates into a lot of interior volume. Most boats on the used market today feature an L-shaped galley to port. It is small but highly functional, with two deep sinks, a stove and oven, standard 12-volt fridge and clever storage lockers for trash, cutting boards and cutlery. It would be challenging to stow gear and provisions for an ocean crossing, but that can be said about almost any 34-foot boat. The aft cabin is accessed from the galley and includes a good-sized double that runs fore and aft. Many new boats have athwartship berths that are not very useful while underway. The aft cabin also has a big hanging locker and additional storage under the berth.

The head is opposite the galley and includes all the usual accoutrements. Amidships, or actually aft of amidships, is the perfect spot for a head on a small boat, much better then squeezing it behind the V-berth. The nav station and electrical panel are forward of the head. The saloon features an L-shaped settee to port, at least most boats do; as mentioned earlier, the first boats had the galley running either side of the saloon. The table is small but opens up to accommodate as many people as you'd ever want in a 34-foot boat. The forward V-berth cabin is spacious and includes a hanging locker, with drawers opposite and bookshelves above the bunk.

It is often the details that separate a good boat from an average one and that's the case with the Hallberg-Rassy 34. Small features like a diesel interior heater, backup manual pumps and efficient lightning came standard on the 34. The more you probe around these boats the more you like them, and that is not always the case with other boats.

Engine

The standard power plant for the HR 34 is the Volvo Penta MD 2030, a 20-horsepower diesel with a saildrive transmission. Readers know that I don't particularly like saildrive lower units as they are prone to corrosion and more vulnerable to collision. So why do manufacturers use them? They have advantages, the foremost being that they don't require as much space as a straight transmission with a prop

shaft, stern tube, stuffing box, strut and cutless bearing. Be sure to check the lower unit on any used boat with a saildrive for signs of corrosion. Also carefully check the sealing gasket.

Access to the engine on the HR 34 is from behind the companionway and it's adequate. The engine was reported to have a bit of vibration, but this was corrected at some point during the production run. These engines are extremely reliable and very fuel-efficient. Owners report that when motoring at 6 knots in flat seas the engine uses around half a gallon of fuel per hour. The fuel tank capacity is 155 liters, or roughly 40 gallons.

Underway

One of the best reasons to consider a Hallberg-Rassy 34 is its lively sailing performance. This is not a clumsy cruiser just claiming to be a good performing boat, it is a sailboat first that also just happens to be a nice cruising boat. Just look at the hull shape. There is enough of a forefoot to reduce the tendency to pound but not too much to slow the boat down. The balanced rudder is well aft and provides good control even while running before big seas.

The powerful seven-eighths double spreader rig delivers plenty of horsepower. Frers' speed diagram shows the 34 capable of reaching at 8-plus knots without a spinnaker, and near 9 when the chute is flying and the gods align. Upwind performance is more than adequate with speeds of 6-plus knots in moderate breezes and seas. Polars of course can be misleading in the real world, but the real world evidence supports the fact the HR 34 is a sweet sailing boat. My friend, Crister Leferdahl, crews on a 34 that is actively campaigned in Stockholm and he tells me they have done very well during several seasons of hardcore racing.

Conclusion

The HR 34 is an expensive late-model used boat with prices ranging from $150,000 to more than $200,000. It is also a high-quality, versatile boat that is capable of crossing an ocean or racing across the bay in style. I have always admired boats that are simply at home on the sea, and that's the best definition of the Hallberg-Rassy 34.

Tartan 34

This classic earns enduring respect
with its sailing qualities and S&S pedigree

Classic is a wonderfully subjective term when used to define sailboats, especially fiberglass boats. What separates a classic from just another successful production boat? Ask 20 sailors and you'll likely receive 20 different answers. Fearless correspondent that I am, let me roll up my pants, flip off my flip-flops and wade into this debate.

My version of a classic fiberglass sailboat includes a distinctive design that ages gracefully, one that can't be classified as typical of a certain period but instead helps define that period and somehow transcends it. A classic must be well engineered and solidly built, it should represent the best construction ethos of its day. As a fiberglass boat, it needs to have had a long and successful production run and a faithful ongoing following. Most importantly, it must be well proven within its design parameters. The Valiant 40 was designed to cross oceans, and it certainly has crossed oceans. The tough and fast J/35 still wins races, and the Ensign, an enduring, affordable

daysailer, introduced thousands to the magic of sailing. These are very different boats yet all classics. What about the Tartan 34?

Designed by Sparkman & Stephens in 1967, the T34 went into production the next year and by the time the molds were pushed out into the parking lot 10 years later, 525 boats had been launched. The keel centerboard hull design capitalized on the quirks of the old CCA rule and also afforded shallow water sailors a high quality, big boat option that performed well in a variety of conditions. Douglas and McLeod Plastics, and later when the company evolved into Tartan Marine, did, for the most part, an excellent job building the 34. The majority of boats built are still sailing. And, as I gaze down the canal at a nearby 1970 Tartan 34, it is clear that the boat has aged very well indeed. The Tartan 34 has the earmarks of a classic, hence the C you'll often see after the 34. This not only differentiates between the updated 34 introduced in 1985, but also implies a certain, well-earned status.

First impressions

I just returned from a little jaunt in my kayak to register my first impression of the Tartan 34, for the umpteenth time. The boat has a springy sheer, a rakish entry and a jaunty stern. Yes, the result is a stubby LWL of 25 feet but it sure looks nice, the way those of us who discovered sailing in the 1960s and 1970s think a boat should look. The trunkhouse is a bit boxy, especially forward, yet it's somehow distinguished. There is no gimmickry in this design, and students of S&S's early fiberglass period will recognize the pedigree. Olin Stephens, in his design comments noted, "There is nothing outstanding or unusual about it; everything just seemed to work well." The coaming boards add a nice visual touch although they

TARTAN 34

LOA 34'5"
LWL 25'
Beam 10'2"
Draft board up 3'11"
   board down 8'4"
Displacement
   11,200 lbs.
Ballast 5,000 lbs
Sail Area
   473-527 sq. ft.

do hit you right in the small of the back when seated in the cockpit; ah, details.

Below the waterline the 34 features a long, shallow, swept-back fin keel with a centerboard. The story goes that the hull shape was inspired by the S&S America's Cup contender INTREPID. The rudder is fairly well aft and skeg hung. The board up draft is just 3 feet, 11 inches. Displacement is a moderate 11,200 pounds, slightly less than the Morgan 34 and Ericson 35, comparable boats of the day, and the 5,000 pounds of internal ballast corresponds to a 44-percent ballast-displacement ratio. The short waterline produces a displacement-length ratio of 320. Before you scoff, consider that the Tartan 34 was a class winner of the 1968 SORC and other early boats captured the Port Huron-Mackinac race and the Marblehead to Halifax race. The 34 was a thoroughbred in its day and even by way of comparison still performs adequately, especially off the wind. The PHRF rating is around 189.

Construction

The hull is solid fiberglass and the deck is balsa or plywood cored. Later Tartans, like the 37 and 41, also used cored hulls. The hull is sturdy, to say the least—a result of the fiberglass construction philosophy that insisted thickness does matter. The layup was not sophisticated and the hulls were resin rich, but there is no disputing that they have held up very well over the years. The hull and deck are joined on an inward flange, bedded and bolted through the teak toerail.

The lead ballast is internal, placed in the keel cavity and fiberglassed over. The rudder is fiberglass over foam. The teak-faced bulkheads and furniture facings are tabbed to the hull and few structural issues have been reported. The mast is keel stepped. There is a lot of teak on deck, and depending on the level of maintenance, this can greatly influence the appearance of an old 34.

What to look for

During the years I have been writing the Used Boat Notebook I have corresponded with many different owners and owners' associations. The Tartan 34 Association ranks near

TARTAN 34 PRICE DATA

		Low	High
BUC Retail Range	1970	$20,700	$23,000
	1975	$30,400	$33,800
		State	Asking
Boats For Sale	1970	WI	$29,900
	1974	MD	$23,000
	1978	MI	$34,900

the top when it comes to providing honest information for prospective buyers and its new Web site, which can be accessed through www.tartanowners.org, is excellent. One of the articles that you can download is written by Jack Waddell, who sails hull No. 215 Vixen Hull. Waddell lists several common problem areas to be aware of when purchasing a 34.

He noted the centerboard pivot and lever should be checked carefully when the boat is on the hard, there is an access plate on the side of the keel. Over the years these parts wear, making it difficult to raise and lower the board. The 34 centerboard is unique in that it can be locked in position at whatever depth you desire; a great trim feature, although some argue that the board should either be completely up or down only. A locking board also eliminates the kick up action during a grounding, and can result in board or keel damage.

The second issue Waddell notes is subdeck delamination. This certainly is not a problem unique to Tartan, many early glass boats with balsa and plywood cores have the same problem. Be sure to sound the decks carefully. Severe delamination will be apparent just from walking around, the decks will feel spongy and creaky. Typical problem areas are around the chainplates, stanchion bases, grab rails, etc. Waddell points out that the spot where the forward edge of the coachroof meets the deck is particularly prone to gelcoat crazing and delamination. What's the cure for deck delamination? If it is minor, it's probably best not worry about it, just make sure any suspect deck fittings are well bedded to pre-

Tartan 34   SAILING Magazine's Value Guide

 PRICE: The Tartan 34, like many quality boats of this era, has become very affordable. Compare what $25,000 buys in a newer boat.

 DESIGN QUALITY: A venerable and versatile S&S design, the 34 sails well off the wind and is a proven overall performer. The centerboard opens up thin water areas off limits to deeper draft boats.

 CONSTRUCTION QUALITY: Tartan did a good job building the 34, however, certain features have not aged well. Balsa cored decks are a potential problem and in some cases materials used were not the best.

 USER-FRIENDLINESS: An easy boat to handle under sail, good for singlehanding. Best when sailed flat. The interior is not overly comfortable and unless extensively updated, some of the systems can be very old.

SAFETY: There are handholds above and below, wide side decks and good sea berths. The boat does however, heel early and as a shoal-draft centerboarder, it has a relatively high center of gravity. With that said, 34s have been all over the world.

 TYPICAL CONDITION: For the most part, 34s have aged well, and seem to have been well cared for. However, some boats on the used market are now more than 35 years old, and that's an old boat no matter how you slice it.

 REFITTING: Although tight quarters make some retrofit projects difficult, there is great engine and tank access, two of the most onerous tasks to deal with during a retrofit.

 SUPPORT: The 34 has a devoted following and active owners' association. Track them down at www.tartanowners.org. Ideas and advice for repairs and upgrades are posted and class President Deane Holt will direct your query to a knowledgeable source.

 AVAILABILITY: With more than 500 built there is always a good selection of 34s on the market. Best areas seem to be the Chesapeake and Great Lakes. A quick search on www.yachtworld.com turned up 13 boats for sail.

 INVESTMENT AND RESALE: Owning an older boat can be costly, especially if you maintain it in good condition. Low initial cost softens the blow of spending money to keep the boat in top condition.

 OVERALL 'SVG' RATING

vent any further water penetration. If it is major, it's a big job to tear out the core from below and replace it. Look at other 34s first before tackling this job.

Water intrusion in the foam rudder is a common problem as is excessive wear on the lower rudder bearing, so both items should be checked. On the earliest boats the original through-hull fittings were gate valves. These boats also incorporated brass pipes with nipple valves as well. The cockpit scuppers are solid pipes that exit just above the waterline, a bad arrangement. Almost all boats now have seacocks, but if this upgrade hasn't been done, do it immediately. Leaks in the aluminum fuel and fiberglass water tanks are also potential problems. Fortunately the tanks are easy to get

to under the port and starboard settees, making repairs or replacement possible without major surgery to the interior.

On deck

While in many ways the 34 is a small boat, certainly by modern standards, the 9-foot, 3-inch-long cockpit is quite spacious and arguably the boat's best feature. Tiller steering was standard and is still common although many boats also came from the factory with wheel steering or have been converted. Tillers leave the cockpit less cluttered and feel good under sail. If the boat has a pedestal and wheel, it is quite far forward, which allows the helmsman to tuck under the dodger.

Winch islands to port and starboard are well placed for shorthanded sailing, making the 34 easily handled alone or by a couple. A substantial bridgedeck keeps green water from sloshing below and there is a lazarette seat inside the aft coaming. Early boats led the mainsheet aft, an inefficient and cumbersome arrangement that also served to crowd the helmsman. Most 34s have refitted a traveler just aft of the bridgedeck. This became a standard arrangement when the boom was shortened slightly in the early 1970s to make the boat rate better under the emerging IOR rule. Ironically, while the loss of a small amount of sail area doesn't help the 34's light-air performance, shortening the boom did relieve the excessive weather helm. A roller-reefing boom was also standard, although you'll likely find most 34s with some version of slab reefing.

The side decks are wide and easy to navigate. Grabrails along the coachroof are well placed. The single spreader mast has an air draft of just under 45 feet. The narrow 10-foot, 2-inch beam allows for tight sheeting angles when beating. Deck fittings were typical of the period, with some being chrome. However, most have been replaced with stainless.

Down below

Typical of 1960s era boats, there is not a lot of elbow room down below. Still, not everybody wants a boat with two double cabins and a stall shower. The Tartan 34 interior is functional and includes good sea berths and well-placed handholds. It also has a very classy aura with its teak finish. While the Tartan plaid cushions are like rings on a tree stump, accurately dating a boat, they're easy to change. The original cabin sole is cork, which provides good nonskid but also holds dirt. The small space is offset by a full 6 feet, 2 inches of headroom that is carried all the way into the forward cabin.

The interior plan includes a V-berth forward with a hanging locker to starboard and the head opposite. The saloon features opposing settees, each with a built-in lee board and a bulkhead mounted table. The starboard settee stretches under the bureau and the raised back support is not particularly comfortable. Although on some early boats the fuel tank was located under the cockpit sole, most 34s

have a 26-gallon aluminum tank under the port settee. A 36-gallon fiberglass water tank is under the starboard settee. The port side settee is L-shaped and encloses the engine, which is positioned on the centerline. This added settee seems a bit misplaced but you can't beat the engine access.

The small galley is to starboard. A two-burner alcohol stove was standard, although many boats will have been upgraded to either a nonpressurized alcohol system or propane, and there is enough room to retrofit a small stove and oven. The icebox tucks up under the bridgedeck and has a handy access hatch in the cockpit. A small sink faces aft. The quarterberth to port is good sized and makes another sea berth as well. A fold-up countertop serves as the chart table, and the seat is the head of the quarterberth. A simple electrical panel is located nearby.

Engine

The original engine was the ever popular Atomic 4. Late in the production run a 25-horsepower Farymann diesel became an option but not a popular one. However, many boats have retrofitted diesels, which are safer, more fuel efficient and usually provide more punch. The Westerbeke 30 and Universal 25s are common replacements. Engine access beneath the L-shaped settee in the saloon is terrific.

Underway

The primary reason the Tartan 34 is considered a classic is because of the way it sails—the boat handles well in a variety of conditions. Although many of Olin Stephens' designs are known as demons to weather, the 34 also shines off the wind, a typical feature of centerboarders. The 34 is efficient downwind, with an optimum jib angle of 173 degrees, which is deeper than many modern fin keeled boats. The 34 is initially tender, especially when carrying an overlapping genoa, but as the wind pipes up she stiffens up. Like almost all boats, but especially of centerboarders, the 34 likes to sail on its feet.

Jim and Joanne Matthews sail their 1973 Tartan 34 HEATHER out of Pensacola on the Gulf Coast. Although they're in the market for a larger, liveaboard cruiser, they just can't part with their beloved 34.

"This boat has just been a joy to own," Joanne said. "And Jim has finally repaired or replaced everything." The Matthews casually race HEATHER but really enjoy the boat for cruises that can last up to a couple weeks. "We are very comfortable aboard, although I would like a little more room in the galley."

Jim said that he usually ties in the first reef in the main at around 15 knots while carrying on with full 135-percent furling genoa. When the wind tops 22 knots, the second reef balances the boat nicely and a large headsail can still be carried. He also said that keeping the centerboard down reduces weather helm. "Power reaching in 15 knots, we'll easily do 6.5 knots," said Joanne, who helms when racing. "And we have occasionally topped 7."

Conclusion

With prices ranging from $20,000 to $35,000, the Tartan 34 is an excellent value on the used boat market. And the boat does hold its value. The original owner of HEATHER bought the boat new in 1973 at the New York Boat Show for $23,000. The Matthews bought the boat in 1993, 20 years later, for $23,000. And if they sold her today, they'd likely get somewhere around $23,000. Besides, at any price, how often can you own a classic?

C&C 35

Handsome, well-built racer-cruiser charms
with its impressive performance and affordability

The C&C 35 is a survivor and, some claim, a classic. I sure wouldn't argue with them. Designed by Cuthbertson and Cassian in 1969, the boat was originally called the Redwing 35 and was built by George Hinterhoeller. The name was changed to the C&C 35 after Hinterhoeller merged with C&C Yachts. The C&C 35 was developed during the waning period of the CCA rule, when the IOR was emerging, but before it changed from an idealistic handicapping system to more of an intrusive developmental rule. And that may be why the 35 has survived and thrived—it is an undeniably handsome boat designed to sail well, not rate well, and good looks and good sailing characteristics never go out of style. The C&C 35 WALLOON is one of the only boats to win the Port Huron to Mackinac Island race under both rules.

The C&C 35 was in production for six years, one of the company's longer runs. This was an era when builders retooled frequently and designs were rarely produced for more than a couple years. In fact, the C&C 35 underwent major changes in 1973 and as a result,

boats built prior to that are known as the MK I and those built afterward, the MK II. A total of 350 boats were launched. Interestingly, my friend, Fort Lauderdale surveyor Paul Anstey, built the C&C 35 on license in his boat shop in Poole, England, during the early 1970s. There were around 20 English-built 35s.

First impressions

Although both versions of the boat are similar in appearance, there are some notable differences, especially below the waterline. Both boats have a modest sheerline with fairly long overhangs, at least by today's standards. The LOA of the MK I is 34 feet, 7 inches and the LWL is 27 feet, 6 inches, revealing an overhang ratio of about 20 percent. The hull has a bit of flare forward and a springy stern with a slightly reversed transom. The underwater sections show rounded bilge sections, and although the boat was considered flat and beamy in its day, it seems softer to modern eyes. The cabintrunk on the MK I featured a distinctive

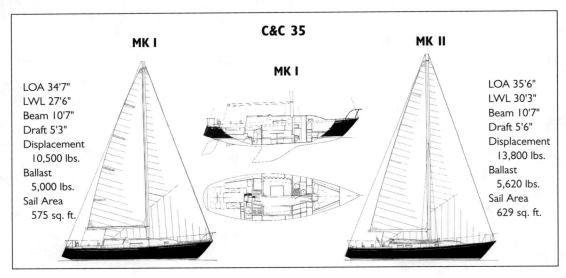

C&C 35

MK I

MK II

MK I

LOA 34'7"
LWL 27'6"
Beam 10'7"
Draft 5'3"
Displacement
  10,500 lbs.
Ballast
  5,000 lbs.
Sail Area
  575 sq. ft.

LOA 35'6"
LWL 30'3"
Beam 10'7"
Draft 5'6"
Displacement
  13,800 lbs.
Ballast
  5,620 lbs.
Sail Area
  629 sq. ft.

spray dodger molding. The MK II replaced this molding with a slight rise in the trunk. The MK I has a single long portlight in the saloon while the MK II has two smaller ones.

Below the water, the MK I has a swept-back shark fin keel shape and an odd scimitar-shaped spade rudder trailing aft. The shape of this rudder, designed to keep the leading edge in turbulence-free water, was changed to a more balanced, freestanding blade on the MK II. The aft sections were also changed, flattened a bit, to take advantage of the IOR rule. The ballast was increased by 600 pounds in the MK II and the sail area increased by 50 square feet. Interior modifications combined to add nearly 30 percent to the displacement. Although the MK II has a more modern hull shape, and an LWL 2 feet, 9 inches longer, 35 owners who still race the boat prefer the performance of the lighter MK I.

Construction

The 35 predates C&C's extensive production of cored hulls, and the hull is made of relatively thick, solid, hand-laid-up fiberglass. However, the deck is composite with a balsa core. The hull and deck are joined on a standard flange and bonded chemically and mechanically. The overall construction is typical of the time, fairly heavy and not overly sophisticated. It is always interesting to read old reviews of the 35. Writers in the early 1970s considered the 10,500-pound 35 MK I to be almost radically light.

Bulkheads are securely glassed in place as is most of the interior infrastructure. Some secondary bondings have not held up well, but that's a sign of age more than a problem with the original construction. The keel is externally fastened with stainless fasteners, and the rudder stock is also stainless steel. The rudder is foam and fiberglass. Transverse floors are constructed of glassed-over plywood and can be subject to delamination. C&C's finish work was high quality, although the extensive use of Formica definitely dates the boat.

What to look for

The first thing to remember is that most C&C 35s are over 30 years old. It is remarkable, really, how well the boats have aged, espe-

C&C 35 PRICE DATA			
		Low	High
BUC Retail Range	1970	$21,200	$23,600
	1975	$31,100	$34,500
		State	Asking
Boats For Sale	1970	MA	$24,900
	1972	NC	$29,900
	1975	MI	$38,000

cially because almost all 350s have been raced hard at some point during their lives. When you begin inspecting boats on the used market, look for a 35 with a new engine. The original power plant was the well-loved and much maligned Universal Atomic 4. This venerable gas engine is reliable and cheap to repair or replace; still, I'd look for a boat with a retrofitted diesel, an upgrade that doesn't seem to drastically alter the asking price. Late in the production run some MK II models were fitted with small Westerbeke diesels, which many owners have repowered over the years.

Leaks are a common ailment in most 35s, particularly at the hull-and-deck joint and around the portlights. Bedding compound that has lost resiliency primarily causes these leaks. Remember that, while it is a straightforward task to re-bed the ports, curing a chronic leak in the hull-and-deck joint is more challenging. Also, check the keel bolts, as some owners noted that iron washers were used, which of course have likely rusted and will need to be replaced.

While in the bilge, look closely at the floors for signs of cracks, rot or delamination. The main bulkhead also needs close examination: Check to see if the bonding is fractured. Naturally check all the age-related items, especially old seacocks, hose clamps and other below-the-waterline fittings.

On deck

The cockpits of the MK I and MK II have a few differences to be aware of. The MK I features a cockpit traveler just forward of the helm, effec-

C&C 35

 **PRICE:** With prices ranging from around $20,000 to around $40,000 the 35 is a good value on the used market. Canadian boats may be the best deals because of the favorable exchange rate.

 DESIGN QUALITY: The C&C design has aged gracefully and is undeniably handsome. I suspect we will still be writing nice things about this boat 10 or 20 years from now, a sure sign of a timeless design.

 CONSTRUCTION QUALITY: C&C built good boats, especially early on before the company was beset with financial troubles. Check for rusty keel bolts and leaks in the hull-and-deck joint.

 USER-FRIENDLINESS: The MK II is a bit more user-friendly than the MK I, which isolates the helmsman. Still for the most part, the boat is easy to handle.

 SAFETY: The MK II cockpit features a secure coaming and stout bridgedeck, a feature missing on the MK Is. Overall, the solid construction and quality construction add up to a safe boat.

TYPICAL CONDITION: Although most 35s were raced at some point in their life, they seem to have held up well. C&C owners are a dedicated group by and large, and most boats appear to have been upgraded along the way.

 REFITTING: The 35 has been out of production for a long time, which complicates finding parts. However, the boat has decent access for most refit projects. The 1970's engineering and electronics may seem ancient. Parts for C&C are available from South Shore Yachts on the Web at www.niagara.com/sailboat.

 SUPPORT: Although C&C is back in business, it is a different company without much connection to the old models. However, the Internet is buzzing with C&C sites; one of the best ones is www.cncphotoalbum.com.

 AVAILABILITY: With more than 350 boats built there is usually a good selection of boats on the market. The Great Lakes area has the best selection.

INVESTMENT AND RESALE: It is hard to go too far wrong with a C&C 35. Not only will it please you on the water, it is easy on the pocketbook as well. When it is time to sell, the market is well established.

OVERALL 'SVG' RATING

tively creating separate steering and trimming stations. On the MK II the traveler was moved forward, usually above the companionway.

The MK II has a substantial bridgedeck, a nice safety feature, while the MK I has a low-cut companionway with just a small sill, making it necessary to keep the bottom washboard in place in wet conditions. Both cockpits have a low coaming that hits you right smack in the small of your back, so seat cushions are a big help. Also, the helm station is well aft, effectively leaving the helmsman exposed to the elements, although the low-profile cabintrunk does provide good visibility from the cockpit, especially looking to leeward past a big genny.

The side decks are fairly wide, considering the overall beam is just 10 feet, 7 inches.

The chainplates are located well inboard, as are the headsail tracks, allowing for narrow sheeting angles. Original deck hardware has likely been updated by now, although some boats have been maintained in near original condition, a testament to the overall high quality of the boat.

The original nonskid surface is most likely well worn by now, and it is also possible that the decks and cabintrunk have been painted. Many owners used a one-part paint that does not hold up very well and may be peeling; this was the case on both boats I looked at in South Florida. There were different sailplans for each model. The MK II had a tall rig option and many owners opted for a slightly shorter boom.

Down below

The interior plan is nearly identical in both models. After stepping below, there is a small chart table to port. The navigator sits on the foot of the quarterberth, a typical arrangement. A small U-shaped galley is to starboard. A two-burner alcohol stove was standard, although it's probable this has been updated. If a propane stove has been installed, be sure to check the system carefully. Sometimes the gas bottle is placed in the cockpit locker, which is not sealed and definitely not safe.

A single sink near the centerline faces aft and drains on either tack. The icebox compartment is rather small and will need better insulation to be efficient if upgrading to refrigeration. For short cruises the galley is more than adequate as there is plenty of storage and decent counter space. Incidentally, this arrangement is reversed on the MK II; the galley is to port and the nav desk and quarter berth to starboard.

The saloon includes a dinette to port with a settee opposite. I like a dinette arrangement because it keeps the cabin sole clear without having to fold a table up and out of the way. My kids always spend a lot of time around the dinette table when we're underway.

The shallow bilge does not allow room for tanks, which were located under the settee and quarterberth on the two boats I looked at. The cabin sole is molded fiberglass, practical and a bit sterile. The head is actually spacious for a 1970's vintage boat with a vanity and wash basin. There are two hanging lockers opposite, which I find a curious use of space. I guess you needed more room for blue blazers back in those days. The double V-berth is long and comfortable, and the cabin is lined with shelves and has lockers underneath the bunks and drawers below.

Engine

As noted earlier, the original engine was an Atomic 4, 30-horsepower gas auxiliary. These engines, which were first built in 1947, were installed in almost every boat under 40 feet until the mid-1970s. And, those that haven't been replaced are usually still running. They are pretty simple really, just keep the plugs, distributor and rotor clean, have a decent set of points, add gas and air and the thing will run and run. However, the Atomic 4 doesn't have enough umph to push the C&C 35 into a chop, and gasoline engines are dangerous. Late model MK IIs were offered with the option of a 15-horsepower Westerbeke diesel. Owners who have repowered more recently often have chosen the Yanmar 3GM series engines, or the 25-horsepower Universal diesel that has the same footprint as the Atomic 4.

Underway

The reason for buying an older C&C 35 is simple: It's for the sailing. These boats sail beautifully. Whether you are out for an afternoon, club racing under PHRF, pushing the boat in the Bermuda Race or just cruising, the 35 impresses with its performance and handling. By the way, in the 1997 Annapolis to Newport Race, a 1971 MK I finished third overall.

Both models are easily driven in light air, although the lighter MK I is faster. However, reaching or running in a good breeze, the MK I, with its scimitar-shaped rudder can be a handful and intriguing broaches are not unknown. The MK II is a bit stiffer, and with a more conventional rudder, easier to handle off the wind.

Both models are close-winded and few owners report excessive weather helm. The nature of the rig calls for flying overlapping genoas, which by design can load up the helm. Steve Purdy, who has sailed his 1973 MK I from Virginia to Nova Scotia, sums up the 35's performance like this: "easy to handle and comfortable for two to cruise, but still fast enough to enjoy racing and to be competitive." Not a bad combination for any boat.

Conclusion

The C&C 35 is an enduring favorite on the used boat market. It is a handsome, high-quality, fine-sailing boat with a proud pedigree that can be purchased for less than $35,000. Maybe that's why many sailors consider the 35 to be a classic.

CS 36 Traditional

A Canadian-built racer-cruiser that's well-mannered yet tough enough for the heavy stuff

The virtues of the sweet sailing CS 36 are not well known south of the border; it's one of those fine Canadian-built boats that seems to have fallen off the radar screen for many American used boat buyers. The CS 36 is a high-quality, versatile boat with a proud pedigree. Designed by Raymond Wall, who was for many years the chief designer and engineer for the venerable English firm of Camper & Nicholson, the 36 was introduced at the 1978 Toronto Boat Show. By the time the Tony Castro-designed CS 36 Merlin replaced the Traditional model in 1987, more than 300 CS 36s had been launched, including many that went into service in The Moorings' Caribbean charter fleet.

The original name of Canadian Sailcraft Company was shortened in 1971 to CS, and the company was a quiet success story. Founded by Paul Tennyson in the early 1960s, his small plastics laminating firm began building boats in 1964. Its first boats included a 15-foot daysailer designed by George Cuthbertson and a 12-foot catamaran. The company's first big

boat was the CS 27, also designed by Wall and launched in 1977. The success of the 27 prompted the company's move from a small plant in Toronto to a larger facility in nearby Brampton, Ontario.

The CS 36 followed on the 27's heels and a popular 33 joined the fleet the following year. Castro, who trained with Ron Holland, replaced Wall as the firm's in-house designer in 1984 and contributed designs for the 30, 34, 40, 44 and the Merlin 36. Without much fanfare, CS, which is sometimes confused with the successful Canadian builder C&C, became one of Canada's top builders. In 1986, its best year, CS produced nearly 200 boats. Unfortunately, CS could not weather the economic downturn of the late 1980s and early 1990s, and by 1992 the company was reduced to auctioning off most of its tooling.

First impressions

The CS 36 was euphemistically named the Traditional to set it apart from the later Merlin 36. It had a low-slung, modern profile when first introduced. However, unlike other modern boats of the time that seem woefully outdated today, the 36 is still a handsome boat—a sure sign of sound original design work. The pinched reverse transom, an appendage left over from the IOR days, is easily recognized

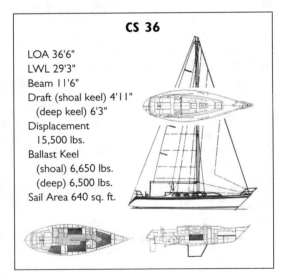

CS 36

LOA 36'6"
LWL 29'3"
Beam 11'6"
Draft (shoal keel) 4'11"
(deep keel) 6'3"
Displacement
15,500 lbs.
Ballast Keel
(shoal) 6,650 lbs.
(deep) 6,500 lbs.
Sail Area 640 sq. ft.

because it is almost always the same color as the wide cove stripe that flows into it, which was a distinctive and attractive styling touch. The sheer is fairly flat and the cabintrunk is low and sleek without a trace of wood. The fine entry has a moderate bow overhang that was a feature of many racer-cruisers in the 1970s and 1980s.

Below the water, the CS 36 has a moderate forefoot that trails into a powerful fin keel. The standard draft is 6 feet, 3 inches, although an optional 4-foot, 11-inch shoal-draft model was popular with boats destined for the Chesapeake Bay. Aft of the keel there is a bit of bustle and the rudder is mounted on a partial skeg. With a displacement of 15,500 pounds, the CS 36 was moderate for its day, heavier than the Catalina 36 and quite similar, at least by the numbers, to the S2 11.0. The displacement/length ratio of 276 puts the boat in the cruiser category today and suggests that it should be able to stand up to a blow without the micromanagement that lighter, flatter boats require. A sloop rig, the single-spreader mast with an air draft of 52 feet, 10 inches, supports 640 square feet of sail area that translates into a sail area/displacement ratio of 16.5. Most 36s have a PHRF rating of about 120 to 125.

Construction

The CS 36 has a solid fiberglass hull, unlike the later Merlin and many other similar boats of the day, including C&C boats, which for the most part had balsa or foam-cored hulls. Wall was adamant about this construction feature because he didn't like the idea of cored hulls. His views were shaped by the rugged conditions common in the English Channel and North Sea that tend to make designers more conservative. The deck, cabintrunk and cockpit sole are balsa cored. The hull-and-deck joint is on an inward flange and through-bolted on 4-inch centers.

CS used a combination of efficient molded liners and more traditional bonding techniques. Bulkheads are tabbed to the hull and deck and further secured in place by molded liners and molded hull stringers. Molded pieces are used for a partial headliner, interior modules and cabin furniture bases. Overall the construction is very well done and

CS 36 PRICE DATA

		Low	High
BUC Retail Range	1981	$47,900	$52,600
	1984	$62,200	$68,400

		State	Asking
Boats For Sale	1981	CA	$65,000
	1985	Canada	$64,800
	1986	NC	$61,000

older CSs have aged well. The lead keel is externally fastened and the fiberglass rudder is foam filled with a stainless steel stock.

What to look for

The first thing to look for is a Traditional 36 as opposed to the Merlin, which was in production from 1987 to 1992 and is usually a bit more expensive. Although the two have similar profiles, the Traditional 36 displaces 2,000 more pounds and carries an additional 700 pounds of ballast. Also, early Traditional 36s had shorter spars imported from England. Unless you are planning some high-latitude sailing, look for a boat with the taller rig.

According to several reports, CS was hard hit by the pox plague of the early- and mid-1980s. Most boats will have had one or more bottom jobs by now so it's important to try to find out the blister history of the boat you're considering. Other owner complaints are few and far between. Apparently water-logged rudders are a common problem, something that's anything but unique with foam filled rudders. Also, the CS 36 was originally fitted with gate valves and if these haven't been changed to seacocks they should be. The 1985 CS 36 that I inspected at the Miami Beach Marina has original Marelon ball valves that are functional and don't corrode, although they're vulnerable in a lightning strike. Carefully inspect all age-related items, especially the standing rigging.

One last item to consider in selecting a used boat is location. Many boats seem to be located in Canada and on the Great Lakes, but there are

CS 36 Traditional

PRICE: Price is not the prime reason for choosing a CS 36, but quality always comes at a cost. Diligent research and careful shopping can likely uncover a clean, well-equipped 36 for around $50,000.

DESIGN QUALITY: Wall's design has aged very well indeed. The boat is more cruiser than racer these days, the logical evolution, but the 36 offers an appealing blend of performance and seaworthiness.

CONSTRUCTION QUALITY: The CS 36 is understated in appearance but beneath the bland fiberglass profile the construction is top quality. The solid glass hull is an advantage—as the boat ages, it is one less potential problem.

USER-FRIENDLINESS: Easy to race and easy to cruise, sounds like the definition of user-friendly.

SAFETY: Solid construction, high ballast-to-displacement ratio, stout bridgedeck and ample handholds above and below make for a safe boat. The lifelines and stanchions could be beefier.

TYPICAL CONDITION: This rating would likely be higher but some of the 36s down in the islands have been sailed hard and put away wet.

REFITTING: The use of molded liners limits creativity and access when it comes to refits. The engine is not easily removed for repowering and other areas of the boat are not easy to work on.

SUPPORT: Although CS is out of business, an active owner's group offers advice and support. Find them on the Web at www.closereach.com/csoa/cs36.htm.

AVAILABILITY: With a large production run that lasted until 1987 there is usually a good selection of boats for sale at any one time. A quick check of Yachtworld.com and BoatTrader.com turned up nearly 15 boats.

INVESTMENT AND RESALE: The CS 36 has held its value well over the years, as most quality products do, and there is no reason to expect this to change, especially as new boat prices continue to soar.

OVERALL 'SVG' RATING

---

also a good number available in the Caribbean. The freshwater boats, with their overall lack of corrosion, would clearly be my first choice, especially over a boat in from the islands that was used hard in the charter boat trade.

On deck

The T-shaped cockpit, while not spacious, is well set up for both coastal and offshore sailing. The Edson pedestal and wheel is located well aft and the molded helmsman's seat increases visibility and makes long steering stretches more comfortable. T-shaped cockpits in general allow easy access to the wheel, although the cockpit seats are often not quite long enough to stretch out on. The single lever engine control is mounted in a user-friendly position on the port

coaming, instead of down by your feet or through the wheel spokes on the pedestal.

There is a stout bridgedeck, which is often overlooked on today's designs. Most sail controls are led aft. Lewmar 30s and 40s were the standard halyard winches, mounted on the aft end of the trunkhouse. Lewmar 43s were the standard primaries, which are mounted on the coaming just out of reach of the helmsman. Most CS 36s seem to have converted to mid-boom sheeting with the traveler mounted over the companionway. The original design had the traveler running across the bridgedeck.

Original deck hardware was first-rate and CS offered features usually found on larger boats, including a stainless steel stemhead fitting with double anchor rollers, an external anchor locker and enclosed fair leads for the mooring lines. Rod rigging was an option, although most boats are fitted with 1-by-19 wire. The handrail on the cabintrunk is made of functional and low-maintenance stainless steel. The bow and stern double rail pulpits are top quality but the original aluminum stanchions are a bit light. The molded nonskid surface on the boat I inspected was well worn.

Down below

The interior plan is fairly standard for an aft-cockpit 36-foot cruiser, however the teak joinerwork and overall workmanship is very nice. The forward cabin includes a V-berth double with a nice array of drawers and lockers underneath. The head is to starboard and includes a teak grate that covers the shower sump. The standard toilet was a high-quality Wilcox Crittendon. The saloon features an L-shaped settee to starboard that converts to a double berth, and with the straight settee opposite makes a good sea berth with the addition of a lee cloth. Two table arrangements were available—a fixed centerline table or bulkhead-mounted foldaway version. There is decent storage in lockers and shelves above and behind the settees, although the water tanks occupy the space beneath the settees.

The galley is immediately to port when you drop below. The stainless steel countertops are impressive and most functional. There is a single sink, a three-burner stove and oven and a decent-size icebox/refrigerator. There are large fiddles for when working underway, a dedicated trash bin and outboard lockers for food stowage. The foul weather locker next to the companionway can also be accessed from the cockpit locker—a feature rarely found on a small boat. The nav station is opposite the galley and includes a good-size chart table with shelves above. The electrical panel is outboard and there are three drawers below. The head of the large quarterberth doubles as the nav station seat and some previous owners have added custom cushions to serve as seat backs.

Engine

A couple of different engine models were available including a three-cylinder Volvo 28-horsepower and a 33-horsepower Mitsubishi. Most boats were fitted with a 30-horsepower Westerbeke coupled with a British Leyland block. Although the CS 36 is an easily driven hull, this is just enough engine for serious cruising and it will be hard pressed to push the boat into a choppy head sea. Access is primarily from behind the companionway and through a side panel in the quarter cabin. The aluminum fuel tank holds 35 gallons, translating into a realistic range under power of 250 to 300 miles.

Underway

A friend of mine, Gary Ward, delivered a CS 36 from the East Coast to The Moorings charter base in Tortola several years ago. He remembers the boat to be well mannered in a blow and surprisingly dry down below even when blasting along to weather. The boat was fitted with a belt-driven, wheel-mounted autopilot and it steered the entire trip. Ward told me that the boat topped 7 knots frequently on a close reach, and that they completed the 1,200-mile passage from Charleston, South Carolina, in eight days, averaging 150 miles a day.

Owners report that the main and No. 1 genoa can be carried up to about 20 knots. The helm doesn't load up easily and the boat is well balanced. The cockpit design lends itself to having a dedicated helmsman and a trimmer, but the boat is easy to handle and responds when sailed aggressively. The CS 36 is that rare combination, satisfying to race locally, capable of winning its class in the Bermuda or Mackinac races, and tough enough for serious bluewater cruising.

Conclusion

Prices for used CS 36s range from around $40,000 for an early boat to around $70,000 for a later model. You can find other 15- to 20-year-old 36-foot production boats for less money, but few match the inspired design and quality construction of the CS 36. This boat belongs in the same quality category as Sabre and Tartan.

Morris Justine 36

A handsome and all-around capable Down-Easter

Mention the Morris 36 these days and most sailors conjure images of the spectacular new Sparkman & Stephens designed daysailer/weekender being built by the highly respected Maine builder. However, the original Morris 36, which is better known as the Morris Justine, is no slouch and just happens to be the company's best-selling model to date. A graceful Chuck Paine design, the Justine 36 is superbly engineered and well proportioned. It is just large enough to be a genuine cruising boat with a nice turn of speed but small enough to be nimble and easily handled. Whether your sailing schedule allows for an afternoon gliding along Penobscot Bay or a month making your way to Nova Scotia, the Justine 36 will be right at home.

Launched in 1983, 33 boats were built as the Morris Justine 36. Another seven were produced with a modified transom and called the Morris 38, otherwise the two boats are identical. Between the two models there are usually three or four on the used market, and

they tend to be located in the Northeast, or occasionally on the Chesapeake Bay. Morris quality doesn't come cheap, yet the Morris Justine 36 is old enough that its price curve has flattened out. It has gone from being expensive to being a solid value. With prices hovering around $200,000—a little below for an early boat, a little above for a later boat—the Justine is still a lot of money but it is clearly a good value as well. If you're not convinced, take a look at what $200,000 buys in a new boat and then climb through a Justine 36 and compare.

Tom Morris has been building boats for more than 30 years, and he's been working with Chuck Paine for almost that long. Morris Yachts has turned out more than 200 semi-custom sailboats, ranging from around 20 feet to more than 60 feet. I recently spoke with Tom and as we chatted on the phone he told me that he was gazing out in the yard at a lovely Justine 36 that had been freshly painted. Morris, speaking softly in a voice somehow mixed with both pride and humility, noted that, "although the boat is 15 years old, it is hard to tell it from a new boat. I fully expect that people will be sailing Justine 36s 50 years from now, and that is something that makes me feel good."

These days Morris Yachts focuses on large boats, and builds just a handful—about six—each year. This limited production provides Morris with an unusual luxury for a successful builder; he doesn't have to compete against his own boats on the secondhand market. In fact, used Morrises are an essential part of his business as new owners bring them back to the factory to be updated. "It is rare for someone to buy a used 36 and not bring it to the factory," Morris said, "and I love to see the old boats come back." Of course, he has a soft spot for the Justine 36; it's named after his wife.

MORRIS JUSTINE 36

LOA 36'3"
LWL 29'6"
Beam 11'7"
Displacement
  15,602 lbs.
Ballast 6,500 lbs.
Draft
  deep-keel 5'4",
  shoal 4'6"
Sail Area
  627 sq. ft.

First impressions

The Morris 36 is understated, it is really a classic Maine-built boat. There is nothing about it that shouts out, "notice me." Instead, it quietly wins you over with its elegant lines and obvious quality, and the closer you examine the boat the more you admire it. I'd put the Justine 36 on my short list of favorite boats to row out to in a crowded harbor. The sheerline is just subtle enough, the long cabintrunk is a little boxy but it reeks of Down East tradition, and in general, the boat looks at ease in the water, which is the mark of a no-compromise design. Paine's early hull shapes were deceptive. At first glance they look like a lot of fin and skeg boats, but the keel shape is refined and Morris has always looked for ways to keep his boats light. An LWL of just less than 30 feet and a moderate displacement of 15,600 pounds translate into a fast hull. Most Justine 36s have the optional 4-foot, 6-inch shoal-draft Schell keel, which opens up just about any cruising ground. The rudder is hung on a beefy skeg and the propeller is mounted in an aperture.

Construction

The hull is hand-laid solid fiberglass and Morris was one of the first builders to use vinylester resin. Rib Core, a rugged system of floors and stringers, is an internal hull stiffener. For the most part the boat is built without molded liners and all bulkheads and facings are securely tabbed to the hull. In fact, a close examination of this neat, clean tabbing that extends three inches illustrates the overall ethos of the build. The only fiberglass pan is the sole in the head, where it is practical. Tom Morris told me that everything in the boat that might need to come out, can come out through the companionway, including the tanks and diesel. An advantage of building a boat without liners is that it is open to customization, a key element of any Morris sailboat.

    The deck is cored with half-inch, end-grain balsa, except in high-load areas where it is solid glass. The hull-and-deck joint incorporates a small bulwark, which not only provides for a strong, relatively leak-proof joint, but also makes the deck more friendly when going forward. The lead ballast is external and bolted

MORRIS 36 PRICE DATA

BUC Retail Range		Low	High
	1990	$155,500	$171,000
	1996	$233,000	$267,200

Boats For Sale		State	Asking
	1989	ME	$229,000
	1990	ME	$189,000
	1993	FL	$210,000

to a keel stub. This arrangement offers the advantages of external keels and still provides for a decent sump in the boat. Interiors differ in both layout and finish. Some boats are finished with teak veneers and others with white laminates and teak trim, which is usually preferred.

What to look for

The Morris 36 has aged very gracefully, indeed, and documented problems are few and far between. Morris says that most boats that find their way to the yard opt for updating more than refitting. Typical projects include adding high-tech sails and sail control systems. Replacing the standing and running rigging are also pretty typical updates. Naturally electronics may need updating as well. Bigger projects include re-powering. Early boats came with a three-cylinder 28-horsepower Volvo and later boats with a comparable Yanmar. Morris says that swapping engines requires reworking the engine beds but that process also provides the opportunity to clean, paint and upgrade the compact engine compartment. One complaint about the original construction is that it didn't include an oil drip pan beneath the engine and this is the right time to add one.

    Other items to look for include making sure of just what model you have. A few boats were built with an optional tall rig, but it isn't much taller—a whopping couple of inches—so don't expect these boats to be turbo-charged. The deep-keel model probably provides slightly better upwind performance but most

Morris Justine 36

 **PRICE:** Yes, the Justine 36 is a good value but it is still expensive, especially when compared to other 15- to 20-year-old 36-footers. You have to make a commitment to quality.

 **DESIGN QUALITY:** Chuck Paine hit the mark with this handsome, capable and deceptively fast boat. It is truly a fine example of an all-around boat, a dying breed. The only complaint is a lack of room below.

CONSTRUCTION QUALITY: Tom Morris builds, and more importantly, engineers top-quality boats. He blends solid construction techniques, a commitment to state-of-the-art materials and the touch of an artist in every boat.

 **USER-FRIENDLINESS:** The Justine 36 is easy to handle, both under sail and power, and the seakindly motion is easy on the crew and boat. The systems are well laid out. The interior is small but practical and comfortable for a couple.

SAFETY: The Justine 36 pushes all the right safety buttons without ruining the aesthetics. The cockpit is deep and secure, the lifelines are well supported and the rigging provides plenty of options when the going turns nasty.

 TYPICAL CONDITION: Morris owners make big investments in their boats, new and used, and generally take very nice care of them. The fact that many boats have been factory maintained means that they are in good shape.

 **REFITTING:** The nature of the build makes the Justine 36 a good candidate for retrofitting. Of course it may not need much work, just updating. You can access most areas of the boat, although in some places it will help if you're small and agile.

SUPPORT: Tom Morris fully expects every Morris-built boat to come home to the shipyard in Bass Harbor sooner or later. The detailed records maintained on each boat are invaluable to future owners.

 **AVAILABILITY:** Tom Morris just doesn't build enough boats. Of course, that's the way he wants it. At any given time there will be two or three Justines on the market.

 **INVESTMENT AND RESALE:** The Justine 36 has held its value well. Original owners are now selling their boats for about what they paid for them. In these days of shrinking production it is a safe bet that top-quality boats will hold their values well into the future.

OVERALL 'SVG' RATING

---

boats left the factory with the shoal keel. Morris 38s, which are newer, cost proportionately more and the only thing they offer is the modern transom. One big advantage of buying a used Morris is the file kept on each boat. Morris tries to maintain accurate records, from ownership to equipment changes for each boat, so prospective buyers can know the true story of the boat they're considering.

On deck

The cockpit is not expansive but this isn't a boat designed to cram a lot of people aboard. Steering may be a tiller but more likely it's a wheel system. The visibility from the helm is only adequate, especially with a dodger in

place, but the cockpit is deep with four drains, which is a nice trade-off at sea. There are lockers port and starboard and coaming is angled to spare your lower back and also doubles as a seat for a better view. The mainsheet traveler is forward with midboom sheeting. On a smaller boat, and the Morris 36 is a small 36-footer, this arrangement is a necessity. And the system can work without sacrificing too much efficiency when the mainsheet leads are laid out to reduce friction and the hardware is top quality.

One of Tom Morris' favorite features is the molded bulwark, which in typical Morris style is low slung, blending naturally into the flow of the deck. The nonskid provides good traction and the 27-inch stanchions, double lifelines, teak handrails on the coachroof and stout pulpits give a sense of security. The stemhead fitting usually features just one anchor roller and the hawse feed for the ground tackle leads it below. I prefer an external chain locker.

Most 36s have a cutter rig with a mobile staysail stay. I like this arrangement. It is nice to sail as a sloop sometimes, especially when close tacking and removing the staysail to a less intrusive position really makes maneuvering easier. The mast is a single spreader section and the shrouds are set just inboard. The deck hardware is variably first class, Harken blocks, Lewmar winches, and tracks and stainless from Hinckley.

Down below

The Justine 36 interior might surprise you; it is not luxurious, nor even elegant. It has a spare, utilitarian feel, and although the workmanship is excellent, it isn't boastful. Although no two 36s are exactly alike, most feature two types of finish—either teak veneers on the bulkheads or white laminates with solid teak trim. I prefer the white look, it is more in keeping with the Down East philosophy of the boats, brighter and tends to better accentuate the fine joinerwork in the trim pieces.

The standard layout includes a V-berth forward. The hanging locker is to port with the head compartment opposite. No, there is not a separate shower stall but there is a teak grate over the sump and everything else you need. The saloon usually includes a centerline table with leaves, and settees to port and starboard. Most boats came with at least one pilot berth and often two. I love pilot berths. They are the best place to snooze, out of the traffic flow and in the center of the boat. They also open up the saloon, a nice feature on a narrow boat. However, many people can't resist converting the pilot berths into cabinetry.

The galley is to starboard and includes one large and one small sink, a two- or three-burner stove and oven, a good-sized icebox and a reasonable amount of counter and storage space. The electrical panels are mounted below the companionway steps, in the galley, which is not the best location for keeping them dry. The navigation station is opposite the galley and faces outbound. A swing out stool seat is not wildly comfortable and some 36s have retrofitted better chairs. The quarterberth is also to port. An aft cabin model was also offered, which features a private quarter cabin, but few boats were built with this option.

Engine

As noted earlier the original engine was a three-cylinder 28-horsepower Volvo but a variety of engines were fitted per owner requests. These engines were reliable and ran well but are expensive to maintain and repair. Later models were fitted with Yanmar marine diesels, and many boats have had engine rebuilds or replacement along the way. Access is only adequate from behind the companionway steps but this is a function of a lack of space, not poor design. The fuel capacity is usually listed at 37 gallons. The boat handles well under power, and efficient hull shape helps fuel economy. Many 36s are fitted with folding propellers like the Max Prop, which not only enhances performance and maneuverability but also reflects the loving care Morris owners spoil their boats with.

Underway

"The Justine is extremely well balanced," Tom Morris said, and although I generally have a healthy skepticism of builders and designers, for some reason I believe him. A well-balanced boat is easy on the crew and gear, especially self-steering equipment. It is also rewarding to sail a balanced boat because it responds to attention and quickly lets you know when it needs a bit of love. The Morris 36 has a moderate sailplan and can carry a fair amount of sail when the wind pipes up. Morris says he built the boat with Chuck Paine's 20/20 rule in mind. When the wind or angle of heel hits 20, either knots or degrees, it is time to tie in the first reef in the mainsail.

I spoke briefly with a Morris 36 owner on the dinghy dock in Lunenburg, Nova Scotia, this past summer. He had sailed his boat up from Marblehead a few weeks before and told me that despite a lot of light air and inexperienced crew he was often charging along at more that 7 knots with an asymmetrical chute.

I was impressed as I watched him sail onto a mooring in the harbor. Tom Morris knows of a couple of boats that have crossed the Atlantic and one that circumnavigated.

Conclusion

The Morris Justine 36 is lovely, well-designed and thoughtfully built. It is a terrific all-around boat and will please even the most discriminating sailors. It is pricey, but not when compared to similar boats and certainly not when compared to new boats of even lesser quality. If you have dreamed of owning a new Morris but can't get beyond the steep prices, consider a used one. I suspect the Morris Justine will continue to hold its value and I know that it will deliver a lot of pure sailing pleasure.

PDQ 36

A well-built nimble-sailing cruising cat designed for families not charter companies

I recently spent a week in the postcard perfect, pastel-splashed village of Hopetown in the Abacos, and it drove me crazy. We rented a house, thinking it would be relaxing, but it just wasn't my cup of rum. After an hour or so sitting on the beach, I would invariably slink away to the town dock and enviously watch the boats come and go. One afternoon as I was lamenting my landlubbing existence, a PDQ 36 cruising cat came gliding through the narrow channel and picked up a mooring in the congested harbor under sail. Although I later learned that electrical problems had rendered the boat's engines useless, it didn't diminish the superb seamanship of the crew and the nimble performance cat.

PDQ Yachts was formed for the express purpose of building cruising cats. The Canadian company set up shop in the old Whitby Boat Works facility in Whitby, Ontario, and tapped into the local skilled labor force. A few years ago the company moved into a new nearby state-of-the-art production facility, but it continues to laminate in the Whitby Boat

Works building. Its first boat, a stylish but slightly stubby 34-foot cat, was launched in 1989. The boat debuted successfully at the Annapolis show, and PDQ has ridden the cruising cat wave ever since. In 1991 the hulls were extended to accommodate stern steps, creating the PDQ 36.

Designed by Alan Slater, the 36 has been consistently updated through the years and is still in production today. The current model is the PDQ 36 Capella. Overall, around 100 PDQ 36s have been built, making it one of the most successful cruising catamarans manufactured in North America. This article will focus on the older, pre-Capella models, which can occasionally be purchased for $150,000 or less, a solid value in the high-priced cruising catamaran field.

First impressions

Few sailors are ambivalent about cruising cats—you either like them or you don't—and a new generation of sailors openly wonder why anyone would buy a monohull. Despite a two-tiered cabintrunk, the PDQ is handsome in profile, partially due to clever styling with a cove stripe and portlights on the cabintrunk deflecting your eye from the high freeboard that is a feature of most cruising cats.

Performance and safety ratios used for monohulls also apply to cats. With a displacement of 8,000 pounds, the PDQ 36 has a displacement-to-length ratio of around 90, which varies slightly with the model but clearly accounts for its lively performance. (Racing cats usually fall between 50 and 80, while heavier cruisers fall between 100 and 120.) Naturally beam-to-length ratio is a common measurement used to compare cats. According to multihull designer Chris White, a simple rule of thumb is that the overall beam should be half the waterline

PDQ 36 MARK II 34

LOA 36'5"
LWL 34'4"
Beam 18'3"
Draft 2'10"
Displacement 8,000 lbs.
Sail Area 490 sq. ft.

length for the right mix of stability and performance. The PDQ 36 is right on the mark with a beam of 18 feet, 3 inches and an LWL of 34 feet, 4 inches for a ratio of just over .5.

"The PDQ 36 is one of my favorite models," said John Sykes of 2Hulls, a Fort Lauderdale brokerage specializing in multihulls. "It sails better than most comparably sized cats and holds up well."

Most PDQ 36s on the used market are masthead sloops, with a sail area of 490 square feet. (A sporty fractional version was offered but few if any sold.) The U-shaped hulls have stub keels that improve upwind performance, although the overall draft is still just 2 feet, 10 inches. The bridgedeck clearance is adequate. On the foredeck, the PDQ 36 has two tramps and a partial bridgedeck. The interior arrangement has two doubles forward, a single head and a saloon.

"The PDQ 36 is an owner's boat," Sykes said. "It wasn't designed for the charter trade, as a result they don't linger on the market."

Construction

The PDQ 36 construction scantlings reflect the serious cruising intent of the design and a commitment to quality by the builder. The hulls are solid fiberglass below the waterline and cored with Klegacell or Corecell foam above. Vacuum bagging is used to ensure uniform resin flow. Cruising cats need to be as light as is practical, but they have to be strong enough to withstand the stress caused by two hulls. In many ways, multihulls are more of an engineering challenge than building a ballasted monohull. The decks are also foam cored, except in areas where high-load fittings are attached. Those areas are solid fiberglass. The glass is triaxial knitted fabric, and epoxy or vinylester resin is used exclusively throughout the laminating process.

The hull and deck are joined on an outward flange with 3M 5200 adhesive and stainless fasteners. The keels, which are NACA foils, are secondary bondings and won't breach the watertight integrity of the hulls should they sustain damage from a collision or grounding. They are also designed and built to support the weight of the boat when it is hauled or careened.

PDQ 36 PRICE DATA

BUC Retail Range		Low	High
	1992	$109,500	$117,000
	1997	$164,500	$180,500

Boats For Sale		State	Asking
	1990	MD	$ 99,000
	1996	SC	$159,900
	2000	NC	$209,000

Although some sailors swear by centerboards or daggerboards for better upwind performance, the fixed keels on the PDQ make more sense in a cruising boat. Centerboards are engineering nightmares, and besides, a stub keel will generate lift to weather if it's the right shape. The small rudders, which are also foil shaped, are mounted on small skegs on the long-range cruiser models.

What to look for

The PDQ 36 has been consistently upgraded and improved, consequently, there are model changes to be aware of. In 1990-91 the original PDQ 34 was stretched to 36 feet, which improved the overall look of the boat significantly. In 1994 the MK II Classic and Mark II LRC came on the market. The primary difference was that the Long Range Cruiser came with inboard 18- or 27-horsepower diesel saildrive engines instead of outboards. Other changes in the Mark II LRC included increased tankage, beefier standing rigging and safety bars at the mast. The Mark III, introduced in 1998, continued with the Classic and LRC distinctions. The most noteworthy feature of the Mark III was the popular optional hardtop bimini. Later on, the mainsheet traveler was moved to the top of the hard-top.

Whatever model you choose, be sure the surveyor checks the deck for signs of leakage and subsequent delamination. If the boat you are looking at is 10 years old, carefully inspect the standing rigging. Beyond that, I haven't identified many specific problems to watch for with used PDQ 36s for two reasons: The boats

PDQ 36

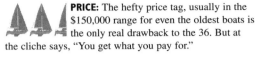

 **PRICE:** The hefty price tag, usually in the $150,000 range for even the oldest boats is the only real drawback to the 36. But at the cliche says, "You get what you pay for."

 **DESIGN QUALITY:** Alan Slater's design is an excellent blend of performance and comfort in a fairly small package. The PDQ 36 doesn't try to do too much, and that is refreshing.

 **CONSTRUCTION QUALITY:** The boats are well built, with vacuum-bagged cored hulls above the waterline and solid glass below. Top-quality materials and fittings are used throughout.

USER-FRIENDLINESS: The 36 is a particularly easy boat to handle, and the loads are rarely overwhelming. Two widely spaced engines make handling under power a joy, once you learn the nuances of twin screws.

 SAFETY: Robustly constructed, nimble under sail and a secure cockpit add up to a safe boat. However, the side decks are narrow and the stanchions could be taller on the classic models.

 **TYPICAL CONDITION:** Most PDQs are still young and all the boats I have seen on the used market are in good shape. This reflects the caring attitude of owners and quality construction and fitting out.

 REFITTING: PDQ designed the boats with refits in mind—a rare but wonderfully responsible attitude for a builder.

 SUPPORT: Owners mention good factory support, even with used boats. Contact PDQ at its Web site www.PDQyachts.com or call the company at (905) 430-2582. The company also maintains a brokerage section.

 **AVAILABILITY:** If you have your heart set on a PDQ 36 don't tarry when one becomes available, there is rarely much of a selection on the used market.

 **INVESTMENT AND RESALE:** The 36 has held its value well for the first 15 years, and there is no reason to suspect anything different in the future. PDQ is well established in the market and well respected.

OVERALL 'SVG' RATING

---

are very well made, and they are, for the most part, quite young, especially by *Used Boat Notebook* standards.

On deck

Although the cockpit is certainly spacious, it is deep and has a feeling of security not always found on cruising cats. The wheel is mounted on the bulkhead to starboard. Older boats employed a push-pull steering system, similar to those on outboard powerboats. Newer boats have the better pull-pull system. There is good visibility from the raised helmsman seat, although it is hard to see forward from any other spot in the cockpit. Chances are good that the boat will have a large bimini, which makes it very difficult to see the mainsail but is an absolute necessity for sailing in the tropics. The

companionway door is smoked acrylic and difficult to secure in a blow.

The mainsheet traveler spans the cockpit on an aft bridgedeck, and the primary sheet winches are within reach on the aft section of the cabintrunk. Halyards are usually routed aft to the forward end of the cockpit. Most PDQ 36s will be equipped with Spinlock rope clutches, Harken roller furling on the forestay and Lewmar winches. The deck-stepped spar is by Isomat.

The side decks are quite narrow, which means that you will likely step on top of the trunk when going forward. Just keep an eye out for the boom. The forward bridgedeck is small. Small storage lockers are located forward in each hull. The trampoline sections are well supported and are a great place to hang out under sail. The nonskid surface is excellent, typical of the fine glass work throughout the boat. Handrails are stainless steel. There are also plenty of Lewmar deck hatches for terrific ventilation.

Down below

"The interior plan is one of the PDQ 36's most appealing features," Sykes said, "primarily because of what it doesn't have." While you will certainly find PDQs available for charter, the boat was conceived as a cruiser and not as a tax deduction. It doesn't have four double cabins with en suite heads. It does have a practical arrangement that is well suited for extended cruising.

The saloon features a large table with comfortable wraparound settees and unobstructed visibility. I have made four offshore round trips between Florida and New England in a similar cruising cat, and one of the things I liked best was being able to duck inside while on watch without losing visibility. Three steps carry you down into each hull. The starboard side features a full-sized chart table amidships and a large molded head compartment with a separate shower aft. The port hull houses the galley, which usually includes a two-burner stove and oven, double sinks and a generous amount of counter space. Monohull sailors are always struck by the lack of fiddles.

Aft to port is an optional cabin that was designed to the individual owner's needs. You may find a double with over and under bunks, a workroom, an office or even a miniature dive shop complete with compressor and tanks. Most PDQ 36 Classics simply have another sleeping cabin while most LRC models are more creative. The two double sleeping cabins are forward, side by side on the bridgedeck. I prefer fore-and-aft bunks on any boat. These spacious cabins include queen berths with overhead deck hatches and large hanging lockers. The interior finish is practical and workmanlike. PDQ is more concerned with making sure there is access to almost any part of the hull than with elegant teak joinerwork, an admirable trait.

Engine

The primary difference between the Classic and LRC models is that the latter features in-

board diesels while the former has outboards. Although Sykes said that some customers prefer the simplicity of outboards, most would opt for inboards if available. The outboard arrangement is clever. The engines, usually 9.9-horsepower four-stroke Yamaha or Honda models are mounted in lockers below the cockpit seats. They provide plenty of push and can be tilted up when not in use, eliminating all drag. Another advantage is that they can be removed and hauled into the shop for servicing, and while they are heavy to heft, saving the expense of having a mechanic come to the boat might make it worth the effort.

The diesels are usually either 18-horsepower two-cylinder Yanmars or 27-horsepower Volvos. Saildrives do create drag and eventually become maintenance issues with the lower units submerged continuously; however, the advantages of a diesel are worth it. Although outboards are much better than they used to be, they are not as reliable or rugged as a small diesel. Also, with a diesel you can throw on an efficient alternator. The Volvo 27 comes standard with a 55-amp alternator, allowing you to be able to carry and charge larger batteries and use a host of 12-volt gadgets and gizmos, from water pumps to autopilots. The port-side engine is accessed through the aft cabin, and you reach the starboard engine through a hatch in the cockpit.

Underway

Cruising cats are a permanent part of the sailing landscape, and no longer have to defend their existence with outlandish claims of performance. They sail great off the wind, adequately upwind, and best of all, they don't heel. They will not keep up with cruising monohulls when hard on the wind, but will be 25 to 50 percent faster off the wind. Within that framework there are a lot of variations, and by all accounts the PDQ 36 performs very well. "The sea trial always clinches the deal," Sykes said. "The PDQ 36 simply outperforms most of its competitors."

Chester White, who owns an 11-year-old 36, noted that he likes the blend of solid performance, flat sailing and shallow draft. A well-equipped PDQ 36 makes the annual off-shore passage from New England to Antigua every November and ties up near the Hylas 49 that I deliver along the same route each year. That can be a tough sail, and a boat has to be prepared for serious weather.

Most PDQ 36s will come with a full-batten main, a roller-furling genoa and a cruising chute. Boats set up for bluewater cruising will likely have a storm jib as well. The mast is certainly not towering, but one of the advantages of cruising cats is that good performance is available without the need for a lot of sail area. The loads are rarely excessive, even in a blow. And while double digits are certainly common when reaching in a stiff breeze, the PDQ 36 is really more of an all-around 7- to 8-knot boat, which, incidentally, is great going for a 36-foot cruising boat.

Conclusion

The PDQ 36 is an intriguing cruising option. It offers good performance, spacious deck and interior layouts, shoal draft and flat sailing. It is solidly constructed and holds its value on the used market. In fact, it can be difficult to find used boats. Designed as a family cruiser instead of a charter boat, the PDQ 36 has proven itself as an offshore sailer. It may be expensive, but when measured against a comparable monohull, which needs to be 10 feet longer to have comparable accommodations, the value becomes obvious.

Express 37

*A fast, fun, one-design racer
turned cruiser from the ULDB era*

The Express 37, like many West Coast flyers, traces its roots to Santa Cruz, California. In the 1980s this funky city on the north shore of Monterey Bay was the hotbed of ULDB development. Designed by the late Carl Schumacher, the 37 was commissioned by builder Terry Alsberg, who was already producing the popular and very fast Express 27.

The design criteria for the 37 was clear from the beginning. Schumacher and Alsberg wanted an off-the-wind rocket ship that was big enough and tough enough to stand up to the rigors of long-distance offshore racing. And they achieved their objective almost immediately. Introduced in late 1984, the first Express 37s finished first, second and third in class in the 1985 Transpac Race.

Alsberg, who learned his trade working for ULDB guru Ron Moore, did a terrific job of building the Express series, which later included a 34-footer. Some say he built the boats too well, and by 1989 his shop was in trouble and soon out of business. Of course these were

difficult times for all sailboat builders. In all, 65 37s were built and for the most part, they're concentrated in San Francisco Bay, Southern California and Long Island Sound. Small fleets are also located in Seattle and on the Great Lakes. However, one-design fleets are dwindling as the Express 37 has to some extent begun the natural, if sad progression from racer to cruiser, albeit a true performance cruiser. The Express 37 is also something of a cult boat and the few used boats that turn up for sale don't linger on the market.

First impressions

The Express 37 is deceptive, at first glance it doesn't look like an offshore-capable thoroughbred, it can be easily mistaken for a run of the mill, racer-cruiser style production boat. But don't be misled, this is a boat that you have to sail to appreciate. In profile, the sheer is almost straight but there is nice entry angle to the bow. The broad stern features a reverse transom. The low-slung cabintrunk is short and concentrated amidships. A careful inspection of the underbody lines reveals flat, flared sections forward and this, no doubt, helps the 37 surf on even modest waves. The keel is a narrow-cord foil slightly raked aft. The balanced rudder is placed well aft. Weight is centered in the middle of the boat to keep the ends light and buoyant and again to facilitate getting up on top of the water.

The double-spreader rig is moderate in proportion and the sailplan includes a large, relatively low-aspect main and smaller, high-aspect headsail. This rig has been coined a "masthead fractional rig," which handles like a fractional rig but delivers more horsepower and trims more efficiently. Displacement numbers seem to vary, the original design called for 9,500 pounds of displacement and 4,500

EXPRESS 37

LOA 37'1"
LWL 30'10"
Beam 11'6"
Displacement 10,000 lbs.
Ballast 4,500 lbs.
Draft 7'3"
Sail Area 638 sq. ft.

pounds of ballast. According to some reports, Schumacher claimed the finished boat weighed in closer to 11,000 pounds and the two boats on **www.yachtworld.com** list displacement at 10,000 pounds and 10,500 pounds respectively. Take your choice, anyway you cut it, the ballast/displacement ratio is more than 40 percent—the Express 37 is a stiff boat designed not only with ocean racing in mind but also the blustery conditions of San Francisco Bay.

Construction

To a build a light boat that can stand up to the demands and loads of serious ocean racing, you have to build it well, and that was certainly the case with the Express 37. The hand-laid-up, vacuum-bagged hull is balsa-cored and Alsberg was one of the first builders to use vinylester resin in the outer layers to prevent blisters. The deck is also balsa-cored and joined to the hull on a typical inward flange and bonded with 3M 5200 and stainless screws.

Molded liners are used throughout the boat, including separate pans for the head, galley and other furnishings. These liners look a bit stark and limit access to the hull and deck but they are practical and allowed Alsberg to really control weight. There are structural floors that provide excellent athwartship support. Few if any hull problems have been reported by owners. Indeed, the 37's hull is known for being virtually bulletproof. Also, the older Express 37s that I have examined are remarkably free of gelcoat crazing and cracking; the original fiberglass work was excellent.

What to look for

There are some documented problems to look for when you get serious about an Express 37. However, because the problems have been identified, in most cases they will have been already take care of. Specifically, when loaded up the No. 1 genoa tracks caused the decks to flex and potentially crack. The switch to Kevlar headsails, which didn't stretch and transferred the load to the tracks and the deck instead, apparently caused this problem. Bartz Schneider, who sails his 37 on San Francisco Bay and is a valuable source of information on the boat,

EXPRESS 37 PRICE DATA			
		Low	High
BUC Retail Range	1985	$55,400	$62,800
	1987	$59,400	$65,300
		State	Asking
Boats For Sale	1985	MI	$55,000
	1986	MD	$62,000
	1987	NJ	$74,900

notes that the problem is rectified by backing the tracks with U-shaped aluminum extrusions mounted below deck, which then serve as full length backing plates for the track.

Another problem, primarily on early boats, was the lack of tabbing on the bottom of the main bulkhead. In some cases, the bulkhead, which was a bit thin anyway, cracked. Starting around hull No. 20, the bulkhead beefed up, to ½-inch width and was thoroughly tabbed to hull. Of course, any boat that has been raced and sailed hard will have wear and tear issues. Be suspect of an extensive sail inventory on the listing sheet, chances are most are tired and not worth devoting space inside the boat to. Also, find out how old the standing rigging is, rod rigging was standard and is difficult to determine problems from a visual inspection. The condition of the running rigging will be more obvious.

On deck

Although there is little doubt that the deck layout was designed for racing, it is surprisingly easy to convert to a more cruiser-friendly arrangement, especially shorthanded cruising. All mast and sail control lines are led aft to the cockpit and can be controlled from a position standing in the companionway. This is not a bad system, it keeps crew weight centered and safely in the boat. The cockpit is set up for efficient sail trimming, with the mainsheet traveler on a bridge just aft of the companionway, the primaries outboard and the tiller well aft. A few boats came with wheel steering and others have been retrofitted but the boat is made for tiller steering.

Express 37

 **PRICE:** A new Express 37 in 1985 cost about $80,000 and that's about what you will pay for one today, it is a lot of boat for the money.

 DESIGN QUALITY: Schumacher hit the mark with this boat, it flies off the wind, tracks well to weather and can be sailed short-handed. It also has reasonable accommodations in the standard model while the MK II is ready to cruise.

 CONSTRUCTION QUALITY: Terry Alsberg did an impressive job of building the entire Express line. Light and strong, they have been sailed hard and put away wet for years and for the most part are still going strong—a testament to solid construction.

USER-FRIENDLINESS: An exciting boat to sail, you don't need to be a pro to get good performance, although, to sail it to its potential you will need a serious crew. Accommodations are functional and can be upgraded.

SAFETY: The robust construction is a prime safety feature, although typical of most performance boats, stanchions, handrails, etc., are on the small side.

 TYPICAL CONDITION: The boats have been sailed hard and yet they seem to hold up well. Most owners have been devoted, although their devotion is usually expressed in terms of more go-fast gear.

REFITTING: The Express 37 can be modified for cruising, or revamped for serious racing, whether it be one-design, PHRF or club racing. Liners make structural changes challenging, but lack of a formal interior is actually a plus.

SUPPORT: Express has long been out of business but the owner's association is active. Check out the Web site at www.express37.org.

AVAILABILITY: Only 65 boats were built and they seem to change hands reluctantly. Selection is best on the West Coast or around Long Island Sound.

 **INVESTMENT AND RESALE:** The Express 37 has held its value extremely well. Basically, you should be able to sell the boat for what you paid for it if you maintain it. Typically, you won't get back what you put into it, but that does not make the 37 unique.

 OVERALL 'SVG' RATING

A tapered aluminum mast was standard; these boats were built before the rush to carbon spars. Navtec rod rigging was also standard. Deck hardware included Merriman tracks and Lewmar winches. Teak handrails on the cabin-trunk and forward toerails lend a bit of security on deck, but should be expanded if you are converting to cruising. The class rules kept the sail inventory under control, and basic sails include a No. 1, No. 3 jib and 1.5-ounce spinnaker in addition to the main. A No. 4 jib and additional spinnaker are considered optional sails.

Down below

While nobody will confuse the interior of the Express 37 with a Cabo Rico, it is functional and reasonably comfortable. The interior finish includes a teak-and-holly sole and a smattering of ash and oak trim, teak ceiling strips and large expanses of molded fiberglass. The arrangement is straightforward, with a makeshift V-berth or sail storage in the bow. An enclosed head is next and the saloon includes a bulkhead-mounted table and opposing settees that convert into pipe berths. There isn't much storage as tanks take up the space below the settees, although there are small overhead lockers along the hull sides.

The galley lines up to starboard with a small stovetop and icebox. The sink is mounted amidships, behind the companionway steps, which is inconvenient to say the least, but at least it drains on either tack. The nav station is opposite the galley and includes a large chart table and decent seat. The aft end of the boat is more or less open, with quarter berths to port and starboard.

The MK II Express 37 featured a much better interior plan. Not only is it finished nicer but the arrangement is much improved. There is a real V-berth double, a comfortable saloon, a U-shaped galley and a double quarter cabin aft to port.

Unfortunately only 10 MK IIs were built. However, if you are looking to cruise the boat then search for a MK II first. Even if you can't find one to buy, find one to climb through, it will give you plenty of ideas for modifying the standard boat.

Engine

Before hull No. 25, the standard engine was the Yanmar 2GMF, 2-cylinder 18-horsepower model. Afterward, Alsberg upped it to the 3-cylinder 3GMF, the 27-horsepower model, which pushes the boat along smartly. Of course you don't buy an Express 37 to motor around, and chances are the boat you buy will have the original engine and it won't have many hours on it either. Access is terrific, primarily because the aft end of the boat is open, although it can be loud down below when the engine is running.

Underway

This is what it's all about and it is the reason you buy an Express 37—the boat sails brilliantly. Designed to fly off the wind, the 37 also sails fast upwind.

"The boat just has great bone—it is tough, I'd sail mine anywhere," said Schneider, the San Francisco Bay fleet captain and 37 devotee.

It has to be to stand up to 20 years of racing in the bay. While it is not at its best upwind in light air, the 37 finds it stride when the wind pipes up. Extremely close winded, the boat can carry decent headsails even blasting to weather, although the typical technique of dumping the main to keep the boat relatively flat is definitely the fastest way to sail. The Express 37 PHRF rating seems to range around 70.

And when you crack the sheets, well, that's another story. In heavy air you must keep the boat under control. Schneider tells a story of sailing off Point Conception in big winds and burying the bow while charging down a wave at 17 knots. It never pays to outrun the waves. Double-digit speeds off the wind are commonplace. Although class rules allow for up to eight crew, the boat can be sailed safely even in, as Schneider calls them, "gnarly conditions offshore," short-handed. The boat is light but so are the loads.

Conclusion

The Express 37 offers exhilarating performance both on and off the racecourse. And although one-design fleets are shrinking, most 37s have a lot of speed left in them. Also, following the trend of their boats, as racing sailors get older and migrate toward more casual sailing, a logical decision might be to convert a 37 into more of a cruising boat. With prices hovering around $80,000, the Express 37 is a terrific value.

Lagoon 37

This charter favorite is also a well-built cruising cat with a proven offshore record

Looking back at those not so faraway days in the early 1990s, it seems logical that wide-bodied catamarans with enough deck space to host a neighborhood block party, and four double cabins below, would become key additions for charter fleets all over the world. And so they have. What seemed less likely is that catamarans would become viable options for cruising sailors. But cats have made significant inroads into the cruising market too. Last year I was surprised to note how many cats were squeezed into the marina in Horta, in the Azores. There were dozens. Fifteen years earlier, a cat crossing the Atlantic was still something of an anomaly. Ten years ago they were a cult, now they're part of the cruising fraternity. One early production catamaran built with private ownership in mind was the Lagoon 37. Introduced in 1993, this sleek cat was built for Jeanneau's Lagoon division in a joint venture with TPI composites in Rhode Island.

Designed by Marc Van Peteghem and Vincent Fleury Michon, the 37 is in many ways a scaled down version of their successful Lagoon 42. The 37, however, seems more manageable, and the three-stateroom layout is ideal for a cruising family. Sure, plenty of 37s made their way into charter service, but many didn't and these are the boats to search out on the second-hand market.

While new catamaran prices are steep, to put it gently, a couple of decades of production has finally produced enough inventory for used prices to reach a level where they are comparable to monohulls. With a bit of careful shopping, a mid-1990s Lagoon 37 can be purchased for around $150,000, and when you consider it has the space of a 45-footer or larger monohull, that's not a bad value.

First impressions

The Lagoon 37 does not have the stately ship-like bridge ports that distinguish current Lagoon models. Instead, the sleek cabintrunk is sloped aft with two large forward ports and three to each side. The look, ironically, is more modern than today's boats, but does not result in as much interior volume or light. The hulls include NACA-shaped stub keels that are not

LAGOON 37

LOA 36'9"
LWL 33'4"
Beam 20'2"
Draft 4'
Shoal Draft 3'4"
Displacement 11,883 lbs.
Sail Area 849 sq. ft.

all that stubby. The draft is 4 feet, a bit more than comparable models like the Fountaine Pajot Athena and Prout Snowgoose. And while 4 feet might limit some gunkholing, it does help the 37 track well and the boat is well known for its ability to point. Bridgedeck clearance is around two feet.

The fractional rig has an air draft of just less than 55 feet, which is practical for inland waterway work and still offers plenty of horsepower in moderate breezes. A sail area of 849 square feet, combined with a displacement of nearly 12,000 pounds, translates into a sail area/displacement ratio of 26.1. The Lagoon 37 is no lightweight, the displacement/length ratio is 143, so the boat needs a bit of breeze to find its stride but it won't be overpowered when the trades get testy. This boat was designed with tradewind sailing in mind.

Construction

Hulls and deck-structure feature Baltek end-grain balsa cores, sandwiched between bi- and tri-axial cloths held together with vinylester resins. Catamarans are subjected to a variety of forces working in different directions, and top-quality material components are as important as good construction techniques. Lagoon didn't skimp on materials. Each hull includes watertight bulkheads fore and aft. The hulls and bridgedeck are essentially molded together and married to the deck and cabintop on a flange. The joint is laminated, not through-bolted. The fiberglass work is very well done. My daughters and I spent a fair bit of time aboard a Lagoon 37 in Spain last summer. The English family cruising the boat was in the process of finishing up a circumnavigation and I was impressed how good their 12-year-old boat looked.

The forward crossbeam is heavy aluminum, with an upward striker for support. The crossbeam is mounted in brackets on each hull that allow the hulls to work slightly without loading the aluminum, a system that has been proven by the thousands of bluewater miles. Support of the deck-stepped mast is accomplished by means of a stainless compression post that in turn rests on a beefy wooden member supported by the forward structural bulkheads.

LAGOON 37 PRICE DATA

BUC Retail Range		Low	High
	1994	$115,200	$126,500
	1996	$119,500	$131,000

Boats For Sale		State	Asking
	1994	FL	$159,000
	1996	Caribbean	$166,000
	1996	Caribbean	$171,000

What to look for

The first thing to look for is the specific model you want. If for some reason the 4-foot draft presents a real problem, a shoal-draft model of 3 feet, 4 inches was offered later in the production run. Also later in the production run, a galley-up option, meaning the galley was in the saloon and not down in the port hull, was also offered, although both of these features are rare. It is important to note that the Lagoon 37 had a second life as a Moorings 37. Although the hulls are the same, the interior is designed for charter work.

In terms of structural issues, Lagoon owners report very few problems. Look for signs of stress around the cross-member brackets. Also check the swage fittings on the beefy shrouds. Our English friends re-rigged the boat early in their trip when cracks were detected. If the boat had been chartered there will be all the normal signs of wear and tear, from a worn-out cabin sole to an assortment of nicks and bruises in the gelcoat and teak joinerwork. Ex-charter boats can be good buys, but be prepared for complete refits including sails, running rigging, new trampoline and more. Ex-charter boats will often have a lot of hours on the twin Perkins, and the price of repowering two new engines can be a shock.

On deck

The deep, spacious cockpit is at once comfortable and yet still feels secure for offshore sailing. It is clearly one of the 37's best features. The seats wraparound two fixed tables. You

Lagoon 37

 PRICE: There is no denying that cats are expensive, but a 10-year-old Lagoon 37 represents a good value.

 **DESIGN QUALITY:** The hull and deck design is capable and comfortable, the interior arrangement is a bit iffy.

 **CONSTRUCTION QUALITY:** The Lagoon 37, built by TPI, was well built with excellent materials. The used boats have held up very well.

 USER-FRIENDLINESS: A large comfortable cockpit, easy access to the swim steps and a great deck make the boat user-friendly. The sailplan is not overwhelming and the controls are well thought out. The interior is spacious.

SAFETY: Cats are, by design, a lot safer than many people realize. Basically unsinkable, even in the incredibly rare event of capsize, they will float upside down. The capsize issue is not really relevant these days as more and more cats, including Lagoon 37s, complete ocean voyages.

 TYPICAL CONDITION: Private boats rank higher, and ex-charter boats may rank lower. Try to find a private boat first.

 REFITTING: Easy access to the engine room makes maintenance and repairs easy. Overall, access is good, especially by production boat standards.

SUPPORT: Lagoon, now part of Groupe Beneteau, continues to be one of the leading catamaran builders in the world. It offers decent support for its used boats. Go to www.cata-lagoon.com. A good source for multihull information is www.multihull-maven.com.

AVAILABILITY: Although the 37 was a popular design, it was soon replaced by the 38 so availability is somewhat limited. The best places to look for boats are in warm-water areas, particularly the Caribbean Islands.

 INVESTMENT AND RESALE: The initial price of the Lagoon 37 was more than $200,000 in 1993, and the boat has held its value pretty well, at least until recently. I suspect a Lagoon 37 purchased for $150,000 today will prove to be a decent investment, at least by used boat standards.

 **OVERALL 'SVG' RATING**

are down low when seated anywhere but the helmsman chair, making it difficult to see forward. This is just a fact of catamaran life you have to get used to. The seatbacks are a bit abrupt and good cushions are essential. The helm chair is supported by a sturdy, double-legged pedestal. Visibility from the helm is adequate, although with a bimini or hardtop it is impossible to see what the mainsail is up to.

Bulkhead-mounted wheels take a bit of getting used to —you can't steer by putting your legs into it, although I always find myself trying anyway. Access to the molded swim steps on each hull is terrific. Davits mounted on the bridgedeck support a large dinghy between the hulls, although the lifting tackle may need additional purchase. The mainsheet traveler is aft, spanning most of the bridgedeck, and trimming the traveler is always the first option. Tacking is when you realize the beam

is just over 20 feet as you scoot across the cockpit to haul in the sheet.

While the side decks are wide there are no handholds on the cabintrunk and you feel a bit exposed until you can clutch the shroud. The forward tramp may need to be replaced if it's worn or feels spongy. The tramp is a great place to tarry when underway. There are large lazarettes forward and a decent-sized chain locker amidships. There are also two deep lockers in each hull aft. Ironically, the best locker space is found in the end of each hull—the section of the boat that really shouldn't be overloaded.

Down below

Unlike other cruising cats, the Lagoon 37 is nicely finished down below with solid teak trim, teak veneers and white laminates. While two overhead hatches offer adequate ventilation it would be nice to have an opening forward port as well. The plan includes a large saloon with a huge U-shaped settee and a dinette that can seat up to eight. This arrangement consumes the saloon. The galley is in the port hull, although it is still somewhat open to the saloon. The galley is spacious and includes a three-burner cooker, double stainless sinks, and a large refrigerator/freezer.

Both hulls feature queen cabins forward, with good storage provided in cubby-style and hanging lockers. These fore and aft berths are tucked up into the bridgedeck, and are not just part of the hulls, making them genuine queen-sized berths. The starboard side also includes a double cabin aft, and the charter models squeeze a walkthrough head in between. The main head is aft in the port hull, and it is expansive with a full, standup shower and room to move around. The nav station, featuring a fold-down chart table and the electrical panel, are in the starboard hull. This arrangement is cramped and I suspect most chart work will be done on the saloon table.

You will either really like the simplicity and openness of this plan or it will strike you as a waste of space in the saloon. I think it's an ideal arrangement for a true cruising cat.

Engine

The original engines were Perkins MD 20, 18 diesels. Our English friends noted that the engines were reliable but felt the boat was underpowered. Access is excellent, however. The starboard engine is located beneath the aft bunk and the port engine is aft of the head. Both engines are easy to work on and maintain. The fuel capacity of 50 gallons is a bit light, but then again, weight is always an issue with multihulls. These stingy engines each burn about one-half gallon an hour while pushing the boat along at close to 6 knots. When you spot cruising Lagoon 37s at anchor or in a marina they often have plastic fuel cans lining the deck. Twin screws are one of the best features of cruising cats. The Lagoon 37 handles well under power, and you always have a complete set of spare parts aboard.

Underway

The hull and keel shapes make the Lagoon 37 more weatherly than some of its competitors, although it does need a bit of breeze to get going. We concluded that our Kaufman 47 monohull made faster passages overall than the Lagoon 37 our English friends sailed around the world, but this was also due to different sailing philosophies. They sailed with two small children and always depowered the boat in a blow and in the evening. Also, if a cruising cat is overloaded it quickly translates into lost performance, and they had their boat stuffed with gear.

While it is hard to generalize, owners report typical speeds of 7 knots upwind in moderate breezes and sailing inside of 45 degrees apparent. Off the wind, even when loaded, the Lagoon 37 shines, and our friends noted a top speed of 16 knots in the Indian Ocean. The big roachy main can produce a bit of weather helm, and needs to be reefed early to maintain balance with the headsail. The Lagoon 37 has an overlapping genoa, which is effective when reaching in the trades. Downwind sailing is best accomplished with an asymmetrical chute.

Conclusion

The Lagoon 37 is a well-engineered and sturdily constructed cat that has a proven track record as an offshore cruiser. If you are looking for a boat for a year's sabbatical in the Caribbean, take a hard look at this handsome cat.

Pacific Seacraft 37

Traditional and good-looking, this cruiser's uncompromising seakindliness is made for bluewater cruising

It is a bit unusual for a boat like the Pacific Seacraft 37 to appear in the *Used Boat Notebook* for the simple reason that it's still in production. The boats that have been profiled over the years, despite typically long and successful production runs, are no longer available as new boats, which makes them good values on the used market.

Introduced in 1978 the Pacific Seacraft 37, or as many still refer to it, the Crealock 37, is an impressive world voyager, and it continues to be in demand by serious sailors looking for a high-quality bluewater cruiser. Naturally the newer boats will be quite expensive (the base price of a brand-new model is around $200,000), but early models sell for less than $100,000.

W. I. B. (Bill) Crealock has designed a slew of fine cruising boats over the years, including the handsome Cabo Rico 38 and the husky Westsail 42. Less well known as a writer, Crealock's 1978 memoir, *Vagabonding Under Sail*, is a wonderful book describing his early days sailing all over the world. I remember finding the book at Michigan State University and feeling like I had discovered a hidden treasure.

Surprisingly, the Pacific Seacraft 37 traces its origins back to Clipper Marine. In the mid-1970s, the company began tooling to build a 37-foot bluewater cruiser that would be tough and affordable, something to compete with the Westsail 32. Clipper Marine went broke before any boats were built and the boatbuilding company Cruising Consultants acquired the molds. The result was the first edition of the Crealock 37. Cruising Consultants built 16 boats in 1978 and 1979 before selling out to Pacific Seacraft. The rest, as they say, is history. Pacific Seacraft will soon be launching hull number No. 263. Of that number most have put plenty of bluewater miles under their keels and have nosed their fine bows into harbors all over the world.

First impressions

The Pacific Seacraft 37 marries a traditional look with a quiet but uncompromising attitude. With a shapely canoe stern, sweet sheerline, low freeboard and long bow overhang, the PS 37 is a handsome boat by any definition. However, a closer inspection reveals practical features expressly designed for sea duty. The cutter rig does not include a bowsprit with the potential for rig and structural damage, and all sail controls are led aft to a well-protected cockpit. If good looks alone were driving the design, the trunkhouse might have been lowered. However, Crealock understands the importance of maximizing room below without compromising the basic hull shape and the need for handholds on deck that are located at a useful height. Below the waterline the large fin keel is cutaway fore and aft, the rudder is hung on a full skeg and the propeller is completely protected.

PACIFIC SEACRAFT 37

LOA 36'11"
LWL 27'9"
Beam 10'10"
Displacement
 16,200 lbs.
Ballast 6,200 lbs.
Draft
 deep 5'10"
 shoal 4'11"

Under sail the PS 37 performs surprisingly well and has logged many fast passages, which may come as a bit of surprise after glancing at performance parameters. The boat's displacement/length ratio of 334, for example, is nothing to brag about, especially when compared to cruisers like the Island Packet 37 and Gozzard 37, which check in at around 270. This number, however, is very deceptive, since the PS 37 is narrow and heels early, thereby extending the waterline significantly. Also, displacement figures are inherently inaccurate when it comes to cruising boats and the loads they carry.

One admirable aspect of the Pacific Seacraft 37's performance is that the hull almost never pounds in a seaway and the boat can be easily handled with a small crew. So many times, heavier cruisers turn in faster passages than lighter ones simply because the crew is better rested because it didn't need to micromanage its boat.

Construction

Pacific Seacraft builds stout boats, and its construction techniques are conservative and well proven. The hull is solid fiberglass, and while the company does offer optional balsa or foam layers, these are for insulation purposes only. Early hulls were not immune to the boat pox that swept the industry in the 1980s, but today's boats include vinylester resin in the first laminate to prevent blisters.

A full-length molded liner supports the hull with several recesses for bulkheads, floors, furniture fittings and engine beds. There are drawbacks to molded linings: They are hard to secure to the hull, limit hull access and restrict different interior configurations. However, Pacific Seacraft uses numerous bonding points to make sure that the liner is firmly glassed in place.

You can't argue with the results: few if any 37s have reported structural hull damage, even after hard groundings.

The deck is plywood cored, which is unusual in a boat of this quality, but once again, the results speak for themselves; deck delamination does not seem to be much of a problem, even in boats more than 20 years old. Most boats use plywood under high-load areas any-

PACIFIC SEACRAFT 37 PRICE DATA			
		Low	High
BUC Retail Range	1985	$ 82,700	$ 89,900
	1990	$108,500	$119,500
		State	Asking
Boats For Sale	1980	CA	$115,000
	1989	MN	$139,900
	1996	MD	$170,000

way, locally replacing the more common balsa cores. The hull-and-deck joint incorporates the molded bulwark to form a box joint that is strong and dry. A teak caprail covers the joint.

The mast is deck-stepped and the compression post is tied into the main bulkhead. The main bulkhead is both fiberglassed and bolted in place. The ballast is an external lead casting, fastened to a large keel stub with hefty stainless steel bolts.

What to look for

Older Pacific Seacraft 37s have aged very well indeed, especially considering that many have sailed far and wide. Solid original construction and a seakindly hull shape are a good combination when it comes to maintaining a boat's integrity through the years.

From a production standpoint, an important change occurred in 1988 when vinylester resin was added to the first laminate to prevent osmotic blisters. The boat has been built to ABS standards for many years, and in 1993 the original mat and woven roving was replaced with biaxial roving as the standards changed.

Some owners have reported problems with the aluminum fuel tanks, located in the bilge. The seawater sloshing in the bilge can find its way into the tank through the fittings at the same time accelerating corrosion on the exterior. The water tanks are actually part of the hull liner and should be carefully inspected.

For the most part Pacific Seacraft uses first-rate deck fittings. The overhead hatches made by Bowmar, however, are not very well constructed and have been known to leak.

Pacific Seacraft 37

 **PRICE:** Quality doesn't come cheap, with prices ranging from $80,000 for a very early model in rough condition, to well over $200,000 for a recent model.

 DESIGN QUALITY: Crealock's design is ideal for bluewater cruising. The hull is fast enough to roll up miles on passage and stand up to gales without wearing out the crew.

 **CONSTRUCTION QUALITY:** There is really nothing special about the material or the technique, however the execution is superb. The boats have held up well, which is the ultimate test of original construction.

 **USER-FRIENDLINESS:** Easy to handle, especially for a cruising boat. The systems are relatively simple and well engineered. The only drawback is the lack of living space, but that is the nature of the design.

SAFETY: From the husky bulwark and stout stanchions, to well-placed handholds and a deep cockpit, the 37 is a very safe boat indeed.

 TYPICAL CONDITION: Most boats have been sailed far and wide, however the original construction and dedication of most owners to maintain their boats translates into clean boats on the resale market.

 REFITTING: The molded interior liner limits creativity when it comes to changing the interior plan, and makes it difficult to complete wiring and plumbing upgrades.

 **SUPPORT:** Because the boat is still in production and because Pacific Seacraft is a customer service-oriented company, there is plenty of support from the factory, even for their oldest used boats. Links to owner's groups can be found on the company's Web site www.pacificseacraft.com.

 **AVAILABILITY:** With 263 boats afloat, there is always a good selection of used boats for sale. They seem to be widely scattered across the county.

INVESTMENT AND RESALE: The initial price may be high, however, there is a very good likelihood that you will be able to get your money back when you sell.

OVERALL 'SVG' RATING

On deck

The deep cockpit exudes a sense of security. The seats are long enough to sleep on, and the backs are angled for good support. The cockpit sole is actually a well-sealed access hatch to the engine compartment—a great feature. The starboard locker is quite large. Coamings have built-in winch handle boxes, and there is a propane locker on the aft deck, behind the cockpit. The bridgedeck is narrow, but certainly up to the task of keeping green water out of the cabin. New boats feature Whitlock steering, while older boats may have an Edson system.

A midboom sheeting arrangement keeps the cockpit uncluttered as the traveler runs just forward of the companionway. All sail controls are usually led to the cockpit, although there isn't a lot of room on the aft end of the trunkhouse, especially when tucked under a dodger.

The molded nonskid surface is quite aggressive, and seems to hold up well even on older boats. A substantial bulwark, with 30-inch stanchions mounted on the vertical face, and stout teak handrails mounted on the cabin-top make it safe to move about the deck, even in rough conditions. Pacific Seacraft didn't skimp when it came to fittings. The cleats are oversized and well secured, and the hawsepipes forward must please the pilots who inspect the boats before passage through the Panama Canal. The husky dual anchor rollers and internal chain locker can be accessed from the forepeak.

Although the Pacific Seacraft 37 has been rigged as both a sloop and a yawl, most are true cutters. The typical sailplan includes a main with two reefs, a fairly heavy staysail and a high-cut, 120-percent yankee. It is not uncommon to find both headsails set up for roller furling.

The chainplates are outboard and through-bolted through the topsides. While this doesn't foster tight sheeting angles, remember that the 37's beam is less than 11 feet, which means that the angles are not much different than a beamy boat with inboard chainplates. The aluminum mast has an air draft of 47 feet, 9 inches.

Down below

The interior arrangement isn't fancy, but as Don Coleman at Pacific Seacraft says, "It works." The forward cabin is deceptively large, usually set up with an offset double to starboard instead of a V-berth and a comfortable chair tucked in to port. There are also two hanging lockers opposite the head. By today's standards the head seems rather plain. But it does have a shower, sink, commode and good storage. What else do you need in a head?

The saloon features a straight settee to port and a convertible double to starboard, which drapes around the table. Both make excellent sea berths, especially the starboard double with the table serving as a leeboard. Deep shelves behind the settees, with fiddles designed to keep everything in place, swallow up books and small items.

The chart table is to port, with a quarter berth behind. This is called a double, but it really is better suited for a single, or as it will likely become, the onboard miniwarehouse. The galley is to starboard and is set up for preparing a meal at sea. Deep stainless sinks face forward, and the stove is outboard. For years Pacific Seacraft has used Force 10 cookers, arguably the best in the business. The fridge/icebox faces aft.

The joinerwork is not fancy, but it's clean, tasteful and functional. The teak interior, especially in the older boats, can seem a bit dark. The headroom is more than 6 feet, 3 inches and ventilation is excellent with overhead hatches and opening portlights. Handholds are well placed. The interior arrangement is just about perfect for a cruising couple.

Engine

By the late 1980s four-cylinder Yanmars became the standard power plant. Most boats will have the 4JHE rated around 50 horsepower, giving the easily driven, 16,000-pound PS 37 plenty of punch. Wallace notes that he easily motors along at 6 knots, burning about one gallon per hour. Most early boats were fitted with a smaller Universal diesel.

The hatch in the cockpit sole makes repowering much less of a procedure than it would be trying to squeeze an engine through the companionway. In fact, overall access is excellent whether it's through the companionway, through the cockpit hatch or through a third panel in the quarterberth. The aluminum fuel tank holds 40 gallons, which is not enough for serious voyaging. It is not unusual to see 37s carrying extra fuel in jugs on deck.

Underway

The Pacific Seacraft 37 has sailed just about everywhere, and its cruising exploits have been well documented. What comes as a bit of surprise to many owners is how well the boat sails. "I sail at 6 knots or more all the time," explains Wallace, the recently retired chief justice of the Illinois Supreme Court. Wallace, who took delivery in Chicago, sailed south from Annapolis to Florida. "We had a variety of conditions, from calms to gales, and the boat never gave me an anxious moment."

The cutter rig is easily balanced, and the boat adapts readily to self-steering. The cutter rig is also well suited to heavy weather, as the headsail can be shortened and finally rolled in completely with the staysail acting as a storm jib.

Downwind, the cutter is not particularly efficient, and some type of drifter or cruising spinnaker is necessary to maintain speed in light air. When the wind pipes up, the 37 finds its stride, even when a large sea is running. Several owners have reported touching double digits while surfing down trade wind seas. Long passages that average better than 150 miles per day are common. However, the most underrated performance factor is seakindliness, as nothing wears out the crew or the gear faster than a quick, pounding motion. The Pacific Seacraft 37 is a "swisher," not a "pounder."

Conclusion

The Pacific Seacraft 37 is a nearly perfect cruising boat for a couple. The interior may seem small when compared to more modern designs, but the point of cruising isn't to bring all your worldly goods with you; it's to leave them behind. The boat is well constructed and brilliantly designed. The only drawback to the boat is the price; however, if you are willing to buy an older boat, you may be able to launch your cruising dreams sooner than you think.

O'Day 37

Affordable coastal cruiser with accommodations perfect for living aboard

The O'Day 37 caused a stir when it was introduced in 1978. It was one of the first center-cockpit models less than 40 feet long that actually looked and behaved like a sailboat, not a powerboat with a mast. Aesthetically it was a big improvement from the company's other center-cockpit boat, a stubby 32-footer introduced a few years earlier. The 37 was an immediate success, popular with sailing schools, charter companies and sailing families longing for private accommodations. While hard-core sailors continue to eschew center-cockpit designs, and see them as heretics in the world of pure sailboats, most of us recognize and appreciate their practical appeal. And when it comes to practical, the O'Day 37 stacks up well against all comers, especially when you factor in price; a late model 37 in good condition usually sells for around $40,000. Liveaboard sailor Jim Schrader, who has cruised up and down the Atlantic coast during the last five years in his

1982 37, LEE WARD, puts it simply, "The best thing about the boat is the cabin arrangement."

First impressions

The sheerline of the O'Day 37 is vintage mid-1970s, with just a subtle dip amidships but nothing extreme. In spite of a wide cove stripe, your eye tends to follow the cabintrunk and cockpit coaming, giving the impression that the boat has more freeboard than it actually does. The sloop rig is relatively low aspect with an air draft of 47 feet and a long boom, working sail area is a moderate 594 square feet. The stem is nicely raked and the forefoot trails into a sweptback fin keel that again, is straight out of C. Raymond Hunt's 1970s de-

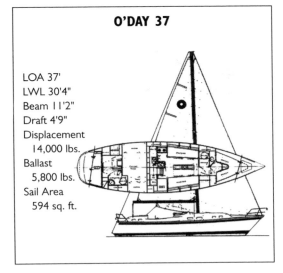

O'DAY 37

LOA 37'
LWL 30'4"
Beam 11'2"
Draft 4'9"
Displacement
 14,000 lbs.
Ballast
 5,800 lbs.
Sail Area
 594 sq. ft.

signer manual. The rudder is supported by a large, full skeg.

The displacement of 14,000 pounds was moderate in its day, less than the Tartan 37 and more than the Islander 36. The 6,000-pound lead keel translates in to a ballast/displacement ratio of nearly 43 percent. For a sensible coastal cruiser the numbers look good, displacement/length ratio is 224 and sail area/displacement is 16.35. The O'Day 37 won't win many races but it has better than average overall performance, is fairly stiff and has a good motion in a seaway.

O'DAY 37 PRICE DATA

		Low	High
BUC Retail Range	1980	$28,600	$31,800
	1983	$33,400	$37,100

		State	Asking
Boats For Sale	1978	NY	$43,000
	1982	OR	$37,000
	1983	MD	$43,500

Construction

Founded by Olympic sailor George O'Day in the late 1950s, the company was one of America's original fiberglass builders and produced many legendary boats, especially small boats. The 37 was built during the period when the company had been sold to the conglomerate Bangor Punta, which also variously owned Ranger, Cal and Jeanneau. I recently looked closely at LEE WARD, which is hull No. 194. I found it to be in very nice shape, and the condition of a 25-year-old boat, even one that has been well maintained, reveals a lot about original construction.

O'Days were not meant for rugged bluewater sailing—they were built to the production standards of the day—and yet they have held up pretty well over the years and many have logged thousands of offshore miles. The one-piece hull is solid fiberglass, and not particularly heavily laid up. The deck is both balsa, and in places where more support is required, plywood cored. The hull and deck are joined on a flange and chemically and mechanically fastened. A rubrail was a nice option.

The rudder is high-density foam covered with a thin outer layer of fiberglass and includes a beefy stainless steel shaft. The ballast is lead, internally placed in the keel cavity and fiberglassed over. The bulkheads are teak and plywood and are well tabbed to the hull. From 1980 on, O'Day used bronze through-hull fittings below the waterline and surprisingly good quality hardware and fittings in general during a production run that produced hundreds of boats before it was phased out in 1984.

What to look for

A quick survey of the 37 owner reviews on a variety of Web sites produced a few common problems, most of which were confirmed by discussions with Schrader. Most owners complained that the original hatches and especially the plastic port lights need upgrading, and in most cases, replacement. The flush mounted forward hatch is prone to leaking. Some boats had deck prisms (or skylights) forward and these also leaked. The solution was usually just to remove them.

Deck delamination may or may not be an issue, and this is one item to make sure the surveyor checks. You can usually spot this malady yourself with a careful inspection of the deck around the chainplates and where the cabintrunk and deck converge and forward around the chain locker. Delamination reveals itself with telltale creaks and groans as you put a bit of weight on the suspect areas. Also, the original standing rigging included swaged terminals and if they haven't been replaced they will need to be. In fact, most riggers suggest upgrading the rig every 10 to 12 years, so even if the boat was re-rigged previously, it may need it again, especially if you plan to cruise extensively.

On deck

The deep cockpit is cozy, in the words of one owner, and lends a feeling of security. The pedestal crowds the entry into the aft cabin, however the 28-inch wheel is just the right size for getting around. Visibility from the helm,

O'Day 37

 **PRICE:** With prices ranging from the mid-$30,000s to the low $40,000s, the O'Day 37 is genuinely a lot of boat for the buck.

DESIGN QUALITY: This design may not be everyone's cup of tea, but it achieves what it set out to achieve. It's a decent looking, comfortable coastal cruiser that performs well through a variety of conditions.

CONSTRUCTION QUALITY: Built to production boat standards, time has proven that the original workmanship and materials were more than adequate. Deck delamination and blisters should be watched for.

USER-FRIENDLINESS: A comfortable living arrangement and cozy cockpit make this a cruising-friendly boat. Visibility and deck mobility are not great.

SAFETY: The design translates into a soft motion and the boat is relatively stiff. The crowded deck and nonskid make moving about while underway a bit tricky.

TYPICAL CONDITION: Although many boats were originally chartered or school boats, most have been converted to family cruisers. Some boats on the market seem to have been sorely neglected. Be wary of boat prices that seem to good to be true.

 REFITTING: According to several owners in the throes of refit projects, the 37 is not the easiest boat to work on. Parts are still widely available.

 **SUPPORT:** The owners' association has plenty of information on line at www.Odayowners.com. There are many 37 owners listed and the best way to get accurate information is from a fellow owner.

 AVAILABILITY: With a large production run there is always a good selection of boats available. The Chesapeake Bay, East Coast and Florida seem to offer the most boats for sale.

INVESTMENT AND RESALE: The 37's price has stabilized as more sailors realize that it represents a solid value on the used boat market.

OVERALL 'SVG' RATING

---

usually an advantage of a center cockpit, is average at best but at least the helmsman can easily access the main and headsail sheets. Although the aft cabin is entered from the cockpit, the addition of a fully enclosed bimini makes the main cabin, cockpit and aft cabin feel like one well-connected working and living area. There are good-sized lockers beneath the cockpit seats. The mainsheet is led aft to a triangular block and tackle arrangement on the aft deck and is controlled with a small winch. It's completely out of the way and utilizes efficient end-boom sheeting. The genoa tracks are located directly outboard of the cockpit, with turning blocks aft for the sheet leads. While this arrangement makes lead adjustments easy, it also makes for flapping sheets in the cockpit when tacking.

The single-spreader mast is deck stepped. The chainplates are mounted in the middle of the narrow side decks, which makes going forward a bit awkward. The chainplates are also difficult to access from down below. Double lifelines were optional but most boats on the used market seem to have them. The bow and stern pulpits are beefy and well supported. A molded toerail with a teak cap offers deck security although you will find most 37s have gelcoat worn nearly smooth. Long teak handrails line both cabin tops. An external chain locker is handy, although the cast single anchor bow roller is a bit undersized.

Down below

The disadvantage of a center-cockpit design is that space in the main cabin is usually sacrificed, and this is the case with the 37. After dropping below, the small galley is immediately to port. A two-burner, counter top alcohol stove was standard, although most owners will have upgraded the cooker. If a propane system has been retrofitted be sure to check the installation carefully. Double stainless steel sinks were standard, although one sink is quite shallow, and pressure hot and cold water was also an unusual standard feature. The icebox is typical of its day, fairly large and modestly insulated, if you plan to live aboard and cruise in warm climates you'll need to improve the insulation. A small chart table is opposite the galley.

The main cabin features opposing settees with a drop-leaf table between. Some owners have removed the table for added space. By the way, the 1980 brochure notes that off-white shag carpeting was listed as an option. There are shelves above and bulk storage below the settees. The finish is in teak and the joinery work is simple but very well done. Teak grab rails overhead are well spaced and the headline is foam backed vinyl. It's a good reach up to the rails; headroom is 6 feet, 4 inches. The forward head is rather small, although it has everything you need. A generous hanging locker is opposite to starboard. The forward cabin includes a V-berth with a removable filler insert. The cabin is separated from the head and main cabin by somewhat flimsy folding doors.

The roomy aft cabin, the feature that really defines the 37, offers a large athwartships double berth with storage below. Additional storage is found in a hanging locker and in teak-faced drawers and shelves. The private aft head includes a fiberglass liner and a shower.

Engine

The standard engine was a four-cylinder, 32-horsepower Universal diesel. This is a reliable machine and many of the boats have original, i.e. high hour, engines. Still, an O'Day 37 that has been repowered is worth paying a bit more for on the used boat mar-

ket. Schrader says that despite being loaded for cruising he still makes close to 6 knots without too much effort, at least in flat seas. The standard aluminum fuel tank carries 28 gallons, which corresponds to close to 300 miles with the stingy Universal. Engine access is not as good as it should be from behind both companionways. Accessing the stuffing box is particularly challenging, and one owner notes that he installed a dripless model to solve the problem.

Underway

Almost across the board owners report that the 37 finds its stride when the winds start blowing, and that it needs a lot of trim and coaxing to keep moving in light air. Schrader notes that once the winds hit 10 knots the boat comes alive and sails smartly up to 20 knots when he considers reefing the main. Although the sheeting angles are not overly tight, the boat is fairly close-winded and tracks well. It is also dry upwind, which is not always the case with a center cockpit simply because you're closer to the spray. Schrader described one nasty Gulf Stream crossing with winds gusting to 30 knots and the seas at 15 feet.

"The boat felt rock steady in the water, we had two reefs and tiny headsail and never felt threatened. We were zooming along at 7 knots and the ride was OK." He also notes that the boat sails well under autopilot, explaining, "she balances easily."

Conclusion

The O'Day is a nice example of an affordable coastal cruising boat. Although many boats were originally chartered or school boats, most have been retrofitted into family cruisers. If your budget is between $30,000 to $45,000 and a private aft cabin is high on your priority list, take a hard look at the O'Day 37, it just might surprise you.

Prout Snowgoose 37

While not as flashy as modern cats, this cruiser's built to sail the oceans

Just a few weeks ago I returned from delivering my boat across the Atlantic. While holed up in the Azores I saw three Prout Snowgoose 37s in the jammed-packed marina in Horta. Of course this isn't surprising; when you mention the Snowgoose 37 to an experienced multihull sailor their likely response will be, "Oh, what a great cruising boat. It's a real bluewater boat." Unlike more modern cruising cats that boast double-digit speeds and hotel-like accommodations, the Snowgoose is renown for its rugged construction and seakindliness.

The boat was built to cross oceans, not to fill Caribbean charter fleets. Somewhere around 500 boats have been built, and, although statements like this are impossible to confirm, I have been told that nearly 100 have completed circumnavigations. "If you have $100,000 and want a cat to sail around the world, you'll probably end up in a Snowgoose," said John Sykes, who owns 2Hulls, a large multihull brokerage in Fort Lauderdale, Florida.

Monohull sailors tend to think that cruising catamarans are a new phenomenon. New is a relative term. The Prout family began building cats in the 1950s, and their boats have been well known and respected in the United Kingdom and Europe for half a century. In fact, a 1963 Australian-based Prout catamaran just completed its third circumnavigation. It's only recently that catamarans have earned similar respect on this side of the Atlantic. I remember seeing an old Snowgoose 35 on Lake St. Clair when I was kid in the early 1970s and it seemed odd and exotic at the time. I wondered if it was safe to be out on the lake in a catamaran when the weather turned nasty. I was a bit chagrined to later learn that the boat had been sailed over from England. Although Prout has had its financial struggles recently, its older models, especially the Snowgoose 34, 35 and 37, are held in high esteem.

First impressions

The Snowgoose 37 doesn't look like a world cruiser. Compared to many of today's cruising catamarans which, I confess, strike me as looking a bit bulbous, as if over-inflated, the Snowgoose seems a bit outdated and rather pedestrian. The solid bridgedeck forward is not as sexy as a trampoline and the 15-foot, 3-inch beam makes the boat downright skinny. The double-ended hulls don't offer stern scoops and easy access swim steps. The cockpit is, at least by catamaran standards, rather compact. However, as soon as you step aboard the Snowgoose 37 you realize that it's a solid, serious boat. It has a bearing in the water that most monohull sailors would recognize.

The wide, dark stripe that encapsulates the ports around the cabintrunk distinguishes the boat as a Prout. The hulls, which were among the first cats to have rounded bilges, show a slight reverse sheer. The Snowgoose 37, which saw the bulk of its production in the 1980s, and its later

PROUT SNOWGOOSE 37

LOA 37'
LWL 33'
Beam 15'3"
Displacement 5,600 lbs.
Sail Area 570 sq. ft.

evolution, the Snowgoose Elite, both trace their lineage to the legendary Snowgoose 35, one of the most successful production catamarans. A relatively low-aspect cutter rig makes for a working sail area of 570 square feet. The single-spreader mast has an air draft of less than 50 feet.

Construction

The Snowgoose 37 is not, by any means, a lightweight. The displacement of more than 5,600 pounds is heavier than some modern monohulls of a similar length. The early hulls, which include molded stub keels, are solid fiberglass, while new models are solid below the waterline and cored from the waterline north. As mentioned earlier, the bridgedeck is solid, and although this adds weight it also provides rigidity between the hulls that a single crossbar can't match. The bridgedeck clearance is not as high as more modern designs and this will result in plenty of water action between the hulls. The deck on the older boats is balsa cored, while some newer boats have been cored with other materials. When you drop below and see the generous use of teak you quickly realize that saving weight was not the prime construction concern. While most cats rely almost entirely on modular construction, the Snowgoose 37 is built more traditionally with bulkheads and furniture facings securely tabbed to the hull. I recently inspected a 1994 Snowgoose Elite that had just returned from a two-year Caribbean cruise and double Atlantic crossing. There were no signs of deck delamination, gelcoat crazing or leaks. Marine surveyor and Snowgoose owner Jack Allinson notes that his 20-year-old boat shows only minor gelcoat crazing and is structurally sound. "I hope to sail it for another 20 years," he said.

What to look for

The first thing to look for is the right Snowgoose 37. Although it is hard to find information pinning down exact hull numbers, somewhere around 1986 the updated Elite model went into production. The primary difference is that the Elite is 12 inches wider than the standard Snowgoose, and as a result is slightly roomier down below but also a tad heavier and two inches deeper in draft. Of course, with a draft that's still

PROUT SNOWGOOSE 37 PRICE DATA

BUC Retail Range		Low	High
	1985	$ 79,000	$ 86,800
	1990	$110,000	$121,000

Boats For Sale		State	Asking
	1980	MA	$ 93,400
	1985	NY	$120,000
	1992	FL	$125,900

less than three feet it isn't really much of an issue and the extra interior volume is worth the two inches. The hull shape of the Elite is slightly different. Unlike the standard Snowgoose which has two transom-hung outboard rudders, the Elite rudders are slightly smaller and located below the waterline.

Most Snowgoose 37s have single engines with a rotating, retractable sonic drive gear. While this gear is efficient—John Sykes claims it comes close to matching the performance of twin screws—it is not perfect and can be expensive to repair. Be sure to have it carefully inspected by a mechanic who actually knows something about it. Also, pay close attention to the wiring; most boats have had owner-installed electronic additions over the years and the original wiring was not the boat's best feature. In fact, an interesting aspect of the Snowgoose 37s on the market is that most boats have been retrofitted for offshore cruising—sometimes this is a good thing and sometimes it isn't. The discount offered by a boat with a limited inventory may not only save you money but a lot of aggravation too. Instead of dealing with worn-out equipment you can start fresh.

Naturally, all age-related issues, especially if the boat has been cruised extensively, should be carefully inspected. Standing and running rigging and the condition of the steering systems are particular items to check.

On deck

The cockpit is quite comfortable but small when compared to more modern cruising cat designs. If you're heading offshore, that's not a negative.

Prout Snowgoose 37

SAILING Magazine's Value Guide

 PRICE: The price of a Snowgoose 37 must be compared to other catamarans, not other monohulls. It is one of the few bluewater cats available for anything approaching $100,000.

 DESIGN QUALITY: There is nothing flashy about the design, it is relatively slow and not all that roomy. But the boat has been proven in the one place that counts—on the ocean—and its record is extraordinary.

 CONSTRUCTION QUALITY: Prout builds solid boats and the Snowgoose 37 has held up very well. Strength is emphasized over weight savings and the workmanship and fitting out are top quality.

 USER-FRIENDLINESS: An easy boat to handle in most conditions with all lines led aft. Flat sailing and a reasonable motion (as long as you are not beating into choppy seas) along with a well-thought-out interior make for a user-friendly boat.

 SAFETY: Unlike most cats, the Snowgoose 37 was designed for bluewater sailing. The boat features sturdy construction, an enclosed cockpit, a solid bridge deck, well-designed sail controls and stout fittings.

 TYPICAL CONDITION: Although the Snowgoose 37 has aged well, most boats have been seriously cruised and often times the equipment is well worn.

 REFITTING: A relatively easy boat to work on and unlike other cats accessibility is decent due a traditional build. Parts are available but information is limited.

 **SUPPORT:** Despite the large production run there isn't an active owners' group, at least not one that I found. John Sykes at www.2hulls.com is a good source and at any time he has several Snowgoose cats on the market. Also, surveyor Jack Allinson is a font of Snowgoose information, his Web site is www.allinson.com.

 AVAILABILITY: There are always plenty of boats on the market although the clean ones tend to sell fairly fast. Florida, the Caribbean and Europe are good markets.

 INVESTMENT AND RESALE: The Snowgoose is a boat that you can purchase, retrofit for a world cruise and sell it afterwards and not loose much money. What more can any sailor ask for?

 OVERALL 'SVG' RATING

The bulkhead-mounted wheel is to starboard and because of the relatively low profile visibility is good from the helm, even with a full bimini and dodger enclosure. That is not always the case with smaller cruising cats. One well-known model requires that you peer through the cabin ports to see forward from the helm.

All sail controls are led to the cockpit and there is a clever stainless steel fairlead and a vertically-mounted winch to facilitate hoisting the sails. There is a large storage locker under the cockpit sole and access to the engine. One advantage of a single engine is the ability to center the weight on the bridgedeck instead of placing hundreds of pounds of metal in the end of each hull, which is exactly where you don't want it. The mainsheet traveler is aft, and although there is plenty of travel, it's not as long as most newer cat travelers. There is, however, a useful aft deck behind the traveler. The main companionway includes a thick, bi-fold Plexiglas door that can be closed quickly in ugly weather.

The side decks are narrow. Fortunately there is a stout stainless grabrail that is at just the right height as you make your way forward. The double lifelines and stanchions are tall, oversized and extremely well supported. Also, there is a lifeline across the bow, a nice safety feature. Overall the deck fittings are robust. The double anchor rollers are designed to host serious ground tackle. The solid bridgedeck allows for two large forward lockers, which gobble up fenders, lines, jerrycans and the like and keep the deck clean.

The anodized aluminum spar is deck stepped. Most boats are cutter rigged, and most have both the genoa and staysail roller furled. The main will likely have a decent-sized roach and be fully battened.

Down below

The Snowgoose 37 and the Elite came with two interior plans. The family layout includes a full queen berth forward and two spacious double cabins aft. The forward cabin is open to the saloon, with keeps it airy but limits privacy. However, this is an ideal place to sleep at anchor, you can simply raise your head and peer out the forward portlights to make sure you haven't dragged. The saloon includes wraparound settees and a large table. The Snowgoose 37 is not as bright below as some cats and the headroom in the saloon is around 5 feet, 8 inches. However, the use of teak and quality joinerwork lends a feeling of elegance that is rare on a cat.

Forward in the starboard hull there is a changing station, locker storage, a full-length bookshelf and two hanging lockers for the queen cabin. The galley takes up the center of the hull. Although the hulls are relatively narrow, the galley is more than adequate with a unique three-sink basin and a three-burner stove and oven. It is a very secure area to cook, especially because cats don't heel much. And while some prefer a "galley up," meaning in the saloon, the Snowgoose 37 arrangement is an excellent compromise. Although it's technically a "galley down," the partial saloon bulkhead is low, allowing the cook to be part of the social scene and still out of the way. The refrigerator and freezer are located under the bunk in the aft cabin, which I am sure at times is inconvenient.

Each aft cabin includes a double berth, a hanging locker, a seat and vanity and deep shelves forward of the bunk. These cabins don't have a lot of elbow room, especially when compared to more modern designs. The port hull houses a roomy navigation station with a clever folddown seat and a real chart drawer. There is plenty of room for instruments and radios and the electrical panel is located on the forward bulkhead. The head is all the way forward and it's quite large. A single head is sensible, and is one of the primary reasons why the interior plan works well.

The open plan is identical to the family plan except that the settees in the saloon continue all the way forward, eliminating the third cabin. They do, however, convert into a nice sized berth.

Engine

The vast majority of Snowgoose 37s were manufactured with a single engine. Typically this has been two-, three- or four-cylinder diesel ranging between 30 and 40 horsepower. Common engines are the Volvo MD series and three-cylinder Yanmars. Regardless of what engine is used, access is excellent through hatches in the cockpit and aft deck. The 35-gallon fuel tank is also located under the cockpit. The most unique feature of the engine is the stern drive unit. Most boats have the Sonic Drive by Sillette. This stern drive is, to use the English word, "steerable" meaning that it turns as you turn the wheel and offers good steering control in both forward and reverse. It is also retractable, which along with the small skegs protecting the rudder make it possible to beach the Snowgoose 37.

Underway

Allinson, who has sailed his 1984 hull No. 216 Snowgoose, OWN N SUN II, from the East Coast to the islands, notes that his boat manages 6 to 7 knots in most conditions. It's not fast but it is consistent, and it doesn't need to be micromanaged, making it an ideal passagemaker. Allinson says that unlike modern cats that rely on a huge, roachy mainsail, the Snowgoose goes best when the big genoa is drawing. He also notes that punching the boat upwind in choppy conditions is challenging and that there is a lot of water action below the bridgedeck.

Allison, who often singlehands, appreciates the ease of handling three smaller sails from the cockpit instead of dealing with a large mainsail. One of the Snowgoose owners in the Azores told me that during two Atlantic crossings he has averaged 150 miles per day, and he was quick to add that he doesn't push the boat. The Snowgoose 37, with its flexible cutter rig, balances easily and handles well under autopilot.

Conclusion

The Snowgoose 37 is a solid, capable world cruiser with a proven track record. It may not be as flashy as newer-designed cruising cats, but when the ocean is in an unpleasant mood the last thing on your mind is flashiness.

Cabo Rico 38

*Timeless design and sturdy build are the hallmarks
of this accomplished cruiser*

First impressions, as they say, only get one chance, and few boats make a more lasting mark than the Cabo Rico 38. This winsome cutter, draped in teak, inspires dreams of quitting your job and sailing to faraway places. It's just that kind of boat. Bill Crealock pushed all the right aesthetic buttons when be designed the 38.

Crealock stated in his design notes, "The Cabo Rico 38 hull shape is the one in which everything came together best."

It's been more than 25 years since the first hull was laid in Costa Rica, and close to 200 boats and thousands of bluewater miles later, it is not cavalier to refer to the Cabo Rico 38 as a classic. You can list it next to other legendary long-keeled cruisers like the Bermuda 40, Bristol 40 and Shannon 38.

Cabo Rico is an unlikely success story. The company was founded in the mid-1960s by John Schofield, who managed British Leyland's Rover plant in San Jose and molded sailboats in his spare time. His first boat of note was the Crealock-designed Tiburon 36,

launched in 1971. He didn't make many Tiburons, but occasionally you will come across this stout ketch on the used boat market.

The first Cabo Rico 38 was completed in 1977. Although the offshore marine industry in Taiwan was beginning to dominate the cruising boat market in the late 1970s, and consumers were warming to the idea of foreign-built boats, building boats in Central America still carried the stigma of the banana republic. Could they really build decent boats in Latin America? The solid construction and sheer beauty of the Cabo Rico 38 proved that indeed they could.

Cabo Rico came of age when Edi and Fraser Smith took over the company in the late 1980s. The company quickly expanded the range of production and today it builds five models ranging from 36 to 56 feet. They also took over David Walter's Cambria yachts, and continue to produce the sleek 46 along with the innovative Mark Ellis-designed Northeast motorsailers. Although the Cabo Rico 38 is still technically in production, very few are ordered these days as the company focuses on bigger boats. The real market for 38s is in used boats and prices range dramatically, from an asking price of $84,000 for a 1978 model to nearly $200,000 for a more recent edition.

First impressions

In a 1993 review, *SAILING*'s Chris Caswell declared, "The 38 has not succumbed to the fickleness of style and remains just as pretty today as when it was first introduced." Well, I will back up Caswell's claim. Eleven years after his review the boat still is awfully darn pretty. It has a timeless quality. The sweep of the hull includes a clipper-style bow with a sprit and handsome teak carved trailboards and a fair bit of overhang. The counter stern is

CABO RICO 38

LOA 41'
LOD 38'
LWL 29'3"
Beam 11'6"
Draft 5'
Displacement
  21,000 lbs.
Ballast
  7,800 lbs.
Sail Area
  778 sq. ft.

narrow and no doubt seakindly in a following sea. If you appreciate traditional boats you'll find the Cabo Rico's sheerline a thing of beauty. The cabintrunk is relatively low profile and blends nicely into the cockpit coamings.

Below the waterline the hull is slack in the bilges and the full keel is slightly cutaway in the bow. The rudder is attached to the trailing edge of the keel and the propeller is an aperture and completely protected. And while this keel shape may seem obsolete to some, it sure produces a nice ride at sea. The 38 may pitch a bit in a seaway but it will never pound, and a soft motion is the most underrated design feature on any boat. The rig was intended as a cutter, not a modified sloop, so the spar is a bit farther aft than a typical sloop. The mast is keel stepped. The working sail area of 778 square feet translates into a sail area/displacement ratio of 16.3, which is more moderate than you might suspect.

Construction

Naturally, a 25-year production run will result in many construction details that have changed, evolved and improved as materials and processes become better. However, one thing has remained constant, the boat is solidly built for the purpose of ocean sailing. The hull layup is interesting. Although sometimes it's reported that the hull is balsa cored, that is a bit misleading. A layer of balsa coring is added to what is essentially a solid fiberglass hull and then covered with a thin skin. The balsa is not necessarily a structural part of the hull, instead it is for thermal and sound insulation. Fiberglass floors stiffen the hull and support a fiberglass subfloor—there is no wood to rot in the bilge. The teak-and-holly sole is laid over the subfloor, making it very solid. The lead ballast is internal and placed into the keel cavity in several sections. Earlier boats had internal iron ballast, it has been reported that the change occurred around hull No. 40.

The deck is balsa cored in the traditional sense. A shoebox joint, incorporating the raised bulwark and teak caprail join the hull and deck. Most boats had teak decks although it is not uncommon for owners to have removed them. Recent models likely have omitted this once de rigueur option. Only a few

CABO RICO 38 PRICE DATA

		Low	High
BUC Retail Range	1985	$ 99,000	$109,000
	1990	$138,500	$152,000
		State	Asking
Boats For Sale	1981	OH	$ 89,500
	1988	FL	$129,900
	1993	TX	$189,000

molded liners are used during the build, for the most part the bulkheads and furniture facings are plywood with teak veneers or solid hardwoods and securely laminated to the hull. Speaking of teak, it is one of the hallmarks of the Cabo Rico 38. The boat is finished with locally grown teak with a light honey color and used liberally both on deck and down below.

What to look for

Warren and Marti Fritz of Kalamazoo, Michigan, recently purchased a 1984 model in Fort Lauderdale, Florida, and then shipped it home to Lake Michigan. While the survey revealed typical age-related issues, it had a few serious recommendations. One item that turned up was blisters on the hull, and although it wasn't serious, the Fritz's are planning to do an epoxy bottom job this winter. Another issue to look for are teak deck troubles. If there are many missing bunks, cracked caulk, and some of the planks seem to be proud, be wary of subdeck delamination. While teak decks provide terrific nonskid and look lovely, they are expensive to repair or replace.

Other common problems include leaks, especially around the scuppers on deck and at the chainplates. These leaks usually reveal themselves down below. Also check for evidence of mast boot leaks. Fortunately, the mast step, which is directly below the table, is a fiberglass bridge spanning a couple of floors.

The original engine was the venerable Perkins 4108, and as these workhorse engines age, they usually start to burn oil. The front

Cabo Rico 38

 PRICE: This is still the major obstacle to owning a Cabo Rico 38, they are pricey. However, if you are willing to consider older models, then this becomes less of a factor.

 DESIGN QUALITY: Some will argue that this is a dated design, and they are right. It is also a proven design, tested in the real world of cruising, year in and year out.

 CONSTRUCTION QUALITY: The 38 is solidly built and well engineered. The interior craftsmanship is superb. Older boats have held up well, considering that most have been sailed hard. The generous use of teak on deck, including teak decks, does require plenty of maintenance.

 USER-FRIENDLINESS: Cutters are a bit overrated when it comes to ease of handling, even with a club footed staysail. The cockpit is designed for offshore sailing, and not as comfortable as more modern cockpits.

 **SAFETY:** A very secure cockpit and deck make the Cabot Rico 38 safe in a seaway. The interior is also well designed with handholds and there is no open space to go careening across. The soft motion also eliminates crew fatigue.

 TYPICAL CONDITION: This rating would be higher but all of the exterior teak demands attention. Typically an owner has the boat looking great when it goes on the market but if it takes a while to sell, the varnish weathers and the boat begins to look neglected.

 REFITTING: Accessibility is good for adding components. However, the original workmanship is of such high quality it is difficult to maintain the standard, most owner-fitted add-ons are obvious.

 SUPPORT: The company, based in Fort Lauderdale, is quite helpful in answering requests about specific 38 items. Also, with the boat still in production, parts are available. Visit www.caborico.com for more information.

 **AVAILABILITY:** Just less than 200 boats were built and although they change hands rarely, there are enough boats out and about to always have a decent selection on the market. You must be prepared to travel if you want to look at more than one.

 INVESTMENT AND RESALE: The 38 has held its value very well over the years, and is only affordable now because of age. It is hard to imagine, in this time of limited production, that Cabo Rico 38s will sell for much less than they do now.

 OVERALL 'SVG' RATING

and rear seals are also prone to leaking as they age, so don't be horrified if the bilge reveals some dark mysterious fluids. The 4108 is imminently repairable, and surprisingly, will also usually run just fine even if the seals are not in great condition.

Be sure to check the status of the standing rigging. Swage terminals were used on the shrouds and stays, and if they haven't been changed out recently, factor that job into your purchase price. Also, pay careful attention to the bobstay fittings, the lower one is actually below the waterline and prone to corrosion.

Headsails on cutters don't age as well as those on sloops as they need to be dragged around the staysail stay on every tack, so check the conditions of the headsails. Also, very early boats had a plywood cockpit sole that was prone to rot. One other note, Cabo Rico built a pilothouse model 38, although it is rarely seen on the used boat market.

On deck

The Cabo Rico is a big 38-footer, at least on deck. This sounds silly, but the LOA is actually 41 feet when you include the bowsprit and raised bulwarks, and the wide side decks give it a big boat feel. The cockpit can happily accommodate four, and still includes a bridgedeck, decent-sized lockers and a large lazarette and aft deck. Most boats have Edson pedestal steering with a stainless wheel rim and teak spokes. The seat backs are a bit abrupt, at least by today's standards, but the cockpit is very secure, especially when a spray dodger and bimini are in place. Some boats have aft facing portlights that make it uncomfortable to lean back against the cabintrunk.

Sail controls may be led aft. The mainsheet traveler is forward of the companionway, with a midboom sheeting arrangement that frees up cockpit space in exchange for less leverage on the main. Most boats have a club jib boom for the staysail, which clutters the foredeck, although it allows the staysail to be self-tending. Some owners have converted the staysail to roller furling, and in the process, have eliminated the boom and rigged staysail sheet leads instead. Cabo Rico used Isomat spars, and while these spars are not the most robust, they seem to hold up very well.

The side decks are easy to navigate, even when it is blowing, and the stanchions are tied into the bulwark for additional support. While most boats on the used market will have teak decks, those that don't will have various forms of nonskid. There are plenty of teak handrails, including clever athwartship mounted rails on the aft end of the cabintrunk. All the way forward there is an extremely useful storage space beneath a teak grate. The bowsprit hosts twin stainless anchor rollers and the windlass is usually sandwiched between the staysail stay and boom.

Down below

The Cabo Rico 38 interior is stunning. The joinerwork is completely captivating. While the most recent 38s have actually cut back on teak, most boats on the used market will be bathed in honey-colored teak with a high-gloss varnish finish. You really have to search to find a bare fiberglass surface. Ventilation is supplied through several overhead hatches and opening portlights.

Although there are many varieties when it comes to the interior plan, the two most common arrangements are the A and B plans. The B plan, which seems to be the most desirable, includes an offset double berth forward. This is followed by a head with a separate shower stall and a hanging locker opposite. The B plan also includes a small L-shaped settee to port with a table hinged on the main bulkhead. The locker behind the teak table is a work of art. Opposite is a straight settee.

The U-shaped galley is to port and includes double sinks, a two or three burner stove outboard and a huge refrigeration/icebox compartment. In fact, you need to be tall just to bend over and reach down to the bottom of the box. The galley is compact but filled with clever storage spaces, and most boats have removable panels for the sinks and stove top to increase counter space. The nav station, such as it is, is opposite the galley and there is a large quarterberth aft to starboard, although it is a stretch to call it a double. The A plan is almost identical except that it includes a standard V-berth and straight settees and a fold-up table in the saloon. Don't be surprised to encounter variations on either of these plans as some owners opted for custom interiors.

Engine

Several different diesels have been used during the 38's long production run. Early boats had the workhorse Perkins 4108, while others had the comparable Westerbeke 46-horsepower model. Later boats have four-cylinder Yanmars and it should be noted that the most recent 38s have moved the engine forward under the galley sink. Most boats on the used market have the engine beneath the companionway steps. Access is decent, although it is much improved in the newer boats. The 56-gallon fuel tank is fiberglass. One owner highly recommended a feathering prop to help control the boat in reverse.

Underway

The Cabo Rico 38 wasn't designed or built to win races, or even for casual daysailing, she was meant for bluewater cruising. However, with a generous sailplan its performance is better than many suspect. According to Fritz, who sails JUBILATE on Lake Michigan, as soon as the wind reaches 10 knots the boat accelerates to 6 knots. "It's uncanny," he said.

The cutter rig is not wildly efficient sailing up wind. It is, however, made for reaching. Most boats are set up with a high-cut yankee forward to fill the foretriangle with the staysail. The yankee not only offers better visibility than a genoa, it is easier to tack. The cutter rig also balances easily and adapts to self-steering. One advantage of a "non-swim step transom" is that it is better suited for mounting a windvane self-steering device.

Fritz really likes the motion, or lack there of. "We were used to sailing lighter boats," he said. "It came as a pleasant surprise to realize that JUBILATE never pounds, not even in the worst Lake Michigan chop, and that's saying something."

That soft ride is a major reason why the 38 is popular with many long-distance voyagers. The 38 stands up well when the breeze pipes up and most owners note that they don't reef until the wind reaches 20-knots-plus. The ability to carry sail in a fresh tradewind is vital for a cruising boat, that's when you rack up the miles. And when it is time to shorten up, the 38 will press on with a reefed main and staysail, which incidentally, is an ideal sailplan for heaving-to.

Conclusion

The Cabo Rico 38 is an exceptional cruising boat. With prices for older boats in the 80s, this lovely cutter is now a viable option for most cruisers. Besides, it might be worth a few extra bucks just for the compliments.

Privilege 39

This well-built cat makes for a capable world cruiser

The Privilege 39 is a terrific boat for a family of six to sail around the world. It is a fine boat for knocking around the Caribbean on a sailing sabbatical. It's not a bad boat to start a charter business with either. Get the point? The Eric Le Ferve-designed Privilege 39 is a versatile and capable cruiser. And with prices for used models at or below $200,000 it is also a very good value. If you need proof, spend an afternoon carefully inspecting one of these solidly built cruising cats and then see what $200,000 buys in other cruising catamarans.

Privilege was the brand name for Jeantot Marine. Founded by Rene Bernard and Philippe Jeantot in 1985, the company capitalized on Jeantot's fame. He was the winner of the first BOC singlehanded around-the-world race and later created the Vendée Globe Challenge. Whether his reputation helped the company is hard to determine, but his thousands of miles of bluewater sailing definitely shaped the way Privilege catamarans are built. The boats are ruggedly constructed and genuinely designed for ocean sailing.

"They (Privilege catamarans) are cats that monohull sailors relate to. They seem to be able to transition into a Privilege easier," said Christine Buttigieg of the Catamaran Company in Fort Lauderdale. "They are solidly built, each one is semicustom, they don't seem as stark as other cats and they really hold up at sea."

First impressions

If you climbed the mast and viewed the Privilege 39 from that perspective its most distinctive feature becomes obvious, the large area of solid bridgedeck forward. Sure it adds a bit of weight but it also adds rigidity and strength. It provides secure deck space for working on the boat and for supporting the forward crossbar. It sets Privilege apart from other builders who just string a net between the hulls supported by an aluminum extrusion.

When viewed in profile, the 39 hulls appear to be raised and the sleek, two-tiered cab-intrunk flows naturally from the hull lines. In its day, it was modern catamaran styling. Today, it seems dated. The 39 has a 36-foot waterline and a 21-foot beam, which adds up to a lot of square footage. There is adequate bridgedeck clearance and the fine entries of the hull are known to have a good motion in a seaway. The shallow fixed keels translate into a draft of 3 feet, 6 inches. Overall displacement is just a whisker under 14,000 pounds. The mast height is just over 50 feet above the waterline and working sail area is approximately 850 square feet.

Construction

Each Privilege 39 was built on a semicustom basis. Unlike most cruising cats, the interior features hand-cut wooden bulkheads and furniture facings instead of molded liners. One of

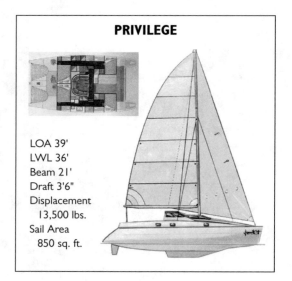

PRIVILEGE

LOA 39'
LWL 36'
Beam 21'
Draft 3'6"
Displacement
   13,500 lbs.
Sail Area
   850 sq. ft.

the reasons Privilege boats have been more expensive than their competitors is the company doesn't take advantage of scale production techniques. The boats are literally built the old-fashioned way, which is unique in the multihull universe. The interior joinerwork is excellent. The fiberglass sculpting is also excellent.

The 39's hulls are composite, cored from the waterline up and solid from the waterline down. The deck is cored throughout, except in areas of high loading. The hull-and-deck joint incorporates the expansive bridgedeck on a flange. The forward crossbeam is heavy gauge aluminum and mounted on a universal joint that allows a bit of flex and movement in the hulls. The upward V-shaped striker helps carry the load for the forestay.

What to look for

The Privilege 39 is also called the Privilege 12, representing its metric length. It is also sometimes called the Alliaura 39, the name of the company that purchased Privilege in 1996. However, shortly after the company was sold, the new Marc Lombard-designed 395 went into production. Don't confuse the two models, the 395 is an extension of the Privilege 37 and sells for a lot more. Otherwise, they are all the same boat, which was in production from the late 1980s through the late 1990s.

In general the Privilege 39 has held up very well. A 1989 model in Fort Lauderdale that has been sailed hard and put away wet requires just a bit of love and elbow grease to be ready for sea. Be wary of former charter boats. The 39 has the four-cabin layout and many boats were in charter fleets. Former charter boats can sometimes represent terrific values but they can also require costly refits that can quickly defeat the advantages of a reduced selling price. Remember, if you need to repower, you are talking about replacing two engines, which certainly adds up.

On deck

The Privilege 39 has a huge cockpit, even by catamaran standards. The T-shaped helm station is aft on the port side. It feels more like the helm of a twin-wheel monohull and I prefer it to the bulkhead mounted wheels of most simi-

PRIVILEGE 39 PRICE DATA

		Low	High
BUC Retail Range	1992	$173,000	$191,000
	1994	$195,000	$215,000
		State	Asking
Boats For Sale	1991	MD	$206,000
	1992	FL	$205,000
	1995	Caribbean	$226,000

larly sized cats. It is, however, often exposed to both sun and spray. I like the way the sail controls are led to sailing stations on either side, freeing up the cockpit for socializing. The mainsheet traveler runs the length of the cockpit and is easily accessed from either side. The cockpit includes a lovely teak table and loads of storage. Indeed, that's a Privilege trademark, lots and lots of storage, both on deck and below. Teak seats aft seem positively elegant in this age of molded fiberglass madness. Most boats will be fitted with davits that allow a good-sized dinghy to be slung between the hulls. Most boats will also have an array of solar panels mounted above the davits. Unlike some cats, the bimini top may or may not cover the entire cockpit. The swim steps seem a little small and difficult to access, especially by today's standards.

In general, Privileges have heavier rigging than most catamarans, again emphasizing their commitment to offshore sailing. The mast is supported with uppers and lowers, which is unusual and welcome, and the staysail stay's chainplate is well supported in the solid forward section of the bridgedeck. Most 39s are set up as cutters, with the staysail furling as well as the lighter headsail. Some boats are rigged to fly screechers, otherwise known as drifters. Small items like hefty pulpits and well-supported stanchions also set the Privilege 39 apart. The two small triangular areas of net forward provide a nice spot for sunbathing and watching dolphins gambol between the hulls. The anchoring arrangement includes a husky stemhead fitting and Bruce

Privilege 39

 PRICE: Cruising catamarans are not cheap. However, some are definitely better values than others, and the Privilege 39 is a quality boat at a fair price.

DESIGN QUALITY: There is nothing revolutionary or even extraordinary about the 39's design; however, it is well proven on the oceans and charter bases of the world.

CONSTRUCTION QUALITY: From excellent fiberglass work to fine woodworking, by catamaran standards, the 39 is a well-built boat.

USER-FRIENDLINESS: The aft helm station has positives and negatives. The visibility is good, the instrument panel is good but the exposure is not. The four-cabin interior maximizes the extra space provided by the large bridgedeck.

SAFETY: This is where the Privilege 39 shines. The solid construction, well-supported rig, large bridgedeck and easy to navigate deck add up to a safe boat.

TYPICAL CONDITION: Ex-charter boats drag this rating down. The truth is: chartering is hard on boats, even boats with full-time crews.

REFITTING: Unlike many charter boats that are constructed entirely from molded tools, there is decent access to most parts of the 39. There is also a track record of turning former charter boats into family cruisers.

SUPPORT: Although the company is still in business, there isn't much support here in the United States. There is not an active owner's association and you need to speak French to make sense of the Web site. Christine Buttigieg is a good source of information. You can reach her at www.catamarans.com or at (954) 727-0016.

AVAILABILITY: There is always a good supply of 39s on the market. The best selection is always in Florida and the Caribbean. If you are serious about a 39 it's worth your while to make a trip to the islands. Chartering is also a good way to see if you want to invest in a 39.

 INVESTMENT AND RESALE: Privileges are in general more expensive than some of their peers, but they are also quality boats that hold their value. Most of the depreciation has been wrung out of the 39.

OVERALL 'SVG' RATING

anchor roller. The chain locker is in the bridgedeck, and unlike cats without a solid forward section, the ground tackle does not need to be led a long way aft. From well-placed teak handrails to aggressive nonskid to lower shrouds to grasp, the Privilege 39 is friendly on deck, even in a seaway.

Down below

The Privilege 39 has a surprisingly handsome interior set off by plenty of cherry or mahogany woodwork. Even the expansive portlights are nicely framed in wood. The 39 has a warmth about it that I like. The layout on other hand is not my favorite. Access to the saloon is through wooden doors from the port side of the cockpit. A large aft opening port and all

around forward ports makes the saloon light and airy. A large U-shaped settee draped around a table dominates the saloon. A forward facing nav station is to starboard. This is a nice spot to sit while underway. The forward and side visibility is more than adequate and you are out of the weather.

The galley is down, meaning that it's stashed into the port hull. While models differ, most include a single sink, 12-volt refrigeration opposite, a two- or three-burner non-gimballing stove and again, ample storage in well-placed bins and lockers. Each hull features two double cabins. The forward cabins in each hull include athwartship bunks, which makes good sense and is yet another advantage of the large bridgedeck. This arrangement allows for large locker space and forward facing portlights. You can lie in your bunk and see if the anchor is dragging. Heads are located in the walkway of each hull and the aft bunks are also situated athwarthships. Overall ventilation is excellent provided by numerous deck hatches and opening portlights.

Engine

The original engines were 29-horsepower Volvo diesels with saildrive transmissions. Access is through the lazarettes on the aft end of each hull. Several of the boats on the market have re-powered with Yanmar diesels. Either set of engines have enough oomph for the Privilege 39 to motor at 8 knots and still maintain decent fuel economy. The total fuel capacity is 400 liters, translating into just over 100 U.S. gallons.

Underway

Several Privilege 39s have circumnavigated and many others have crossed oceans. In fact, almost every 39 available for sale on our side of the world will have crossed the Atlantic on its own bottom. That speaks volumes about the boat's seakindliness. How does it perform in the more pedestrian world of daysailing or knocking around the coast for a weekend? Just fine, but it's not as lively as monohull sailors might think. The Privilege 39 is not a lightweight cat, and it's not overflowing with sail area. It will attain double digits while reaching in tradewind conditions but only 7 or 8 knots upwind. And that is nothing to be ashamed of. The motion is not as rapid as on some faster cats and that's a positive.

Conclusion

I like the concept and the execution of the Privilege 39. It's a genuine cruising cat, capable of fast passages and not daunted by heavy weather. If I were in the market for a catamaran to take my family on a circumnavigation, I would begin my search by zeroing in on the Privilege 39.

Cal 39

Bill Lapworth's revolutionary performance cruiser still shines today

Jack Jenson, the builder, and Bill Lapworth, the designer, combined their unique talents to produce several memorable boats during the nascent days of fiberglass boatbuilding, otherwise known as the 1960s. Jenson Marine was better known by its brand, Cal, and just take a look at the company's boats for 1965: The Cal 20, 25, 28, 34, 36 and, of course, the 40—literally a hall of fame lineup.

Yes, these were the glory days for Cal but they didn't last. Jenson sold the company shortly afterward to Banga Punta, a corporate monolith, which later sold it to Lear Siegler, an even larger, soulless conglomerate that built everything from vacuum cleaners to nuclear warheads. Somewhere along the way, as boats became inventory instead of the inspirations of idealistic men, the magic waned. And yet, if you ask yacht brokers around the country what model Cal they would most like to list, there is a good chance they'd say a mid-1980s Cal 39.

CAL 39

LOA 39'
LWL 31'6"
Beam 12'
Draft (standard) 6'8"
Draft (shoal) 5'6"
Displacement
   17,000 lbs.
Ballast 7,000 lbs.
Sail Area
   692 sq. ft.

Launched in 1978, the Cal 39 was built during the hectic period when Cal's manufacturing shifted to Tampa, Florida, and then up to Fall River, Massachusetts, as the company struggled to re-establish its identity. Still, when all the glass cures, it is really the design that carries the day, and in typical fashion Lapworth was ahead of the curve with the 39. It was a genuine performance cruiser before there really was such an animal, and as such, the design not only seems less dated than others from this period, it is still highly desirable as a capable and affordable cruiser. Somewhere around 150 39s were built and unlike many forgettable boats of this time, the Cal 39 has maintained its financial value.

First impressions

Like many Lapworth designs, the Cal 39 does not overwhelm you when you first see it bobbing between pilings. If you step back and look closely you'll note that the boat has a subtle but handsome sheerline and that the coachroof flows naturally with the curve of the deck. Freeboard is moderate, which translates into low when compared with today's boats, and there is a fair bit of overhang forward and a rakish reverse transom. The hull shape looks right, the boat rides smoothly in the water, like it belongs there, and the boat grows on you the longer you stare at it.

Below the waterline, the 39 has a moderate forefoot that trails into a large fin keel. Two keels were available—the standard 6 foot, 8 inch deep-draft and a 5 foot, 6 inch shoal-draft model. Displacement is 17,000 pounds resulting in a displacement/length ratio of 257, which means that the boat can be loaded up and still sail well. The spade rudder is placed well aft, a Lapworth hallmark, and results in excellent steering control, especially when running in big seas. Two rigs were offered—the standard keel-stepped spar with an air draft of 55 feet and the optional tall rig that adds a few feet to the mast and about 50 feet of sail area. The sail area/displacement ratio is a respectable 16.2, not a light air demon but a very good all-around performer—just what I want in a cruising boat.

Construction

The construction of the Cal 39 was in keeping with other boats built by Bangor Punta and later Lear Siegler, including O'Day, Jeanneau and Ranger sailboats. And while these boats are not well known for their construction they have held up well over the years. The Cal 39 hull is solid glass and laid up fairly robust. The deck is balsa-cored in most places and plywood was used in high-load areas. The hull-to-deck joint is the conventional inward facing flange and is both chemically and mechanically fastened.

The interior bulkheads are securely tabbed to the hull and a molded liner is used on the cabin sides and overhead liner. The finish is quite nice, actually better than most would suspect with excellent joinerwork and teak

CAL 39 PRICE DATA			
		Low	High
BUC Retail Range	1980	$ 47,100	$ 51,500
	1985	$ 60,000	$ 65,900
		State	Asking
Boats For Sale	1978	CA	$ 49,900
	1982	FL	$ 57,000
	1987	MA	$ 62,000

trim. The ballast is lead and the rudder is foam with a thin layer of glass over it.

What to look for

There were actually several different models of the Cal 39. The first one was the boat that replaced the legendary Cal 40 in 1971 and was in production just a few years. The 39 covered in this article went into production in 1978 and is sometimes called the MK II. The MK III was introduced sometime around 1981 and included an expanded aft cabin and other subtle changes. Finally, another 39 was introduced in 1994 when Cal made a brief, ill-fated comeback. These later boats, designed by C. Raymond Hunt and Associates, are quite nice but much more expensive than the MK II and IIIs. Also, production was very limited.

Early Cal 39s came standard with Perkins 4108 diesels, a reliable engine that is easy to work on and still easy to find parts for. Later boats had a four-cylinder Universal and others had Pathfinder diesels. Almost without fail owners complain about the Pathfinder, which was a marinized Volkswagen Rabbit engine. It is interesting to note that of the 15 39s listed for sale at **www.yachtworld.com**, six have been repowered with Yanmars. I'd look for one of these first.

Draft, both water and air, drive used boat prices. For many cruisers the 6-foot, 8-inch standard keel is, all puns aside, a major drawback, the 5-foot, 6-inch shoal model is more desirable. Also, the hard-to-find tall rig is in demand as you can always shorten sail but it is

Cal 39

PRICE: If you have been looking for a used boat for coastal and or offshore cruising in the 38- to 40-foot range, you will quickly realize what a good buy a Cal 39 is. You can find them for less than $60,000 and, with a bit of luck, under $50,000.

DESIGN QUALITY: Lapworth hit the mark with this design. It sails well and has a very comfortable, well-thought-out interior. It is not sexy but it has aged nicely.

CONSTRUCTION QUALITY: There is nothing extraordinary about the build, but there is also nothing particularly shoddy. Built like most 1970s and 1980s cruising boats.

USER-FRIENDLINESS: A relatively easy boat to handle under sail and power, especially for a near 40-footer. The interior space is well utilized. The cockpit is a bit cramped and not wildly comfortable.

SAFETY: The lifelines and stanchions are typical production quality and could stand to be beefed up for offshore work. Handrails are well placed and secure. Nonskid is usually worn.

TYPICAL CONDITION: Many 39s have been cruised or lived aboard and others were originally put into charter service. However, you can also find a nice model that has been retrofitted for cruising.

REFITTING: According to several owners in the throes of refit projects, the 39 is not the easiest boat to work on. Parts are still widely available.

SUPPORT: There is no factory support available and a lot of confusing and conflicting information on the Web. Dan Dalrymple edits the "Old Cal Homepage," at http://pages.sssnet.com/go2erie/calhome.htm.

AVAILABILITY: About 150 were built and it seems there are 10 to 20 on the market at anytime. If you want a Cal 39 you can find one.

INVESTMENT AND RESALE: You are not likely to lose money if you purchase a Cal 39. The boat is widely recognized as a terrific value for a nimble cruiser and in demand.

OVERALL 'SVG' RATING

---

harder to raise your mast. Some owners have noted deck delamination and leaky hull-to-deck joints but both seem more exception than rule. The rudder can also be a problem and should be carefully examined during the survey. One last item, try to find the history of the boat, quite a few 39s went into charter service.

On deck

The Cal 39 has a seagoing cockpit and to some that is not a compliment. There is no denying that with its substantial bridgedeck and short seats separated from the helm station that it is small, especially by today's standards. However, the tradeoff is that classic argument that smaller is safer, it holds less water in dirty weather and a smaller cockpit results in a more spacious interior. It is also efficiently laid out, that is if the traveler has been moved to a posi-

tion over the companionway. There is good visibility from the slightly raised helm seat and the winches can be reached from the helm.

There is a locker to port and one aft, which had been converted to a gas locker on the 1979 model I climbed through in Fort Lauderdale. The companionway is offset to starboard to make room in the aft cabin, but not to a degree to make it dangerous when heeling.

The side decks are wide, although the nonskid is likely well worn. If you are considering painting the deck you will need to apply nonskid to the paint. There are teak grabrails along the coachroof and the stanchions and lifelines seem well supported. A teak toerail looks great when it is varnished or freshly oiled, but it is a pain to maintain, especially because an outer headsail track is mounted on top of it. An inner track on deck allows for close sheeting angles. Most boats have double anchor rollers forward and a shallow external chain locker. The single-spreader spar is beefy and keel-stepped. Be sure to check the wire terminals on the standing rigging for cracks and crevice corrosion.

Down below

The Cal 39 interior is surprising. This was one of the first boats to feature an aft cabin in an aft-cockpit model. The port cabin is small but the two private staterooms were a real attraction when the boat was new and still is today. Despite a typical teak finish, the cabin is fairly bright with two or three large overhead hatches and eight portlights, most of them opening. However, many boats have plastic portlights, be wary of broken dogs and cracked frames.

The 39 MK III included a sink and large hanging locker in the aft cabin and some models came with an enclosed aft head at, unfortunately, the expense of the nav station. Personally I think a second head on a boat this size is a waste of space. The standard interior plan includes an L-shaped galley opposite the aft cabin, or in the case of the MK II, opposite the large quarterberth. The galley usually includes a three-burner stove and oven, large double sinks facing forward and a good-sized, 8-cubic-foot icebox.

The saloon has a settee and table to port and sea berth settee to starboard. The nav station is usually to port as well and features a decent sized chart table. Tanks take up much of the storage under the settees. The forward cabin is the owner's cabin with an en suite head, hanging locker and large V-berth. The head can also be accessed from the saloon. The original teak-and-holly cabin sole is not well supported and may need work.

Engine

As noted earlier, the Cal 39 came with a variety of engines and many have been repow-

ered. The original engine was the Perkins 4108, a 50-horsepower model that delivered about 30 horses at the prop, but that was enough to push the boat through the water at 6 knots. Fuel capacity is 45 gallons. Later engines include a Universal 44 and a 50-horsepower Pathfinder. Although I owned a boat with a Pathfinder and had little trouble, some 39 owners are not pleased with this marinized VW machine. Engine access is poor, from behind the companionway. One owner summed up this limitation succinctly, "That's why God made skinny people."

Underway

The Cal 39 is a very sweet sailing boat, at home in blue water or knocking about the bay. Many 39s have been retrofit into serious cruisers and owners rave about the seakindly motion and good turn of speed. The powerful hull shape can carry sail in a blow and can also be loaded up with stores without sacrificing too much performance. Owners report that the 39 needs a bit of a breeze to get moving. The narrow hull shape heels early and then stiffens up and also rolls running before a following sea. However, it also has enough oomph to surf when the conditions are right.

The boat is close winded, especially by cruising boat standards, and this is an underappreciated feature. This past summer in the Mediterranean found me hard on the wind seven days in 10, and I was thankful I had a fast, nimble boat. Most stodgy cruisers we encountered were steaming along under power.

Conclusion

The Cal 39 is an ideal boat to consider for long-range cruising, especially if your budget is under $70,000 and you need private accommodations but don't want to sacrifice good sailing.

Passport 40

*Sweet sailing cruiser designed for
comfortable world cruising*

Good things come to those who wait, or at least that's what my parents told me, and, worse still, that's what I tell my kids. Maybe it's even true. Take the Passport 40 for example. It has always been considered a top-quality bluewater boat, and now it is finally old enough to be considered a solid value as well. Designed by Robert Perry and built in Taiwan, the Passport 40 is well named, it is a boat that can punch your ticket to see the world. Yes, it's still pricey, an early to mid-1980s model will usually sell for somewhere between $120,000 to $160,000, but compare what that same money buys in a new, or even just a newer boat, and it isn't much of a comparison.

The Passport 40 was launched in 1980 and remained in production through 1991, with 148 boats built. Many have cruised extensively and all are still sailing. In some way, the Passport 40 and other similar vintage Perry designed cruisers trace their roots, or at least their basic underwater hull shapes, to the Valiant 40. Although not a double-ender like the Valiant, the

Passport 40 was considered a performance cruiser in its day. Although it is heavy by today's standards, it remains a nimble, easily handled boat that performs well in the trade winds for which it was designed. Perry's combination of a traditional style deck with a modified fin and skeg underbody produced a very successful formula for cruising boats.

Wendell Renken commissioned Perry's design and was the original developer and distributor of the Passport line, which eventually included models ranging from 37 feet to 52 feet. Renken was one of many Americans in Taiwan in those days, and in their own, less than subtle way, these Yanks helped lay the foundation for Taiwan's world-class boat-building industry. Today Passport yachts are manufactured and imported by Wagner Stevens Yachts in Annapolis. Thomas Wagner, who has been associated with Passport from the beginning, is a great source of information on all Passports.

First impressions

The Passport 40 is a handsome boat. I remember spotting an early model in the St. Martin lagoon almost 20 years ago. I hopped in the dinghy and rowed over and introduced myself. I just had to find out what kind of boat it was. The bow rakes gently aft and the reverse transom is broad—there is nothing harsh about Perry's lines. The beam is a moderate 12 feet, 8 inches. The coachroof extends well forward, in fact the foredeck is quite small, making it tough to stow a hard dinghy. The portlights are distinctive with two smaller bronze ports framing a longer one amidships.

Below the waterline a relatively deep forefoot trails into a powerful fin keel. As mentioned earlier, the rudder is skeg hung. I know this hull shape is outdated but I have logged

PASSPORT 40

LOA 39'5"
LWL 33'5"
Beam 12'8"
Draft 5'9"
Displacement
  22,771 lbs.
Ballast 8,500 lbs.
Sail Area
  771 sq. ft.

thousands of offshore miles with this type of keel and rudder arrangement and I have great confidence in it. Two keels were available, the standard draft is 5 feet, 9 inches while the shoal model slices all of 6 inches off the bottom of the keel. A sloop rig was standard, although almost all boats have been fitted with a staysail stay, usually the removable type. Part of the original design objective was to allow the boat to be sailed under main alone and be easily sailed singlehanded. Total working sail area is 771 square feet.

Construction

The hull is solid fiberglass, heavily layed up with layers of 24-ounce roving, 1.5-ounce mat and polyester resin. The Passport 40 predated the switch to blister preventing vinylester resins yet blisters do not seem to be much of a problem, even with boats that have toiled for years in the tropics. A look below the teak-and-holly cabin sole reveals stout transverse floors. The hull is further stiffened with longitudinal stringers. The iron ballast is encapsulated in the keel cavity. Lead would have been better but most Taiwan boats of this period used iron because it was more widely available and much cheaper.

Early boats had marine plywood cored decks. The plywood was cut into small sections and infused with resin around the edges. Later boats were cored with Airex foam. Most of the boats have or at least had teak side decks, which were a thick, five-eighths inch and applied with a lot of Thiokol. They're not the usual problem they are on other boats of this vintage. Some boats, especially later models, came with molded nonskid. The hull-and-deck joint is through-bolted on an inward flange and incorporates a raised bulwark. Bulkheads and furniture facings are securely fiberglassed to the hull. There is a lot of external teak besides the side decks, including handrails, eyebrows on the coachroof, and a lovely caprail. Also, the teak joinerwork below is exceptional.

What to look for

The prime reason the Passport 40 has held its value so well over the years is that it has aged

PASSPORT 40 PRICE DATA

		Low	High
BUC Retail Range	1984	$113,000	$124,000
	1986	$127,000	$139,500

		State	Asking
Boats For Sale	1981	CA	$125,000
	1983	MA	$144,000
	1986	NY	$154,500

very well. Another factor cannot be ignored. The Passport 40 has never been a cheap boat and in most cases owners have been able to afford the required maintenance and often lavished their boats with care. There are, however, a few specific items to watch for.

Teak decks are a mixed blessing. They look great and provide terrific nonskid when wet, but they are also a maintenance issue and a potential source of leaks from the myriad of fasteners that hold them in place. Be sure to have the decks carefully inspected although old Passport 40s rarely if ever turn up with delaminated subdecks.

Another area to check is the chainplates. A recent sale of an older 40 in Fort Lauderdale, Florida, revealed badly corroded chainplates during the survey. The chainplate covers are easily removed from the deck, and this is the first place to look. If the caulking is old or missing, probe the area further from down below. Like all boats more than 10 years old, the standing rigging should be carefully inspected, and if original, it should be replaced before heading offshore. The fuel tanks on early boats were made of black iron and were usually glassed over, which in theory stopped them from rusting from the outside in. Later boats had aluminum tanks.

The brightwork is a big job on a Passport 40 but it is also a big part of why the boat looks smart when all trimmed out. A boat whose brightwork has been let go might save you a few shekels, and although it's not expensive to bring the wood back into shape, don't underestimate the time and work required to

Passport 40

PRICE: Quality doesn't come cheap. However, with many boats 20-plus-years old, the price has become realistic.

 DESIGN QUALITY: Robert Perry hit the mark with this design. The Passport 40 handles well in a variety of conditions and is comfortable above and below deck.

CONSTRUCTION QUALITY: These boats are well engineered and very well built. Upgrades during the production run kept the quality high.

 **USER-FRIENDLINESS:** An easy and rewarding boat to sail for both bluewater veterans and new cruisers. The systems are well thought out and the interior is livable.

SAFETY: A seagoing cockpit, effective teak decks, a molded bulwark and well-placed handholds make the Passport 40 a safe boat on deck. The solid construction is the ultimate safety feature.

 **TYPICAL CONDITION:** Passport 40s have aged well and seem to be well cared for by previous owners, a combination that makes most boats on the used boat market in good shape.

REFITTING: The boat was designed with accessibility in mind. However, the original high level of craftsmanship means that you must find skilled workers to complete cosmetic jobs.

 SUPPORT: Thomas Wagner at Wagner Stevens Yachts is a font of knowledge about the boat. Visit the Web site at www.wagnerstevens.com. An active list serve can be found at www.Sailnet.com.

 **AVAILABILITY:** The production run of almost 150 boats means that there are always several Passport 40s for sale at any given time. The West Coast and the Chesapeake Bay seem to be where more boats are available.

 **INVESTMENT AND RESALE:** Although the initial price is steep, the Passport 40 holds its value well, especially today during these times of limited big boat production.

OVERALL 'SVG' RATING

---

prep teak and meticulously apply multiple layers of varnish.

On deck

The Passport 40 has a near ideal seagoing cockpit. It is comfortable for three or four people with wide seats and angled coamings that are nicely trimmed in teak. There is a stout bridgedeck and large drains should an errant wave or two crash aboard. There is a large locker to port. The standard 36-inch Epson destroyer wheel seems a bit undersized and the boat I examined in Palm Beach had a larger, teak-rimmed wheel that was lovely. Individual engine controls require reaching through the wheel to manipulate, I'd prefer a single-lever control on the pedestal base. The primary winches are positioned fairly far aft, allowing the helmsman to

trim the headsail without leaving the wheel. All other sail controls are led aft through a beefy coaming that provides a perfect base for the cockpit dodger. The mainsheet and traveler are just forward of the coaming, clearing space in the cockpit but still rigged far enough aft on the boom to provide good purchase.

The side decks are fairly wide and the molded bulwark lends security when going forward. The stanchion bases are vertically mounted for strength and overall the deck fittings are robust and top quality. I like the bronze fairleads that are fitted through the bulwark and caprail; they're handsome and practical. The mooring cleats are huge at 10 inches. Deck hatches were originally Atkins and Hoyle, later in the production run they were replaced by Lewmar hatches. A husky stainless steel stemhead fitting with a single anchor roller was standard along with a manual windlass. Many owners opted for the double roller and most boats will have upgraded to an electric windlass by now.

Down below

The interior of the Passport 40 is simply lovely. The woodwork is superb, from the solid teak staving on the bulkheads to the rounded joints fashioned into handholds in the galley and nav station. Remember, the rich teak finish coated with many layers of satin varnish makes for a fairly dark interior, however.

It is hard to generalize about the interior plan as each boat was more or less custom built. According to Wagner, about half of the Passport 40s came with a head-forward layout followed by a Pullman berth. The other half featured a traditional V-berth, followed by a head with a separate shower. Owners seem to favor the head-forward plan as it allows the forward hatch to be left open longer (a little spray in the head is no big deal, a little spray in your bunk is not nice) and pushes the bunk aft a bit, which is always more comfortable when sleeping underway.

The saloon has either a U-shaped or L-shaped settee draped around a lovely teak table. Some boats mount the table along the partial bulkhead dividing the galley, allowing it to fold up, creating a roomier saloon. There are lockers and bookshelves above and outboard of the settees. Thick, four-inch cushions were standard. The nav stations vary, usually they're opposite the galley to starboard and can be forward, aft or outboard facing. All boats feature a double quarter cabin aft. The large galley invariably includes two deep stainless sinks, a very well-insulated top loading icebox/refrigeration and a propane stove and oven.

Engine

The old reliable Perkins 4108 diesel was the original engine and you will still find them on some Passport 40s. Boats with the U-shaped settees usually feature the Perkins due to the clearance beneath the table, while boats with the L-shaped settee had Yammers, which were used on later boats. Either way access is terrific, and good access almost always translates into better maintenance. Parts are still widely available for the 4108 and it is an easy engine to work on. With that said, a boat with a quieter, more efficient Yammer would be preferred. The fuel tanks were originally black iron encased in fiberglass to prevent corrosion with a total capacity of 105 gallons. A three-bladed prop was standard but most boats on the market seem to have upgraded to a feathering propeller. According to several owners, performance under power is more than adequate, with 1,800 to 2,000 RPMs on the 4108 translating into 5 to 6 knots depending on conditions.

Underway

The sweet sailing characteristics of the Passport 40 just may be its most endearing feature. Almost all owners boast how well the boat handles. Words like "predictable," "swift" and "nimble" dominate their comments. Fast passages are de rigueur for Passport 40 sailors. They also speak highly of the soft ride, and as my readers know, I am always extolling the merits of an easy motion at sea. The less the boat works, the less the crew works, and the more enjoyable the passage.

Specifically, the Passport 40 sailplan allows it to make way in light going, but it really thrives when the wind perks up. Most owners report reefing the main at around 20 knots and others talk about the nice balance when the staysail is in use. The boat does not make much leeway and easing the traveler usually eliminates weather helm. For a cruising boat the Passport 40 is reasonable close winded. When conditions turn nasty, it is nice to be able to drop or roll in the headsail, set the staysail and carry on with a deeply reefed main. One owner noted how he skirted deadly Hurricane Mitch offshore and came through unscathed.

Conclusion

The Passport 40 is a world class cruising boat, equal parts rugged voyager and elegant yacht. It is a boat that you can be proud of and one that can carry you to any corner of the globe. Now that the price compares with a new 35-foot production boat, it's even affordable. It was worth the wait.

Pearson 40

*Lively offshore or thin-water cruiser
is one of this builder's best*

Pearson Yachts was one of the grand old sailboat companies, one of the founding fathers so to speak, of the fiberglass revolution that liberated sailboat manufacturers from the dictates of wooden planks and frames. In spite of the new material's potential for radical behavior, Pearson established its proud reputation by building solid, moderately proportioned boats that appealed to mainstream sailors. The legendary 28-foot Triton designed by Carl Alberg was Pearson's first success story. Many others followed, including the Bill Shaw-designed 30 that sold in record numbers, and many popular, if unspectacular cruisers including the 365 and 424. Occasionally, Pearson veered off course and produced innovative designs that caught the sailing public off guard. One was the Pearson Flyer, a 30-foot one-design rocketship that was just ahead of its time. Another was the Pearson 40.

When the P40 was introduced in 1977 it was loaded with features that broke the Pearson mold. The hull was balsa cored with a unique

whale-shaped underbody and a deep centerboard. The hull shape, which was similar to Ted Hood's centerboarders of the time, was a risky departure from form for Pearson. The deck, however, is the P40's most recognizable feature. Following the lead of the earlier Ericson 39 and Tartan 41, the P40 deck is genuinely flush. It looks racy, sexy and although the deck has proved utilitarian for cruising, it divided sailors into two camps when the boat first came out—either you loved the look or you didn't.

Unfortunately for Pearson, more people didn't and production was halted after four years with just 71 boats built. The short run, at least by Pearson standards, is a pity because Shaw, the designer and Pearson's general manager, lavished attention on the P40. Not only is the construction top rate, the interior finish is also better than most Pearsons. The P40 is one of those boats that has fallen through the cracks of the used boat market, and that can work to the advantage of the used boat buyer, especially if they are in the market for a lively cruising boat with a budget in the $50,000 to $60,000 range.

First impressions

Naturally the flush deck commands attention. There are those who simply love flush decks,

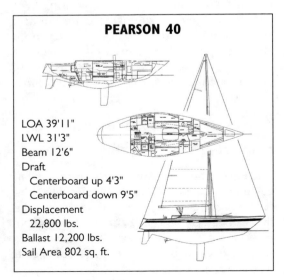

PEARSON 40

LOA 39'11"
LWL 31'3"
Beam 12'6"
Draft
   Centerboard up 4'3"
   Centerboard down 9'5"
Displacement
   22,800 lbs.
Ballast 12,200 lbs.
Sail Area 802 sq. ft.

and Chip Lawson counts himself among them. Lawson is an experienced sailor and the driving force behind the spirited P40 owner's association. "I am a flush-deck guy," he said. "From the day the boat was first introduced I knew I wanted to own a P40, it just took me awhile to pull it off."

While the deck is the signature feature, the unique underbody is what separates the P40 from other boats. Nearly round, there is a trace of a keel at the lowest point and the original rudder is mounted on a full skeg. The tendency is to think that stability has been compromised, but that is far from the case. The boat is fairly heavy, displacing nearly 23,000 pounds. Lead ballast of 12,200 pounds, or more than 50 percent, keeps the boat on its feet. The angle of positive stability is 129 degrees and that's a good number for offshore work. The board-up draft of just 4 feet, 3 inches opens up shallow cruising grounds that are normally off limits for 40-footers, emphasizing the versatility that devotees love. With an air draft of just under 60 feet the P40 carries 802 square feet of working sail, quite a bit more than the similar-sized Tartan and Ericson.

Construction

The P40 was one of the few boats that Pearson built with a cored hull. Like the earlier Tartan 41, the balsa coring was more of a hull stiffener than genuine core between thin layers of glass. The hull is heavily layed up, and although all boats are more than 20 years old, the hulls tend to be in good shape. Lawson, who has tracked down most P40 owners, notes that hull core problems are almost unheard of. Decks were also balsa cored and delamination problems are also rare. Materials were typical of the time, including polyester resin used throughout the laminating process.

The hull-and-deck joint is on an inward flange and is mechanically fastened through the toerail. Pearson did a good job of tabbing in bulkheads and other secondary bondings, and its fiberglass work was almost always of a good quality. The lead ballast is internal mounted in the small keel cavity. The centerboard trunk is also stashed away in the stub keel and as result does not protrude into the cabin.

PEARSON 40 PRICE DATA

BUC Retail Range		Low	High
	1979	$55,800	$61,200
	1981	$60,200	$66,200

Boats For Sale		State	Asking
	1979	NY	$49,500
	1980	CT	$59,000
	1981	TX	$64,900

What to look for

The first thing to look for is a boat with a new, MK II rudder, although it is unlikely that you will find one. This new rudder is a classic example of how an active owner's group can not only sustain interest in older boats but also dramatically improve them. The original rudder was frequently overloaded and at least one boat lost the rudder racing in the Pacific. Lawson and a group of owners approached designer Roger Marshall and he designed a new, partially balanced spade rudder. Dick Dowall has extensively sailed a P40. "The new rudder is very well balanced and eliminates the downwind, deep reaching IOR concerns of the pinched stern," he said.

Lawson added that the new rudder made a world of difference, as the rudder was really the only drawback to the way the boat handled. While only a few boats have opted for the new rudder so far, the owners' association Web site has plenty of information about the project.

Chainplate problems are also well documented and many boats have already replaced the originals with an updated design. There is an excellent illustration of how to retrofit new chainplates on the Web site. Up to hull No. 60 the boat had discontinuous standing rigging and some owners have opted to change to continuous wire, eliminating the need for extra terminals and turnbuckles aloft which are difficult to tune. The original Navtec turnbuckles should be replaced.

Another feature to look for is a P40 that has a converted transmission. The original en-

Pearson 40

 PRICE: Although the asking prices seem to be creeping up a bit, it is still possible to find a P40 for around $60,000, which is a very good buy.

 DESIGN QUALITY: The design is innovative, one of those boats that you love or hate. The whale bottom is not for everybody but the boat is well proven both on the ocean and nosing around in shallow water.

 CONSTRUCTION QUALITY: Pearson did a nice job with the P40 and overall construction is good. The balsa-cored hull does not seem to be a problem, although issues with rudder and chainplates need to be addressed.

 USER-FRIENDLINESS: Sails well with a small headsail and is easy to handle from the cockpit. The interior is comfortable and the boat is usually not overloaded with complicated systems.

 SAFETY: The deep cockpit is secure, if a bit cramped, and the flush deck is safe in heavy weather, although the handholds require crouching or crawling when going forward. There are plenty of handholds below, and the centerboard does not compromise structural integrity.

 **TYPICAL CONDITION:** Most boats on the used market seem to have been well cared for, although even the youngest P40 is more than 20 years old.

 REFITTING: Although bigger boats usually cost more to refit, oftentimes the job is easier due to better access. Common projects include upgrading the transmission and updating the rudder.

 **SUPPORT:** Although Pearson is out of business, the huge National Pearson Yacht Owners' Association can be found at www.pearsoncurrent.com. Better yet, the Pearson 40 Owner's Association, at www.pearson40.org is loaded with useful information and photos. Class President Chip Lawson is a font of knowledge and eager to share what he knows about the boat.

 AVAILABILITY: This rating is a mixed bag, if boats are not available it is because owners like to hang on to their boats—a negative for used boat buyers. Unfortunately, only 71 boats were built.

 INVESTMENT AND RESALE: The P40 has held its value well over the years. The cost of upgrades can be expensive but that's the case with many used boats.

 **OVERALL 'SVG' RATING**

---

gine, a 37-horsepower Westerbeke 40 included a Paragon transmission and a V-drive gear. I am no fan of V-drives in general, but according to Lawson, the Walters V-drive is not the problem; the Paragon transmission is.

"The switch to a more robust and more reliable Borg Warner Velvet Drive is not difficult, and if you buy a rebuilt gear, it's not all that expensive—definitely worth the trouble," Lawson said.

On deck

Like most boats of this era, the pinched stern dictated by the IOR rule results in a fairly narrow cockpit. Still, the deep cockpit is more than adequate for cruising with long

seats and large lockers. The wheel is placed well forward, another one of those design features that you either like or don't, although you can't deny that the visibility is terrific. Dowall, who sailed with his wife from their homeport of Newport, Rhode Island, to the Caribbean and back a few years ago, clearly likes the arrangement. "The wheel forward makes short-handed sailing a dream," he said. "Access to winches, sheets, halyards and the instruments is great. Also, the helmsman can steer from under the dodger if need be."

The flush deck makes going forward easy and offers a friendly platform for sail handling. It is also ideal for dinghy stowage and lounging about in fair weather. In heavy weather, however, you have to bend over to reach the teak handrails that are mounted well inboard. Stanchions and double lifelines are well supported. The mainsheet traveler is mounted forward of the companionway with a midboom sheeting arrangement. Most boats are set up with inboard and outboard headsail tracks. The double-spreader spar is a beefy section and keel stepped. Many boats will have updated deck gear, and if you find a boat with self-tailing winches consider it a nice perk.

Down below

Unlike the innovative hull and deck designs, the interior plan is straightforward. A decent sized V-berth cabin is forward with a small dressing seat and plenty of storage. The head is next aft to port with a hanging locker and a bureau opposite. The saloon includes a drop-leaf centerline table that accommodates six and pilot berths with built-in leeboards. It is hard to resist not turning these berths into storage areas but they do make excellent sea berths, up and out of the traffic flow. The settees are a bit stiff backed but they do slide out to make comfortable berths.

The U-shaped galley is to starboard and includes double stainless sinks and the stove with oven located outboard. There is ample counter space, useful fiddles and a huge fridge. The surfaces are covered with Formica. There are numerous lockers for food and utensil storage behind the stove and facing aft, in fact, the amount of storage throughout the P40 is impressive.

A large navigation station is opposite the galley. The desk can accommodate a full-sized chart with storage below. There is also space to mount instruments and repeaters on the partial bulkhead. A small quarterberth is aft, which has been converted to storage on most boats.

The interior is nicely finished with mahogany and ash. In his designer remarks Shaw is effusive in his praise of the joiner-work and overall finish, claiming, "the interior of the 40 is my proudest achievement." The 6-foot, 3-inch headroom is surprising considering the flush deck and it is not as dark below as one might suspect. Several overhead hatches and sidelights provide light and decent ventilation.

Engine

The standard engine was the Westerbeke 40, a 37-horsepower diesel, but some boats came with a 4107/4108 Perkins, which is comparable in horsepower. The placement of the engine requires a V-drive transmission, making accessing the stuffing box a challenge. The P40 is a candidate for a dripless stuffing box.

Many owners consider the boat underpowered. Dowall puts a new, larger engine on his wish list, but notes that the Westerbeke is good on fuel consumption at 1,800 rpm, which translates into a 600-mile-plus motoring range. Lawson claims that the addition of a feathering-type propeller improves performance. This is especially helpful in reverse, as V-drives are notorious for poor performance when working astern.

Underway

Both Lawson and Dowall comment on how easily driven the P40 is and how a large, overlapping genoa is not necessary in most conditions, at least for cruising purposes. The high-aspect-ratio main combined with a working jib or small, fairly high-cut genoa keeps the boat moving smartly. Lawson sails with a yankee and several boats, including the Dowall's Endeavor have been converted to cutters.

Lawson notes the boat is a touch tender and he usually ties the first reef in the main when the apparent wind nears 20 knots. The boat is quick and fairly close winded although the centerboard needs to be deployed to track well. The full board-down draft is 9 feet, 5 inches although it can be partially lowered in shallow water or for trim. Off the wind, especially with the board up, the P40 flies, although like many IOR boats it can be squirrely running before big seas. The Mark II rudder improves downwind steering dramatically.

Lawson recently sailed his boat around the bottom of Florida from Tampa to Melbourne and encountered a variety of conditions. He was impressed with how well the boat handled rugged conditions in the Gulf Steam.

"The wind was gusting to 30 knots from the northeast with nasty steep seas, you know, the square waves found only in the Gulf Stream. The boat did great. The crew, on the other hand, needed a break," he said.

The Pearson 40 has completed numerous offshore passages, including at least one transpacific run.

Conclusion

The Pearson 40 is an intriguing boat. It is comfortable and offshore capable and yet the centerboard design allows for gunkholing in the thinnest of waters. It is an ideal boat for my local cruising grounds, the Bahamas and Florida Keys. With asking prices usually around $60,000 the boat is a terrific value. Be warned, used P40s do not linger on the used boat market.

Venezia 42

Nicely designed former charter cat turned family cruiser

We were nearly 100 miles off the coast of North Carolina when the ugly front moved offshore and walloped us. I was delivering a Venezia 42 cruising catamaran from Martha's Vineyard to her home base in West Palm Beach, Florida. Appropriately named NEXT WAVE, I knew the boat well having logged more than 5,000 offshore miles on biannual north-to-south deliveries. Still, I had not encountered a genuine, spray in the face, heart in your hand, Force 9 gale and was apprehensive about how the boat would respond. Primarily a monohull sailor, I suspected the worst.

The winds blasted us from the northeast and then veered to southwest. We were obliged to pound into wild, confused 15- to 20-foot seas, difficult conditions for any boat to handle. I was pleasantly surprised. Rather, I was shocked to discover that with just a deeply reefed main the Venezia was able to forereach effectively, comfortably bobbing along on top of the water instead of plunging into it. Making

way at 3 or 4 knots at 60 degrees off the wind, we rode out the storm without much stress.

There was slamming between the hulls as the rush hour water raced by and we made a bit of leeway, but I never doubted the Venezia's integrity. In fact, with the autopilot in control we were able to stand our watches from inside the saloon staying warm and dry while enjoying the drama outside through the large aft facing windows and forward ports. It was almost like watching an IMAX film!

Although there are many claims as to just who is responsible for launching the cruising catamaran revolution, few dispute that the French were the first to tool up and build big cats as production boats. Fountaine Pajot was one of the early players, launching its first cruising catamaran in 1983, the 37-foot Louisiane. The boat's surprising popularity convinced Fountaine Pajot to concentrate on building catamarans instead of the 420s, 470s and IOR prototypes that had previously been the backbone of its factory near La Rochelle. The 44-foot Casamance in 1985 was in many ways the forerunner of today's cruising cats. The hulls were expanded for more interior space and daggerboards were exchanged for less efficient but trouble-free fixed keels, or winglets.

The Venezia was launched in 1992 and remained in production until the Bahia 43 came on line in 2000. Nearly 200 Venezias were built and most went directly into charter service. These boats have done their duty and many are now available on the used boat market. A quick search on **yachtworld.com** turned up more than 20 boats, ranging in price from $180,000 to more than $270,000 for a nonchartered owner's version. Expensive, yes, however, when you compare those prices to new cruising cats, the value, even for a tired, ex-charter boat becomes obvious.

VENEZIA 42

LOA 42'
LWL 41'
Bridgedeck Length 27'3"
Beam 23'
Draft 3'11"
Displacement 14,960 lbs.
Sail Area 978 sq. ft.

First impressions

The Venezia caused quite a stir when it was introduced at the Paris boat show. Not only was the basic design quite futuristic looking—some say it looked like a spacecraft—but designers Joubert and Nivelt included the now famous visor. This feature, which has become a Fountaine Pajot trademark, extends the coachroof beyond the forward portlights, sheltering the saloon from the sun without restricting visibility or light while creating a very sleek cabin profile.

The Venezia is not a light boat, at least not by multihull standards. The dry displacement is nearly 15,000 pounds. This is a genuine cruising catamaran and can carry a bit of load without immediately immersing the hulls and destroying performance. The hulls have a narrow entry and the bows are nearly plumb, the waterline length is 41 feet. The substantial bridgedeck is just over 27 feet long, giving the boat a feeling of rigidity and accounting for some of the weight.

Bridgedeck clearance is around 2 feet, however, in a seaway there is a lot of dynamic water action between the hulls and a fair bit of slamming. The two fixed keel stubs have a draft of just less than 4 feet and the working sail area is 968 square feet. The fractional rig includes a big, roachy, full-batten mainsail.

Construction

The Venezia's hulls are a sandwich construction with vacuum bagged PVC foam cores. The outer skins are hand-laid fiberglass with isophthalic polyester resin. The core is then bonded with regularly spaced couplers, linking the two skins into a single, sturdy unit. From the beginning Fountaine Pajot used isophthalic gelcoats on the hull and decks to prevent osmosis. Overall, the fiberglass sculpting is superb, the boat is filled with compound curves and yet you almost never see a stress crack. The molded nonskid is intricate and effective. A stout aluminum thwart supports the hulls forward with a channel running aft between the trampolines as a lead for the ground tackle.

Many of the interior components are molded composites, a practical production technique but the result, at least cosmetically, is a somewhat sterile look down below. The interior

VENEZIA 42 PRICE DATA

		Low	High
BUC Retail Range	1993	$169,000	$186,500
	1997	$221,000	$243,000

		State	Asking
Boats For Sale	1993	Caribbean	$200,000
	1994	MD	$229,000
	1997	Mediterranean	$286,000

is trimmed with mahogany panels but multihull builders are always battling the weight issue seeking better performance by keeping off the extra pounds. Eliminating copious amounts of heavy joinerwork is often the first step.

What to look for

The first thing to look for is the cabin arrangement that you want. Most Venezias have four double cabins and two heads. Some have fitted the forwardmost sections of each hull with single berths, bringing the total number of private cabins to six. This is a dead giveaway that the boat was chartered as the two extra berths often served as crew quarters. The two aft cabins feature athwartship doubles while the forward cabins have fore and aft doubles. The rare owner's version will have converted one of these cabins into an office, and when you see this arrangement it's a tip off that the boat might well have been privately owned.

Most Venezias you inspect will be ex-charter boats and that is why the boat is affordable, at least by cruising cat standards. Look for normal signs of wear and tear and factor in new fabric and possibly foam for all cushions, which is not an inexpensive retrofit item.

Be wary of high hours on the Yanmar diesels, they are not very convenient to work on, although since they are saildrives they are easy to pull out and replace. Of course, you are talking about two engines, one in each hull, and that conveniently doubles the price. Be sure to check for excessive corrosion on the saildrives and carefully inspect the seals and small cooling filters.

Venezia 42

PRICE: Prices have finally started dropping as more cruising cats hit the market. Still, dollar for dollar, big cats are more expensive than comparable monohulls.

DESIGN QUALITY: The futuristic design still looks good and the boat is seaworthy and comfortable. It is not as swift as other less "cruising/chartering" oriented cats.

CONSTRUCTION QUALITY: Nicely built, these boats have proven themselves in charter fleets the world over, and that is tough duty.

USER-FRIENDLINESS: The boat is well set up for shorthanded sailing and powers brilliantly. The cockpit however can be difficult to see from and at times you find yourself looking through the ports even in the cockpit.

SAFETY: It is not fair to compare cruising cats to either performance multihulls or monohulls, they stand alone and have an impressive track record. The sliding doors aft and poorly designed escape hatches compromise safety.

TYPICAL CONDITION: Considering that most boats have been chartered hard and put away wet, this is an impressive rating. There isn't much cosmetic change, however be alert for high hours on the engines—repowering two engines is expensive.

REFITTING: Although it's an easy boat to work on, it has French idiosyncrasies that can be maddening. Still, as a lover of wine I refuse to jump on the bandwagon and bash the French.

SUPPORT: There is not a lot of support from the factory and there is not an active owner's association. One good source of information is John Sykes at TwoHulls in Fort Lauderdale at www.twohulls.com.

AVAILABILITY: There are always Venezias on the market and if you are willing to consider traveling to exotic charter destinations you can make great buys. I know of a boat for sale in the Seychelles that might sell for $150,000.

INVESTMENT AND RESALE: These boats have held their value very well during the past 10 years and with new boat prices so high I suspect they will continue to do so into the future.

 OVERALL 'SVG' RATING

Pay particular notice to the escape hatches located in each head. These hatches, which allow you to "escape" in the unlikely event of a capsize, protrude beyond the hulls and take a beating from the wave action. They often leak and the completely inadequate plastic handles and latches have often been over tightened. We had a dangerous situation when one of these hatches gave way and we had to lash it in place with a broom handle. Also check the lashings on the forward trampolines, especially if the nets seem droopy.

On deck

The deck and cockpit are simply huge and as you make your way about the boat you quickly realize that 42 feet of LOA times 23 feet of beam adds up to a lot acreage. The Venezia's wraparound cockpit can comfortably seat more people than you should ever have on a boat at one time. Although I must confess, on a long passage the shallow seats and fairly straight backs can leave you longing for a more traditional cockpit. There is usually a large table to port and plenty of storage space in the aft lockers and under the sole. The bulkhead-mounted helm is perched to starboard, with a fighting-chair-style helmsman's seat. The arrangement is definitely better suited for basketball players and almost unmanageable for short people. Each hull has wide swim steps for easy water access and also for hopping into the dinghy. Most boats have dinghy davits as well.

The mainsheet traveler runs the entire width of the cockpit, along the aft coaming, a great feature for trimming the powerful main. All other sail controls are led aft, usually to the port side coachroof. Fountaine Pajot used good quality deck hardware and sailing gear and most boats will have a combination of Lewmar and Goiot fittings.

Roller furling was standard on the headsail with slab reefing on the main. Standing rigging consists of a single upper, with jumpers, and partial backstays that make it difficult to pay out the boom. There are two deck lockers forward, although the placement of the water tank limits storage.

The trampolines are a terrific place to sprawl out and relax, both at anchor and under way. I fondly remember an hour spent watching a pod of gamboling dolphins race between the hulls. I was stretched out on the tramps, the autopilot was driving and, as Dave Barry would say, "I am not making this up," one of the crew was playing the guitar and singing— I swear.

Down below

The Venezia has the classic "galley up" arrangement in multihull speak. You enter the saloon through sliding glass doors—there is really no other way to describe them. The galley is to port and usually includes a two-burner stove, single sink and small front-loading 12-volt fridge. In typical French fashion, the galley works well despite limited counter space. (By the way, there are no fiddles because there's no heeling.)

There is storage for pots and pans below while provisions are usually stashed under the settee cushions. A large oval table is to port with a wraparound settee. The nav station is also to port, with a partial bulkhead serving as a base for repeaters and instruments on one side and the less than state-of-the-art electrical panel on the other.

The two aft cabins include a large hanging locker and storage with drawers below. Many similarly sized cruising cats locate the engines beneath these berths. By placing the engines in aft lazarettes, Joubert and Nivelt created a lot more storage space and improved the quality of life when motoring—the noisy beast is not right beneath your bed. The heads are about amidships in each hull and are not particularly roomy. Some owner versions have converted one head to a dedicated shower.

The forward staterooms have berths running the entire width of the hull with smaller hanging lockers inboard. The areas forward are good for storing light gear, fenders, etc., unless they have been set up as sleeping quarters. Either way, main access is through a hatch on deck. We used these cabins for our cooks when we chartered two catamarans in Belize a few years ago. Incidentally, seven people were aboard a Venezia for eight days without any sense of crowding.

Engine

The Venezia is powered by twin Yanmars. Most boats will have 28-horsepower models, although a fairly common upgrade or retrofit was to go with the three-cylinder 37-horsepower 3GM. Access is at the bottom of the lazarette, which is convenient unless of course anything is stored in the lazarette. Once the locker has been emptied and the wooden hatches opened access is still limited. At least with saildrives you don't need access to a stuffing box and stern tube. The batteries and main switches are usually in the port lazarette.

Handling a cat with twin screws is a true pleasure, especially for traditional monohull sailors who have spent years trying to con their heavy, unwieldy, long-keeled boats in and out of marinas. With a screw in each hull it is possible to make the Venezia turn in its own length. Although there is some skill required to operate twin screws, once you get the hang of it you'll love it. Fuel capacity is around 90 gallons in two tanks, which translates into 45 gallons per engine, or about 60 hours of motoring. We motored long stretches on one delivery up the coast and it was not uncommon to steam along at 8 knots at moderate rpms in smooth water.

Underway

The first time you sail a heavily loaded cruising catamaran you just might be disappointed. Not that there is anything wrong with the way they sail, they are just not as fast as you might expect. On three round trips up and down the coast, we averaged about 150 miles of non-current miles a day, or about 6 knots. At times we zipped along in low double digits and at other times we labored upwind at 5 knots. One feature that almost everyone loves is the lack of heeling. A feature of the Venezia that isn't as loveable is the quick motion in a chop and the slamming of water ricocheting between the hulls.

We were always able to carry more sail than I expected and by the time I brought the boat back south for the last time I realized I didn't need to reef the main until the wind was nearly 20 knots. The boat sails upwind well with a flat, high-cut 105-percent No. 3. Overlapping genoas are not worth the trouble, it is far more efficient to pop the asymmetrical chute as soon as the wind opens up. One passage north we flew the chute day and night for three days and kept the boat moving smartly despite light airs.

Conclusion

I like the Venezia very much and I would strongly consider buying one if I were in the market for a cruising catamaran. It is a terrific family cruiser, well built and a solid financial value. I suspect my daughters would like having their "own side" of the boat. And keeping your gin and tonic upright when sailing is not a bad selling feature either.

Beneteau First 456

A sturdy cruiser that will offer performance for years to come

The Beneteau First 456 is one of the largest boats we've profiled in the *Used Boat Notebook* column and I think one of the best values. Designed by the prolific, versatile and immensely talented German Frers, the 456 began life as a powerful, ocean-racing machine, racking up wins in most major offshore races during the early and mid-1980s. While many ex-racing boats seem dreadfully outdated at age 20, a fate that I suspect awaits some of today's uncompromising designs, the 456 has gracefully aged into a capable and comfortable performance cruiser that can still surprise around the buoys, especially if it is blowing.

Beneteau launched the First Series in 1979 with the sleek, ultra modern Jean Berret designed 30. Although it seems passé today, Beneteau should have patented the term "performance cruiser," as the First Series turned out to be quite successful both as racers and later as cruisers. Berret followed up the 30 with the First 38, and Frers delivered designs for a 42 and the 456. The 456 was launched in 1983 and remained in production for four years. Hundreds of boats were built and many were sold in the United States. Other 456s were sailed across the pond and remained on this side of the Atlantic. A recent quick search on **Yachtworld.com** revealed more than a dozen 456s for sale in the United States and Canada.

First impressions

Forty-five feet is about the ideal length for the angular, hard-edged look that came to represent most First Series boats, and in some ways helped set the stage for the shape of yacht design that continues today. While the smaller boats in the series tend to look clipped and ungraceful, Frers really hit the mark with the 456. The bow is nicely raked and although the overhang might be slower than today's snub-nosed, waterline-stretching stems, it sure is handsome. The sheer is relatively flat but the long run of the hull and moderate freeboard makes the straight line visually appealing. The sleek cabintrunk slopes to meet to the deck just forward of the mast. The broad reverse transom predates the stern step phenomenon.

Below the waterline the 456 has a deep, and I do mean deep, high aspect fin keel. The standard draft is 7 feet, 11 inches and that translates into 8 feet-plus when loaded for cruising. Fortunately, many boats that were sold in the United States had the optional 6 foot, 3 inch shoal draft.

The rudder is a balanced spade and positioned well aft, offering good steering control in most conditions. A close inspection of the underwater profile reveals one of the 456's best characteristics. Unlike other performance boats of this era, the 456 is not a pounder, and it won't knock your fillings out when sailing upwind.

The forefoot has more bite to it than today's Farr-designed First Series boats, and while the hull shape is still plenty fast, it isn't as flat or as prone to lifting out of the water and slamming back down. Motion is probably the most important factor in cruising boat design and one the least discussed and most

BENETEAU FIRST 456

LOA 46'1"
LWL 39'5"
Beam 14'1"
Draft (Standard) 7'11"
Draft (Shoal) 6'3"
Displacement 26,561 lbs.
Ballast 10,340 lbs.
Sail Area 970 sq. ft.

abused by designers. The designed ballast-to-displacement ratio of 45 percent helps account for the 456's stiffness in strong breezes.

Construction

Beneteau blends production efficiency with traditional construction techniques to build affordable and strong boats that have proven themselves on countless ocean crossings. In fact, it's safe to say that more Beneteaus have crossed the Atlantic on their own bottoms than any other boat. With that said, I confess to having mixed feelings about the partial molded liners that Beneteau uses as a structural grid system. The 456 liner is just a couple feet high and contains molded floors and longitudinals that stiffen the hull. The liner is then fiberglassed to the hull, in essence creating a hull within a hull. The system works; Beneteaus have reported few structural problems over the years. In fact, at a recent Annapolis Boat Show the Beneteau sales people were tossing around the figure of 5 million sea miles logged by Beneteaus. Heck, they're catching up to McDonalds! Still, liners do limit access to and can potentially come adrift of the hull.

The 456 hull is solid fiberglass and relatively thick. The deck is balsa cored and the hull joint incorporates the aluminum toerail. Many 456s came with teak decks, a feature that I would try to avoid when shopping for a used boat. Beneteau has always done a nice job of fiberglass sculpting and the 456 deck mold is intricate. Gelcoat cracking and crazing is rare and the molded nonskid seems to hold up well.

The iron keel is externally fastened with stainless bolts supported by a molded in backing plate. The nuts are then covered with resin slurry, which is not a good idea. The rudder stock is stainless steel and the quadrant is aluminum. The mast is keel stepped. Bulkheads are tabbed in place and supported by the liner. The joinery work is surprisingly nice, and the overall engineering reflects the fact that Beneteau has built a lot of boats over the years; they know what works and what doesn't.

What to look for

The first thing to look for is a First 456 without teak decks. While teak decks are undeni-

BENETEAU FIRST 456 PRICE DATA

		Low	High
BUC Retail Range	1984	$ 73,500	$ 79,700
	1987	$ 89,700	$ 98,600

		State	Asking
Boats For Sale	1983	FL	$117,000
	1985	MD	$105,000
	1986	Mediterranean	$145,000

ably handsome, they are a chore to maintain and a source of problems. Unfortunately, teak decks were actually standard for much of the production run so many 456s have them. Also, check the deck carefully for signs of delamination, especially around the chainplates. Water damage to the bulkhead below is often a sign that the chainplates are leaking.

The early First Series boats were hard hit by the dreaded pox that swept through the industry in the 1980s. Beneteau, unlike most builders, had the wherewithal to do the right thing and told owners to take their boat to the yard, have a complete bottom job done and send them the bill. The result was that Beneteau established an impressive reputation in this country and almost all their boats had professional blister jobs done.

If you find a 456 that has been re-powered, usually with a four-cylinder Yanmar, consider it a plus. The original engine, likely the venerable Perkins 4108, is tough and reliable but just doesn't provide enough horsepower for a boat that displaces around 25,000 pounds when loaded for cruising. Some boats came with the 56-horsepower Perkins 4154 and others with a 60-horsepower Pathfinder diesel by Volkswagen. Another potential problem is with the keel bolts. Some owners have reported keel bolt leaks or gaps in the keel-to-hull joint. I would suggest a careful inspection before deciding upon a repair. If you do have to drop the keel, it is a big job, not least of which is breaking up the resin that covers each bolt. Also, some owners report problems with the rudder bearings, especially if the boat had been out of the water for a long time. Other less serious but

Beneteau First 456

PRICE: The First 456 is terrific value in a large performance cruiser. You should be able to find a clean model for less than $120,000. By way of comparison, see what $120,000 buys at a new boat show.

DESIGN QUALITY: The Frers design blends a performance hull with spacious accommodations. It is also quite seaworthy. The 8-foot draft will be a problem for many U.S. sailors.

CONSTRUCTION QUALITY: Beneteau's record speaks for itself, their boats have more ocean crossings than any other. Still, some production efficiencies, including the use of hull liners, are less than ideal.

USER-FRIENDLINESS: For a big, performance-oriented boat, the 456 is relatively easy to handle. Most sail controls can be reached from the helm. Runners are a bit of a pain.

SAFETY: A stout bridge deck and plenty of handholds below are safety features. Low and not overly stout lifelines and stanchions could be better.

TYPICAL CONDITION: The 456s on the used market are in surprisingly good shape, especially since many had former lives when they were campaigned hard.

REFITTING: As is the case with many production boats, refitting is tougher because of the use of liners and other construction efficiencies that make later refits more complicated.

SUPPORT: The Beneteau owner's group, at www.beneteau-owners.com, has a lot of useful information and dialog among owners. The Beneteau USA site, www.beneteauusa.com, has data about all models.

AVAILABILITY: Hundreds of 456s were built and many are for sale on this side of the Atlantic. If you include Europe and the Caribbean in your search, availability goes up to 5.

INVESTMENT AND RESALE: The 456 has held its value well over the years and should continue to do so into the future. The boat is a solid value in the marketplace.

OVERALL 'SVG' RATING

---

annoying problems include drooping fabric hull liners and original French electrical systems that were undersized.

On deck

The 456 cockpit is deceptively large, moderately comfortable and safe in heavy seas. In fact, the substantial bridgedeck makes it somewhat of a gymnastics maneuver to get below, especially if a dodger is rigged. Lewmar winches were standard, and most 456s, even the early ones, came with self-tailing primaries.

The foredeck includes a double bow roller and a large, divided, external chain locker that can house serious ground tackle. The pulpits, stanchions and lifelines are a bit on the light side. The genoa tracks are inboard for tight sheeting angles and many boats have a load bearing, adjustable system lead to the cockpit.

This feature is really useful on large boats, especially with a roller furling headsail that requires frequent lead changes. Isomat spars were standard and the standing rigging is beefy. Most 456s are set up with running backstays to keep the mast from pumping. Owners have mixed feelings on whether or not the boat needs them.

Down below

The 456 came with a variety of interior layouts. The forward cabin plan might include two doubles to port and starboard, with upper and under berths, or a pullman double berth with a vanity and writing desk opposite. In either arrangement the head is forward. The aft cabin plan features either two quarter-cabins, with small double berths, or a single, owner's cabin with a full-sized double. Boats that went into charter service often had the four-cabin arrangement. However, the most popular plan includes two doubles forward and the single owner's cabin aft. My friend Steve Maseda just purchased a 1984 456 with the pullman cabin forward and the owner's cabin aft, and unless you need a lot of small staterooms, this is the most desirable plan for cruising.

The saloon features wraparound settees and seating for eight at a centerline table with fold-out leaves. Most boats have pilot berths. The water tanks are under the settees, limiting storage space, however the shallow bilge leaves little choice when it comes to tank placement. The large nav station is to starboard and the L-shaped galley is opposite. The galley usually includes a three-burner stove/oven, double stainless sinks and a poorly insulated icebox compartment with 12-volt refrigeration.

Engine

The standard engine was the Perkins 4108, which is the same engine Beneteau used in both the First 38 and First 42. It is not uncommon to find a re-powered 456, so be sure to check the installation carefully. The standard prop was a small two-bladed model, which didn't help performance under power but did reduce drag under sail. Engine access is adequate from behind the companionway and through the aft cabins. The 55-gallon, stainless steel fuel tank is located forward of the engine. Like most fin and spade boats, the 456 handles well in reverse once you gather way on.

Although the 4108 is a bit small for the 456, don't necessarily assume the engine has to be replaced, even if it has high hours. The 456 is easily driven under sail, and motoring is required only in the calm conditions.

Performance

"It's all about performance," Maseda says, "even in a cruising boat. I am not looking to

win races but sailing is so much more enjoyable when the boat is performing at an optimal level." Maseda has owned an interesting assortment of boats, including a Melges 24, an Olson 30 and a Gulfstar 50 that he took a year-long sabbatical aboard with his family 10 years ago. "I am ready to go cruising again, but my years in sport boats has spoiled me, I need some speed."

The 456 should deliver the speed he's looking for and still provide enough creature comforts to make long-term cruising enjoyable. The 456 sails best when kept on her lines; the mantra "flat is fast" applies. However, the boat is set up for large, overlapping headsails so sometimes it's impossible not to bury the rail. The powerful masthead sloop is in its element close reaching, and according to owner Walker Montgomery, speeds of 8-plus knots are easy to attain if there isn't much of a sea running. Montgomery, who sails his 456 out of Galveston Bay, says that the boat handles well running and reaching, even in heavy seas in the Gulf of Mexico.

Montgomery finds that his 135-percent roller furling headsail provides the versatility needed for most conditions. An alternative to a roller furling headsail is essential for serious cruising and a good option is the Gale Sail, available through ATN Inc. Maseda recently sailed from Tarpon Springs to Bradenton off Florida's Gulf Coast. He covered 35 miles in just over five hours. "The winds were moderate and I was impressed with how nice the boat moved through the water," he said. The helm was light and easily balanced. I think I am going to like this boat."

Conclusion

The Beneteau First 456 is an excellent choice for a performance oriented cruiser with spacious accommodations. Prices range from around $100,000 for an older model that might have been a charter boat, to $140,000 for a clean owner's model. Anyway you look at it, the 456 delivers a lot of boat for the money.

Irwin 52

The boat that started the deck-saloon revolution

The Irwin 52 was a trend-setting boat. It was a deck-saloon cruiser before there were deck-saloon cruisers. What's more, the Irwin 52, with more than 250 hulls launched, may be the most popular big boat, 50-foot-plus, ever built. These beamy ketch-rigged cruisers offered no apologies for their motoryacht-like interior accommodations, spacious cockpit, wide side decks and raised bulwarks. It boasts of good performance under power as well as sail. Hmm, come to think of it, those features sound awfully familiar? When you take a look at many of today's larger cruising boats, it seems that Ted Irwin was a visionary.

Ironically, the Irwin 52 has a better reputation today, 30 years after it was first introduced, than it did when new. Ted Irwin was an enigma in the industry. He was a designer, builder and world-class sailor, and during the early 1980s, his company was the largest privately owned sailboat firm in the country. He sold a lot of boats, especially big boats. Irwin claims to have built more sailboats longer than 50 feet than anyone in the world. Still, despite his consistently innovative designs, his company garnered a reputation for producing cheap boats. Ask sailors who came of age in the 1970s and 1980s what they think of Irwins and they'll likely scowl.

However, time has shown that some complaints about Irwin's quality have turned out to be spurious. Older Irwins, especially the larger models, are in high demand on the used market. "If you can find a Series II 52 for a good price, even after totally refitting the boat, you'll make money," said Gene Gammons. Gammons knows of what he speaks. These days he is a yacht broker but previously he was the project manager for the Irwin 52 and his Web site, www.irwinyachts.com, provides a wealth of information about all Irwin models. He worked side-by-side with Irwin for years.

Launched in 1976, the Irwin 52 caught the sailing world off guard, suddenly it was possible to own your own small ship. While many 52s were employed as crewed charter boats there is no denying that privately owned models started the shift toward larger cruising boats.

IRWIN 52

LOA 56'
LWL 44'
Beam 15'4"
Draft
  Centerboard
    up 5'6"
  Centerboard
    down 12'6"
Displacement
  46,000 lbs.
Ballast
  16,000 lbs.
Sail Area
  1,421 sq. ft.

First impressions

The Irwin 52 has plenty of freeboard and a moderate sheer accentuated by a rakish bowsprit. The raised aft deck irked purists, who still existed in the 1970s, but provided plenty of headroom for the luxurious aft cabin, and along with the wide cove stripe, became something of a 52 trademark. It does take some getting used to when navigating the big step on deck, especially in the dark with lumpy seas. The cabintrunk includes large side and forward facing ports that flood the interior with light. I remember the dire warnings we experts issued about taking "big windows" offshore. Today most sailors can't get enough of the deck-saloon concept.

Although Irwin knew that he had to build cruising boats if he wanted to stay in business, his heart was always in performance boats. The 52 sports a generous rig with more than 1,350 square feet of working sailing area. The underbody is refined with a cutaway long keel and a partially balanced rudder. The 52 moves under sail. Indeed, with its long 44-foot waterline it reaches along at 8 knots steadily. I have logged a lot of miles delivering 52s and I am always impressed with how well they sail. Although it is not particularly close winded, the Irwin 52 is a much better performer than other big cruising designs of the period, including the clipper bow designs of Bill Garden and blunt bowed Out Island series by Charlie Morgan. Most 52s were centerboards with a board-up draft of 5 feet, 6 inches. The original air draft of 67 feet made the Intracoastal a no-fly zone, although you may well find the boat you're considering has had the rig shortened to less than 65 feet.

Construction

The bugaboo with Irwin Yachts is just how well built were they? While some of the smaller models have not held up well over the years, the bigger boats, built to heavier scantlings, have endured pretty well. The construction of the 52 evolved over the years. Early boats had solid glass hulls while later boats, after the Series II was introduced in 1982, had Klegecell coring from the waterline up. All models featured plywood cored decks. And while plywood is not the best material for this purpose because it is heavy and prone to rot, Irwin mitigated the latter issue at least by using four-inch squares saturated with resin. The box joint of the hull and deck includes the wide bulwark and a handsome teak caprail.

Early models were classic production boats using three massive interior pans. These molded units were tabbed to the hull. As with any large secondary bonding, there is the potential for problems, and it limits access to the hull. Also, these pans restricted the interior options—the layout was the layout and you either took it or left it. The Series II boats featured all wood interior construction with bulkheads and facings fiberglassed directly to the hull, which allowed customized plans.

IRWIN 52 PRICE DATA

		Low	High
BUC Retail Range	1981	$109,000	$119,000
	1986	$135,000	$149,000
		State	Asking
Boats For Sale	1976	FL	$169,000
	1982	FL	$124,000
	1985	Caribbean	$249,000

What to look for

The key to making a smart purchase of an Irwin 52 is to know just what model you're looking at. Series II boats, which were substantially upgraded and are easier to retrofit, were introduced in 1982. This is not always reflected in the price of used 52s. It seems as if owners and brokers just look at other boats on the market and price theirs accordingly. This can work to the advantage of the savvy shopper. Also, don't confuse the 52 with the 54, which is quite easy to do because they are basically the same boat. The 54 replaced the 52 in 1988 and typically costs significantly more.

In addition to typical age-related issues, one problem common to most 52s was the iron maststep. It was down low, in the bilge, and over the years it corroded. This is a well-known problem and may have been addressed by previous owners. Also be wary of delaminated floors around the mast, which were glassed-over wood. These members were often used to mount new gear, from watermakers to air conditioning compressors, and if the holes drilled for fasteners were not well sealed they were prone to delamination. Other problems may include leaking chainplates, spars in need of repainting, and spider cracks and delamination on deck. Also, 52s were manufactured during the pox period, and most boats will have had a blister repair job or two somewhere in their past.

On deck

The Irwin 52 cockpit transformed center-cockpit design. Unlike most center cockpits of

Irwin 52

PRICE: The 52 just may be the best-priced big cruiser on the market. You can find a boat in decent shape for around $150,000. Take that same budget to a boat show and compare.

DESIGN QUALITY: Ted Irwin really shook the world with this design. It was the first deck saloon. It sailed well and the centerboard arrangement made it a great boat for shallow water destinations like the Bahamas.

CONSTRUCTION QUALITY: If only they had built these boats as well as they were designed they would have been classics. Of course they would not have been affordable then . . . the old tradeoff.

USER-FRIENDLINESS: The livable interior is extremely user-friendly, in port. Underway, it is a bit different. The many systems are a mixed bag; they offer convenience but at the cost of time spent dealing with them.

SAFETY: There is safety in size, and the bulwarks and wide decks are niece features. The overall construction could be better and it is tough to function down below in a seaway.

TYPICAL CONDITION: It seems the 52 has reached the point where many boats on the market have already gone through refits. The value of the 52 has steadily risen as a result of caring owners.

REFITTING: This depends on the model, pre-1982 boats are harder to work on, or at least to alter, and even new boats can be frustrating with older systems needing to be replaced.

SUPPORT: Gene Gammons is the best source of information. E-mail him at captaingene@msn.com. His Web site is good source of information: www.irwinyachts.com.

AVAILABILITY: When it comes to big boats, the 52 had one of the most successful production runs and there are always plenty of boats on the market. Florida and the Caribbean seem to have the most boats listed for sale.

INVESTMENT AND RESALE: Ironically, after years of having a poor reputation, the stock in older, large Irwins has risen dramatically. You will get your money out of a 52 if you take care of it.

OVERALL 'SVG' RATING

the time, it was large, comfortable and not just squeezed into the space above the engine room or distorted to allow for headroom in the pass-through to the aft cabin. You can sleep comfortably on either side. Sitting at the wheel it seems like you are looking downhill at the bow, the visibility is terrific but you do feel a bit exposed—you can really feel the freeboard. Early boats came with Barlow or Barient winches. The midboom mainsheet included a triangular arrangement on deck designed to displace the mainsail loads in lieu of a traveler but it was not wildly efficient. On a boat I delivered we ripped two of the mainsheet blocks out of the deck. Sail controls may or may not be led aft, and most boats on the used market have conventional spars with slab reefing.

The wide side decks and substantial bulwarks are great features of the Irwin 52. The stanchions are tall but only adequately sup-

ported. Early boats had the pulpits screwed to the teak caprail, later boats had them through-bolted. Handrails on the trunkhouse are the perfect height to be useful. The aft deck features huge lazarettes. "This is the place for bikes, sails, awnings and other gear that cruisers need but have no place to store," Gammons said. Forward, the bowsprit houses double anchor rollers and there is a large chain locker forward. Hawsepipes through the bulwark enclose mooring lines, although on early models in particular, the deck hardware was a bit undersized, especially for a 44,000-pound boat.

Down below

Interiors sell boats. It was just as true in the 1970s and 1980s as it is today. And few boats have more inviting interiors than the Irwin 52. Whether or not you want to head offshore in this interior is another question but for coastal cruising and living aboard it is hard to beat. A friendly Australian family recently purchased one of the last Irwin 52s built and moored it behind my house to prepare it for the long crossing home to Sydney. "The three-cabin layout is perfect for the kids," Donna said. "I like all the room to work on and add new systems," Brett told me, adding with a laugh, "Of course all that room means you can spend a lot of money too."

As mentioned earlier, models prior to 1982 all featured the same plan. This includes a drop-down galley to starboard, a large nav station to port and a palatial saloon. The aft cabin has an athwartship double and private head and shower. Forward, there is a large V-berth, a quarter cabin with upper and under berths and a second large head. There is no shortage of elbowroom. Series II models often used the same basic plan, however changes included island berths in both fore and aft cabins and different uses of the quarter cabin.

Decadent features like a stand-up fridge and freezer, ample counter space in the galley, including a breakfast bar with built-in stools, air conditioning, generator, hanging lockers that are sized like closets, and a full shower with enough tankage to make long, hot showers possible, make the 52 a good choice for those having a hard time downsizing from the land life to boat life.

Engine

Most 52s came standard with the Perkins 4-236 85-horsepower diesel. These workhorse engines are well respected by industry pros. They are reliable, relatively easy to work on, and although they've been long out of production, parts are still widely available. The engine is located beneath the saloon cabin sole, and access is terrific. This position also makes repowering an easier proposition. Most center-cockpit models have the engine squirreled away under the cockpit. You need to take a hard look at the mechanical systems in any 52 you are considering. Items like a 7.5 KW Onan generator, LectraSan macerator system and old watermakers seem alluring but in reality they add little value and much aggravation maintaining, repairing or replacing.

Irwin 52s have extensive 12- and 110-volt electrical systems, and if they are original, they will need to be updated. Don't underestimate this job, replacing wiring is time consuming and frustrating, some of the runs are incredibly long. Remember, on pre-1982 boats, access is not very good.

Underway

Although most cruisers buy an Irwin 52 for the size, they are often pleasantly surprised by the sailing qualities. Under full canvas the 52 moves smartly in light to moderate airs and truly comes alive in the trades. Brett and Donna have averaged 165 miles a day so far while crossing the Pacific. They are currently in Tonga and although they've had some mechanical issues with the boat they are pleased with its performance. They are also pleased with its heavy weather capability.

"We had to beat to safe harbor in Cuba to avoid Hurricane Ivan," Brett wrote in an e-mail, "and it was rugged. Force 9 gusting higher, the boat did well with a deeply reefed main, mizzen and staysail."

The versatile sailplan makes Irwin 52 balanced and it adapts well to autopilots. The mizzen can be used to trim the helm, making the autopilot's task easier. Brett and Donna don't hesitate to fly their cruising chute off the wind, although in typical tradewind conditions they find the 130-percent genoa poled out pulls them along at close to 9 knots without any stress. The 52 handles extremely well under power and with a feathering prop it backs true. I know, not long ago I had to back a 52 out of a long canal for a sea trail, and once I gained momentum it was a piece of cake.

Conclusion

If you are interested in an Irwin 52, don't apologize. The boat has design features that can only be found in new boats costing many times more. The 52 represents a unique blend of living space and underway performance. It may not be the ideal ocean crossing machine but it sure makes living aboard a lot less painful. With prices ranging from $125,000 to just over $200,000 it is a lot of boat for the buck.

40 Years of Used Boats

The marketplace is overflowing with great buys

I've been doing a lot of sailing and a lot of traveling lately. In the past few months I have meandered through the Chesapeake Bay, crossed Lake Michigan a couple of times and drifted out to Catalina Island. I've chartered in French Polynesia and taken QUETZAL, my Kaufman 47 cutter, down to Panama and back. And everywhere I go I check out sailboats. Less charitable types, a.k.a. landlubbers, might call it an obsession bordering on addiction. I confess I'm a marina, mooring field and anchorage junkie. As soon as my boat is secure, I launch the dink and row around the harbor. I tell my crew that it's my professional responsibility. After all, I write boat reviews for a living. But they know it has nothing to do with writing, it's all about the boats, something you either understand or never will.

And what have I discovered out there? A lot of used boats. Sadly, but not surprisingly, you don't see many new boats. The few new boats tend to be either relatively affordable production boats, or a handful of tricked-out world cruisers, preparing to, well, cruise the world. You see some new small boats, but not as many as you should.

Statistics don't lie, the new sailboat industry is flat. How flat? According to figures from National Marine Manufacturers Association, 14,400 sailboats were sold in the United States in 2005, up ever so slightly from 2004. However, it was 4,000 fewer than in 2001. Sailboats represented a tiny fraction, around 2 percent of the 864,000 new boats sold in 2005. This figure includes anything that floats, from houseboats to personal watercraft.

The average price of a sailboat, and this includes all makes and models, from an 8-foot Optimist to the new Hylas 66 pilothouse, was more than $44,000. To put that in perspective, the average price of a sailboat in 2001 was $34,000. That's a 25-percent price increase in four years. If you had a sense that boats are getting more expensive, you're right. It's almost impossible to find a new 30-footer for less than $100,000, and you can spend nearly twice that. And when you factor in other costs, including sales tax, dockage, insurance, and maintenance, the picture becomes sadder still.

However, there are a few statistics that work to the average working stiff/sailor's advantage. According to the U.S. Coast Guard, there were nearly as many sailboats afloat in U.S. waters as any other type of boat, more than 1.5 million. Sailboats, unlike small powerboats and other more fragile watercraft, never seem to die. A 40-year old Pearson Ensign is just as much fun to sail today as it was when new, back when SAILING Magazine was a black-and-white regional magazine hitting the newsstands for the first time. This huge inventory of boats supports what is an obvious statistic, for every new sailboat sold, eight used boats change hands. The second-hand market is what really drives the sailing industry. And, it's a buyer's market and always has been. If you really want a sailboat you can find one that you can afford.

It's actually a great time to be looking for a used boat. Not only is the market soft but used boat buyers are equipped with more tools than ever to help make informed decisions. There is a lot of good information out there. SAILING Magazine was one of the first publications to seriously review used boats. The Used Boat Notebook has been a monthly or bi-monthly feature for 10 years and close to 100 boats have been profiled. Other magazines have followed our lead, and offer occasional used boat reviews. The Internet not only provides current, wide-ranging information on boats for sale through a variety of Web sites but also allows prospective buyers to thoroughly research boats they're considering. Online owner's associations make it easy to find detailed information and chat with other owners. Another great advantage of the Internet is that it allows used boat owners to track down long out of production parts and fittings to help them retrofit their old boats.

New boat prices have also had an impact on how many of us care for our older boats. Realizing that new boats may be out of our purchasing league, we take better care of our current boats. I have no statistics to back this up but my casual observations and gut instincts tell me that older boats are better maintained than ever before. There's a certain responsibility that goes with keeping your old boat in good sailing condition. An old, abandoned fiberglass sailboat is an environmental nuisance. Also, you never know how much pleasure that old boat sitting on a trailer behind the garage just might give you if you take the time to get it back in shape. Remember Spray, Joshua Slocum's famous sloop? She was propped up in a field when a friend gave her to him. "The ship proved to be a very antiquated sloop called the Spray, that the neighbors declared had been built in year 1." Slocum rebuilt her and became the first man to sail solo around the world. Spray may be the most famous used boat of all.

During my recent travels, three different used boats caught my eye. At Marina Carenero in Bocas des Toro, Panama, I tied up next to an old but immaculate Peterson 44. A handsome center-cockpit cruiser, the boat was a 1978 model that looked brand new. I was shocked to find out that the boat was just finishing up a six-year circumnavigation. Unfortunately the owners were not around, having returned to the states for a brief visit home. However, Mac, the marina owner, gave me the details. The boat was owned by a couple in their 60s, who had left San Diego and headed across the South Pacific. They spent a season down under before crossing the Indian Ocean. They then angled up the Red Sea into the Mediterranean where they tarried for a couple of years. Then they crossed the Atlantic to the Caribbean. In Panama, they were making plans to transit the canal and head for home. And their boat looked no worse for the wear.

The Peterson 44 is a well-known, affordable bluewater boat. The hull has a soft sheer,

the deck house profile is low, the fin keel and skeg hung rudder have moderate proportions and a generous sailplan keeps the boat moving in light air. About 200 44s were built during a short six-year production run in late 1970s and early 1980s. Later, the Kelly Peterson 44 and 46 replaced and updated the original design.

A quick survey of www.yachtworld.com, one of the best Internet sites for used boat listings, shows six Peterson 44s for sale, ranging from $110,000 to $130,000. Most models have already been retrofitted once, and documented problems like leaking water tanks and the faulty heel on the rudder bearing have already been dealt with. The interior features an aft cabin that is accessed through a cockpit hatch or a stooped walkthrough from the saloon. The galley is well set up for cooking underway and a dinette to port is a practical arrangement for cruising. That couple has probably finished their circumnavigation by now, and I suspect their boat still looks like new.

At the docks of Milwaukee's South Shore Yacht Club I spied a squeaky clean Tartan 37. Another great old boat, this Sparkman & Stevens design had to be at least 30 years old. Admiring it from the dock, I took in the measure of a modern classic. Relatively low and sleek, the T-37 has modest sheer and a proud reverse transom. The teak toerail was freshly varnished. I couldn't see the keel, but I knew that the long fin was shallow because I could see the centerboard winch in the cockpit. Board up draft is just 4 feet, 2 inches. The rudder is hung on a skeg. A sloop rig with a short boom, the T-37 was designed during the days when huge genoas ruled the waves.

The T-shaped cockpit is a study in function nicely fused with comfort. The side decks are wide and the chainplates are well inboard making for a friendly and safe foredeck. The boat was not fit out for racing or cruising, just for sailing. And it was scrubbed to an extent that you needed sunglasses to look at. The Tartan 37 is a fine example of a quality used boat at an affordable price. Nearly 500 of the older S&S 37s were built during a 13-year production run that ended in 1989. Prices vary, but with a bit of legwork you can find a nicely maintained and equipped Tartan 37 for less than $60,000. Sure the interior may be dark by today's standards and not quite as roomy as

Used Boats 1970–2005 | SAILING Magazine's Value Guide

 **PRICE:** Boat prices represented a far smaller percentage of household income in 1970 than today. Sailboats cost 15 percent of average annual household income in 1970 compared to 70 percent in 2005.

 **DESIGN QUALITY:** Today's used boat buyer has a much more interesting selection of designs to choose from. In 1970 most boats had similar, long-keel narrow-beam hull shapes.

 CONSTRUCTION QUALITY: A lot is made of the strength of early fiberglass boats, but they were resin rich, making the hulls thick but not necessarily strong. Today's construction techniques and materials are remarkable.

USER-FRIENDLINESS: Today's boats are extremely user friendly. If you said a couple could easily handle a 50-footer in the late 60s people would have thought you were nuts.

SAFETY: Newer designs are loaded with safety features, but some sacrifice ultimate stability for increased interior volume and sacrifice sea motion for increased speed potential. I think old boats were just as safe as today's boats.

 TYPICAL CONDITION: Today's used boats are better maintained. This is simply my own observation, no science to back it up, but because boats represent such a large investment they warrant looking after.

 REFITTING: Refitting today is dramatically easier. Part sources, tools and products have all evolved. Refitting older boats is common, back then, folks tended to think of buying new instead.

 SUPPORT: A tough call, so many boatbuilders are out of business. Sailboat manufacturers have not been overly responsive to the needs of used boat buyers. In some ways, the used boat market today is why the new boat market is so small.

 AVAILABILITY: Today is a golden period but it won't last. While boats built in the 70s and 80s are still viable, soon they'll be relics. Very limited production today will cause availability of good used boats to decrease as the years go on.

 INVESTMENT AND RESALE: Because new boat production is decreasing and prices increasing, the value of quality used boats will increase. An investment today will keep up with inflation for years to come.

 OVERALL 'SVG' RATING

those glitzy new boats at the show. But few boats sail any better through a range of conditions, and that dark teak interior sure seems more palatable when you compare what $60,000 buys on the new boat market.

Cruising around the mooring field in Two Harbors, Catalina, I spied a pale blue-hulled Rawson 30. This was one of the old ones, probably built in the mid to late 1960s and it was a little rough around the edges. But it was set up for cruising, California style. It had solar panels all over the deck, a huge wind generator, a monster TV antenna and floating alongside, a super slide. I only saw one crewmember, a three- or four-year-old blond kid scooting around the deck naked. The boat was obviously his home.

The Rawson 30 is better known on the West Coast, where hard-core cruisers know it as an affordable bluewater boat. A heavy, full-keeled cruiser designed by William Garden, they were built by Ron Rawson in Redmond, Washington. Plenty of freeboard and a boxy cabintrunk resulted in a lot of room below for a 30-footer. Interior quality varied dramatically as most were kit boats, meaning that owners bought the hull and deck and finished the interior themselves. This was a West Coast trend in the 1960s and 1970s, when cruising first evolved as a lifestyle and it was cool to a have a funky boat.

Four Rawson 30s are listed on **yacht-world.com**. A 1964 model, which has completed a circumnavigation but looks tired, can be had for less than $10,000. A refurbished pilothouse model with a new diesel is asking $27,000. At either end of this range, you are looking at a very affordable and capable boat. Your bluewater cruising dreams don't have to be derailed by a lack of money.

So forget that tired excuse that sailing is too expensive. The used market is vast, there are boats to fit every sailor's needs. And no matter how much or how little you spend on a boat, the dynamics of wind, water and sail are the same. The power, the peace and sense of fulfillment that only sailing can offer is defined not by the price of the boat, but by the measure of a sailor's spirit. And if you see someone rowing around the anchorage checking out your boat, say hello.

PART 2

Ten Great
New Boats
to Sail Around
the World

Tartan 3400

Intelligent design marks the evolution of the 34-foot Tartan

For years Tim Jackett, Tartan's chief designer, has done a commendable job of blending the proud Tartan pedigree with exciting new designs that embrace technology. The new 3400 is his latest example. Small touches like the wraparound cockpit coaming, and other more prominent features like the low-profile cabintop, are unmistakably Tartan. Thirty-four feet is sacred ground for Tartan, and the Fairport, Ohio-based company has a tough act to follow with the 3400. The first Tartan 34, known these days simply as the Tartan Classic, was designed by Sparkman & Stephens and launched in the 1960s. When combined with later 34 Mark II models built in the 1980s, nearly 1,000 Tartan 34s were built. While the 3400 salutes this storied past, it is not riding on its coattails. This exciting new boat is all about the future, the 3400 fairly lists with fresh thinking.

Jackett, who is also Tartan's chief operating officer, has created a performance-oriented, high-volume hull that is remarkably easy to handle. The sailplan includes a power-

Moderate winds and gloomy skies did nothing to dampen the spirits aboard the Tartan 3400 during a test sail on Chesapeake Bay—the boat was lively and comfortable.

TARTAN 3400

LOA 34'5", LWL 30'5"
Beam 11'11"
Draft 6'6" (Fin),
   4'11" (Beavertail),
   3'11"-7' (Keel/Centerboard)
Displacement 10,800 lbs. (Fin),
   11,000 lbs. (Beavertail),
   11,800 lbs. (Keel/Centerboard)
Ballast 3,500 lbs. (Fin),
   3,700 lbs. (Beavertail),
   4,000 lbs. (Keel/Centerboard)
Sail Area 620.18 sq. ft

ful full-batten main and a self-tacking 100-percent headsail. A furling reacher is rigged and ready to deploy the moment you fall off the wind. A carbon fiber mast and boom are standard. One day this won't seem out of the ordinary but for now there's no disputing the 3400 is ahead of its time. The epoxy hull construction is sophisticated, strong and light. I had the opportunity to test sail the 3400 recently and came away impressed. The boat lends new meaning to the phrase, intelligent design. The 3400 includes features generally reserved for the owners of big, incredibly expensive, semi-custom boats.

The details

The Tartan 3400 hull is a composite of unidirectional E-glass, epoxy resin and CoreCell linear polyurethane coring. Through the use of resin impregnation machines, Tartan achieves a glass-to-resin ratio of 65 percent to 35 percent. The equation is simple: More glass and less resin equals strong, light hulls. The foam coring provides panel stiffness, sound and thermal insulation. The hull is vacuum-bagged to make sure there are no voids and then post-cured for 24 hours at 145 degrees, just to make sure the epoxy goes off. Pound for pound, an epoxy post-cured hull is dramatically stronger than a traditional hand-laid hull using more common polyester resins. The Tartan 3400 hull includes a 15-year structural and blister warranty.

The 3400 deck is cored with Baltek AL 600 balsa. Core "windows" or areas of solid, reinforced laminate, are used wherever deck hardware is mounted. This technique limits core exposure and possible delamination down the road. Tartan does not through bolt deck hardware. Instead, stainless fasteners are drilled and tapped into aluminum plates in the deck. The obvious advantage is that hardware can be removed without the hassle of dealing with nuts and headliners below. When done well this method is perfectly adequate, especially on smaller boats. The hull-to-deck joint is the time-tested method of laying the deck on an inward facing hull flange. A T6 aluminum flat bar is molded in, forming a full sheer length backing plate.

The hull shape includes a clean entry that won't pound too much when sailing upwind in a blow. Full, flat aft sections create speed potential when sailing off the wind and cockpit and interior volume. Jackett has hit upon an ingenious concept with interchangeable keels.

"Innovative geometry in the attachment of the keel allows you to tailor-fit your 3400 to your sailing area," Jackett said.

Three keel configurations are offered. The bulbed fin, with a draft of 6 feet, 6 inches offers the best overall performance. An all-around 4-foot, 11-inch beavertail keel offers more moderate draft and the keel/centerboard option, a longtime Tartan trademark, is ideal for shoal-draft sailing. The board-up draft is just 4 feet. However, if you change your sailing area or just your attitude, you can order a different keel, have it shipped to the yard, and installed. This will become an alluring feature when Tartan 3400s hit the secondhand market. The rudder is made with high-density foam covered with epoxy skins. The stock is stainless steel and the rudder stuffing box is bronze, traditional and quality material choices that are well proven.

Jackett's plan was to create a genuinely fast boat that required minimal sail handling. These days it seems designers are searching for this Holy Grail in an attempt to lure new blood into sailing and to keep their plants working. Jackett hit the bullseye, the Tartan 3400 sails brilliantly and yes, it's a breeze to handle. With the 100-percent headsail unfurled tacking is simply a matter of turning the wheel. In theory, deploying the reacher is also a snap, unfortunately we didn't have this sail available for our test sail.

We had moderate conditions near Annapolis as we cleared Back Creek and hoisted sail. In 12 knots apparent we sped up to 6 knots on a tight reach. Sheeting in we sliced through the chop created by an armada of impatient powerboats. Designers and builders invariably claim that their hull shape won't pound in a seaway, and they're usually not

The handsome yet functional interior is finished in varnished cherry, and the overall layout lends a spacious feeling.

telling the truth. The 3400 hull didn't pound, the motion was very soft, even upwind in a two- and three-foot chop, I was duly impressed. Easing off the wind we longed for the reacher, however with just the working sails we zoomed along at 6-plus knots.

On deck

The 3400 is littered with Harken deck hardware, from winches to the traveler mounted forward of the companionway. Yes, it's time to mention the midboom sheeting dilemma again, but hey, I seem to be the only one left in the world who worries about boom loading so I am just going to drop it. Speaking of the boom, Jacket calls his carbon section a "trough." It's designed to help, with the aid of lazyjacks, to gather up the mainsail. When you're ready to tidy up you simply pull over the boom-stored sail cover and call it a day. Maybe it's just in my mind but I swear you can feel the difference a carbon fiber mast makes. The ride seems softer, quieter, there isn't as much pitching.

The 3400s mast is built by Novis Composites and is painted with white Awlgrip. The jib stay, which terminates just aft of the stem, is 7/8-rigged on the spar. The floating reacher luff is masthead rigged to really power things up off the wind. The 3400 has an air draft of 55 feet. Other numbers of interests? The ballast/displacement ratio is 34 percent, the sail area/displacement ratio is a respectable 18.8 and the displacement/length ratio is a fast 171.3.

Down below

The interior is handsome and functional but not designed to be all things to all sailors. I like it. Finished in varnished cherry, the top-quality workmanship is obvious the moment you drop below. In keeping the overall ethos of the boat, structural bulkheads are bonded to hull and serious fiberglass timbers carry keel and mast loads. The plan includes a double cabin forward and another aft. A single head opposite the galley to starboard frees up space in both the forward cabin and saloon. The forward cabin is a bit tight, reflecting the fine entry, however the berth is a genuine double

Granicote sink and a two-burner Force 10, along with plenty storage space, make the galley a joy to cook in.

and there are two hanging lockers. The main cabin features opposing settees and a small drop-leaf table with a center storage bin and two drawers.

Jackett has employed slightly angled counters and half bulkheads to lend a sense of spaciousness below and there are well-placed teak handholds throughout. The galley includes a two-burner Force 10 cooker and a nine-inch molded Granicote single sink. There is storage in cherry faced lockers above the stove and below the sink. The well-insulated icebox is decent sized but refrigeration is optional. The navigation station is opposite the galley. It's easy to justify eliminating the nav station these days, especially in boats less than 40 feet, and I applaud Jackett for allotting space for what I still consider to be the most important spot below. The single head is good sized and includes a separate shower.

You realize the Tartan 3400 is just 34 feet by some of the specs and capacities. The freshwater tanks hold 60 gallons, not bad for a boat of this size but not enough for cruising without frequent stops. The two standard batteries are Group 27, these could be upgraded for more amps and oomph. Tartan has gone with corrosion-free Forespar Marelon valves both above and below the waterline. The 27-horsepower Yanmar diesel with a saildrive provides plenty of punch, is quite and extremely fuel efficient. The aluminum fuel tank holds 25 gallons and a single-lever control facilitates smooth handling under power. Engine access is excellent from behind the companionway and through side panels.

Under sail

Back in the cockpit, we chased shifting breezes around the bay. The visibility from behind the 40-inch destroyer wheel is good and the sail controls are all led aft. An experienced sailor can singlehand the 3400. The cockpit seat backs are angled for comfort and the deep well will feel secure offshore. There is a good-sized locker to starboard, a dedicated propane locker and a sleek cutout for a swim step and telescoping ladder astern.

After tacking one more time we made our way toward Back Creek. We flopped the jib over, paid the main out and eased along wing and wing. Apparent winds fluctuated around 5 knots and our speed was about the same. I went forward. The side decks are wide and easy to navigate. The stainless stemhead fitting incorporates a single anchor roller. In fact, the stainless work is impressive, from the beefy 10-inch mooring cleats to the deck hatches, it seems like everything was shiny stainless steel. Well, not everything, the toerails and handrails were varnished teak. This is a Tartan after all.

The Tartan 3400 is an exciting new model from one of America's premier builders. It combines thoughtful, high-tech construction, good performance and easy handling. It is also handsome and just feels right in the water. The 3400 extends Tartan's run of creating classic 34-footers.

Southerly 110

*This English-built cruiser is equally at home
in the shallows as it is crossing the deep ocean*

Like every Southerly, the Rob Humphreys-
designed 110 blends fresh thinking, quality
construction and the unique option of skinny-
water sailing or bluewater passage making.
And while this handsome 35-foot, 6-inch
swing keel, twin-rudder cruiser is now turning
heads in North America, sailors on the other
side of the Atlantic have long appreciated the
innovation that accompanies the introduction
of each new Southerly model.

Built by Northshore Yachts Ltd., in Chich-
ester, England, the first swing keel Southerly
was launched in 1978. More than 700 boats
have been built since then and they've not only
proven their mettle as world cruisers, they've
also put to rest any questions about the safety
of taking a swing keel boat offshore. In addition to the 110, the Southerly line includes the
37-foot 115 and the 135, a robust cruiser with
an LOA of 45 feet, 6 inches. There are raised
saloon versions of the 110 and 135. Northshore
also builds the rugged Fisher pilothouse motorsailers and the traditional, Robert Harris-
designed Vancouver series.

*The Rob Humphreys-designed Southerly 110
moves along nicely in spite of the fickle breeze on
Tampa Bay.*

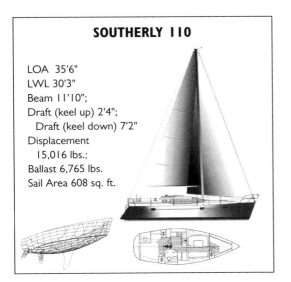

SOUTHERLY 110

LOA 35'6"
LWL 30'3"
Beam 11'10";
Draft (keel up) 2'4";
  Draft (keel down) 7'2"
Displacement
  15,016 lbs.;
Ballast 6,765 lbs.
Sail Area 608 sq. ft.

I recently had the opportunity to sail the
Southerly 110 on Tampa Bay. Although the light
breeze and gentle sea state didn't really test the
boat, I was impressed with the 110's ease of
handling and steady bearing in the water. Within
minutes of clearing the dock we had the main
and genoa drawing nicely as we eased out of the
channel under sail. I was pleased to have John
Hiltunen from the factory in England and U.S.
dealer David Bagaus aboard.

The details

The term "swing keel" might be a bit misleading, there is nothing lightweight or small boat-
like about the 110's keel arrangement. The keel
box, or cavity, is an integral part of the hull and

the 4,455 pounds of fixed ballast is cast iron. This section is strong enough for the 110 to dry out in tidal harbors with no adverse effects to the hull and also offers transverse stiffening to the swing keel unit. The 2,310-pound airfoil-shaped swing keel is also cast iron and incorporates a stainless steel pivot at its leading edge. A hydraulic ram, powered by an electric motor, raises and lowers the keel. Naturally there is a manual backup system. The swing keel can actually absorb a shock load better than a fixed foil, and upon impact will retract back into the hull, rotating on its pivot and sparing the boat more serious damage.

The keel can also be trimmed, by means of a push button at the helm, to various positions. In deep water sailing upwind, the keel is lowered to its full 7-foot, 2-inch length and the 110 tracks like a demon. Off the wind, it can be raised to a more advantageous point. Nosing into a shallow anchorage the keel can be raised completely and the 2-foot, 4-inch draft will certainly be appreciated.

The "other" interesting feature of the 110's underbody is the twin rudder system. Canted on both sides of the gently rounded buttocks, these semi-balanced blades offer excellent steering control. In fact, under most conditions the 110 will steer itself, at least for awhile. And while this doesn't eliminate the need for an autopilot it does mean that the pilot will work less and be more efficient. The rudders are angled to avoid grounding when the 110 is beached or drying out.

The 110's hull is hand laid up fiberglass, solid below the waterline and composite cored from the waterline up. Over the years Northshore has molded hulls for Camper Nicholson, Trintella, Bowman and others—this is the company's specialty. The deck is balsa cored except in areas of high stress loading where plywood is used instead. The hull and deck joint is both chemically and mechanically bonded and covered by a teak caprail. Structural bulkheads are securely fiberglassed to the hull. The boat is solid—it just has the feeling of a 40-footer.

On deck

The 110's cockpit is at once comfortable and also designed for offshore work. The helm is

A secure and comfortable cockpit, designed for offshore sailing.

positioned well aft and the molded pedestal houses the compass, engine instruments and a single lever throttle control. The Whitlock Cobra system provides smooth steering. The view from the helm is adequate over the relatively high cabintrunk. The primaries are Lewmar 44 STs mounted on the coaming. At first they seem undersized until you remember this is only a 36-foot boat. Sail controls are led aft to rope clutches and Lewmar 16s. Single line slab reefing is standard. The mainsheet features midboom sheeting with much discussed advantages and disadvantages: cockpit space versus boom purchase and loading. Most people choose cockpit space. There are two decent-sized lockers and a deep lazarette to port. European builders tend to tout the open stern not as a swim step but as a simplified means of boarding when Med mooring. Either way it is hard to imagine any new boat with a conventional transom anymore.

Selden spars are standard and North American sailors should consider the optional tall rig. A solid Selden vang is also standard issue as is Furlex headsail furling gear. The deck gear is first rate, I particularly like the beefy midship cleats for controlling spring and breast lines when coming alongside. A raised bulwark, aggressive nonskid and well-placed stainless grab rails offer security when moving about the deck in seaway. A double, stainless steel anchor roller can accommodate serious ground tackle. The standard anchor is a 33-pound Bruce.

The large saloon windows flood the interior with light and lend a sense of spaciousness.

Down below

Large saloon windows flood the interior with light and lend a sense of spaciousness. The joinerwork is finished in either solid cherry or cherry-faced plywood and the workmanship is excellent. The interior plan is open, functional and efficient. If this was a multihull or power-boat it would be called a "galley-up plan." Upon dropping below, the galley is to port, and overlooks the saloon. Twin sinks face forward and a two-burner cooker is outboard. There is a lot of counter space and adequate storage in lockers behind the stove and under the sink and in four large drawers. An L-shaped full-length stainless rail not only keeps the cook away from hot surfaces but also provides a welcome handhold when preparing meals underway.

The nav station is opposite the galley and includes a clever instrument console for repeaters. Another stainless railing is well placed to keep the navigator in place and also to keep the crew on their feet as they make their way forward. The electrical panel is located below the chart table, and I know this is a wimpy complaint, but it is a bit uncomfortable to bend down to access the panel. The large head is located aft of the nav station. One head makes sense in a boat of this size. I like the dedicated oilskin locker in the head, which is just next to the companionway.

The saloon has a C-shaped dinette to port and a settee and sea berth opposite. There is good storage under the seats, except below the

aft end of the dinette where the 45-gallon stainless steel water tank is located. Warm water sailors should consider adding more ventilation in the form of either an overhead hatch in the saloon or opening ports. The forward cabin, which is a bit tight, has a single port berth that converts to a double when necessary. An optional arrangement includes an additional overlapping single berth to starboard. The aft cabin on the other hand is surprisingly spacious. A genuine double berth is offset to starboard with a large vanity and desk to port. Two hanging lockers and a host of drawers and lockers present plenty of storage space. The head can also be accessed from the aft cabin.

There is good access to the engine compartment with hinged panels fore and aft, and in fact the engine box can be completely removed for serious maintenance and repair. A three-cylinder Yanmar 29-horsepower diesel is standard. The 40-gallon stainless steel fuel tank is located below the sole next to the nav station. The Yanmar 3M30 is particularly fuel-efficient and the fixed three-bladed propeller gives the 110 plenty of punch through the water. Without pushing the engine we steamed along at close to 6 knots when we motored back to the dock after our trial.

Under sail

Out on the Bay the wind was fickle. One moment it would fill in at 10 knots apparent and we'd accelerate to 5 knots and then it would falter. Just as advertised the 110 was well balanced and only needed occasional nudges on the wheel to maintain course. We experimented with keel trim and setting the keel couldn't be easier. A lighted control gauge indicating just how much keel is deployed is located on the pedestal. As expected, the 110 tacks much cleaner with the keel down and also tracks up wind better. Whenever we angled off the wind, the keel came up in degrees until when we were running, then it was all the way up. Trimming the keel is simple, just part of the routine and offers a lot of performance pluses.

As we glided along John Hiltunen filled me in on the history of Northshore Yachts Ltd., and also told of many notable voyages completed in swing keel Southerlies. And while any boat I own must be bluewater capable, what really had me thinking about the Southerly 110 was all the shallow water in my home waters. I have longed to explore the broad expanse of Florida Bay and nose up into the jungle rivers of Everglades National Park. I have also dreamed of cruising the shimmering flats off the west coast of Andros Island in the Bahamas, but my deep-draft boats have always kept me at arms length from these unspoiled cruising grounds. The Spanish have a proverb that says it's not the length of a man's life that matters, but the width. The Southerly 110 makes a sailor's world a bit wider.

Hanse 400

*Fast features and a flexible interior combine
to make this a true crossover boat*

The Hanse 400 is something of a throwback. Don't misunderstand me; this sleek new design from Judel/Volijk & Co. is thoroughly modern, from its efficient fractional rig to innovative epoxy construction and flexible interior arrangement plans. With its reverse sheer, long waterline and low-profile cabintop the Hanse 400 has "today" stamped all over it. (It's a look I like.) So why is it a throwback? Like many top-quality production boats from the 1970s and 1980s, the Hanse 400 refuses to be easily classified. It's not a dedicated bluewater cruiser and it's not a flat-out racer. It is, however, a lot of both. The marketing team at Hanse Yachts calls it the crossover concept, a fast boat with a terrific interior. In the old days we called it a racer-cruiser. Pardon the cliché but the more things change, the more they stay the same. When it comes to sailing that's not a bad thing.

Hanse Yachts has quietly established a presence in the American marketplace. Strolling the docks of major boat shows I am always

In spite of the fickle Chesapeake Bay breeze, the Hanse 400 slips along nicely showing a real turn of speed.

HANSE 400

LOA 39'7"
LWL 35'4"
Beam 13'3"
Draft standard 6'5",
  shoal 5'4"
Displacement 18,739 lbs.
Ballast 6,426 lbs.
Sail Area 1,137 sq. ft.

intrigued to inspect the latest model from this progressive German builder. Hanse's first boat was a 29-footer introduced in 1993. This model, originally built in Sweden as the Aphrodite 291, established Hanse's reputation for melding quality and affordability. The company's next project was converting the former Finngulf 33 into the Hanse 331. The Hanse factory, a former wooden boatyard, is located on the Baltic coast at Greifswald where boats have been built since 1361. Today Hanse builds six original and highly innovative designs ranging from 31 feet to 53 feet.

I recently sailed the new Hanse 400 on a cool day on the Chesapeake Bay. The conditions were light to moderate, a typical bay day with winds fluctuating between 8 and 15

With a rod-kicker and single-line mainsail reefing system, the Hanse 400 is ready for easy sail handling.

knots. I hopped from the photo boat onto the wide swim step and introduced myself. Within seconds, the self-tacking jib was unfurled, the main trimmed and we were off and sailing on a lively close reach.

The details

The hull of the Hanse 400 is laminated with epoxy resins and vacuum bagged to keep the resin-to-glass ratio low. The clever sandwich construction features foam coring below the waterline and balsa coring above. Although most Hanse 400s will be sailed as performance cruisers, close attention is paid to paring weight. The use of epoxy typically results in a 10- to 12-percent weight savings over traditional fiberglass laminating techniques. A grid of floors and stringers stiffens the hull and provides support for the lead ballast that includes a cast iron keel shaft. Two keel options are offered, the standard, rather narrow-chord fin with a draft of 6 feet, 5 inches or a shoal model with a 5 foot, 4 inch draft.

Hanse is unique among production builders in that it allows owners to virtually custom design the interiors of their boats. The new 400 has 18, that's right, 18 interior variations. Hanse has developed computer operated jigs in a sophisticated woodshop that facilitate this kind of customization. This kind of fresh thinking no doubt attributed to the Hanse 400 being named the European Boat of the Year in the class for boats up to 12 meters.

On deck

Back on the bay, I made my way behind the pedestal and took the leather-covered wheel. The 400 responded to small course changes immediately and accelerated smartly. The rod link steering system is not only highly reliable, it takes a lot of the slop out of the helm. The rudder features an aluminum shaft. This is another example of Hanse engineers looking at ways to save weight. A little here, a little there, but it all adds up to better performance. I confess, I prefer harder stainless steel when it comes to rudderstocks. However, self-aligning needle bearings keep the rudder true, limiting potential wear and tear and more and more builders are employing aluminum alloys for rudder stocks.

The visibility from the helm was excellent. Indeed, the overall cockpit design is very well thought out. All control lines are led aft under fiberglass covers, keeping the deck clean and uncluttered. While midboom sheeting, with the traveler forward of the companionway, is standard, a clever cockpit mainsheet arrangement for racing is optional. This is a good way to hush critics of midboom sheeting like me. Harken winches and hardware are standard. There's a large locker to starboard, but this depends on the interior selected. The opening transom makes for easy access to the swim step, which includes a hot and cold water deck shower.

Wide side decks and well-placed stainless steel handrails made it easy to work my way forward. There is a good-sized external chain locker but if you intend to use the 400 for serious cruising you'll need to beef up the anchoring arrangement. I like the integrated fitting forward for housing the whisker pole and the amidships cleats for spring lines. The standard deck equipment is top quality.

The 9/10 rig includes a double spreader, deck-stepped spar with an air draft of 64 feet. Technically the 400 will slip under the 65-foot fixed bridges on the Intracoastal Waterway, but you'll need nerves of steel and some flexible antennas. An efficient single-line mainsail reefing system led to the cockpit is standard as is a rod kicker. The working jib led to a forward traveler is completely self-tacking. The headsail lead tracks are well inboard and we were able to drive the 400 well inside of 40 degrees apparent without stalling. A 140-percent North Sails genoa and a gennaker are options but highly recommended. The rig has room for plenty of adjustment, and the split backstay features a six-part adjuster led to port. Harken roller furling gear is standard.

Down below

You'll either be completely enchanted by the interior styling of the Hanse 400 or it will catch you off guard and take some getting used to. I like it. No, make that, I really like it. It's clean, practical, bright, well executed and very original. It's an alluring blend of Scandinavian simplicity and German practicality, and it works. The trim wood is beautifully finished in light silk cherry or the standard classic mahogany. Bulkheads are white laminates, creating a sense of space and light. The concern for weight applies to the interior as well. Doors are foam-filled sandwich construction and the cabin sole is synthetic. As mentioned earlier, there are many different arrangements to choose from but a few basics are included in all the plans.

Once you drop below the galley is to starboard. It features a long counter aft and forward facing double stainless sinks with lockers below. The plumbing fixtures are elegant and simple, like you'd find in a Berlin apartment. A two-burner stove is located outboard. The 12-volt fridge, with access from both the top and front, is standard. The dark laminate counter tops are trimmed with handsome fiddles and a practical stainless handrail. The main head is opposite the galley and includes a large shower stall.

A couple of different arrangements are available in the saloon. Most 400s include a U-shaped settee draped around a dining table to starboard. To port, you can opt for a settee, seats with a fold-out table between or swivel seats. There are modular style lockers with shelves between. The nav station, or office desk, is usually located in the forward cabin. And speaking of cabins, there are several different options. Our test boat was fitted with a single aft cabin to port, tucked under the cockpit and a huge storage/work area to starboard. This is an ideal arrangement for cruising. Twin

The offset Pullman berth in the forward cabin is just one of many options available for the interior layout.

aft cabins are also possible, a combination best suited for chartering. In either case, the aft cabins include a hanging locker, a double berth and decent storage.

The forward cabin may or may not include an en suite head. I'd opt against it and go for the additional legroom instead. Do you really need two heads in a 40-foot boat? The double berth can be either a traditional V-berth style or an offset Pullman. You can choose between two hanging lockers or one locker and a lovely curved writing desk that, as mentioned above, doubles as the nav station. Considering I don't have enough hang-up clothes to fill one locker this choice is a no-brainer for me. There are shelves above the bunk and storage below.

Ventilation is adequate with several opening portlights and a couple of overhead hatches. The systems are well engineered and, for the most part, easily accessed. The electrical panel includes gauges for both fuel and water. Two 70-amp-hour batteries are standard and would need to be upgraded if you planned to spend much time aboard. Tanks are stainless steel, but they're not very big. Total water capacity is 300 liters, or about 80 gallons, while the fuel is just half of that.

A Yanmar 3JH4, 40-horsepower diesel with a saildrive and two-blade prop is standard. The engine is accessible from behind the companionway steps and through panels in the aft cabin. The engine room is well insulated and during our trials I was impressed by the lack of noise below. These new Yanmars are wonderfully efficient, and combined with the 400's easily driven hull shape this translates into excellent fuel efficiency. The engine didn't have to work very hard to push the 400 along at more than 6 knots.

Under sail

The fickle winds sprang to life and we took advantage to fall off onto a reach. Even with the small headsail the performance was impressive. We clipped along at 5.5 to 6 knots on a deep reach and immediately sped up when we brought the wind forward a bit. Sail handling is a snap, and it won't be difficult for a reasonably experienced sailor to singlehand the 400 under most conditions, especially if an autopilot is fitted. The ability to singlehand a boat means that the designers nailed the proportions just right. We executed a few quick jibes before hauling the sheets in for a few tacks. The 400 came through the wind efficiently, pivoting on its fin in a snap. The acceleration was impressive, especially considering that a fleet of obnoxious powerboats had raised a decent chop.

With a base price less than $200,000 it's clear that the new 400 model continues Hanse's tradition of combining innovation and quality in an affordable package. I look forward to seeing more Hanse models at next year's round of boat shows.

J/133

*Cruising or racing, performance comes first
in J Boats' 43-footer*

"The cruiser comes before the racer, just look at the brochure." It was hard to tell if Rich Sterns of J Boats Midwest was joking or not as he tweaked the mainsheet. It was not hard to feel the new J/133s impressive acceleration. It was a seat of the pants sort of thing, no need to look at the speedo, the boat just heeled slightly and powered up. Sterns has the soft touch of a professional helmsman, which of course he was for many years before making a recent foray into the equally challenging world of selling boats. When I glanced at the B&G instruments mounted above the companionway, we were sailing impressively close to the wind, in less than 10 knots true, and cutting through the Lake Michigan chop at close to 8 knots. Sure the word "cruiser" might be placed on the left side of the slash before the word "racer" on the brochure, but like all Js, terrific performance is the 133's raison d'être.

Although the 43-foot J/133 is squeezed between the 40-foot J/120 and the 48-foot J/145, it is more closely related to the J/109,

The asymmetrical spinnaker flown from the sprit is easy to set and a breeze to douse with the ATN chute snuffer.

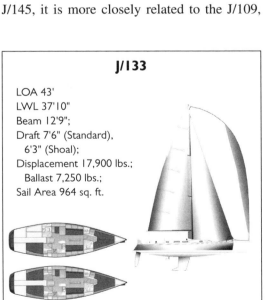

J/133

LOA 43'
LWL 37'10"
Beam 12'9";
Draft 7'6" (Standard),
　6'3" (Shoal);
Displacement 17,900 lbs.;
　Ballast 7,250 lbs.;
Sail Area 964 sq. ft.

the successful 35-footer that was introduced in 2002. Like its smaller sister, the J/133 combines an easy to handle rig that delivers consistently fast sailing with genuinely comfortable accommodations. The long waterline and relatively narrow beam result in an efficient hull shape that doesn't need to be over steered. When the boat is in the groove, you find yourself just nudging the wheel from time to time.

The details

The sailplan calls for a manageable 105-percent roller-furling headsail, a retractable sprit for flying an asymmetric spinnaker without the need for crew and a full-batten main that can either drive the boat at hull speed or be used for nimble maneuvering around the marina. The folks at J Boats simply don't like motoring and believe that happiness is directly proportional to time spent under sail.

The J/133 hull and deck are molded by TPI Composites, using the patented SCRIMP system. This well-proven process places the entire laminate in a dry mold. A vacuum eliminates air voids and then just enough resin is infused through feed tubes to wet the laminate. The resulting balsa-cored hull is light, very strong and extremely durable.

The hull-and-deck joint is bonded with aircraft-grade methacrylate adhesive, a completely chemical joint without the leak potential of mechanical fasteners. The main bulkhead is actually fiberglass, epoxied to the hull and deck, and unlike most veneered plywood bulkheads, it won't delaminate and also can absorb and flex with the unpredictable stresses of the sea. A molded structural grid, comprised of keel floors and longitudinal stringers, stiffens the hull and provides support for the mast step and engine bed.

The antimony-reinforced foil shaped keel is externally fastened to a molded stub with stainless bolts. The standard draft is 7 feet, 6 inches, although a shoal-draft 6-foot, 3-inch keel is an option. The high-aspect rudder blade and stock are carbon fiber. I realize that many builders are using carbon fiber for stocks, and I understand the advantages of not mixing materials, still, I am wary of a carbon fiber rudder stock. High-quality bearings are essential to eliminate any wear on the stock. And there are plenty of boats out there cruising with this arrangement and no problems.

On deck

The J/133 cockpit is designed for efficient sail handling yet it is deceptively comfortable. The cockpit seats and aft deck area offer nice perches to trim and steer from respectively. A Harken mainsheet traveler, complete with Black Magic series blocks, is mounted on the aft end of the seats, just forward of the helm. Although you have to climb back to the wheel, it is easy to control the main from the helm. The steering system is by Edson and a 60-inch

The cockpit is designed for efficient sail handling but it is deceptively comfortable.

Diamond series wheel with an elkhide grip is standard. Most steering is done from the side, where the visibility and feel are best.

Harken 56.2 STA are used for the primary winches with 48.2 STAs serving as secondaries and for the mainsheet and halyard winches. Reefing and furling lines are led aft making the J/133 one of the few performance boats that can be sailed by a couple, or even singlehanded. The halyards were not led aft, thank goodness. This is an inefficient place to hoist a sail from and also results in a mass of line in the cockpit and on the aft end of the house. A port locker is designed to carry a six-man liferaft and there are two decent-sized lazarettes. The propane locker to starboard is vented and drains overboard. The stern step flows artfully within the hull lines and includes a clever telescoping ladder.

The J/133 has a low-slung trunkhouse with stainless handrails and wide side decks. I really like the integral molded toerails forward of the mast and J Boats always does a terrific job on nonskid. Remember the brochure—this a cruiser-racer, and to back up that claim, the deck includes an external anchor locker, a standard dodger and provisions for a bimini top. And of course the retractable carbon fiber sprit is standard. I'm not sure if this is a cruising or racing feature. I do know that it makes handling an asymmetric spinnaker dramatically easier, and let's face it, A-sails are the reaching sails of both the future and the present.

The double-spreader mast is a custom designed auto-claved carbon fiber section from Hall Spars. The mast step is a custom epoxy

The handsome interior is elegant in a no-nonsense way and is finished in cherry with well-executed joinerwork.

piece bolted to a centerline longitudinal stringer. The boom is aluminum and a Hall QuikVang is standard. The standing rigging is Navtec continuous rod led to single pod chainplates. Although the rig is just a shade fractional there are no checkstays or runners, which really simplifies sail handling. An Antal mainsail track is standard and a Harken MKIII 2.0 furling system is standard issue on the forestay. Indeed, Harken gear is in evidence all over the boat, including the adjustable headsail car system that is led to the cockpit.

Down below

The J/133 offers two interior plans. The standard layout includes three private sleeping cabins, the optional arrangement includes a single aft cabin, a second head and the V-berth forward. The handsome interior is at once elegant, albeit in a no-nonsense New England fashion. The joinerwork is well executed and the finish is cherry with satin varnish. The 6-feet, 4 inches of headroom lends a feeling of spaciousness, and considering the limitations of a performance hull, designer Rod Johnstone does an excellent job of using the available space.

The forward cabin includes a generous V-berth, even with the sprit tube housing above, and there is a lot of storage underneath. A hanging locker, dressing seat and vanity are to port, with the dual access head to starboard. The instrument transducers are easy to check below a hatch in the sole. The head is not overly large, but how much time do you spend in there any-

way? It has all the necessary features including a shower.

The saloon has settee berths port and starboard with storage behind and cabinets above with a small shelf between. Finding places to stow gear and provisions will be a challenge for any long-range cruising plans, though. The drop-leaf table has a center liquor cabinet. Halogen lighting is used throughout the boat and the ventilation is excellent with two hatches and nine opening portlights.

The U-shaped galley is on the small side although it includes double stainless sinks, a three-burner Force 10 cooker, a dry goods locker and reasonably sized icebox. Refrigeration is optional. The cook is well supported on either tack and husky fiddles will keep the ingredients on the counter. The nav station is opposite the galley and is one of the best features of the interior plan. With the advent of cockpit mounted plotters, many designers are quietly conspiring against traditional chart tables—I think its an outrage, or at least disappointing. The J/133 nav center can handle a real chart, not just a chart kit, has a well-supported seat and room for repeaters and books.

The aft cabins on the standard model are identical. They include double berths, full-length shelves above the bunks and hanging lockers. In the two-cabin model, the port cabin is replaced by a second head, and unless you need the privacy, this is the preferred arrangement.

A 54-horsepower, four-cylinder Yanmar diesel with a Saildrive SD 40 transmission and folding two-bladed prop is standard. I like that J has opted to make a Racor fuel filter standard as well as a 125-amp Power Max alternator. The standard house batteries are two AGM105-amp models, but I'd like to see more amperage. The 50-gallon aluminum fuel tank is housed under the port settee. The engine is well insulated: it's hard to hear it running in the cockpit.

Under sail

Back on deck, I took the helm. Every time I steer a big J I am impressed with the finger-tip steering control. The sailplan makes sense. We were making good progress upwind with the North 105-percent jib and full main. Easing off the wind, Rich demonstrated how easy it is to set the sprit and hoist the chute. The Chicago waterfront hurried by as we sped toward Navy Pier flirting with 10 knots. We had to slow down to let the photo boat catch up. Johnstone understands that many sailing areas in North America have light winds in the summer and the generous rig on the 133 will drive the boat efficiently without big headsails. However, the same plan will cope with heavy conditions as well. This is the ethos of the boat, to be able to sail efficiently through a range of wind conditions without changing headsails and to be able to fly the asymmetrical chute without a lot of fuss, muss or extra crew.

The wind started to diminish as we jibed the chute and headed south. A snuffer is a key part of the spinnaker plan, and the ATN sleeve gobbled up the A-sail easily. Setting the jib we worked our way back into the harbor, short tacking without raising a sweat and sailing at 30 degrees apparent. The only reason we fired up the engine was so that I could say I steered the boat under power. Yes, the J/133 motors along nicely, touching 7 knots at 2,400 rpms, but I suspect it will take many years of sailing to rack up a lot of engine hours.

The J/133 is an impressive addition to the J Boats fleet. It's a lively performer with genuine cruising accommodations. However, the best feature of the J/133 is that it is an absolute pleasure to sail, and that, after all, is what a sailboat, be it a cruiser-racer or vise versa, is all about.

Hunter 45CC

Comfort, sailability and style mark a new direction

The crew at Hunter is excited about their latest center cockpit cruiser. And for good reason, this striking design continues Hunter's relentless effort to raise the bar on quality and innovation while maintaining a commitment to building boats people can actually afford. I suspect Hunter's competitors are not quite as excited.

The 45CC replaces the popular 456 and early sales clearly indicate that this model is going to pick up where the 456 left off. Like all Hunters, the 45CC contains design inspiration by company founder Warren Luhrs. However, the boat has Glenn Henderson's fingerprints all over it. Henderson is Hunter's director of engineering and chief designer.

"To design a center cockpit is something of a challenge because of the location of the cockpit," he said. "We took a long time playing with floorboard height, the flow of the boat fore and aft and the center of gravity. If you look at the 45CC from the side it is hard to tell it's a center cockpit because it's so sleek and streamlined." Naturally Henderson is a tad bi-

Hunter's chief designer Glenn Henderson's roots as a race boat designer shows in the improved performance of this new generation.

ased but I must admit his comments are right on the mark.

In keeping with all his designs, Henderson worked hard to keep the overall profile low. The wraparound windshield and soft deck contours give the boat a contemporary look and yet there is something purposeful and practical about the design that I like. Like all big Hunters the boat is comfortable, yet the 45CC is designed and engineered for serious

HUNTER 45CC

LOA 44'3"; LWL 39'2";
  Beam 14'6";
Draft 5' (shoal), 6'6"
  (deep);
Displacement 22,936 lbs.;
Ballast 7,389 lbs. (shoal),
  7,237 lbs. (deep);
Sail Area 962 sq. ft.
  (standard),
  883 sq. ft. (furling),
  956 sq. ft. (furling
  with vertical
  battens)

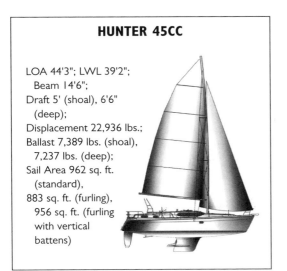

cruising and you can feel it the moment you climb aboard. We recently tested the boat in the Atlantic waters off St. Augustine, Florida. The conditions were on the light side, still the 45CC offered a surprising turn of speed and when it was time to return to the city marina the boat nimbly slipped down the inlet channel under main and cruising spinnaker.

The details

The hull is sensibly constructed with solid fiberglass laminate from the waterline south and balsa coring in the topsides. Forward sections also contain Kevlar reinforcements for strength and fracture resistance in the advent of a collision. The hull shape features a keel stub with external lead ballast externally fastened. This method of construction serves to lower the center of gravity and actually combines the best of both worlds when it comes to the internal vs. external ballast debate. The keel stub provides a sump area in the bilge, while the external ballast offers advantages in a hard grounding. Speaking of grounding, Hunter's director of offshore testing, round-the-world sailor Steve Pettingill, does just that with every new model. "I give the people on the beach a scare, when I repeatedly run the boat aground. But we really do test these boats, we want to see how everything holds together in a real world situation," Pettingill said.

A structural grid that provides hull stiffness and internal support is bonded to the hull with Plexus, a powerful bonding agent developed for the aerospace industry that has been nicknamed "fiberglass fusion." This grid

Belowdecks the 45CC really shines with top notch fit and finishes. A cheerful saloon and dinette.

forms the basis for Hunter's completely modular construction and the process eliminates the need for secondary bonds. Once the grid is lowered into place, there is no moving it. Yes, the alignment is critical. Hunter's efficient construction techniques have been honed over the years and translate into savings for the consumer. The early days of modular construction were not always pretty, but Hunter's current boats are extremely well engineered. In addition, Hunter continues to upgrade the components used in construction and the 45CC includes fittings and materials from Lewmar, Corian, Edson, Harken, Selden, Yanmar and a host of other top manufacturers. Another standard feature sailors will appreciate is a 360-degree rubrail with a stainless guard for those times when the fenders are in the wrong spot when coming alongside.

On deck

A well-designed cockpit is critical in a center cockpit boat simply because space is at a premium. Our test boat was fitted with a folding wheel that opened up space without the need for removing the wheel from the pedestal. The comfortable seats are covered with Flex-teek, Hunter's synthetic teak that looks great, provides decent traction and requires no maintenance. One advantage of a center cockpit is that it typically affords good visibility from the helm and this is definitely the case with the 45CC with its low-slung coachroof. There is a clever integral handrail on the huge pedestal, a large fold-out table and two coaming lockers.

All sail controls are led aft and our test boat included an electric halyard winch to starboard. A stainless arch, a Hunter trademark, supports the Harken mainsheet traveler with leads and stoppers led down each side. This frees up additional cockpit space and is an important safety feature as the mainsheet and boom are out of harm's way. Hunter has worked hard to make its boats easy to handle and the 45CC is no exception. The robust arch also forms a natural, all weather support for the bimini top.

The double-spreader spar by Seldon features Hunter's B&R rig. Henderson is a firm believer in fractional rigs, declaring, "I'll never design another masthead rig." A large main powers the 45CC and the standard jib is a barely overlapping 110-percent genoa. Vertical battens allow the optional furling main to maintain a bit of roach and nice overall shape. Henderson also believes that a boat should be easily driven and not require mountains of canvas to attain hull speed. He describes a matrix that combines the sailplan, the keel and the balanced spade rudder working in harmony to create lift while keeping the CG as low as possible. The headsail includes Furlex roller furling gear standard. The jib tracks are well inboard setting up tight sheeting angles. A rigid vang is standard.

Hunter has done a superb job of fiberglass sculpting and the nonskid on deck provided firm footing as I made my way forward. A beefy stainless steel stemhead fitting with double offset anchor rollers, an external chain locker and an electric windlass are all standard. The stanchion bases are supported by threaded aluminum backing plates. The double lifelines include three opening gates. The stern rail seats are a great place to tarry while underway or at anchor. Two large transom lockers gobble up gear and our test boat was fitted with optional fender holders. The swim platform is a bit narrow but a clever telescoping stainless ladder makes it easy to climb back aboard after a swim. And of course there's a hot shower for a quick rinse.

Down below

The spacious interior is bathed in natural light. Hunter's level of interior finish has steadily improved and the teak joinerwork in the 45CC is first class. The plan is fairly typical of most large center cockpit cruisers but the overall sense of spaciousness is unique. From the foot of the elegant, slightly curved companionway steps, the galley is to starboard. U-shaped with a handsome molding that doubles as a practical fiddle and handhold, the galley is located in the center of the boat—perfect for cooking underway.

There is plenty of counter space, two sinks, and a side-by-side front-loading fridge and freezer. This arrangement may not be as efficient as a top loading system with six inches of foam and hatches you can barely lift, but it sure is convenient. The two-burner gimbaled stove faces outboard. I particularly like

A nicely appointed owner's aft cabin.

the glass cabinets behind the stove and the built-in coffeemaker next to the microwave.

The nav station is opposite the galley, and the pivoting, sumptuous easy chair is the nav seat I have been dreaming of for 25 years. Designed for the new Raytheon E series multifunction displays, the nav station is set up for paper-free wayfaring. No thanks, I still like charts and I am happy to report that the nav desk is large enough to plot on and to store once folded charts inside. The saloon includes a large, furniture-quality table to port that accommodates six comfortably and a settee to starboard. Our test boat was fitted with all the bells and whistles including a flat screen television on the port main bulkhead. A great design feature is the single level floor. Many center cockpit designs have small steps between cabins that are annoying in port and dangerous at sea.

The forward stateroom features a V-berth without the need for a filler cushion, it's a real double berth complete with a seven-inch mattress and easy access storage below. There's a cedar-lined hanging locker and a dressing seat to starboard. There is also plenty of headroom and excellent ventilation. The en suite head includes a stall shower and Corian vanity. The interior is chocked full of small innovations and features that help define a new quality ethos for

Hunter. From windshield shades, to overhead fluorescent lighting, to standard smoke and carbon monoxide detectors in every cabin, Hunter has not skimped in the fitting out of the 45CC.

The master stateroom aft justifies any compromises of a center cockpit design. It is elegant, comfortable and refreshingly practical. Yes, the centerline queen berth with a real mattress will be difficult to sleep in underway, but it sure will be nice when the boat is tied up or swinging on the hook. And when you analyze how much time you spend underway versus at rest, even hard-core liveaboard cruisers generally are in port 10 nights for each night spent at sea. There are convenient bench seats on each side of the berth, two cedar-lined hanging lockers, and Corian covered nightstands with stainless fiddles. There is ample storage in drawers and lockers and terrific ventilation with seven opening ports and a large overhead hatch. The private aft head includes a clever bi-fold door for the shower.

The 45CC comes standard with a 75-horsepower Yanmar diesel and a three-blade prop. Access to the engine is excellent, especially from a side panel in the aft walk through. The vanity tilts out of the way in the aft cabin to allow unobstructed access to the stuffing box. Seventy-five gallons of fuel translates into more than 500 miles of range for this fuel-efficient engine and easily driven hull shape. All tanks have gauges and overall the mechanical systems are first rate. Through-hull fittings below the waterline are bronze and most pumps, compressors and other components are easily accessible. Indeed, this was a major design factor.

Under sail

Out on the Atlantic, we put the 45CC through a rigorous test under power, spinning the boat in its own length several times. There is a bit of wash from the large prop but that's a fair trade for 7 knots of speed. Satisfied with the boat's performance under power, we canned the engine and unfurled the sails. The wind fluttered around 10 knots. We sailed south, on a close reach, touching 6 knots. The ride was smooth despite a light chop and the helm was balanced. Indeed, I let the wheel go for minutes at a stretch. Pinching up, we sailed inside 40 degrees apparent with ease and only started pinching when we neared 30 degrees apparent. Tacking was easy with the small headsail and trimming the main is done primarily with the traveler. The 45CC accelerated pretty well for a serious cruiser and I confess, I was surprised by the soft ride.

Cracking off onto a reach we set the asymmetrical chute. One disadvantage of the swept-back B&R rig is that you can't pay the main out very far, which makes deep reaching tough. However, the sails set nicely at about 120 degrees off and we skipped along at nearly 6 knots. Hauling in the sheet, we easily carried the chute while reaching up at 70 degrees. Heading back toward the inlet we tacked downwind, which is something of a misnomer as you actually jibe. We made a series of jibes with the spinnaker. This is also when you appreciate having the traveler overhead, jibes are not as dangerous, and we made short work of the distance back to the marina. Waiting for the old bascule bridge to open we tested the ground tackle. The anchor was a snap to deploy and I was impressed as the Simpson Lawrence windlass easily transitioned between the rope chain splice.

The new Hunter 45CC is a welcome addition to the cruising boat market. It won't be long before you begin to see this handsome sloop anchored in the watery crossroads of the world.

CatalinaMorgan 440

The name says it all—this cruiser blends traditional ruggedness and modern-day styling

Catalina Yachts Vice-President, Gerry Douglas, and I are both old enough to remember the glory days of Morgan Yachts. There was a time, from the late 1960s through the 1970s when Morgan built rugged, roomy and affordable cruising boats that dominated the market. The Morgan Out Island series had production numbers that few builders today would even dream about, excluding Catalina Yachts of course. It is in this spirit that Douglas conceived and designed the new CatalinaMorgan 440.

"It was important to us to keep the Morgan name on this boat," he said as we slipped away from the dock. "But the boat is very much a Catalina too. Hence the double name." Catalina purchased Morgan 20 years ago, but for the most part, the two lines have maintained separate identities. The 440 is the first cruising boat to bear the long-winded CatalinaMorgan name and in many ways it represents the best of both worlds. The 440 combines the rugged features of old school

The CatalinaMorgan 440 brings two great names together in one boat.

Morgans, with the styling, comforts and ergonomics of Catalina.

"I took my time with this design, two years actually, we did a lot of research and talked with a lot of people," Douglas said.

My instincts tell me that it was time well spent, Douglas has really hit the mark with this new raised saloon cruiser.

While the 440 will appeal to a variety of cruisers, Douglas admits that the target customer is a couple whose children are out of the house and are now contemplating a cruising sabbatical or possibly spending their retirement years afloat.

"We wanted the boat to have legs," he said pointing out the ample tankage for fuel and

CATALINAMORGAN 440

LOA 45'3"
LWL 44'7"
Beam 14'
Draft
  fin keel 6'5";
  wing keel 4'11"
Ballast
  fin keel 8,072 lbs.;
  wing keel 8,600 lbs.;
Displacement
  fin keel 25,000 lbs,
  wing keel 25,528
Sail Area 931

water as one example. "And we wanted it to be genuinely comfortable for extended periods of living aboard."

There is no disputing that the 440 will be a very accommodating boat. However, what impressed me is how well the sailing systems are laid out, how nimble the boat is underway and the overall high quality of fit and finish.

The details

The 440's hull shape is meant for blue water, it is not a weekend warrior masquerading as an offshore boat. Catalina claims the 440 is just as happy on a lazy day sail as on a passage but I don't buy it, this is a cruising boat. The stem is nicely raked, which not only looks better than today's blunt-nosed performance boats but also makes it easy to launch and retrieve the ground tackle without marring the topsides. The beefy wing keel is a lead section and attached to the hull with stainless bolts cast in place.

While most production builders use iron keels, Catalina has always used lead. I wonder if Douglas considered internal ballast for the 440. The debate continues over which ballast is better, and although I favor them, encapsulated keels are becoming rare. The rudder is hung on a partial skeg that allows for well-supported upper and lower bearings. The propeller shaft is housed in a molded skeg, making it far less vulnerable and also helps the boat track.

The hull is solid fiberglass below the waterline and balsa cored from the waterline up—a sensible way to lay up a hull. The solid glass sections can survive a serious underwater

The wide cockpit is perfect for entertaining.

impact while the half-inch balsa core offers excellent panel stiffness and insulating qualities. Coated and scored end-grain balsa is used to prevent the possibility of delamination.

The hull and deck are joined on an internal flange and both bolted and bonded together. A lovely teak caprail, incorporating a stainless steel rubrail, covers the joint. It is not very scientific but the new 440 passed my stomping-around-the-deck test with flying colors—the boat is solid. The 440 construction scantlings also include a collision bulkhead just aft of the anchor locker, a critical feature that should be standard on all offshore boats. Catalina offers five-year warranties covering blisters and structural concerns.

On deck

Tucked behind the deck saloon and protected from the elements by a dodger and bimini, the 440s cockpit has a snug feel to it. Most sail controls are led to a standard, powered-up (electric) winch just to port on the aft end of the cabintrunk. There are handy ties to control coiled lines and mesh bags to store them out of sight. The visibility from the helm station is only adequate, considering the raised trunk, but the trade-off for a spacious, light saloon is one most cruisers are happy to make. The Edson pedestal is substantial and has all the bells and whistles. The large cockpit table seats six and also provides leg and foot support in the wide cockpit. I particularly like the cockpit sole, long teak planks are classy and, unlike grates, easy on the feet.

The companionway features a lightweight foldaway door that is convenient in fair weather. Stout hatch boards are ready when the going gets heavy. The starboard cockpit seat lifts to reveal my favorite feature on the 440, the workroom-third cabin.

"We call this area flex space," Douglas said. "We designers are always intent on utilizing every inch of space, sometimes you need an area that is flexible. It can be a workroom when a project demands it or a third cabin when the grandkids are aboard."

This useful space is also accessed from below through the aft cabin. Another feature that is impossible not to like are the comfy seats fitted into the stern rail. Catalina pioneered stern rail seats and now you find them on many boats. The stern step, or swim step, is large and functional. There is a good-sized lazarette to port and also a dedicated life raft locker. Of course there is a hot and cold shower too.

The side decks are wide enough for easy maneuvering and raised bulwark lends security when on deck. The raised saloon puts the handholds at a good height and they're matched by 30-inch lifelines. The stanchions are supported both vertically and horizontally, so you can lean on them. It is a bit of a climb up to the base of the mast, but a molded step between the forward ports makes it easier. The anchoring arrangement is well thought out and includes double stainless steel rollers and a large divided chain locker. Starboard runners eliminate ground tackle chafe. A vertical windlass is standard.

The tapered aluminum mast features double spreaders and has an air draft of 62 feet, making the 440 Intracoastal friendly. The mast is deck stepped but the engineering is interesting. The compression post actually passes through the deck and has a large plate welded in place for a metal to metal connection with the mast. As a result there is no compressive load on the deck. A Leisure Furl in-boom mainsail furling system is an attractive standard feature and demonstrates Catalina's commitment to making the 440 a world-class cruiser. The mainsheet arrangement is innovative and designed to reduce the loads normally associated with midboom sheeting.

Down below

The interior is bright, airy and nicely finished. Catalinas can't compete with the joinerwork of some custom yacht yards but these boats are not trying to. The workmanship is excellent and the price is realistic—that's a much better business plan as evidenced by the fact that Catalina has been one of the world's most successful builders for 35 years. I like that Douglas has not tried to make the interior appeal to every family. The 440 has two terrific cabins and an area of flex space. The saloon, galley and nav station were not sacrificed to make room for more sleeping cabins.

It is only three steps from cockpit to cabin

The bright and airy saloon is packed with comfort features—the dinette table folds cleverly to form a cocktail table.

sole. Once below, the galley is immediately to starboard, which makes it convenient to pass food up to the crew in the cockpit. There are the expected double sinks, three-burner propane stove, and storage lockers including a useful drawer bank with various size compartments. I like the front opening fridge that's easy to reach and the separate top-loading freezer outboard and aft. Opposite the galley is the aft head and nav station. The head is a completely molded unit with a clever fold-away shower compartment. The nav station, which is an oft-overlooked feature nowadays, includes a decent-sized desk and a stand-alone swivel chair that seems to swing or pivot in every direction.

The saloon features a very clever table that can be raised and lowered electrically, and the four corners fold in to create a cocktail table with more leg room. The table is draped by a C-shaped settee. Opposite is what Catalina calls the "sofa." These cushions are shaped for comfort and the center back piece drops down to form a table for drinks or games. The forward and aft seats have reclining backs and foot rests that raise to become ottomans. I'd be overwhelmed with guilt sitting in this wonderful chair while underway, sailing should never be this comfortable.

Back to reality, one the 440's best features is the space below the saloon floor. There is plenty of room for a generator, watermaker and other equipment and also most of the plumbing is led to a central location and is easy to access and troubleshoot.

The owner's cabin is forward and includes a centerline double with large drawers beneath, a deep locker that has enough room for shelves and hanging clothes, and a dressing table. The CatalinaMorgan includes all the small touches that fine yachts offer these days, from mattresses with inner springs to roll out shades on all the hatches, to LED lights that are bright, cool and energy efficient. The forward head is accessed from the owner's cabin and is also a fully molded compartment making it virtually leak proof. The stall shower includes folding doors. Both showers are led to a single dedicated sump, simplifying the plumbing runs.

The aft cabin includes an optional centerline berth but this comes at the expense of the workroom/flex space to starboard. If there is one feature that every cruising boat needs, it's a workroom. I'd be reluctant to opt for the optional bunk. The aft cabin is quite spacious and includes a double berth with a real mattress and a large hanging locker. Douglas proudly showed me how a large locker to port is able to hold two full-sized duffel bags. This cabin is generally the guest cabin and most guests live out of their duffels, or if they do unpack, can't find a place to store the bags. This locker solves the problem. The aft lazarette can also be reached through a clever hatch in the aft cabin making it easy to access the steering system. Douglas should be applauded for making access a priority throughout the boat.

The main engine is a 75-horsepower, four-cylinder Yanmar that offers plenty of punch and is still fuel-efficient. A single tank holds 117 gallons and that translates into a realistic motoring range of 600 to 700 miles. Electrically speaking, three heavy-duty 4D batteries make up the impressive house bank and multistage charger and 50-amp shore power cable are standard. Two water tanks combine to hold 176 gallons of water, of course if you chose the optional washer and dryer you will likely have to add a watermaker as well.

Under sail

Out on Tampa Bay the wind was fluky. One minute we'd have 10 to 12 knots then it would die away. We had the standard mainsail and 135-percent roller-furling jib with Schaefer furling gear. We eased south on a close reach and once the 440 gathered a bit of headway, it sailed quite nicely. The helm was light and well balanced, the autopilot really wasn't necessary. The sail controls were well placed and I had no trouble trimming the genoa from the helm. The mainsheet is trimmed from the aft end of the coachroof. The mainsheet traveler leads are there as well. The Leisure Furl boom makes raising and lowering the main a piece of cake, especially with the electric halyard winch.

Bringing the boat up hard on the wind, we maintained speed to about 40 degrees apparent. The wind eased as we fell off onto a reach and slowly sailed back toward the marina. I have logged many thousands of bluewater miles aboard serious cruising boats and as I conned the CatalinaMorgan toward the channel markers I felt right at home.

Island Packet 440

Tradition and modern thinking combine to make a bluewater cruiser with liveaboard comfort

This powerful new cruiser from Island Packet has Bob Johnson's stamp all over it. It looks like what his boats are supposed to look like. It is a beamy aft-cockpit model without apologies for what it is not, and a pedigree that is pure Island Packet. Naturally it's a true cutter and robustly constructed. It is loaded with innovations above and below deck that make it particularly user-friendly, and it is tailor-made for a cruising couple with ideal accommodations for guests. The 440 is just another example of why Island Packet is revered by its clients, the company knows what they want.

We tested the new 440 on a blustery, rainy morning in Annapolis, Maryland. Broker John Helwege of Gratitude Yacht Sales, Island Packet's local dealer, luffed up as fellow SAILING writer Bob Pingel and I scrambled out of the photo boat and into the cockpit. We hastily introduced ourselves and met Terry and Barbara Jones, who had just placed an order for a new 440 to be delivered in the spring. A little wind and rain had done noth-

Deep reaching the 400 tops 7 knots under main, jib and staysail.

ISLAND PACKET 440

LOA 45'9"
LWL 38'1"
Beam 14'4"
Draft 5'
Displacement
  32,000 lbs.
Ballast 12,000 lbs.
Sail Area 1,131 sq. ft.

ing to dampen their enthusiasm. Hard-hitting journalist that I am, I got right to the meat. "Why did you choose the Island Packet 440?"

"Because we wanted a boat that we could sail anywhere but one that was also comfortable to live aboard," Barbara said.

"We also feel it is a solid value," Terry added. "We want a company we can trust because we're making a big step up from a Catalina 22." He said they were looking forward to an active and early retirement.

I slipped behind the pedestal and took the wheel. The Lewmar "Cobra" rack-and-pinion steering felt solid and was instantly responsive. The sheets were eased and the 440 found its footing on a close reach. The winds were gusting to 20 knots, and with a full mainsail, staysail and genoa we were a bit over canvassed. Still, the 440 punched through the Chesapeake Bay chop without a hint of pounding, and although the flared forward sections kicked up spray, the cockpit was wonderfully dry—a key advantage of an aft cockpit boat that often gets overlooked during the boat show lovefest when prospective buyers ooze over the centerline queen berths served up by center-cockpit competitors. The GPS flashed 7.3 knots and that was without trying. Tweaking the traveler, tightening the mainsail leech line and flattening the staysail translated into 7.9 knots, which we might as well round up to 8. Falling off the wind we continued to flirt with 8 knots, good going for a 32,000-pound dedicated cruiser. The 440 was in its element.

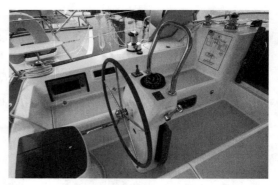

The seaworthy cockpit is comfortable for a crowd.

The details

Island Packet has done a fine job of refining its boats over the years while maintaining trademark features that clearly identify the brand. Long keels and roomy interiors are standard issue for all Island Packets. The 440 is the natural progression from earlier models like the 380 and 420. There are no gimmicks, from the raised bulwarks, to the integral bow platform, to the rakish swim step, the linear flow is natural and refreshingly low profile. The hull form holds its beam well forward and aft, producing less efficiency sailing to weather and more efficiency living down below—a trade-off many cruisers are happy to make. Johnson has stuck by his long keel designs, and the "full foil" keel has proven itself through countless ocean crossings. Off the wind his boats are deceptively fast. This keel shape allows the designer to offer moderate draft, full bilges with a high-load-carrying capacity and a ride that is smooth in a seaway, key ingredients to happy cruising.

The 440's hull is a solid laminate, infused with Island Packet's proprietary pressure-fed roller application system. A molded grid provides structural support. Naturally the ballast is internal and placed in cavities in the wide keel section. The hull is finished with Island Packet's proprietary gelcoat system, Polyclad3, which offers superior protection against blisters, so much so that Island Packet offers a 10-year blister and delamination warranty. The deck is joined to the hull on a molded flange and is both chemically and mechanically fastened. The deck is cored with Polycore, a chemical substitute for foam and wood cores that really helps prevent delamination. Most deck hardware is backed with aluminum plates.

On deck

The 440's cockpit easily accommodated the crowd we had aboard, and even with the boat heeling considerably, the seating was comfortable and secure. The visibility from the helm was good, especially for an aft-cockpit boat. The standard RayMarine sailing instruments are housed in a seahood pod. Reeling in the mainsheet required all of the mechanical advantage offered by the Lewmar Ocean Series 44CST winch, a result of the mid-boom sheeting, but pushing the mainsheet and traveler forward allows for an extensive dodger installation. All sail controls are led aft and can be efficiently worked with the dodger in place. A roller-furling mast is standard, although buyers can request a conventional spar with no cost difference. Hardware throughout is top quality and oversized. There is good storage in the cockpit with two deep seat lockers and clever bins for line tails. Island Packet pays attention to details too. I like the four harness padeyes and the emergency pull strap on the boarding ladder on the stern platform.

The integral bow platform is wide enough to stand on and can support two beefy anchors and associated ground tackle. The

Island Packet's superb workmanship is evident throughout, with designer fabrics and handsome joinerwork. The drop table conceals a nifty liquor locker.

anchor rollers are another impressive Island Packet exclusive and make for both quick deployment and fully captive rodes. The large anchor locker features deck access through a hatch and a watertight bulkhead. This is a great feature on a cruising boat, it is not just a safety feature but also serves as a garage on the foredeck.

The mooring cleats are massive, the stanchions and double lifelines well supported and the stainless steel handrails run the entire length of the cabintop. The molded diamond pattern nonskid offers good traction on the wide side decks. In addition to a standard roller-furling mast, a Hoyt boom is standard on the furling staysail. This clever curved spar helps the staysail maintain shape without the need for barber hauling—it's basically self-vanging and self-tending. A 110-percent genoa is standard and both headsails are controlled with Harken furlers.

Down below

I made my way below and was instantly impressed. Not just by the spacious accommodations but also how quiet and comfortable the interior was as we blasted along on a close reach. The companionway steps are easy to negotiate and the stainless handrails are well placed. The galley is immediately to starboard. I like the slip-resistant molded sole—let's face it, the galley sole is occasionally going to get messy, there is no reason for teak

flooring. The wraparound Corian counter provides plenty of surface area and the fiddles are incorporated into the countertops. A Force 10 stove/oven, a water purification system, a clever slide-out trash bin and a built-in microwave are a few of the standard features that make the 440 galley a pleasure to work in both at sea and alongside.

Access to the aft cabin and aft head are opposite the galley to port. This cabin features an angled island berth, which is a clever use of space. There is also a large, cedar-lined hanging locker and storage beneath the berth and along shelves outboard. The cabin has good ventilation with both an overhead hatch and side portlights. Overhead lights are on dimmer switches. The aft head includes a separate stall shower with folding acrylic doors, Corian counters and a VacuFlush electric head.

The nav station is tucked just forward of the galley to starboard. The inlaid chart table is beautiful although there isn't much room for chart storage. The electrical panel and radio station are outboard, and easily accessed. A quick look behind the panel revealed immaculate, well labeled wiring schemes. The 440 features premium pre-tinned electrical wire.

The fold-up table in the saloon is a terrific feature. It provides a sense of spaciousness when up and can be mounted on either side of the saloon when down. When mounted on the main bulkhead the drop-leaf table conceals a handsome liquor locker. A choice of designer fabrics are available for the plush dual density foam cushions. The teak-and-oak sole, louvered locker doors and teak trimmed fittings represent superb workmanship. There are three overhead hatches and opening portlights down each side. Because the tanks are housed in the bilge, the area beneath the settees is available for storage of gear and equipment. The settees also make excellent sea berths, which is important because both cabins have island berths.

Continuing forward, the owner's stateroom includes an offset island berth, a dressing chair and vanity, and plenty of storage. This is where you feel the beam, most boats don't carry their beam this far forward. And while you can certainly debate the merits of beamy hull shapes underway, there is no disputing the fact that they serve up more space

below. The owner's head, like the aft head, includes a separate stall shower and Corian
counters. Island Packet has made the conver-
sion to electric heads, and while old salts like
me shake our heads, the rest of the world
thinks, "What took you so long?"

The 440's systems are, simply put, top
notch. From the five standard AGM batteries,
including a stand alone engine battery, to the
heavy-duty high-output digital charge con-
trollers, to the pre-wiring needed to add beefy
gear like bow thrusters and a windlass, the 440
is well engineered. A 75-horsepower, four-
cylinder Yanmar is the power in front of a
large three-bladed prop that pushes the 440
along at 7 knots. Overall access is more than
adequate, however daily maintenance items
are very easy to reach. The aluminum fuel tank
is pre-plumbed for additional pickup and return lines, making it easy to install a generator.
There is 160 gallons of fuel tankage which
translates into a realistic motoring range of
more than 800 miles.

Under sail

Back in the cockpit, the rain finally stopped but
the wind held. We headed south, on a deep
reach, and managed to keep the boat moving at
more than 6 knots despite a lack of downwind
running gear. The wide beam helps prevent
rolling and we ambled downwind pleasantly.
Eventually we hauled the sheets in and put the
440 through a series of close tacks. The 110-
percent genoa slipped around the staysail stay
without much trouble, which is not always the
case with a cutter rig. The main and self-tacking
staysail made trimming up a snap. While the
440 won't blow you away with acceleration
it doesn't loose momentum as soon as the wind
eases.

I have been test sailing Island Packet sailboats for many years. It has been a pleasure to
watch them evolve from building small cruising catboats to world-class yachts. The new
440 is a welcome addition to the company's
fleet of accomplished bluewater cruisers.

Cabo Rico 42 Pilothouse

*Robustly built and handsomely styled,
this Chuck Paine cruiser is itching for blue water*

The new Cabo Rico Pilothouse 42 presents something of a conundrum for sailors, just what kind of boat is it? Robustly constructed, it is a proven bluewater passagemaker. At the same time, however, there is something about Chuck Paine's low profile pilothouse and soothing sheerline that provides an air of elegance and a sense of grace that sets the 42PH apart from other hardcore cruisers. There is nothing stark or severe about the boat. And then there is the interior. The practical engineering features and innovative layout are overshadowed by a symphony of blond Costa Rican teak and stunning joinerwork. But don't be fooled by the 42PH's comeliness, this boat is the real deal when it comes to ocean sailing, capable of contending with any of the notorious headlands in comfort and style.

Cabo Rico has been building boats in the Central American country of Costa Rica for nearly 40 years. The company is best known for the Crealock-designed 38 cutter, a legitimate classic that is built on a limited basis

The Cabo Rico 42 Pilothouse struts her oceangoing stuff off Fort Lauderdale, Florida.

these days, and for its homegrown plantation teak joinerwork. In addition to the Cabo Rico line that includes models ranging from 36 feet to 56 feet, it also builds the sleek David Walters-designed Cambrias, and the versatile Northeast 400 motorsailer.

"Our workforce is unique," said company President Fraser Smith. "Our average employee has been with us for at least 15 years. They're our greatest strength." Every Cabo Rico is built on a semi-custom basis.

I recently test sailed the Cabo Rico 42PH in Fort Lauderdale, Florida. I was joined by Tadji Rodriguez, Capt. Mike Ungurean and Fraser Smith. The hull is identical to the traditionally decked 42. Paine describes the refined full keel hull shape as a New England-style hull, and traces its pedigree to its Crealock-designed sisterships. I like the 42's clipper bow.

CABO RICO 42 PILOTHOUSE

LOA 46'6"
LOD 42'6"
LWL 32'2"
Beam 12'8"
Draft 5'3"
Displacement
  26,939 lbs.;
Ballast 10,400 lbs.
Sail Area
  (Cutter Rig)
  1,134 sq. ft.,
  909 sq. ft.

"Yes, the clipper bow looks lovely," Smith said, "but it is functional as well. It keeps the boat dry, and a dry boat is a safe and comfortable boat."

The wind was light as we cleared the docks behind Cabo Rico's U.S. office. We raised sail in the turning basin and steamed out into the Atlantic looking for wind. We eventually rustled up an onshore breeze, shut down the Yanmar and headed south toward Miami. Before long we were sailing at 6.5 knots, skirting the edge of the Gulf Stream.

The details

The 42PH hull is laid up to massive scantlings. A layer of Core-Cell foam is sandwiched between numerous layers of fiberglass, making for a strong and moderately light hull. The deck is also composite construction, with Baltek balsa used as the core material. In keeping with the times, you won't find teak decks on the 42PH, unless of course you really want them. Cabo Rico's overall engineering is impressive. As an example, all through-deck fittings are mounted in a radius of solid laminate, fasteners don't puncture the core, eliminating the potential for delamination.

The hull and deck are joined with a classic boxjoint, featuring inward and outward flanges and incorporating the raised bulwark and teak toerail. Bonded both chemically and mechanically, this is not only an incredibly strong way to marry the hull and deck but this also creates a joint that won't leak. The raised bulwarks also provide secure vertical surfaces for mounting stanchion bases.

Structural bulkheads are tabbed to the hull throughout their perimeter. You won't find molded liners in the 42PH. Beneath the cabin sole, a solid fiberglass subfloor and solid fiberglass stringers eliminate any chance of wood rot in the bilge. A beefy fiberglass bridge that keeps the mast end well clear of any bilge water supports the keel-stepped mast. The ballast is internal lead, placed in the keel cavity that is an integral part of the hull, and then fiberglassed over. This eliminates the need for keel bolts and allows the weight of the fuel and water storage to be kept low in the hull. The debate over internal and external ballast seems to have waned as fin keels have for the most

Cabo Rico finishes its boat with blond Costa Rican teak. The inside helming station is is two short steps down from the cockpit.

part carried the day in sailboat design, but for a serious cruiser I still prefer internal ballast.

On deck

The cockpit seats are nicely sculpted and offer excellent lower back support. Although all pilothouse models suffer from reduced visibility from the outside helm station, Paine's low-profile pilothouse limits this compromise. There are a couple of aft lazarettes and a cockpit locker to port for more than adequate deck storage space. The mainsheet traveler is mounted forward of the companionway, freeing up cockpit space. and all sail controls are led aft.

Our test boat was fitted with the optional self-tacking staysail boom, an arrangement that clutters the foredeck but sure makes sail handling easy. The double-spreader rig is of moderate proportion and the cutter plan features around 1,100 square feet of sail area. The sail area/displacement ratio of 16.88 translates into a boat designed for bluewater sailing. Our boat, hull No. 2, also included a Schaeffer roller boom with an articulating luff track that allows for reefing off the wind. The standard sailplan calls for a high-cut, roller-furling yankee to accompany the staysail, eliminating the need for an overlapping genoa. This is an effective plan for sailing across the wind and makes reducing sail easy in a blow. However, for deep reaching in the trades a poled out genoa is the usual, low-stress alternative to an asymmetrical chute. The standing rigging, which includes increasingly

The nav station is located near the companionway.

rare fore and aft lowers, is heavy duty, and mechanical terminals and a solid vang are part of the standard package.

Stainless steel handrails mounted on the pilothouse, tall and well-supported lifelines, and the raised bulwark lend a real sense of security when going forward, even in heavy weather. The deck hardware is oversized and the double stainless steel anchor rollers and stemhead fitting is well designed. An electric windlass is standard.

Down below

The interior plan is innovative and, considering that this is a 42-foot boat with a modest beam and a real turn to the bilge, the available space is cleverly utilized. Remember, too, that no two 42PHs will be exactly alike as owner input is a key ingredient in every boat.

Dropping below, you enter the pilothouse, and it really isn't much of a drop, more like a couple of easy steps. The inside steering station is to starboard, and surprisingly, the visibility is quite good. The helm chair is comfortable, you can actually sail the boat from below, which is not always the case with pilothouse models. This feature will really pay dividends when motoring on gloomy days on the inside passage, up a Norwegian fjord or along a Patagonian channel.

Across from the helm station is a table and shallow C-shaped settee. This is a delightful, well-lit and ventilated spot to sit, have a meal and take in the world outside. The genius of

the design is what lies beneath and behind the settee. It ingeniously lifts up and reveals a workshop. I like the idea of a workroom, which just may be the most useful space on any serious cruising boat. A surprisingly large double aft cabin is tucked away to starboard.

Continuing forward, the galley is down and to starboard. The counters are finished in Corian and there is plenty of locker space behind and a separate pantry opposite. Across from the galley, our test boat was fitted with a settee and a single unit washer and dryer hidden behind a lovely teak panel. There was also an additional small, easily accessed freezer. This space can also be a third sleeping cabin, an office, or whatever your heart desires. The systems throughout the boat, from lights to latches, are absolutely top quality. The standard equipment list is comprehensive, and ranges from a large inverter to an SSB counterpoise system laid into the hull. And of course, there is all that beautiful teak to admire. Cabo Rico's teak is light, almost honey colored, and when combined with the natural light of a pilothouse design the interior feels bright and airy.

The owner's stateroom is forward and includes an island queen bunk with dressing seats on either side and storage below. This cabin is truly elegant, and a large overhead hatch and opening port lights provide superb ventilation when sitting at anchor. Indeed, I have grudgingly come to realize that the philosophy of placing the owner's stateroom forward makes sense. Underway, the aft cabin and the pilothouse settee offer excellent sea berths, and when you reach your destination, the forward cabin is cool, private and spacious. The en suite head includes a large separate shower stall and tile flooring.

A 56-horsepower naturally aspirated Yanmar diesel is standard and provides plenty of power for the roughly 27,000-pound 42PH. Primary access is below the pilothouse sole and most maintenance items are readily accessible. The sound insulation is amazing, it was hard to hear if the engine was running from the cockpit, and more than tolerable from below. The 72-gallon fuel tank has integral baffles and an inspection port and clean out tube for dealing with contaminated fuel. Range under power is more than 500 miles.

Under sail

Back out on the Atlantic, the sailing was easy. The helm was light as we eased along on a gentle reach. A confused swell would have made a lighter, flatter bottomed boat bounce about uncomfortably but the 42PH barely noticed the chop. A seakindly motion just may be the most important design feature on a cruising boat. A boat that pounds will wear down the crew and is also hard on gear and structural integrity. The 42PH has a soft ride.

Eventually the wind came alive and we were able to put the boat through its paces. Sailing on a close reach, we clipped along at 7-plus knots in about 12 knots true. Hardening the sheets, we sailed capably to 35 degrees apparent with very little helm. It takes awhile to adjust to seeing over the pilothouse. Overall, I was impressed with clean deck leads and how the boat came through the wind efficiently for a long-keeled cutter. Cracking off onto a broad reach, we maintained speed and control although the apparent wind dropped into single digits.

The Cabo Rico 42PH combines the attributes of a well-proven hull shape with brilliant engineering and comfort of a pilothouse design. Of course, practical features aside, the handsome 42PH will also draw compliments wherever it goes.

Lagoon 500

Luxury and sailability abound in this world cruising catamaran

The new Lagoon 500 picks up where the successful Lagoon 440 left off, blending innovation and quality in equal parts. The 500 is truly impressive. From the unique flybridge steering station to the nifty rumble seat cockpit forward to the stunning interior finished in mukali wood, the Lagoon 500 leaves an indelible impression. Designers Marc Van Peteghem and Vincent Lauriot Prevost were given a challenging assignment by the Lagoon management team: Design a catamaran for world cruising that includes just about everything you'd want or need at home. That's right, home; the design premise of the Lagoon 500 was to make the boat as much like a house as possible—albeit a house that can sail at double-digit speeds.

Founded in 1984, Lagoon calls itself determinedly forward looking. It launched its 1,000th boat in 2005. According to U.S. Sales Director Nick Harvey, the company hoped to sell 200 boats worldwide in 2006, with 25 percent of those in the United States. And it's well on its way.

The 500 off downtown Miami. The elegant aft cockpit lies beneath a hard top, and the transom scoops makes for easy access to the water and the tender.

The details

The 500's LOA is 51 feet with a LWL of 49 feet. The beam is 28 feet, which translates into a lot of square footage both above and belowdecks. The overall displacement of 41,005 pounds gives the Lagoon 500 a sense of presence in the water and the generous 1,722 square feet of working sail area provides plenty of horsepower. Our test boat had two 75-horsepower four-cylinder Yanmar diesels and steaming away from the marina we hurried along at 9-plus knots without pushing. The 500 features Lagoon's innovative gull-wing bridgedeck design, that improves clearance and makes the hulls more efficient in the water.

From the waterline down, and at the turn of the deck, the hulls are solid fiberglass, vacuum bagged with vinylester resin. The hull sides, topsides and the bridgedeck are a sandwich construction with balsa coring. This is an intelligent way to marry strength where you

LAGOON 500

LOA 51'
LWL 49'
Beam 28'
Draft 4'6"
Sail Area
   1,722 sq. ft.
Displacement
   41,005 lbs.

need it with the weight savings that make a catamaran what it is. The twin rudders are foam-cored covered with vinylester resin. The rudder stocks are carbon fiber and the steering system is cable. A variety of molds are used in the construction process but there is also some old-fashioned workmanship. The primary bulkheads are securely tabbed to the hulls and furniture facings. Lagoon's fiberglass sculpting is superb. I like the two steps scooped out amidships below the lifeline gates to make for easier boarding when side tied. The 500 is loaded with small innovations that make the boat wonderfully user friendly.

On deck

The 500 includes an elegant aft cockpit for lounging. In many ways the cockpit seems like an extension of the saloon. The steering station is above; a flybridge built into what is a robust cockpit hardtop. You access the steering station via curved steps on either side of the cabintop. There is a surprising amount of room with seating for six. Not surprisingly the visibility is terrific. In fact, it's a bit unsettling at first. With the foldaway bimini top down, we had a bird's eye view of the set of the sails and the Miami skyline.

The sail controls are actually easier to reach from the flybridge than from a standard lower cockpit catamaran. When flying either the drifter or the genoa on a reach, the sheets are led aft to turning blocks, then directed up and inboard to the winches. For windward work there are inboard tracks on the coachroof.

The aft cockpit table is hidden away in an aircraft-style locker in the hard bimini until needed.

The mainsheet traveler is on the aft end of the flybridge, and supported from below by two stainless steel compression posts. The main halyard is led to a standard electric winch just to the right of the helm and the sheet is opposite. By any definition the Lagoon 500 is a big boat but it is also an easy boat to sail.

Climbing down from the helm, you make your way forward on very wide side decks. The diamond nonskid pattern offers good traction and the stainless steel handholds on the coachroof can be reached without bending over—they're chest height. The hatches are recessed so you won't stub your toes. The rumble seat forward is a nice touch and so are the teak seats on each bow pulpit. The anchor rode is channeled to the vertical windlass and large chain locker just forward of the rumble seat. The mast stretches 72 feet above the water. Fractionally rigged, the Lagoon 500 has a versatile sailplan that includes double headsails. The innerstay hosts a flat-cut furling genoa and a lightweight furling drifter for downwind and light air work is flown from the outer stay. One of the advantages of a 28-foot beam is the wide sheeting angles and a pole is not usually necessary when reaching.

The aft cockpit features face-to-face seating with a bracket for a large, handsome teak table. The table is ingeniously stored in an aircraft style locker above. A sliding companionway door and sliding windows in the bulkhead help incorporate the cockpit into the saloon area. The wide swim platforms in each hull are easily accessed from the cockpit via two shallow steps. The steps have lazarettes for stowing snorkel and dive gear and there is a hot water shower on the port hull. You never feel like you're climbing in or out of the cockpit, the entry points are well designed. Three generous-sized lockers accommodate gear along the aft crossmember and there is additional storage under the seat benches. There is a wet bar to port, just before you enter the saloon that includes a sink, pressure water and 12-volt fridge.

Down below

Stepping, not dropping, into the saloon you are immediately struck by the sense of light and spaciousness. Our test boat was elegantly finished in honey-colored mukali wood. The trademark Lagoon shiplike portlights provide natural light and along with the four forward-most opening portlights, plenty of ventilation too. The expansive galley is to port. I prefer the galley up, in the saloon as opposed to down in one of the hulls. The 500's galley is a split-level compromise that works well. A four-burner stove, double stainless sinks with an extra drying sink and large 12-volt fridge are standard. I like the stainless steel counter surface. Storage is primarily under the counter tops and below the floorboards. You could stash enough provisions for an Atlantic crossing under the sole alone.

The forward-facing nav station, looking out through the portlights, is my favorite feature. Often overlooked in today's catamaran designs, the 500's nav station is where you'd likely find me while underway. There are panels for instrument repeaters and a shallow chart drawer. There is a huge L-shaped settee and table arrangement to starboard. Eight people can sit comfortably for dinner. The large cabinet against the mast bulkhead is designed for an entertainment center. In the four-cabin charter version of the Lagoon 500, there is an additional companionway forward of the settee for access to the forward hull cabin.

While the saloon is essentially the same on all models, there are three different cabin arrangements to choose from. Our test boat was fitted with the three-cabin owner's model. Other options include a four-cabin owner's model and a four-cabin charter model. The port hull is the same on all three versions. It includes an aft cabin with a queen berth accessible from three sides, lockers and drawers below and headboard shelves. The aft cabin head includes a varnished wood countertop, stainless sink and separate shower stall tucked away along the outside of the hull. A 12-volt freezer and a locker for an optional washer and dryer are located in the portside gangway.

The port forward cabin also houses a queen berth, cleverly oriented athwartships to provide three-way access. There is a large hanging locker, lockers below the berth and shelves above. The head is forward, and like the aft cabin head, includes a varnished countertop and separate stall shower. Opening portlights and a

The saloon is filled with light and finished in honey-colored mukali wood, and the nav desk is also an inside steering station.

large deck hatch that has a screen and shade built in provide excellent ventilation.

The three-cabin owner's version devotes the entire starboard hull to a single stateroom. The queen berth is aft, with a dressing seat to starboard and lovely bureau opposite. There is a huge hanging locker and plenty of room to change clothes. There is a large settee for relaxing and storage for more clothes than I own. The head is grand, and the shower stall rivals anything you'd find ashore. There is that concept again, home-like. From little touches like light switches, to logical electrical connections in each cabin, the Lagoon 500 has been designed to be your home, as well as your boat. Lagoon knows who its customers are. He or she may well be a new sailor who wants to plunge into serious cruising without sacrificing the comforts of home. They may be operating a business from afar or using the boat as an elegant, floating vacation home.

The systems are well thought out and Lagoon's engineering is always first rate. The standard electrical system includes three large house batteries and one emergency battery. The plug-and-play system is a new concept of electrical distribution with localized junction boxes designed to make tracking problems simple. Simple is the key word. Instead of a massive and confusing panel that looks like it should be on the space shuttle, the 500 features a DC panel controlled with three switches. There are four rotomolded plastic water tanks for a total of 254 gallons.

Most boats will have a watermaker fitted and there is also plenty of room for an optional generator.

The engines are accessed from lockers in the aft hulls. Two 55-horsepower Volvo diesels with saildrive transmissions are standard. Three-bladed fixed props are standard. The lockers are very well insulated, and even from below in the aft cabins it's hard to hear the engines running. Four fuel tanks combine for a 250-gallon capacity, translating into a 1,000-mile range under power.

Under sail

Back on the Biscayne Bay, we hoisted up the full-batten main and unfurled the genoa. Unfortunately the wind was light. However, light air can often be a more revealing test of a boat's capabilities. Contrary to what many sailors believe, a lot of cruising cats perform poorly in light air. Well, don't put the Lagoon 500 on that list. With a true wind at less than 10 knots, we found our stride sailing upwind at more than 6 knots. A little bit of tweaking soon had us approaching 7. It felt like we were on an escalator, there was virtually no motion; it was the easiest 7 knots I have ever experienced. Tacking in light air required backing the headsail before releasing the sheet but the acceleration was impressive. Cracking off on a reach, I gave up the helm and made my way to the rumble seat forward. What a view, what a life. It sure would have been nice to accompany the crew to the Bahamas, where they had a photo shoot scheduled.

Beneteau 523

*Big, beautiful, oceangoing flagship
for a new generation*

The new 523 from Beneteau replaces the Oceanus 50, one of the best-selling big boats of all time and the longtime flagship of charter fleets worldwide. I don't know if we're allowed to say this kind of thing anymore but I am going to risk it. From the moment you first step aboard the 523 you realize that this handsome sloop is completely put together like an elegant French woman, who can not only stand her watch and hand steer through a gale but then turn out a stunning meal afterward. At once a powerful bluewater performer and a supremely comfortable coastal cruiser, the more you look the more you find that every piece is in place to make the 523 appeal to a wide spectrum of sailors.

The prolific design team Groupe Finot has established a solid relationship with Beneteau, including the designs for the company's current models 323, 423 and 473. Instead of re-inventing the wheel with the 523, the team has refined and upgraded what has already been proven through countless miles of ocean sailing and countless hours of chartering fun.

This handsome and elegant sloop is both a powerful bluewater performer and a comfortable coastal cruiser.

BENETEAU 523

LOA 53'1"
LWL 47'11"
Beam 16'
Draft standard 7'6"
 shoal 5'11"
Displacement
 32,800 lbs.
Ballast 10,935 lbs.;
Sail Area 1,625 sq. ft.

Measured by volume the 523 is huge, the LOA is actually a tad more than 53 feet while the beam is 16 feet, carried well aft. However, as soon as you take either of the two helms and put the pedal down, the boat feels surprisingly manageable. In fact, we tacked several times in a span of five minutes as we angled for more sea room during the test sail off the port of Miami. We came through the wind with a minimum of fuss and accelerated quickly. Of course both main and jib sheets are led to self-tailing electric winches, making the close maneuvers a push button affair.

The details

The 523 has clean deck lines and a fast, flat underwater profile, but it is no lightweight, displacing nearly 33,000 pounds. This much boat requires an honest rig and the 523 has one with 1,625 square feet of working sail area. An optional inner forestay adds a staysail to the equation, although the boat is a sloop by design. There are two keel options, the standard deep-draft model that draws 7 feet, 6 inches and the shoal option with a 5-foot, 11-inch keel. Unless shoal depth is critical in the areas where you sail, I'd opt for the standard deep keel; the performance and the motion will be better.

The 523 has a solid fiberglass hull with cored stringers and decks. Beneteau has developed a construction methodology that combines the obvious advantages of scale production with a commitment to building boats that stand up to the demands of the sea. The interior components are prefabricated when possible and efficiently assembled as the boat moves down the line. We can moan and groan about the loss of craftsmanship in today's boats but the truth is that a computer-controlled jig and laser torch makes a cleaner cut than a man with a saw.

Beneteau's joinerwork is exceptional but what is even nicer is that it builds boats, even 53-footers, in a fashion that people can afford. Bulkheads are bonded through 360 degrees and furniture facings are laminated to the liner and hull where applicable. Hull stiffness and support for the externally fastened iron keel is achieved with a grid system in the bilge that in turn is part of the huge hull liner. This liner is essentially a hull within a hull. The rudder stock is carbon fiber.

On deck

The cockpit of the 523 is impressive. It is comfortable for a crowd but still set up for efficient sailing. The dual helms are located well aft, each with a rounded molded seat and depending upon the point of sail one helm always affords excellent visibility. The wheels themselves are bulkhead style. The engine controls are to starboard, which is fine but engine controls on both sides would make coming alongside to port much easier. Each helm station does have full instrumentation.

There is a large drop-leaf cockpit table with a stout stainless steel base for leg support and also a stainless handrail—important fea-

The cockpit of the 523 is impressive, comfortable for a crowd but still set up for efficient sailing. The dual helms are located well aft, and the twin-wheel design creates terrific access to the swim platform.

tures in a wide cockpit. The aft end of the table is designed to house a full-sized chartplotter, visible from either helm. The twin-wheel design creates terrific access to the swim platform that includes a boarding ladder with teak treads and a hot-and-cold shower. There are two large aft lockers and waterproof speakers. I like the life raft locker on the aft deck, it is accessible in a hurry and keeps the raft out of the weather. There is also a convenient wet locker on the aft deck, just in case you are really thirsty after your afternoon swim.

All sail controls save the genoa halyard are led aft. And this makes sense; why clutter up the cockpit with a long halyard tail that rarely is used? The mainsheet traveler is forward of the companionway and a bit on the short side. The rigid vang is standard, which means that you might as well dispense with the standard topping lift. Seven rope clutches to port and three more on the starboard side of the aft end of the coachroof are the circuit boards of sail control. The genoa tracks are nearly 12 feet long and the sheets are led to electric winches easily controlled from the helm stations. The headsail furling line can also be controlled by an electric winch. Just be wary, I like to feel snags when I am a furling in the headsail and electric winches can cause damage.

There is a double stainless steel bow roller and stemhead fitting. A horizontal windlass,

The U-shaped saloon is deceptively large with a versatile, modular table and a bench seat that also serves as a well-placed support when working your way from the companionway forward in a seaway.

which I much prefer to vertical models, is standard. The chain locker is deep, stowing the ground tackle where it should be, low in the hull. The bow pulpit is Euro-styled, meaning that it's open, with a teak boarding step. This allows you to come bow-to when Med mooring, an increasing popular option as sterns become more cluttered with cruising gear. Also, steering in forward is usually easier than in reverse and having the cockpit off the quay affords more privacy. Deck hardware is robust and good quality.

Down below

There are several different interior arrangements available on the 523. The most popular plan features the owner's cabin forward with two spacious double cabins aft. There is also the option of a separate, deck-accessed crew cabin forward. The huge owner's stateroom features a double island berth with bench seats to either side. There are two large drawers under the berth and full-length shelves along the hull. There are hanging lockers to port and starboard and a vanity/desk to port. Halogen lighting is used overhead and this cabin alone has five opening hatches for superb ventilation. Of course when a tropical downpour pops up you'll be scrambling to close them all. The en suite head has plenty of elbow room and a separate stall shower.

This plan puts the table and settee to port with the galley opposite in the saloon. The U-shaped saloon is deceptively large with a versatile, modular table and a bench seat that also serves as a well-placed support when working your way from the companionway forward in a seaway. The feeling of spaciousness comes from pushing the interior components out to the extremes of the hull. This sacrifices storage to some extent, however a close inspection reveals plenty of lockers and shelves. Panoramic panels overhead flood the interior with light but when it's too bright, sleek pearl colored shades can be deployed to diffuse the light and keep the cabin cooler.

The galley is opposite and features a three-burner Force 10 cooker. The 12-volt fridge is front opening, convenient on port tack but tricky on starboard. There is plenty of counter space and forward facing double stainless sinks lean toward the centerline for good drainage. There are lockers above and below. There is a hatch directly overhead and two opening portlights. A galley strap is necessary when cooking in heavy weather. The navigation station is stashed just aft of the galley. The curved wooden seat offers a good platform on either tack. The chart table is more than adequate, especially in these times when many designers dispense with nav stations altogether, and there is a panel for repeaters. The electrical panel is located outboard and offers good access to the wiring behind. The standard electronic navigation package includes Raymarine sailing instruments, chartplotter and autopilot. Radar and PC interface are factory options.

The two aft cabins each have enclosed heads with showers. The berths are legitimate doubles, and there is also room to maneuver so you can stand up to dress. In other words, the cabin is not all bed. There is a small hanging locker, storage under the berth and shelves along the hull. It would be nice to see a dedicated space for a large duffel bag. Lighting and ventilation are excellent, with opening portlights and hatches, features that turn these aft cabins into pleasant living areas and not just sleeping quarters. The optional crew cabin contains a double berth forward and a head. Access is through a large Lewmar deck hatch. Unless you need this cabin for additional crew, I would prefer to see it used as a forward garage—it's a great spot to stow bulky gear like sails and fenders.

The plumbing and electrical systems on the 523 are well laid out, easy to use and access for repairs. The total freshwater capacity is 250 gallons, plenty for a week or more of cruising in the tropics, however most owners will likely add a watermaker. An 11-gallon hot water heater is big enough for several showers. There are meters for all tanks. On the electric side, there are 110-volt outlets throughout as well as well-placed 12-volt sockets. Four 140-amp batteries provide plenty of power for house needs and a single 140-amp battery is isolated for engine starting. A 100-horsepower Volvo diesel pushed us along at 7-plus knots and was very quiet in the cockpit. Access is adequate from behind the companionway and through the aft cabins. A fuel capacity of 119 gallons translates into a cruising range of well over 500 miles.

Under sail

Back on the Atlantic, the winds were fluky. One minute we had 12 to 15 knots true, the next 6 to 8. In the puffs, we clipped along on a close reach with a 140-percent genoa and fully-battened main at 7.5 knots. The helm was very light, fingertip steering from the high side. As the wind eased, the 523 maintained momentum, an advantage of a big boat, and kept moving at near 6 knots. Cracking off onto a beam reach, the 523 really found her stride. I was impressed by the easy access to the headsail sheets from the helm. Two people can handle the boat without a lot of sweat and noise. We could have used a spinnaker for deeper reaching but that is, unfortunately, the nature of new boats tested fresh after a boat show. You have the fake plants and color brochures aboard but no extra sails. Coming back through the wind, we caught a nice lifter and raced back toward Government Cut at 8 knots. Overall, I was pleased not only by the 523's speed but also by its soft motion through the choppy waters near the inlet.

There is little doubt that the Beneteau 523 is another best seller in the making from the world's largest sailboat manufacturer. If your sailing plans call for long-term offshore cruising or occasional coastal escapes, I would take a hard look at the new Beneteau 523.

Appendix I

*Dimensions Defined and Performance and
Safety Indicating Ratios*

Sailboat Dimensions

LOA – Length overall, excluding bowsprits, boomkins, davits etc. Sometimes, and more accurately described as LOD, length on deck. Linear measurements in the book are in feet and inches.

LWL – Load waterline, sometimes called length waterline, or DWL, design waterline. This is the length of the boat as it floats, literally measuring where it touches the water forward and aft. LWL can increase when boats are loaded, or heeled excessively.

Beam – The maximum width of a boat. Beam WL is the maximum width at the waterline, a more useful figure when applying to ratios.

Ballast – Weight, usually lead or iron, measured in pounds and carried in the keel for stability.

Displacement – The amount of water measured in weight that a boat displaces. This amount is equal to the boat's weight, (that's why boats float). This figure is usually noted in pounds although occasionally large boats may have displacement listed in tons. Displacement ratios often use tons, a long ton is 2240 lbs.

Draft – The amount of water required for a boat to float, or the depth of the deepest part of the vessel, usually the keel, below the waterline measured in feet and inches. Some boats will list different drafts depending on the model (i.e., deep, shoal, centerboard).

Sail Area – The square footage of working sails that a boat sets. Usually the sail area is the mainsail and the foretriangle, or normal jib.

Air Draft – The height of the rig, at its highest point, above the waterline, measured in feet and inches.

Performance and Safety Indicating Ratios

These ratios are based on design figures, actual numbers may vary considerably. Use these ratios only as part of a range of factors for selecting a boat, don't over-exaggerate their value

$$\text{Ballast/Displacement} \quad \frac{\text{Ballast lbs}}{\text{Displacement lbs}}$$

This ratio indicates the percentage of ballast to the overall displacement of the boat. A high ratio—above 45%—usually translates into a stiff boat. Modern hull shapes, with deep bulb keels have lessened the importance of this ratio.

$$\text{Displacement/Length} \quad \frac{\text{Displacement in long tons}}{(\text{LWL}/100)^3}$$

This ratio is used to compare the displacement of different hull shapes. Ted Brewer explains concisely that the lower the number, the smaller the waves that will be generated by the hull through the water, and the smaller the wave making resistance. In other words, the smaller the number the faster the hull. Of course, like all of these ratios, there are caveats. Displacement can be calculated in different ways, and LWL changes when a boat is heeled or loaded. Just remember, like any good statistic, these numbers can be tweaked. In broad terms, ultralight boats will have Displacement/Length of under 100, light boats in the 100–200, moderate 200–300, heavy displacement 300–400, and over 400 is considered a sumo wrestler of a sailboat.

SA/
Displacement

$$\frac{SA}{(Disp/64)2/3}$$

This ratio gives an indication of how much sail area is available to push the weight of a boat. Higher numbers translate into faster boats. This figure can be adjusted based on how you measure the sail area, usually it is the main and 100% of the foretriangle. Again, in broad terms, a boat with a SA/D of over 20 can be considered high performance, 18–20 is a good range for ocean racers and performance cruisers, 15–18 for cruising boats and under 15 for boats that need a stiff breeze to move at all.

Overhangs

$$\frac{(LOA - LWL)}{LOA}$$

Developed by Roger Marshall in his excellent book, *The Complete Guide to Choosing a Cruising Sailboat*, this is a simple and useful way to look at the percentage of overhang. Modern boats are extending the LWL at the expense of overhangs. This makes for a faster boat in smooth water, but overhangs are important in a cruising boat because you need reserve buoyancy at the bow and stern. Marshall recommends that a pure cruising boat should have an overhang ratio of 15–20%.

Capsize Screening
Factor or
Capsize Screening
Value (CSV)

$$\frac{Beam}{(Displ./64)1/3}$$

Developed after the 1979 Fastnet Race disaster, this calculation attempts to determine a boat's tendency for capsizing. This ratio is based on the assumption that boats with wide beams are hard to capsize initially but also difficult to right. Heavier boats have less initial stability but are ultimately harder to capsize. The lower the number, the less prone to capsize. 2.0 is a standard of sorts as the maximum acceptable number for offshore boats, under 2.0 is better.

Appendix 2

Glossary

This glossary is not intended to be a complete guide to sailing and sailboat terms. Instead, it is a short list of specialized terms scattered throughout the book and used to describe certain design and construction features.

Aft cockpit – A boat with the primary steering station and sail control area located aft, near the stern, as opposed to a center cockpit boat.

Athwarthships – Across the boat, at a right angle to the centerline.

Auxiliary – The engine in a sailboat, or a boat propelled by both sails and/or an engine.

Balanced rudder – A rudder mounted independently of the keel or a skeg, supported only by the rudderstock. Sometimes called a free standing or spade rudder.

Bobstay – Usually stainless steel wire but sometimes chain, that runs from the stem to the outboard end of a bowsprit.

Boom gallows – A frame, usually over the companionway, used to support the boom without the need for a topping lift. Usually seen on traditional boats only, a solid or rigid vang achieves the same result and is also an important sail control.

Boomkin – A frame or spar extending off the stern to support a backstay or sheet.

Bridge deck – A structural member in the cockpit that helps prevent water from going down the companionway. It can be part of the cockpit seating or just a small sill. Offshore boats need a stout bridge deck.

BUC Guide – A widely accepted private service used by brokers and surveyors providing used boat pricing guides since 1961.

Bulb keel – A fin keel with a rounded flair at the bottom for increased stability, often used on shoal draft keel configurations.

Bulwark – An extension of the topsides, above deck, to form a toe rail.

Camber – Athwartship curve of the deck.

Canoe stern/double ender – A rounded, or in some cases, sharp stern, as opposed to a more common flat stern.

Center of effort (CE) – The center of the sail area.

Center of lateral resistance (CLR) – The center of the underwater plane of a boat. The CLR and CE work in conjunction for balance. If the CLR is ahead of the CE, weather helm will develop.

Center cockpit – A boat with the steering station and most sail controls well forward of the stern, with an aft cabin behind.

Clipper bow – Taken from the clipper ships, a bow entry that has a reverse S shape, or a bow with a concave stem profile.

Club-footed jib – A jib, or often times a staysail, with a boom. Not popular anymore with the advent of roller furling headsails.

Coachroof (trunk cabin, deck house, etc.) – The part of the cabin raised above the main deck.

Coaming – The raised sides of the cockpit.

Compression post – A support, usually tubular but not always, that supports a deck-stepped mast from below.

Cored construction – A method of saving weight and adding strength by using a core material between two thin layers of fiberglass. Most commonly used on decks, with balsa wood as the core. Also used in hulls. Other common cores are PVC and Airex foams. Sometimes called sandwich construction.

Counter stern – A stern that slopes aft as it rises, opposite of a reverse transom.

Delamination – This is usually caused when the core between the fiberglass layers has become wet. The core can rot, or delaminate, and without proper support the actual fiberglass is stressed and can also delaminate.

Dorade vent – A clever type of vent that allows air to pass below but not spray. First used on the S&S designed classic, Dorade, in 1931.

Electrolysis – Electrochemical reaction between dissimilar metals in a saltwater environment.

Fiddle – The edge on a table or counter to prevent spillage when underway.

Flare – The forward part of the hull as it bends outward.

Floors – The athwartship frames (not ribs) that support the hull, located below the cabin sole.

Forefoot – The forward section of the hull below the waterline, the area from the steel to the keel.

Freeboard – The distance from the waterline to the deck.

Gelcoat – A trade name introduced by Glidden in the 50s, it consisted of a flexible polyester resin that allowed a boat to be easily removed from the mold and gave a shiny, smooth finished hull.

Gooseneck – The fitting that joins the mast and boom.

Gunkhole – A shallow, out of the way anchorage or harbor. Gunkholing is the practice of exploring such places at a leisurely pace.

Gunwale – Pronounced gunnel, it is the railing where the deck and topsides meet.

Heave-to – The process and result of bringing a boat into the wind to back the sails and put the tiller down. Boats with long or moderately long keels will be able to ride out gales and even storm conditions. Modern hull designs don't heave-to effectively.

Hull speed – The theoretical maximum speed of a non-planing hull. Quickly obtained by multiplying 1.35 by the square root of LWL.

Hydrodynamics – The study of the flow of liquids around solid objects.

IOR – International Offshore Rule, a much-maligned rule of measuring and rating boats for offshore racing. Gained prominence in the early 70s and inadvertently influenced sailboat design well into the 80s.

Joinerwork – The fine woodwork, specifically in a boat's interior.

Jumper strut – A tubular support system on the forward side of the mast, often to support the staysail stay instead of running backstays.

Longitudinal stringer – Supports that run fore and aft to stiffen the flat surfaces in a hull.

Mast step – A member that supports the base of the mast in the bottom of the boat. Sometimes a bridge spanning a couple of floors is used to support the step.

Mold – The form in which fiberglass is applied to create hulls, decks and molded liners and parts.

One-design – A racing boat that forms a class with other identical boats. Strict controls ensure that the boats have uniformity in construction and outfitting.

Osmosis – Blisters caused by osmosis between the layers of fiberglass. Known as 'the pox' blisters were common in the 70s and 80s when manufacturers used polyester resins almost exclusively. The switch to vinylester resin and strict temperature and environment controls while laminating have greatly reduced the blister problem on newer boats.

Overhang – The distance between the bow and stern and the waterline.

Profile – The view of a boat from a distance amidships, a side view.

Raised deck – A deck without a coachroof or trunk, sometimes called a flush deck, which is used on smaller boats to create room below, although not headroom.

Ratlines – Rope or solid rungs, strung between the stays to form a ladder up the mast.

Rubbing strake – Nowadays more commonly called a rub rail, a protective wood or metal piece, fitted to the hull for protection from scrapes.

Rudder stock – The rod, usually metal but occasionally synthetic, that the rudder is attached to. It may enter the boat through a stuffing box or a rudder tube above the waterline.

Running backstays – Movable or temporary stays set up to support the headsail or staysail. Usually just the weather stay is tensioned.

Saloon – The main non-sleeping cabin in a boat, often and mistakenly called salon.

Scantlings – The structural dimensions and standards of a boat.

SCRIMP – Acronym for Seamann Composites Resin Infusion Molding Process, a laminating technique used by Tillotson-Pearson and others, that is similar to vacuum bagging. Boats are layed up dry, without resin, which is added, or infused later in the process. The system allows for cleaner and more environmentally friendly laminating and also eliminates voids and uneven hand layups.

Seacock – A valve that connects some aspect of a boat's plumbing to the sea, usually used below the waterline where a positive closing action is paramount.

Section – Cross section of a hull plan. Many designers work with 10 sections, each designated as a station.

Settee – A horizontal seat usually found in the saloon that can be converted into a berth.

Sheer/sheer line – The curve of the deck line, or gunwale, as observed from the side, or in profile. Traditional boats usually have more pronounced sheer lines than modern boats. Some boats actually have reverse sheer, where the deck is higher in the middle than the ends.

Side deck – The deck space between the coachroof coaming or side and the gunwale.

Skeg – Part of the aft underbody of the hull designed to support the rudder. A skeg hung rudder is found on many ocean cruising boats, as opposed to the more performance oriented spade or balanced rudder.

Sister ship – Boat of the same design, usually by the same manufacturer.

Spreaders – Supports extending outboard from the mast to spread the shrouds out sideways, increasing the angle the shroud makes with the mast. Depending on the rig, boats can have one or more sets of spreaders.

Stability – There are different types of stability. In general, stability is measured as the force necessary to return a boat to upright from a variety of heeled positions.

Stemhead fitting – The metal fitting that covers the very forward section of the bow, and is supported down the stem. It is generally used to support the forestay and the set up to facilitate anchoring.

Stuffing box – A metal unit used to prevent water from leaking in around the propeller shaft and rudderstock. Old style units are packed with flax, newer units are dripless.

Swage fitting – A terminal end rolled under pressure onto wire, commonly used in standing rigging and lifelines.

Swageless fitting – Mechanical terminals that are applied to wire without swaging, also used in standing rigging applications.

Tabbing – Fiberglass that bonds a wooden bulkhead and furnishings to the hull. Ideally bulkheads should be tabbed on both sides with several layers of glass overlapping several inches.

Tabernacle – A fitting on deck that supports the mast and acts as a hinge for lowering and raising. Usually seen on small boats or sail-boats that spend a lot of time in canals passing under low bridges.

Toggle – Part of the standing rigging, a cast fitting, usually bronze or stainless, that connects the turnbuckle to the chainplate, allowing for some rig movement without bending the turnbuckle.

Transom – The furthest aft athwartship surface of a boat. The name and hailing port are usually posted on the transom.

Tumblehome – The curvature of the hull, first extending outboard from the deck and then inward toward the waterline.

Turn of the bilge – The point of the hull where the topsides curve inward to form the underbody.

Underbody – The hull shape below the waterline.

Wetted Surface – The surface area, measured in square feet, of the underbody.

USED BOAT NOTEBOOK

From the pages of Sailing Magazine, reviews of 40 used boats plus a detailed look at 10 great used boats to sail around the world.

John Kretschmer

Forty Great Used Boats

SAILBOATS 23' – 30'

O'day 23 • Stone Horse • Cal 25 • MacGregor 25/26 • Contessa 26
Tartan 27 • Pearson Triton 28 • Sabre 28 • S2 9.2 • Catalina 30
Olson 30 • Cape Dory 30 • Nonsuch 30 • Pearson 30

SAILBOATS 31' – 36'

Gemini 3000 • Island Packet 31 • Allied Seawind II • Westsail 32
Ranger 33 • Irwin Citation 34 • Beneteau First 345 • Niagara 35
J/35 • Bristol 35 • Ericson 35-II • Islander 36 • Columbia 36

SAILBOATS 37' – 42'

Tartan 37 • Tayana 37 • Endeavour 37 • Swan 38 • Baltic 38 DP
Morgan 382 • C&C 39 • Valiant 40 • Cal 40 • Hunter 40
Bermuda 40 • Morgan Out Island 41 • Whitby 42

TEN GREAT USED BOATS TO SAIL AROUND THE WORLD

Camper Nicholson 35 • Alberg 37 • Shannon 38
Fast Passage 39 • Beneteau First 38 • Tayana 42 • Mason 43
Peterson 44 • Stevens-Hylas 47 • Gulfstar 50

The Original – Same Format – Still in Print

SHERIDAN HOUSE
America's Favorite Sailing Books